ECT:
basic mechanisms

D1526676

EDITORS

Bernard Lerer, M.D.
Jerusalem Mental Health Center,
Jerusalem, Israel
and
Department of Psychiatry,
Wayne State University and Lafayette Clinic,
Detroit, MI, USA.

Richard D. Weiner, M.D., Ph.D.
Psychiatry Service,
VA Medical Center,
Durham, NC, USA.

Robert H. Belmaker, M.D.
Jerusalem Mental Health Center,
Jerusalem, Israel.

ECT:
basic mechanisms

Edited by

Bernard Lerer

Richard D. Weiner

Robert H. Belmaker

1400 K Street, N.W.
Washington, DC 20005

First published by John Libbey & Company Ltd., 80/84 Bondway, Vauxhall, London SW8 1SF, Great Britain, 1984. First published in the U.S.A. by the American Psychiatric Press, Inc., 1986

Phototypeset by Dobbie Typesetting Service, Plymouth, Devon, England
Printed and bound in the U.S.A.

86   87   88   89   5   4   3   2   1

The paper used in this publication meets the minimum requirements of American National Standard for Information Sciences—Permanence of Paper for Printed Library Materials, ANSI Z39.48-1984. ∞™

Library of Congress Cataloging-in-Publication Data

ECT: basic mechanisms.

        Reprint. Originally published: London : J. Libbey, 1984.
        Includes bibliographies and index.
        1. Electric shock therapy.   I. Lerer, Bernard.
II. Weiner, Richard D., 1945–   II. Belmaker,
Robert H.
RC485.E28   1986   616.89′122   86-3507
ISBN 0-88048-237-0 (pbk.)

CONTENTS

Adverse effects

Psychological aspects

Overview

Introduction

B. LERER, R. D. WEINER and R. H. BELMAKER

Jerusalem Mental Health Center, P.O.B. 140, Jerusalem, Israel (BL and RHB); Psychiatry Service, Durham VA Medical Center, Durham, NC 27705, USA (RDW); Department of Psychiatry, Wayne State University and Lafayette Clinic, 951 E. Lafayette, Detroit, M 48207, USA (BL at date of publication).

Therapeutically-induced seizures have played a central role in psychiatry for almost fifty years. The underlying mechanism of action of convulsive therapy has been a focus of interest since Meduna (1935) originated the therapeutic use of chemically-induced seizures and suggested that 'the effect of the epileptic convulsions is that they change the chemical constituents in the organism in a way suitable for the cure of schizophrenia'. Convulsive therapy is no longer primarily used for the treatment of schizophrenia nor has Meduna's (1935) underlying theoretical assumption that schizophrenia and epilepsy (and hence induced seizures) are incompatible, proven to be correct. Cerletti & Bini (1938), who pioneered the therapeutic use of electrically-induced seizures, suggested that 'the electricity itself is of little importance . . . the important and fundamental factor is the epileptic-like seizure, no matter how it is obtained'. Most researchers since Meduna and Cerletti, have been guided by the same basic assumption. Yet ECT still remains an empirical therapy. Its dramatic therapeutic efficacy, in severe depressive illness in particular, continues to constitute a compelling impetus to further research into its possible mode of action.

In spite of its therapeutic efficacy, ECT has always been regarded with considerable misgivings by the general public and much of the medical profession. A number of complex and interrelated factors contribute to public opposition to the use of ECT which, although always present, appears to be mounting. The dramatic nature of the treatment, the use of electricity, the induction of convulsions and loss of consciousness, undoubtedly play a central role. The fact that ECT is an empirical treatment lacking a systematically proven explanation of its mode of action, is clearly also an important factor. To some degree this criticism is unfair in that ECT is by no means the only empirical treatment in medicine and not much more empirical than the less 'invasive' (but not necessarily safer) pharmacological treatments which have partially replaced it. An explanation of 'how ECT works' would nevertheless be of critical importance not only in establishing a scientific basis for convulsive therapy itself but also to our understanding of the mode of action of antidepressant treatments in general. Such an explanation might also provide a potential framework for understanding the nature of the underlying disorders in which ECT is effective.

It is indeed paradoxical that public opposition seems to be increasing at a time when burgeoning research interest might have been expected to give the treatment an added measure of scientific validity. In spite of the enormous practical difficulties involved, efforts to define clinical efficacy and diagnostic indications more clearly have yielded no fewer than six published controlled trials in the past five years, which have compared ECT to simulated treatment (Freeman *et al.* 1978; Lambourn & Gill, 1978; Johnston *et al.* 1980; Taylor & Fleminger, 1980; West, 1981; Ganghader *et al.* 1982). Moreover, extensive data has become available on the nature of ECT-induced memory deficits as well as on the modifications in electrode placement and stimulus intensity that have been undertaken in order to reduce untoward effects. These and other issues relevant to the clinical practice of ECT have been extensively reviewed in

1

recent books (American Psychiatric Associations, 1978; Fink, 1979; Palmer, 1981; Abrams & Essman, 1982) and numerous publications in the literature.

The purpose of the present volume is to provide the clinician and researcher with an in-depth review of the current state of knowledge regarding ECT mechanisms. Since the 1973 book, *Neurochemistry of cerebral electroshock* (Essman, 1973) and the publication of the proceedings of a 1972 symposium 'Psychobiology of convulsive therapy' (Fink *et al.*, 1974), there have been no book-length treatises on this subject. Although most major contemporary reviews of ECT include at least one chapter on ECT mechanisms, it is felt that the importance of this topic, combined with the recent extraordinary resurgence of relevant research activities, particularly in the biochemical and neuroendocrine domains, indicate the need for such a volume. This need is further amplified by the growing concern within the psychiatric profession itself (American Psychiatric Association, 1978; Pippard & Ellam, 1981), that the available body of knowledge regarding all areas of ECT has so far been poorly disseminated and that an undesirable and even potentially dangerous state of ignorance regarding ECT prevails among many ECT practitioners.

Contributors to this volume were asked to present their own research finding~ in the context of a review of other data relevant to the particular area covered. They were also requested, where possible, to relate their findings to specific theoretical hypotheses. The resulting chapters cover major areas of interest such as ECT effects on neurotransmitters and receptors, neuropeptides, neuroendocrine function and cerebral blood flow and their possible inter-relationship. Consideration is also given to mechanisms that may underlie the adverse effects of ECT as well as to the possible contribution of electrode placement, stimulus parameters and psychological factors to ECT mechanisms. A substantial portion of the book is devoted to the neurochemical effects of ECT. This does not reflect the editors' bias but rather the major, current trend of studies on the mechanism of action of ECT and psychopharmacologic treatments in general. That the greater weight of data presented is on the basis of animal rather than human studies again reflects what is being done in the field rather than the editors' preference (which at this stage might be to encourage the latter, as expressed in the concluding chapter).

The major areas covered by contributors to this book may be briefly summarized as follows.

Neurotransmitter and receptor mechanisms
Green reviews the extensive contributions by the Oxford group on changes in monoamine-mediated behaviors following ECS and also addresses the task of correlating changes in biochemical parameters with reported behavioral effects. Modigh *et al.* focus on dopamine receptor changes following ECS with particular reference to behavioral and neuroendocrine effects and possible applications to the treatment of Parkinson's Disease. Effects of ECS on dopamine autoreceptors are reviewed by Antelman & Chiodo on the basis of their electro-physiological studies and form the basis for a novel hypothesis of ECT action. Changes in adrenergic and serotonergic receptors are the focus of Vetulani's chapter, with special accent on correlations between functional measures of receptor sensitivity and changes in radioligand binding. Radioligand binding changes induced by ECS in the adrenergic and serotonergic system are also the central thrust of Kellar's contribution which seeks to define the specificity, time-course and relationship to presynaptic events, of these changes. The work of the Jerusalem group is reflected in chapters by Newman *et al.* on ECS effects on adenosine receptors, by Ebstein *et al.* on ECS effects on noradrenaline release and by Lerer *et al.* comparing ECT and lithium mechanisms. ECS effects on central cholinergic mechanisms are the focus of Atterwill's contribution which also seeks to relate these effects to alterations in the dopaminergic and GABA-ergic systems.

Neuropeptide mechanism
Belenky *et al.* review the evidence for increased functional endorphin activity following ECS and provide preliminary, supporting receptor-binding data. Emrich and Höllt report related human

2

data on CSF β-endorphin changes following ECT and preliminary findings on vasopressin are reported by Bolwig *et al.* in a subsequent section.

Neuroendocrine aspects
Checkley *et al.* review data from human and primate studies on the use of neuroendocrine probes to test whether reported ECS-induced changes in receptor sensitivity are demonstrable in humans following ECT. Albala *et al.* consider clinical applications of neuroendocrine tests in defining clinical indications for ECT, in monitoring improvement and in predicting relapse. Fink undertakes a synthesis of data regarding ECT effects on neuroendocrine parameters and neuropeptides in the context of an hypothesis linking ECT induced hypothalamic changes to the therapeutic effects of the treatment.

Neurophysiological and clinical studies
Silfverskiöld *et al.* report on the effects of ECT on regional cerebral blood flow and stress differences in the effect of unilateral and bilateral ECT. Bolwig discusses the role of ECS effects on the blood–brain barrier and on synaptic proteins in mediating the therapeutic effects of ECT. Weiner *et al.* present data from a study contrasting the effects of stimulus wave form and electrode placement on therapeutic response, memory function and the EEG. Crow *et al.*, on the basis of findings from a controlled, double-blind study of ECT, link a postulated therapeutic specificity of ECT for delusional depression to animal data suggesting an association between adrenergic failure and depressive delusions.

Adverse effects
Squire summarizes his extensive studies on the nature and extent of memory impairment following ECT and discusses the possible role of specific anatomic structures in the development of these adverse effects. This theme is complemented in the previous sections. Weiner *et al.* consider the relative importance of the electrical stimulus versus the induced seizure activity in the production of ECT-induced memory impairment. Bolwig considers the relevance of ECS effects on deep-brain structures to the adverse effects of ECT. A possible link between ECT-induced amnesia and cholinergic receptor subsensitivity following ECS, is suggested by Lerer *et al.* in the final contribution.

Psychological aspects
The possible role of psychological factors in the therapeutic effect of ECT is reviewed by Brown.

Together these contributions provide a full measure of the current state of research on ECT mechanisms. Although it is not *possible* to fit all these data together in terms of any specific theoretical construct at this time, the many perspectives provided do clearly offer the beginnings of a structural framework for understanding the mode of action of ECT. A comparison between the present data as reflected in this volume and those reported nearly a decade ago, reveals numerous areas marked by great strides, many of which are a function of the application of increasingly sophisticated technical approaches allied to novel hypothetical constructs. Given the extent of current research activities in ECT mechanisms, it will indeed be interesting to compare, a decade from now, the present state of knowledge with that available then. Perhaps by that time the framework of data and hypotheses outlined herein will be built upon to the point where a cohesive whole is attained. Such a development might well provide basis for the replacement of electrically-induced seizures by an alternative somatic treatment approach with fewer adverse effects and devoid of controversial aspects. It is to these goals that this volume is directed.

Abbreviations
ECS has been used throughout for electroconvulsive shock or shocks, and ECT for electroconvulsive therapy, where possible distinguishing thus between the experimental and the clinical.

References

Abrams, R. & Essman, W. B., eds (1982): *Electroconvulsive therapy: biological foundations and clinical applications.* New York: SP Medical and Scientific Books.

American Psychiatric Association Task Force on ECT. (1978): *Electroconvulsive therapy.* Task Force Report No. 14, Washington, D.C.: American Psychiatric Association.

Cerletti, U. & Bini, L. (1938): Un neuvo metodo di shockterapie 'L'elettro-shock'. *Boll. Acad. Med. Roma* **64**, 136-138.

Essman, W. B. (1973): *Neurochemistry of cerebral electroshock.* New York: Spectrum Publications.

Fink, M. (1979): *Convulsive therapy — theory and practice.* New York: Raven Press.

Fink, M., Kety, S., McGaugh, J. & Williams, T., eds (1974): *Psychobiology of convulsive therapy.* Washington, D.C.: V. H. Winston and Sons.

Freeman, C. P. L., Basson, J. V. & Crighton, A. (1978): Double-blind controlled study of electroconvulsive therapy and simulated ECT in depressive illness. *Lancet* **1**, 738-740.

Gangadhar, B. N., Kapur, R. L. & Kalyanasundaram, S. (1982): Comparison of electroconvulsive therapy with imipramine in endogenous depression: a double-blind study. *Br. J. Psychiat.* **141**, 367-371.

Johnstone, E. C., Lawler, P., Stevens, M., Deakin, J. F. W., Frith, C. D., McPherson, K. & Crow, T. J. (1980): The Northwick Park electroconvulsive therapy trial. *Lancet* **2**, 1317-1320.

Lambourn, J. & Gill, D. (1978): A controlled comparison of simulated and real ECT. *Br J. Psychiat.* **133**, 514-519.

Meduna, L. J. (1935): Versuche uber die biologische beeinflussung des abaufes der schizophrenia: camphor und cardiozolkrampfe. *Z. Ges. Neurol. Psychiat.* **152**, 235-262.

Palmer, R. L., ed. (1981): *Electroconvulsive therapy: an appraisal.* Oxford: Oxford University Press.

Pippard, J. & Ellam, L. (1981): *Electroconvulsive treatment in Great Britain, 1980: A report to The Royal College of Psychiatrists.* London: Headley (Gaskell).

Taylor, P. & Fleminger, J. J. (1980): ECT for schizophrenia. *Lancet* **1**, 1380-1384.

West, E. D. (1981): Electric convulsion therapy in depression: a double-blind controlled trial. *Br. Med. J.* **282**, 355-357.

4

1.
Alterations in monoamine-mediated behaviours and biochemical changes after repeated ECS: Studies in their possible association

A. R. GREEN

MRC Clinical Pharmacology Unit, Radcliffe Infirmary, Oxford OX2 6HE, England.

1. Introduction

When rats are given a series of electroconvulsive shocks (ECS) either daily for 8–10 days or intermittently, for example, five ECS spread over 10 days, they display enhanced behavioural responses to 5-hydroxytryptamine (5-HT) and dopamine (DA) agonists. These changes have already been reviewed in detail (Grahame-Smith *et al.*, 1978; Green, 1980). In this chapter I shall briefly review these enhanced behavioural responses together with more recent observations on other monoamine-mediated responses. I will then review some of the biochemical changes which occur after repeated ECS and discuss whether any of the biochemical and behavioural changes may be associated. Finally, I will discuss whether enhanced 5-HT- and DA-mediated behaviours can be produced by pharmacological approaches.

Whilst the chapter will concentrate on work performed in the MRC Clinical Pharmacology Unit at Oxford, it will of course briefly cover other relevant work from other laboratories which is discussed in more detail in other chapters.

2. Monoamine-mediated behavioural responses

2.1. Dopamine

The first report on enhanced locomotor responses to the dopamine agonist, apomorphine, following repeated electroconvulsive shock was by Modigh (1975). This was confirmed shortly afterwards by Evans *et al.* (1976) and Green *et al.* (1977) who examined the behavioural responses to tranylcypromine/L-DOPA and methamphetamine. Enhanced behavioural responses following repeated ECS, to treatments which increase dopamine function, have been subsequently reported by Deakin *et al.* (1981), Wielosz (1981) and Bhavsar *et al.* (1981). Using a model which does not rely on motor activity, White & Barrett (1981) have shown a greater sensitivity to the discriminative stimulus properties of both amphetamine and apomorphine after daily ECS for three days. This again suggests increased dopaminergic function.

It has been demonstrated that the enhanced behavioural responses following repeated ECS are not due to increased penetration of the drugs into the central nervous system. Both Modigh & Jackson (1975) and Heal & Green (1978) observed that in ECS-treated rats there were increased locomotor responses following the injection of dopamine directly into the nucleus accumbens. It also appears that intact presynaptic dopamine function is unnecessary for the enhanced responses since unilateral nigro-striatal lesioned rats showed an enhanced circling response to apomorphine following ECS, which is due to the apomorphine acting on the lesioned side (Green *et al.*, 1977). This result does imply that the changes that are occurring to produce the enhanced response are perhaps happening 'beyond' the dopamine synapse. Such

5

an interpretation has received support from two studies. Firstly, Heal & Green (1978) found that ECS-treated rats showed enhanced behavioural responses to injection of dibutyryl cyclic AMP into the nucleus accumbens. This drug acts at the postsynaptic dopamine site but 'beyond' the receptor; that is, it acts to increase dopamine function even when a DA antagonist is present (Heal *et al.*, 1978). Secondly, it was observed that administration of haloperidol shortly before each ECS administration did not prevent the enhanced DA-mediated behaviours occurring (Green *et al.*, 1980).

Finally, it has been demonstrated that enhanced DA-mediated responses occur after repeated chemically-induced seizures. Convulsions produced by either the inhalant convulsant flurothyl (Green, 1978) or the GABA-antagonist drug bicuculline (Nutt *et al.*, 1980) result in enhanced DA-mediated responses. Indeed, following bicuculline-induced seizures, enhanced dopamine-mediated responses were shown to occur sooner (that is, after fewer seizures) than after ECS (Nutt *et al.*, 1980). However, this appeared to be due to the anaesthetic, administered before the ECS, in some way retarding the rate of appearance of the enhanced responses (Cowen *et al.*, 1980). Enhanced responses occurred more rapidly with ECS administration if the animal was not anaesthetised (Cowen *et al.*, 1980). This retarding effect of anaesthetic is not due to it modifying the seizure and making it less severe, although this undoubtedly happens. If the anaesthetic was given up to four hours after an unmodified ECS, the appearance of the enhanced DA-mediated responses was retarded; suggesting that the anaesthetics were in some way interfering with the postictal changes that are initiating those mechanisms responsible for the enhanced responses (Cowen *et al.*, 1980).

Finally, in regard to postsynaptic DA-mediated responses, it has been found that 6-hydroxy-dopamine lesions of the noradrenergic systems in the brain, whilst not altering the behavioural response to apomorphine, abolished the ECS-induced enhancement of these responses (Green & Deakin, 1980).

Serra *et al.* (1981) observed that there are probably changes in presynaptic dopamine autoreceptors. They found that repeated ECS attenuated the sedative response of a low dose of apomorphine. No alteration was seen in this response after a single ECS. This contrasts with Chiodo & Antelman (1980) who observed long-term changes after a single ECS. The location of the autoreceptor studied by Serra *et al.* (1981) is unclear in view of their biochemical data (section 3.1).

2.2. 5-Hydroxytryptamine
The first report of enhanced 5-HT-mediated behaviours following repeated ECS was that of Evans *et al.* (1976) (see Fig. 1) who examined the behavioural responses following tranyl-cypromine/L-tryptophan and 5-methoxy *N,N*-dimethyltryptamine (5-MeODMT). This finding was confirmed in later reports from the same group (Green *et al.*, 1977; Costain *et al.*, 1979) and by Lebrecht & Nowak (1980) using the 5-HTP-induced head-twitch model (a finding that we have subsequently confirmed; Green & Bowdler, unpublished observations). It was again demonstrated that the enhanced 5-HT-mediated behaviours would occur following

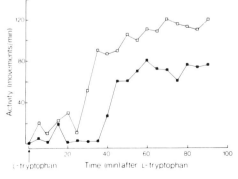

Fig. 1. *Effect of repeated ECS on hyperactivity following tranylcypromine and L-tryptophan*. Rats were given a single ECS each day for 10 d. Some 24 h after the final shock they were injected with tranylcypromine (20 mg kg^{-1}, i.p.) and L-tryptophan (50 mg kg^{-1}, i.p.) 30 min later and hyperactivity measured. Control (halothane anaesthesia only) group (■), ECS group (□). (Reproduced with permission from *Br. J. Pharmacol.*)

chemically-induced seizures, using both flurothyl (Green, 1978) and bicuculline (Nutt *et al.*, 1980).

Enhanced 5-HT-mediated behaviours have been shown to occur under conditions of ECS administration closely mimicking the clinical administration of ECT. That is five ECS given over 10 days (Mon, Wed, Fri, Mon, Wed) to rats administered an anaesthetic and a neuromuscular blocking agent (Costain *et al.*, 1979). The enhanced responses did not occur when the ECS was given in ways not thought to produce therapeutic benefit, for example, multiple ECS in one day or sub-convulsive shocks (Costain *et al.*, 1979; see also Grahame-Smith *et al.*, 1978).

Inhibition of 5-HT synthesis or the administration of a 5-HT antagonist just before each ECS has been shown to prevent the enhanced 5-HT- but not dopamine-mediated behavioural responses (Green *et al.*, 1980). Furthermore, it has been observed that lesions of brain noradrenaline systems, whilst not affecting the behavioural responses to the 5-HT agonist quipazine did prevent ECS enhancing these behaviours (Green & Deakin, 1980). As reported in the previous section, this lesion also prevented ECS enhancing apomorphine-induced behaviours. Finally, enhanced 5-HT-mediated responses have been shown in a model not involving locomotor behaviour. Vetulani *et al.* (1981) observed that repeated ECS enhanced the hyperpyrexia produced by 5-HT agonists.

2.3. *Noradrenaline*

Recently, it has been reported that repeated tricyclic antidepressant administration results in a down-regulation of central α_2-adrenoceptors in rat brain (Smith *et al.*, 1981; Vetulani *et al.*, 1980). We decided to investigate whether changes in α_2-adrenoceptor function could be demonstrated after repeated ECS. α_2-adrenoceptor sensitivity may be tested behaviourally using clonidine-induced sedation (Drew *et al.*, 1979). Following administration of clonidine, rats and mice show a specific type of sedation or hypoactivity which can be rated (Drew *et al.*, 1979). The behavioural parameters rated were: passivity, tactile responsiveness, posture, gait and body sag; full details are given in Heal *et al.* (1981). The clonidine-induced sedation is inhibited by yohimbine but not prazosin.

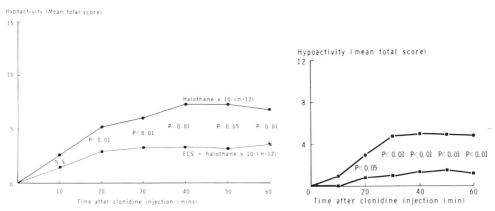

Fig. 2 (above, left). *Effect of repeated ECS on clonidine-induced hypoactivity in mice.* Mice were given either a single ECS while under halothane anaesthesia (■————■) or halothane anaesthesia alone (●————●) once daily for 10 d. Both groups were injected with clonidine (1.0 mg/kg), 24 h after the final treatment. Results were analysed using Wilcoxon's rank order test and where results are significantly different, the significance levels are shown. Twelve mice were used in each group. (Reproduced with permission from *Eur. J. Pharmacol.*)

Fig. 3 (above, right). *Effect of repeated ECS on clonidine-induced hypoactivity in rats.* Rats were given either a single ECS while under halothane anaesthesia (■————■) or halothane anaesthesia alone (●————●) once daily for 10 d. Both groups were injected with clonidine (0.1 mg/kg) 24 h after the final treatment. Results were analysed using Wilcoxon's rank order test and where results are significantly different, the significance levels are shown. 12 Rats were used in each group. (Reproduced with permission from *Eur. J. Pharmacol.*)

Following repeated ECS (once daily for 10 days) mice (Fig. 2) and rats (Fig. 3) showed an attenuated sedative response to clonidine. This attenuation was not observed after a single ECS or a series of subconvulsive shocks. Furthermore, the effect appeared to be mediated through specific mechanisms associated with the α_2-adrenoceptor. Whilst a rather similar behavioural change could be elicited by the administration of the β-adrenoceptor antagonist propranolol, this sedation was not altered by repeated ECS (Fig. 4). In addition, it was found that the decrease in brain MOPEG-SO$_4$ concentration that occurs after clonidine administration was also attenuated by repeated ECS (Table 1).

Recently, we have found that repeated administration of the tricyclic desmethylimipramine also attenuates clonidine-induced sedation (Green et al., 1982a) and Sugrue (1981) has reported that long-term administration of this drug also attenuates the clonidine-induced decrease in rat brain MOPEG-SO$_4$ concentration.

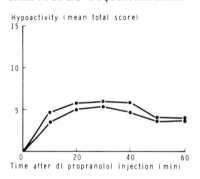

Hypoactivity (mean total score)

Time after dl propranolol injection (min)

Fig. 4. *Effect of repeated ECS on (±)-propranolol-induced hypoactivity in mice.* Mice were given either a single ECS while under halothane anaesthesia (■——■ n 5) or halothane anaesthesia alone (●——● n 9) once daily for 10 d. Both groups were injected with (±)-propranolol (40 mg/kg), 24 h after the last shock. Results were analysed using Wilcoxon's rank order test and there were no significant differences between the two group. (Reproduced with permission from *Eur. J. Pharmacol.*)

Table 1. *Effect of repeated ECS on clonidine-induced changes in brain MOPEG-SO$_4$ concentrations.* Rats were given a single ECS or halothane once daily for 10 d. Twenty-four hours after the final treatment both of these groups plus a group of untreated controls were injected with clonidine (0.25 mg/kg) or saline. 60 min later brain MOPEG-SO$_4$ concentrations were determined. Results are shown as mean ± s.e.m. with the number of observations shown in parentheses. Data were analysed using Student's unpaired t-test

	MOPEG-SO$_4$ concentrations (pmol/g whole brain)		
	Saline-treated		Clonidine-treated
Untreated controls	443 ± 14 (8)	← P< 0.001 →	197 ± 22 (5)
Halothane × 10	416 ± 19 (4)	← P< 0.001 →	238 ± 21 (8)
	n.s.		P< 0.02
ECS × 10	453 ± 76 (5)	← n.s. →	362 ± 35 (9)

Reproduced with permission from Eur. J. Pharmacol. (Elsevier)

3. Changes in neurotransmitter biochemistry and their possible association with the altered behavioural responses

3.1. Dopamine

The behavioural data (section 2.1) suggested that the mechanism of enhancement of DA responses did not involve a change at the postsynaptic DA receptor itself. Biochemical data would support this view. No change in [^{3}H]-spiperone binding in the caudate has been observed after repeated ECS (Bergstrom & Kellar, 1979; Atterwill, 1980; Deakin et al., 1981), nor was any alteration in dopamine-sensitive adenylate cyclase activity observed (Green et al., 1977).

As part of their study on the sensitivity of the dopamine autoreceptor (see section 2.1) Serra et al. (1981) studied the effect of a low dose of apomorphine on the rate of dopamine synthesis. No difference was observed between the control and ECS group on the ability of apomorphine to inhibit dopamine turnover. This raises problems as to the location of the receptors being studied since tricyclics and repeated ECS attenuated the sedative response of the low apomorphine dose but only the tricyclics also attenuated the ability of apomorphine to inhibit dopamine turnover. No change in brain dopamine concentration has been seen after repeated ECS (Evans *et al.*, 1976; Modigh, 1976) nor any change in its rate of synthesis (Modigh, 1976).

3.2. 5-Hydroxytryptamine

There have been several reports of alteration in the rate of synthesis of 5-HT following a single ECS. However, the data obtained have tended to be conflicting. Twenty-four hours following repeated ECS (once daily for 10 days) it seems clear that there is no change in the rate of 5-HT synthesis in whole rat brain (Evans *et al.*, 1976; Modigh, 1976) and more recently we have found no changes in specific brain regions (Green & Cowen, unpublished).

Current research has demonstrated changes in the kinetics of 5-HT uptake into brain slices of cortex prepared from rats given five ECS over 10 days (Minchin *et al.*, 1983) with a significant decrease in the V_{max} and an indication of a decrease in K_m although this failed to reach statistical significance (Table 2). No alteration in the release of 5-HT from slices was seen (Minchin *et al.*, 1983).

Table 2. *Kinetics of uptake of 5-HT into brain slices prepared from rats given repeated ECS.* Results obtained for Lineweaver–Burke plots prepared for 6 or more concentrations of transmitter each point performed in quadruplicate. Number of plots given in brackets. Results show mean ± s.e.m.

	K_m (nM)	V_{max} (nmol 6 min^{-1} g wet wt^{-1})
Anaesthetic (control)	71 ± 10 (7)	0.52 ± 0.06 (7)
ECS	51 ± 8 (8)	0.34 ± 0.05 (8)*

Difference from control: *$P < 0.05$.

With regard to postsynaptic changes, recent evidence has suggested alterations in 5-HT receptor characteristics. Previously it had been reported that the 5-HT receptor was unaltered following repeated ECS; this view being based on [^{3}H]-5-HT binding studies (Bergstrom & Kellar, 1979; Atterwill, 1980; Deakin *et al.*, 1981). However, following the report of the characterisation (using ligand binding) of more than one population of receptor, namely 5-HT$_1$ and 5-HT$_2$ (see, for example, Peroutka & Snyder, 1980), two groups have now reported that there is a marked (35–40 per cent) increase in the number of the 5-HT$_2$ receptors in the cortex following repeated ECS (Kellar *et al.*, 1981a; Vetulani *et al.*, 1981). Since it appears that the behaviours shown to be enhanced by ECS (namely the hyperactivity following tranylcypromine and L-tryptophan or quipazine and the 5-HTP-induced head twitch) are 5-HT$_2$-receptor-mediated (Peroutka *et al.*, 1981; Green *et al.*, 1983) it makes any suggestion that the enhanced 5-HT-mediated behaviours are a reflection of the increase in 5-HT$_2$ receptor number an attractive hypothesis.

3.3. Noradrenaline

It has been known for some years that there are presynaptic changes in noradrenaline (NA) biochemistry following repeated ECS. Turnover of NA is increased (Kety *et al.*, 1967; Modigh, 1976). Modigh (1976), using an *in vivo* technique, suggested that there might be a slight reduction in uptake following ECS. This observation however is not consistent with the observation of Hendley (1976) who examined the kinetics of NA uptake into tissue slices. Following a course of 14 ECS given over seven days, she observed an increase in both V_{max} and K_m.

Recently we re-examined the kinetics of NA uptake into brain slices following administration of ECS in a manner rather closer to the clinical administration of ECT (Minchin *et al.*, 1983). Rats were given five ECS spread out over 10 days, the ECS given whilst the rats were anaesthetised with halothane. Control rats received halothane only. There was no change in the kinetics of NA uptake either 30 min or 24 h following a single ECS (data not shown). However, 24 h after the final of five ECS spread over 10 days, both the K_m and V_{max} for NA uptake were

Table 3. *Kinetics of uptake of NA into brain slices prepared from rats given repeated ECS*. Results obtained from Lineweaver–Burke plots prepared from 6 or more concentrations of transmitter each point performed in quadruplicate. Number of plots given in brackets. Results show mean ± s.e.m.

	Noradrenaline uptake kinetics	
	K_m (nM)	V_{max} (nmol 6 min^{-1} g wet wt^{-1})
Anaesthetic (control)	104 ± 18 (4)	0.83 ± 0.09 (4)
ECS	171 ± 6 (4)†	1.27 ± 0.15 (4)*

Difference from control: *$P < 0.05$; †$P < 0.02$.

elevated (Table 3), the increases being of the same order as those reported by Hendley (1976). It is possible that these changes produce an enhancement of NA uptake from the synaptic cleft into the nerve terminal. This may be an adaptation to increased synaptic cleft concentrations of the transmitter.

There have now been several reports of a decrease in β-adrenoceptor binding in the cortex following repeated ECS (Bergstrom & Kellar, 1979; Pandey et al., 1979; Deakin et al., 1981; Stanford & Nutt, 1982). This change occurs not only after daily ECS for 10 or more days, as in the work cited above, but has now been shown to occur after intermittent ECS administration (Belmaker et al., 1982). The change could be a reflection of the higher synaptic cleft concentrations of NA that are occurring and is a compensatory down-regulation. A down-regulation of β-adrenoceptors has also been shown to occur after repeated administration of certain antidepressants (see review by Green & Nutt, 1983).

What is interesting is that the β-adrenoceptor down-regulation shows regional specificity. Both Kellar et al. (1981b) and Stanford & Nutt (1982) observed decreased β-adrenoceptor binding in the cortex and hippocampus but not the hypothalamus, cerebellum or striatum.

Our observation that repeated ECS attenuated the sedative effect of clonidine and decreased the ability of this drug to lower brain MOPEG-SO$_4$ concentration (see section 2.3) led us to examine the effect of repeated ECS on [^{3}H]-clonidine binding. It was found using saturation analysis that there was a decrease in cortical [^{3}H]-clonidine binding following repeated ECS. The decrease was in the number of binding sites (B_{max}) not the affinity (K_d) (Fig. 5). These data (Stanford & Nutt, 1982) provide the simplest explanation for the lessening of both the behavioural and biochemical effects of clonidine following repeated ECS. Nevertheless, it should be noted that neither Kellar et al. (1981b) nor Deakin et al. (1981) detected any change in [^{3}H]-clonidine binding. However, they were using single concentration analysis.

If the α_2-adrenoceptor is presynaptic, and there are problems in making this assumption (U'Pritchard et al., 1979) then one might suggest that the α_2-adrenoceptor down-regulates in response to a high synaptic cleft concentration of NA (although this does not seem to be an entirely reasonable response of a receptor which is suggested to be present to regulate synaptic cleft concentration of transmitter!).

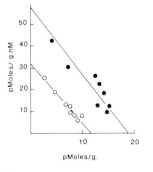

Fig. 5. *Scatchard plots for specific [^{3}H]-clonidine binding in rat cerebral cortex 24 h after the last of 10 once-daily ECS or sham ECS*. Membranes were incubated with [^{3}H]-clonidine over a concentration range 0.1–1.5 nM. B_{max} of ECS group is significantly different from controls at $P < 0.001$ [control 18.9 ± 1.5; ECS 11.7 ± 0.6, $n = 10$]

We have found that repeated desmethylimipramine administration, like repeated ECS, attenuates the sedative effect of clonidine (Green *et al.*, 1982a) and has been reported to also attenuate the brain MOPEG-SO$_4$ concentration lowering effect of clonidine (Sugrue, 1981) and decrease β-adrenoceptor binding (see Green & Nutt, 1983). However, preliminary experiments have not found that repeated desmethylimipramine administration is able to mimic ECS in regard to increasing the behavioural responses to either quipazine or apomorphine (Cowen & Green, unpublished). It thus seems unlikely that either the α_2- or β-adrenoceptor changes in any way initiate the enhanced monoamine-mediated behaviours, although clearly the α_2-adrenoceptor down-regulation is probably associated with the attenuation of clonidine-induced sedation.

3.4. *GABA*

In 1978 we reported that when rats were given a series of electroconvulsive shocks (once daily for 10 days) there was an increase in the GABA concentration in the nucleus accumbens and nucleus caudatus, but no change in the substantia nigra (Green *et al.*, 1978). This change was accompanied by a decrease in the rate of GABA synthesis in these two regions. No changes were seen in rats given either a single ECS or daily sub-convulsive shocks (Green *et al.*, 1978). At the time, it was suggested that these changes might be reflecting a decrease in GABA release in interneurones in these regions (with no change occurring in the main striato-nigral pathway) and that the altered GABA biochemistry might be associated with the altered monoamine-mediated behaviours.

Subsequently, Deakin *et al.* (1981) reported that they were unable to confirm the rise in striatal GABA concentration in rats which had been given ECS during anaesthesia and suggested that the anaesthetic in some way prevented the GABA increase. However, increased monoamine-mediated behaviours are seen in rats following repeated ECS irrespective of whether the rats have, or have not, been anaesthetised during the seizure (Cowen *et al.*, 1980). We therefore recently re-examined the effect of ECS, both with and without anaesthetic, on brain GABA content and investigated whether a change in striatal GABA concentration can be demonstrated at times when enhanced monoamine-mediated behaviours are seen.

In the first experiments rats were given an ECS daily for 10 days and the regional brain GABA content examined 24 h after the final ECS. It was confirmed that at this time there was a statistically significant increase in striatal GABA concentration. An increase was also seen in the hypothalamus but no change in cortex or hippocampus (Table 4). When the ECS was given daily to rats that had been lightly anaesthetised with halothane, there was again an increase in striatal GABA concentration compared to rats given anaesthetic only, even though the anaesthetic administration alone did appear to increase GABA concentration in all brain regions compared to animals that had only been handled (Table 4). It is possible that the failure of Deakin *et al.* (1981) to see a change in striatal GABA content following ECS was because their animals were not killed by microwave irradiation as in the original study (Green *et al.*, 1978) and the investigation being reported here (Bowdler *et al.*, 1983).

Table 4. *Regional brain GABA concentrations (μmol/g tissue) following repeated ECS.* Rats were given either a daily ECS for 10 d with or without halothane anaesthesia and were sacrificed 24 h following the final ECS or 5 ECS under halothane anaesthesia spread out over 10 d (days 1, 3, 5, 8 and 10) or halothane only and sacrificed 24 h following the final treatment. Results are shown as the mean ± s.d. with the number of observations in brackets

	Hippocampus	Cortex	Hypothalamus	Corpus striatum
Handled × 10	2.90 ± 0.12 (4)	2.36 ± 0.22 (4)	4.61 ± 0.40 (3)	3.35 ± 0.61 (4)
ECS × 10	3.29 ± 0.72 (13)	2.29 ± 0.37 (13)	6.38 ± 1.57 (11)§	4.49 ± 0.62 (11)§
Anaesthetic × 10	3.91 ± 0.19 (5)	3.10 ± 0.36 (5)	6.17 ± 1.13 (5)	4.77 ± 0.35 (5)
ECS/anaesthetic × 10	4.66 ± 0.59 (4)	3.30 ± 0.12 (4)	7.41 ± 0.47 (3)	6.18 ± 0.60 (4)§
Anaesthetic × 5/10 days	3.31 ± 0.36 (7)	2.68 ± 1.06 (7)	6.41 ± 2.17 (7)	3.46 ± 0.86 (6)
ECS/anaesthetic × 5/10 days	3.78 ± 0.42 (6)*	2.80 ± 0.36 (6)	7.46 ± 1.32 (5)	5.21 ± 0.98 (5)†

Difference from appropriate control: *$P < 0.05$; †$P < 0.02$; §$P < 0.01$.

We next investigated whether an increased striatal GABA concentration could be seen after administration of ECS in ways which result in enhanced monoamine-mediated behaviours. When five ECS were given over 10 days an increase in striatal GABA concentration was seen (Table 4). Enhanced monoamine-mediated responses can be observed 24 h after a daily ECS for five days when anaesthetic has not been administered (Cowen et al., 1980) and are present for around seven days following the final of 10 daily ECS given to mice (Green et al., 1977). Twenty-four hours after five ECS (once daily), a change in GABA content was seen only in the striatum (handled 4.15 ± 0.61 (6); ECS $\times$ 5: 5.47 ± 0.91 (10), results in μmol/g brain, 32 per cent increase, $P < 0.01$). Similarly, 72 h after 10 ECS (one daily) only striatal GABA was elevated (handled: 3.24 ± 0.20; ECS $\times$ 10: 3.96 ± 0.57 (5), 22 per cent, $P < 0.01$).

As stated earlier, enhanced monoamine-mediated behaviours can be observed after repeated convulsions induced by the inhalant convulsant flurothyl (Green, 1978). Repeated flurothyl-induced seizures did increase the striatal GABA concentration but also increased the concentration in other regions compared to handled controls (Table 5) (see Bowdler et al., 1983).

Table 5. *Regional brain GABA concentrations following repeated flurothy-induced convulsions.* Rats were either handled daily for 10 d or had a convulsion induced daily for 10 d by exposure to flurothyl. Results show mean ± s.d. with the number of observations in brackets

	Hippocampus	Cortex	Hypothalamus	Corpus striatum
Handled	3.01 ± 0.37 (4)	2.19 ± 0.11 (4)	5.24 ± 1.00 (4)	3.87 ± 0.13 (4)
Flurothyl	3.70 ± 0.40 (8)*	2.56 ± 0.18 (8)†	7.11 ± 0.80 (8)†	4.63 ± 0.44 (8)†

Difference from controls: *$P < 0.02$; †$P < 0.01$.

We next performed experiments in which GABA antagonist drugs were given just before each ECS in an attempt to disrupt possible post-ictal changes in GABA neurones (for details see Green et al., 1982b). Rats were given five ECS spread over 10 days (Mon, Wed, Fri, Mon, Wed) during halothane anaesthesia. Control rats were given halothane alone. Both biochemical and behavioural measures were made 24 h after the final ECS. The GABA antagonists bicuculline or pentylenetetrazol were given intraperitoneally 3 min before the halothane (control group) or halothane/ECS (experimental group). Pentylenetetrazol (PTZ) was dissolved in saline and bicuculline dissolve in pH 3 saline. Doses administered were 30 mg/kg for PTZ (which is about 50% of the CD_{50}) and 3.5 mg/kg for bicuculline (which is about 75% of the CD_{50}, because of the rapid inactivation of the drug). At these doses neither drug produces kindling (Nutt et al., 1982).

As expected, the repeated ECS administration resulted in enhanced behavioural responses to both quipazine and apomorphine (Table 6). An increase in striatal GABA concentration was also observed (Table 7). Pretreatment of the rats with either PTZ or bicuculline prevented the enhanced behavioural responses to both quipazine and apomorphine (Table 6). However,

Table 6. *Behavioural responses to apomorphine following five ECS over 10 days and the effect of GABA antagonists before each ECS.* Results expressed as mean ± s.e.m. with number of determinants in brackets. Dose of bicuculline, 3.5 mg/kg; PTZ, 30 mg/kg

		Recorded movements/50 min		
	Pretreatment	Control	ECS	P value
Apomorphine				
	Saline	1527 ± 146 (4)	2412 ± 127 (4)	< 0.01
	PTZ	1354 ± 159 (6)	1551 ± 147 (5)	n.s.
	Bicuculline	1239 ± 264 (4)	1417 ± 203 (4)	n.s.
Quipazine				
	Saline	2063 ± 145 (6)	2901 ± 163 (6)	< 0.025
	PTZ	2351 ± 254 (6)	2548 ± 271 (5)	n.s.
	Bicuculline	2296 ± 265 (4)	2391 ± 403 (4)	n.s.

Table 7. *Effect of pretreatment of rats with GABA antagonists before each ECS (five ECS over 10 days) on regional brain GABA concentrations 24 h following the final ECS.* Results are expressed as mean ± s.e.m. with number of determinations in brackets. Dose of bicuculline was 3.5 mg/kg and pentylenetetrazol (PTZ) 30 mg/kg

Treatment	Pretreatment	Corpus striatum	Hypothalamus	Hippocampus	Cortex
Halothane	Saline	3.45 ± 0.35 (6)	6.40 ± 0.60 (7)	3.30 ± 0.14 (7)	2.37 ± 0.30 (6)
Halothane/ECS	Saline	5.21 ± 0.44 (5)[†]	7.45 ± 0.58 (5)	3.78 ± 0.47 (6)	2.79 ± 0.14 (6)
Halothane	PTZ	4.08 ± 0.26 (4)	5.68 ± 0.72 (6)	3.19 ± 0.11 (6)	2.27 ± 0.13 (6)
Halothane/ECS	PTZ	4.25 ± 0.31 (6)	5.62 ± 0.47 (7)	3.32 ± 0.20 (7)	2.65 ± 0.25 (7)
Halothane	Bicuculline	4.57 ± 0.28 (6)	6.67 ± 0.29 (6)	3.61 ± 0.24 (5)	2.86 ± 0.15 (6)
Halothane/ECS	Bicuculline	3.62 ± 0.22 (6)*	4.99 ± 0.20 (6)[§]	2.84 ± 0.20 (5)*	2.35 ± 0.10 (5)[†]

Difference from appropriate control value: *$P < 0.05$; [†]$P < 0.02$; [§]$P < 0.001$.

interestingly, whilst the behaviours were not enhanced, the animals displayed the hyper-reactivity and irritability associated with repeated ECS (Modigh, 1975). Pretreatment with the antagonist drugs also prevented the increase in striatal GABA concentration (Table 7). Following bicuculline the ECS-treated rats had in fact lower concentrations of GABA in each brain region examined than the control (bicuculline only) group.

Taken together, therefore, all these data (Bowdler *et al.*, 1983; Green *et al.*, 1982*b*) provide reasonable grounds for the supposition that the enhanced monoamine-mediated behaviours might be associated with a change in GABA biochemistry. The increase in striatal GABA concentration occurs 24 h after the last of a series of ECS, given in ways which result in enhanced monoamine-mediated behaviours and is present at other times when enhanced responses are seen (e.g. after five ECS and three days after the last of 10 ECS). Furthermore, administration of GABA antagonist drugs just before each ECS prevented both the enhanced monoamine-mediated behaviours and the change in striatal GABA content.

This does not mean that the change has to occur in the striatum. In the original study a change in GABA concentration was also seen in the nucleus accumbens. We know that following ECS the behaviours mediated by dopamine in this region are enhanced. (Modigh & Jackson, 1975; Heal & Green, 1978). Clearly it is important to confirm and extend the observation that the change in GABA concentration is associated with a decrease in GABA synthesis in specific brain regions (Green *et al.*, 1978) and, if possible, link this to a decrease in GABA function.

One confusing point at present is that Atterwill *et al.* (1981), in a study on the activity of the enzyme glutamic acid decarboxylase in the striatum, found that following repeated ECS there was a small but statistically significant increase in activity, which is unexpected in the light of the observation that turnover might be decreased (Green *et al.*, 1978).

With regard to the characteristics of the GABA receptor following repeated ECS, Deakin *et al.* (1981) observed no difference in [³H]-GABA binding in the cortex and Atterwill *et al.* (1981) also observed no difference in [³H]-muscimol binding in either this region or the striatum. No change has been seen in the characteristics of [³H]-diazepam binding suggesting that this site, which can modulate GABA function, is unchanged by repeated ECS (Bowdler *et al.*, 1983). McNamara *et al.* (1980) did observe an increase in hippocampal benzodiazepine binding after ECS but only after 17 days treatment rather than 10 as in the present study.

3.5. *Opiate peptides*

Green *et al.* (1978) observed that repeated ECS increased the concentration of met[5]-enkephalin in the nucleus caudatus. This finding was confirmed and extended by Hong *et al.* (1979) who showed that the change also occurred in several other brain regions and lasted for several days after the last seizure. They also reported that β-endorphin concentration did not change. Whether these changes are in any way connected with the altered monoamine-mediated behaviours is at present unknown.

4. Can enhanced monoamine-mediated behaviours be produced without the need for a seizure?

In the long term, a major goal in our investigations has been to try and find biochemical and behavioural changes following ECS that might give us a clue as to the therapeutic mechanism of this treatment. Using such data we feel it might be possible to predict pharmacological treatments with a similar high degree of efficacy but, it is hoped, with greater specificity of action and thus perhaps fewer side-effects. To date two approaches have been made to see whether enhanced monoamine-mediated behaviours can be produced by pharmacological treatments.

The first approach involved the use of GABA antagonist drugs in an attempt to alter GABA biochemistry in a similar way to that seen after repeated ECS. Rats were given daily sub-convulsive doses of the GABA antagonist drugs picrotoxin, bicuculline or PTZ. Only after PTZ (daily for eight days at a dose of 30 mg/kg i.p.) was an enhancement of monoamine-mediated behaviours seen and then only to apomorphine (Cowen *et al.*, 1982*b*). The activity response to apomorphine was doubled in the PTZ-treated rats (Table 8) whilst the response to quipazine was not significantly increased (Table 8). A subsequent biochemical study (Green *et al.*, 1982*b*) failed to detect an increase in striatal GABA concentration as is seen after repeated ECS (see section 3.4). However, whilst this does not preclude a change occurring in the nucleus accumbens it does indicate that the mechanism involved in the enhanced DA responses after repeated PTZ might be different.

Table 8. *The effect of repeated administration of sub-convulsive doses of PTZ on the locomotor responses to apomorphine (AP) and quipazine.* Rats were treated daily with either i.p. saline or PTZ for 8 d. Twenty-four hours after the last treatment the locomotor responses to either AP (0.1 mg/kg^{-1} s.c.) or to quipazine (25 mg/kg^{-1} i.p.) were recorded in groups of three rats on Automex activity meters for the period of 50 min following the injection. Numbers represent the mean and s.d. of the total counts during this period, with the number of experiments in brackets. Statistical significance was assessed by Student's *t*-test (experimental animals versus saline controls)

Pretreatment	Drug challenge	
	AP	Quipazine
Saline	856 ± 141 (5)	2936 ± 338 (5)
PTZ (30 mg/kg^{-1} i.p.)	1652 ± 272 (6)*	3572 ± 665 (5)

*$P < 0.001$. (Reproduced with permission from Psychopharmacology.)

With regard to enhanced 5-HT-mediated responses, we have succeeded in producing this effect by pretreatment with β_2-adrenoceptor agonists, including salbutamol and the much more liposoluble compound clenbuterol (Cowen *et al.*, 1982*a*). Acute administration of, for example, clenbuterol was found to enhance 5-HT-mediated behaviours (Fig. 6) in an analogous manner to repeated ECS. However, in contrast to ECS, DA-mediated behaviours were not increased (Cowen *et al.*, 1982*a*). It is at present unclear why β-adrenoceptor agonists should enhance 5-HT-mediated behaviours, but it is clearly of interest in the light of the apparent relationship between intact NA function and enhanced 5-HT responses following ECS.

5. Conclusions

It is clear that there are many changes that occur following repeated ECS. It is probable that some of these changes are involved in the therapeutic effect of ECT, others involved in the side-effects of the treatment and others have no relevance to either. In this chapter I have taken as a basis the enhanced monoamine-mediated behaviours and examined whether these might be associated with any of the biochemical changes.

It seems reasonable to suppose that noradrenaline is associated in some way with the enhanced 5-HT- and DA-mediated responses since lesioning of the NA pathways abolishes the ECS-induced enhancement of these responses. In addition, we, and others, have observed various biochemical changes which occur after other antidepressant treatments (down-regulation of both β- and α_2-adrenoceptors). Furthermore, administration of a β-adrenoceptor agonist results in enhanced 5-HT-mediated behaviours.

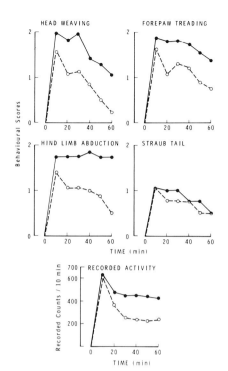

Fig. 6. *Effect of clenbuterol (5 mg/kg) pretreatment on the behavioural responses and recorded activity of pairs of rats following administration of quipazine (25 mg/kg).* Rats were pretreated with saline (o) or clenbuterol (●) (5 mg/kg). Quipazine was injected 15 min later (time zero) and the behavioural responses measured at 10 min intervals thereafter. Results show mean behavioural scores (8 animals in each group) against time after quipazine injection. Head weaving was enhanced ($P < 0.01$) during the period 20–60 min; forepaw treading ($P < 0.02$ at 20 min; $P < 0.05$ during period 30–60 min), hind limb abduction ($P < 0.05$ at 20 min; $P < 0.01$ during period 30–60 min) and recorded activity ($P < 0.05$ at 30, 50 and 60 min; $P < 0.02$ at 40 min) were also enhanced by clenbuterol treatment. Total recorded activity also increased during the 60 min following quipazine ($P < 0.025$). (Reproduced with permission from *Br. J. Pharmacol.*)

GABA also seems to be involved in the enhanced responses. Sub-convulsive doses of PTZ resulted in an increase in DA-mediated behaviours and there are clear changes in GABA biochemistry following repeated ECS. Prevention of these changes abolished the enhanced monoamine-mediated behaviours.

It is reasonable to suggest that the enhanced 5-HT-mediated behaviours are a reflection of the reported increase in 5-HT$_2$ receptor number although the mechanism by which the receptor number increases is unknown. In contrast, there is apparently no increase in DA receptor number and it therefore seems probable that the enhanced behaviours result from the alteration in other modulatory neurotransmitters acting on dopamine neurotransmission. In this regard GABA is a possible candidate since altering GABA function has been shown to alter DA-mediated behaviours (Green *et al.*, 1976; Cott & Engel, 1977).

We would also suggest that the attenuation of clonidine-induced sedation is probably linked to the reported decrease in [^{3}H]-clonidine binding, although it is at present unclear whether this receptor is presynaptic.

It may be that the proposed goal of a pharmacological treatment in place of ECT is not going to be easy to achieve. One can speculate that the success of ECT is due to it changing the function of more than one neurotransmitter system. Noradrenaline and 5-HT biochemistry and function change and these changes may be associated with the antidepressant effect, whilst the increase in dopamine function may result in an increase in 'drive'. It may not be easy to produce a similar diversity of changes with a single drug. However, only clinical investigation with a drug such as clenbuterol will be able to answer such a question. Meanwhile, attempts to link biochemical and behavioural changes will doubtless continue both in Oxford and elsewhere.

Acknowledgements — The studies reported in this chapter are the result of collaboration with a group of colleagues to whom I am indebted. They are Professor David Grahame-Smith, Drs David Nutt, Philip Cowen, David Heal, Michael Minchin, and Ms Julie Bowdler in Clinical Pharmacology, Oxford, Dr Clare Stanford in the Department of Physiology, Oxford, and Dr William Deakin at The National Institute for Medical Research, London.

References

Atterwill, C. K. (1980): Lack of effect of repeated electroconvulsive shock on [³H]-5-hydroxytryptamine binding and cholinergic parameters in rat brain. *J. Neurochem.* **35**, 729–734.

Atterwill, C. K., Batts, C. & Bloomfield, M. R. (1981): Effect of single and repeated convulsions on glutamate decarboxylase (GAD) activity and [³H]-muscimol binding in the rat brain. *J. Pharm. Pharmacol.* **33**, 329–331.

Belmaker, R. H., Lerer, B., Bannet, J. & Birmaher, B. (1982): The effect of electroconvulsive shock at a clinically equivalent schedule on rat cortical β-adrenoceptors. *J. Pharm. Pharmacol.* **34**, 275.

Bergstrom, D. A. & Kellar, K. J. (1979): Effect of electroconvulsive shock on monoaminergic receptor binding sites in rat brain. *Nature* **278**, 464–466.

Bhavsar, V. H., Dhumal, V. R. & Kelkar, V. V. (1981): The effect of some anti-epilepsy drugs on enhancement of the monoamine-mediated behavioural responses following the administration of electroconvulsive shocks to rats. *Eur. J. Pharmacol.* **74**, 243–247.

Bowdler, J. M., Green, A. R., Minchin, M. C. W. & Nutt, D. J. (1983): Regional GABA concentration and [³H]-diazepam binding in rat brain following repeated electroconvulsive shock. *J. Neural Transm.* **56**, 3–12.

Chiodo, L. A. & Antelman, S. M. (1980): Electroconvulsive shock: progressive dopamine autoreceptor subsensitivity independent of repeated treatment. *Science* **210**, 799–801.

Costain, D. W., Green, A. R. & Grahame-Smith, D. G. (1979): Enhanced 5-hydroxytryptamine-mediated behavioural responses in rats following repeated electroconvulsive shock: relevance to the mechanism of the anti-depressive effect of electroconvulsive therapy. *Psychopharmacology* **61**, 167–170.

Cott, J. & Engel, J. (1977): Suppression by GABAergic drugs of the locomotor stimulation induced by morphine, ampetamine and apomorphine: evidence for both pre- and post-synaptic inhibition of catecholamine systems. *J. Neural Trans.* **40**, 253–268.'

Cowen, P. J., Grahame-Smith, D. G., Green, A. R. & Heal, D. J. (1982a): β-Adrenoceptor agonists enhance 5-hydroxytryptamine-mediated behavioural responses. *Br. J. Pharmacol.* **76**, 265–270.

Cowen, P. J., Nutt, D. J., Batts, C. C., Green, A. R. & Heal, D. J. (1982b): Repeated administration of subconvulsant doses of GABA antagonist drugs II. Effect on monoamine-mediated behaviour. *Psychopharmacology* **76**, 88–91.

Cowen, P. J., Nutt, D. J. & Green, A. R. (1980): Enhanced 5-hydroxytryptamine- and dopamine-mediated behavioural responses following convulsion II: the effects of anaesthesia and current conditions on the appearance of the enhanced responses following electroconvulsive shock. *Neuropharmacology* **19**, 901–906.

Deakin, J. F. W., Owen, F., Cross, A. J. & Dashwood, M. J. (1981): Studies on possible mechanisms of action of electroconvulsive therapy: effects of repeated electrically-induced seizures on rat brain receptors for monoamines and other neurotransmitters. *Psychopharmacology* **73**, 345–349.

Drew, G. M., Gower, A. J. & Marriott, A. S. (1979): α₂-Adrenoceptors mediate clonidine-induced sedation in the rat. *Br. J. Pharmacol.* **67**, 133–141.

Evans, J. P. M., Grahame-Smith, D. G., Green, A. R. & Tordoff, A. F. C. (1976): Electroconvulsive shock increases the behavioural responses of rats to brain 5-hydroxytryptamine accumulation and central nervous system stimulant drugs. *Br. J. Pharmacol.* **56**, 193–199.

Grahame-Smith, D. G., Green, A. R. & Costain, D. W. (1978): Mechanism of the antidepressant action of electro-convulsive therapy. *Lancet* **1**, 254–256.

Green, A. R. (1978): Repeated exposure of rats to the convulsant agent flurothyl enhanced 5-hydroxytryptamine- and dopamine-mediated behavioural responses. *Br. J. Pharmacol.* **62**, 325–331.

Green, A. R. (1980): The behavioural and biochemical consequences of repeated electroconvulsive shock administration to rats and the possible clinical relevance of these changes. In *Enzymes and neurotransmitters in mental disease*, eds E. Usdin, T. L. Sourkes & M. B. H. Youdim, pp. 455–467. Chichester: John Wiley & Sons.

Green, A. R., Costain, D. W. & Deakin, J. F. W. (1980): Enhanced 5-hydroxytryptamine and dopamine-mediated behavioural responses following convulsions III. The effects of monoamine antagonists and synthesis inhibitors on the ability of electroconvulsive shock to enhance responses. *Neuropharmacology* **19**, 907–914.

Green, A. R. & Deakin, J. F. W. (1980): Brain noradrenaline depletion prevents ECS-induced enhancement of serotonin- and dopamine-mediate behaviour. *Nature* **285**, 232–233.

Green, A. R., Heal, D. J. & Grahame-Smith, D. G. (1977): Further observations on the effect of repeated electro-convulsive shock on the behavioural responses of rats produced by increases in the functional activity of brain 5-hydroxytryptamine and dopamine. *Psychopharmacology* **52**, 195–200.

Green, A. R., Heal, D. J., Lister, S. & Molyneux, S. (1982a): The effect of acute and repeated desmethylimipramine administration on clonidine-induced hypoactivity in rats. *Br. J. Pharmacol.* **75**, 33 pp.

Green, A. R. & Nutt, D. J. (1983): Antidepressants. In *Psychopharmacology I*, eds D. G. Grahame-Smith, H. Hippius & G. Winokur. Amsterdam: Excerpta Medica, **1/1**, 1–37.

Green, A. R., Peralta, E., Hong, J. S., Mao, C. C., Atterwill, C. K. & Costa, E. (1978): Alterations in GABA metabolism and Met-enkephalin contents in rat brain following repeated electroconvulsive shocks. *J. Neurochem.* **31**, 607–611.

Green, A. R., Sant, K., Bowdler, J. M. & Cowen, P. J. (1982b): Further evidence for a relationship between changes in GABA concentration in rat brain and enhanced monoamine-mediated behaviours following repeated electro-convulsive shock. *Neuropharmacology* **21**, 981–984.

Green, A. R., O'Shaughnessy, K., Hammond, M., Schächter, M. & Grahame-Smith, D. G. (1983): Inhibition of 5-hydroxytryptamine-mediated behaviours by the putative 5-HT₂ antagonist pirenperone. *Neuropharmacology* **22**, 573–578

Green, A. R., Tordoff, A. F. C. & Bloomfield, M. R. (1976): Elevation of brain GABA concentrations with amino-oxyacetic acid: effect on the hyperactivity syndrome produced by increased 5-hydroxytryptamine synthesis in rats. *J. Neural Transm.* **39**, 103–112.

Heal, D. J., Akagi, H., Bowdler, J. M. & Green, A. R. (1981): Repeated electroconvulsive shock attenuates clonidine-induced hypoactivity in rodents. *Eur. J. Pharmacol.* **75**, 231–237.

Heal, D. J. & Green, A. R. (1978): Repeated electroconvulsive shock increases the behavioural responses of rats to injection of both dopamine and dibutyryl cyclic AMP into the nucleus accumbens. *Neuropharmacology* **17**, 1085–1087.

Heal, D. J., Phillips, A. G. & Green, A. R. (1978): Studies on the locomotor activity produced by injection of dibutytyl cyclic 3′5′-AMP into the nucleus accumbens of rats. *Neuropharmacology* **17**, 265–270.

Hendley, E. D. (1976): Electroconvulsive shock and norepinephrine uptake kinetics in rat brain. *Psychopharmacol. Commun.* **2**, 17–25.

Hong, J. S., Gillin, J. C., Yang, H-Y. T. & Costa, E. (1979): Repeated electroconvulsive shocks and the brain content of endorphins. *Brain Research* **177**, 273–278.

Kellar, K. J., Cascio, C. S., Bergstrom, D. A., Butler, J. A. & Iadarola, P. (1981b): Electroconvulsive shock and reserpine: effects on β-adrenergic receptors in rat brain. *J. Neurochem.* **37**, 830–836.

Kellar, K. J., Cascio, C. S., Butler, J. A. & Kurtzke, R. W. (1981a): Differential effects of electroconvulsive shock and antidepressant drugs on serotonin-2-receptors in rat brain. *Eur. J. Pharmacol.* **69**, 515–518.

Kety, S. S., Javoy, F., Thierry, A. M., Julou, Z. & Glowinski, J. (1967): A sustained effect of electroconvulsive shock on the turnover of norepinephrine in the central nervous system of the rat. *Proc. Natl. Acad. Sci. USA*, **58**, 1249–1254.

Lebrecht, U. & Nowak, J. Z. (1980): Effect of single and repeated electroconvulsive shock on serotonergic system in rat brain II — behavioural studies. *Neuropharmacology* **19**, 1055–1061.

McNamara, J. O., Peper, A. M. & Patrone, V. (1980): Repeated seizures induce long-term increase in hippocampal benzodiazepine receptors. *Proc. Natl. Acad. Sci. USA* **77**, 3029–3032.

Minchin, M. C. W., Williams, J., Bowdler, J. M. & Green, A. R. (1983): The effect of electroconvulsive shock on the uptake and release of noradrenaline and 5-hydroxytryptamine in rat brain slices. *J. Neurochem.* **40**, 765–768.

Modigh, K. (1975): Electroconvulsive shock and post-synaptic catecholamine effects: increased psychomotor stimulant action of apomorphine and clonidine in reserpine pretreated mice by repeated ECS. *J. Neural. Transm.* **36**, 19–32.

Modigh, K. (1976): Long term effects of electroconvulsive shock therapy on synthesis, turnover and uptake of brain monoamines. *Psychopharmacology* **49**, 179.

Modigh, K. & Jackson, P. M. (1975): Evidence for a sustained effect of ECS on neuronal structures connected to brain catecholamine neurones. *Abst. 6th Int. Congr. Pharmacol. Helsinki*, p. 172.

Nutt, D. J., Cowen, P. J., Batts, C. C., Grahame-Smith, D. G. & Green, A. R. (1982): Repeated administration of subconvulsant doses of GABA antagonist drugs 1. Effect on seizure threshold (kindling). *Psychopharmacology* **76**, 84–847.

Nutt, D. J., Green, A. R. & Grahame-Smith, D. G. (1980): Enhanced 5-hydroxytryptamine- and dopamine-mediated behavioural responses following convulsions 1: the effects of single and repeated bicuculline-induced seizures. *Neuropharmacology* **19**, 897–900.

Pandey, G. N., Heinze, W. J., Brown, B. D. & Davis, J. M. (1979): Electroconvulsive shock treatment decreases β-adrenergic receptor sensitivity in rat brain. *Nature* **280**, 234–235.

Peroutka, S. J., Lebovitz, R. M. & Snyder, S. H. (1981): Two distinct central serotonin receptors with different physiological functions. *Science* **212**, 827–829.

Peroutka, S. J. & Snyder, S. H. (1980): Long term antidepressant treatment decreases spiroperidol-labelled serotonin receptor binding. *Science* **210**, 88.

Serra, G., Argiolas, A., Fadda, F., Melis, M. R. & Gessa, G. L. (1981): Repeated electroconvulsive shock prevents the sedative effect of small doses of apomorphine. *Psychopharmacology* **73**, 194–196.

Smith, C. G., Garcia-Sevilla, J. A. & Hollingsworth, P. J. (1981): α_2-adrenoreceptors in rat brain are decreased after long-term tricyclic antidepressant drug treatment. *Brain Res.* **210**, 413–418.

Stanford, C. & Nutt, D. J. (1982): Comparison of the effects of repeated ECS on α_2- and β-receptors on different regions of rat brain. *Neuroscience* (in press).

Sugrue, M. F. (1981): Effects of acutely and chronically administered antidepressants on the clonidine-induced decreased in rat brain 3-methoxy-4-hydroxyphenylethylene-glycol sulphate content. *Life Sci.* **28**, 377–384.

U'Prichard, D., Bechtel, W., Roust, B. & Snyder, S. H. (1979): Multiple apparent alpha noradrenergic receptor binding sites in rat brain: effect of 6-hydroxydopamine. *Mol. Pharmacol.* **16**, 47–60.

Vetulani, J., Antkiewicz-Michaluk, L., Golembiowska-Nikitin, K., Michaluk, J., Pilc, A. & Rokosz, A. (1980): The effect of multiple imipramine administration on monoaminergic systems of the rat brain. *Pol. J. Pharmacol.* **32**, 523–530.

Vetulani, J., Lebrecht, U. & Pilc, A. (1981): Enhancement of responsiveness of the central serotonergic system and serotonin-2 receptor density in rat frontal cortex by electroconvulsive treatment. *Eur. J. Pharmacol.* **76**, 81–85.

White, D. K. & Barrett, R. J. (1981): The effects of electroconvulsive shock on the discriminative stimulus properties of d-amphetamine and apomorphine: evidence for dopamine receptor alteration subsequent to ECS. *Psychopharmacology* **73**, 211–214.

Wielosz, M. (1981): Increased sensitivity to dopaminergic agonists after repeated electroconvulsive shock in rats. *Neuropharmacology* **20**, 941–945.

2.

Increased responsiveness of dopamine receptors after ECT — A review of experimental and clinical evidence

K. MODIGH, J. BALLDIN, E. ERIKSSON, A.-K. GRANÉRUS and J. WÅLINDER

University of Göteborg, Göteborg, Sweden; Department of psychiatry and neurochemistry, St. Jörgen's Hospital (KM, JB, (JW); Department of pharmacology (KM, JB, EE); Department of geriatric and long-term care medicine, Vasa Hospital (A-KG).

Introduction

The use of electroconvulsive therapy (ECT) as a treatment for depressive illness has until recently been based solely on empirical clinical experience. In contrast the mode of action of antidepressant drugs has been considered as fairly well established. The therapeutic effect of antidepressant drugs has been associated with the inhibition of re-uptake or degradation of monoamine (MA) transmitters, leading to facilitated monoaminergic neurotransmission.

The difference in scientific status between ECT and antidepressant drugs has, however, been considerably equalized during the last few years. New antidepressant drugs have been introduced which seem to be devoid of effects on metabolism or re-uptake of MA (Zis & Goodwin, 1979) and more attention has been drawn to the fact that antidepressant drugs acutely affect metabolism or re-uptake, whereas the antidepressant effect has a delayed onset. The discoveries that long-term antidepressant treatment changes the responsiveness of MA receptors (for review, see Charney *et al.*, 1981), represents a new area of research on anti-depressant treatment. The development of these receptor changes parallels the time course for the clinical effect fairly well. Moreover, the receptor changes are common denominators for all kinds of antidepressant treatments including the atypical drugs as well as electroconvulsive shock (ECS) and in fact the earliest reports in this field described effects of ECS (Modigh, 1975; Vetulani & Sulser, 1975).

We have, for several years, been studying the effects of ECS on the responsiveness of dopamine (DA) receptors in experimental animals as well as in humans and the following presentation will focus on these changes. The recent findings that ECS also affects 5-hydroxy-tryptamine (5-HT), α- and β-adrenergic receptors will be reviewed elsewhere in this volume.

Animal experiments

Behavioural models

In our first attempts to investigate whether ECT affects postsynaptic catecholamine receptors we utilized the behavioural model illustrated in Fig. 1. A large dose of reserpine, administered to mice, blocks their spontaneous motor activity completely. The motor activity can be restored partially by administration of the DA agonist apomorphine and more completely by administration of apomorphine in combination with the noradrenaline (NA) receptor agonist clonidine. Pretreatment with one ECS daily for seven days (ECS × VII) was found to potentiate the effects of apomorphine alone as well as apomorphine + clonidine. The potentiation required

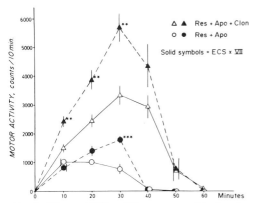

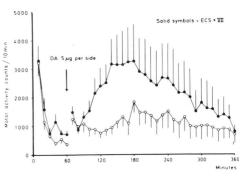

Fig. 1. *Effects of ECS × VII on motor activity in mice induced by reserpine (10 mg/kg i.p.) followed by apomorphine (0.5 mg/kg i.p.) or apomorphine (0.5 mg/ kg i.p.) plus clonidine (0.5 mg/kg i.p.). Each point represents the mean of 7–8 determinations ± s.e.m. Statistical differences between ECS-treated and control mice are indicated. ***P < 0.001, **P < 0.01 (from Modigh, 1975). (Reproduced by kind permission of the Editor, J. Neural Transm.).*

Fig. 2. *Effects of ECS × VII on motor activity in rats administered nialamide, 110 mg/kg i.p. at day 3 followed 1 h later by 5 µg DA bilaterally into nucleus accumbens. Each point represents the mean of 5–6 determinations ± s.e.m. (after Modigh & Jackson, 1975).*

more than a single ECS to develop and persisted for at least a week. The DA agonist potentiating effect of ECS × VII could also be demonstrated in other similar models. Figure 2 shows the potentiating effect of ECS × VII on the psychomotor stimulant effect of DA applied locally, bilaterally, into the nucleus accumbens, indicating that the potentiation is not mediated

Table 1. *In vivo experiments on effects of repeated ECS on DA-receptor function in animals**

Method	Convulsive therapy	DA-agonist	ECS-effect	Observed	Reference
Motor activity	ECS × VII	Apomorphine, i.p.	+	Day 1–7	Modigh, 1975
	ECS × VII	DA in n. accumbens	+	Day 3	Modigh & Jackson, 1975
	ECS × X	Tranylcypromine + L-dopa, i.p.	+	Day 1	Evans et al., 1976
	ECS × X	Metamphetamine, i.p.	+	Day 1	Green et al., 1977
	fluorothyl × VII	Tranylcypromine + L-dopa, i.p.	+	Day 1	Green, 1978
	5 ECS/X days	Apomorphine, i.p.	+	Day 1	Green & Deakin, 1980
	5 ECS/X days	DA or dibutyryl cAMP in n. accumbens	+	Day 1	Heal & Green, 1978
	ECS × X	Tranylcypromine + L-dopa, i.p.	+	Day 1	Deakin et al., 1981
	ECS × VII	Apomorphine D-amphetamine or nomifensine, s.c.	+	Day 1–10	Wielosz, 1981
Stereotyped behaviour	ECS × VII	Apomorphine, i.p.	+	Day 3–10	Modigh, 1979
	ECS × VIII	Apomorphine, s.c.	+	Day 1–4	Serra et al., 1981
	ECS × VII	Apomorphine, s.c.	0	Day 1–10	Wielosz, 1981
	12 ECS/IV weeks	Apomorphine, i.p.	+	Day 4	Globus et al., 1981
	ECS × X	Apomorphine, s.c.	+	Day 1	Bhavsar et al., 1981
Circling behaviour after unilateral nigrostriatal lesion	ECS × X	Methylamphetamine or apomorphine, i.p.	+	Day 1	Green et al., 1977
Catalepsy	ECS × I–X	Haloperidol (antagonist), i.p.	−	Day 1–5	Green et al., 1978
Discriminative test — reinforced behaviour	ECS × III	D-amphetamine or apomorphine, s.c.	+	Day 2	White & Barrett, 1981
Hormone secretion					
growth hormone	ECS × VII	Apomorphine — clonidine, i.p.	+	Day 2	Edén & Modigh, 1977
prolactin	ECS × VII	Apomorphine	+	Day 2	Balldin, 1981
Autoreceptor function					
single unit recording	ECS × I–VI	Apomorphine, i.v.	−	Day 2–7	Chiodo & Antelman, 1980
behavioural inhibition	ECS × VIII	Apomorphine, s.c.	−	Day 1–4	Serra et al., 1981

*ECS indicates electroconvulsion; ECS × 7, one electroconvulsion daily for seven days; day 1-7, effects observed 1-7 days after the last ECS; DA, dopamine; i.p., intraperitoneally; s.c., subcutaneously; + increase; - decrease; 0 no change.

by changes in permeability of the blood brain barrier (cf. Bolwig *et al.*, 1977). These results, which have been confirmed by several independent investigators (Table 1), indicate that ECS increases the responsiveness of limbic DA receptors involved in the regulation of psychomotor behaviour.

Apomorphine-induced stereotypies in rats were also potentiated by pretreatment with ECS × VII and this effect remained statistically significant at day 10 after the last ECS (Fig. 3). The results suggest a similar effect of ECS on DA receptors involved in stereotyped behaviour ie the striatal DA receptors (cf Fibiger *et al.*, 1973; Kelly *et al.*, 1975; Roberts *et al.*, 1975). The effect was confirmed in three of four subsequent studies (Table 1). Wielosz (1981), who found enhancement of apomorphine-stimulated locomotor activity but not of apomorphine-induced stereotypes after pretreatment with repeated ECS, suggested that ECT exerts its stimulant effect on mesolimbic but not on striatal DA receptors. The findings by Green *et al.* (1978) that pretreatment with repeated ECS attenuated the cataleptic response following injection of haloperidol (cf. Hornykiewiez, 1973) and by Green *et al.* (1977) that repeated ECS enhances apomorphine stimulated circulating behaviour in unilateral nigrostriatal lesioned rats, however, argue for an effect of ECT on striatal DA receptors as well. The beneficial effect of ECT in Parkinson's Disease (*vide infra*) lends further support for this contention.

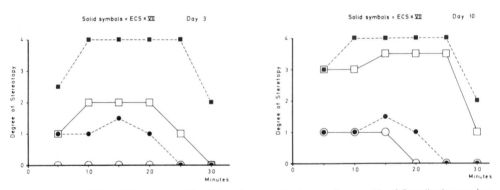

Fig. 3. *Effects of ECS × VII on apomorphine induced stereotypies in rats.* Apomorphine 0.5 mg/kg (squares) or 1 mg/kg (circles) was administered 3 (left) or 10 (right) after the last ECS. Shown are median scores in groups of six animals. Differences in stereotypies between experimental (filled symbols) and control (open symbols) groups were estimated by nonparametric multivariate analysis

$P > 0.05$ was considered not significant (n.s.).

	E - C
Day 3 apomorphine 0.5 mg/kg	$P < 0.01$
apomorphine 1 mg/kg	$P < 0.01$
Day 10 apomorphine 0.5 mg/kg	n.s.
apomorphine 1 mg/kg	$P < 0.05$

(From Modigh, 1979).

By means of single-unit electrophysiological recording, a subsensitivity of DA autoreceptors located in the substantia nigra has been demonstrated following repeated ECS (Chiodo & Antelman, 1980). The phenomenon is confirmed by behavioural studies (Serra *et al.*, 1981) where pretreatment with repeated ECS was found to eliminate the inhibitory effect of small doses of apomorphine on psychomotor activity (cf. Strömbom, 1976). Hence ECT seems to facilitate the dopaminergic neurotransmission by interference with both auto- and postsynaptic DA receptors.

White & Barrett (1981), utilizing reinforced behaviour in rats for measuring their ability to discriminate between low doses of D-amphetamine or apomorphine on the one hand and saline on the other, found that pretreatment with repeated ECS enhanced their discriminative ability.

The result was interpreted as reflecting increased sensitivity of DA receptors in a rewarding system which may have special significance for the antidepressant effect of ECT.

Neuroendocrine experiments

Evaluation of whether the effects of ECT on DA receptors have any relevance on the therapeutic effects of the treatment, requires methods that study the effects clinically. We have investigated whether the dopaminergic influence on growth hormone (GH) and prolactin (PRL) secretion can be utilized for this purpose. As a first step we evaluated this possibility in experiments on rats. The normal secretion of GH in rats, which is pulsatile with peaks in plasma concentrations at regular 3–4 h-intervals, can be blocked completely by the administration of reserpine (Edén & Modigh, 1977). In the following experiments this effect was utilized in order to facilitate estimations of monoamine agonist induced GH secretion. Apomorphine 0.25–5.0 mg/kg induced no measurable release of GH either in animals pretreated with ECS × VII or in control animals. Administration of clonidine 0.25–0.5 mg/kg induced a moderate GH secretion with no significant difference between ECS-pretreated and control animals. The GH-releasing effect of combined treatment apomorphine + clonidine was, however, significantly enhanced by pretreatment with ECS × VII (Fig. 4). The enhancement, in all probability, is induced by apomorphine and the results thus indicate that ECS affects hypothalamic DA-sensitive structures involved in the regulation of GH-secretion. It is, however, also evident from these experiments that DA agonist induced GH secretion is dependent on concomitant activation of α-adrenergic receptors. In subsequent experiments these have been characterized as α_2-receptors (Eriksson et al., 1982).

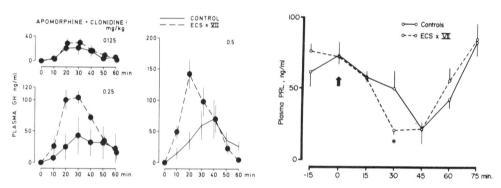

Fig. 4 (above, left). *Effects of combined treatment with various doses of clonidine and apomorphine on GH secretion in rats pretreated with reserpine alone (controls) or ECS × VII followed by reserpine.* Each point represents the mean of 3–6 determinations ± s.e.m. (after Edén & Modigh, 1977)
Fig. 5 (above, right). *Effects of apomorphine (0.5 mg/kg), on plasma PRL levels in rats pretreated with ECS × VII and in controls.* All animals were administered reserpine 4 h before the injection of apomorphine. Each point represents the mean of 5–6 determinations ± s.e.m.
*$P < 0.05$ (from Balldin, 1981).

Pretreatment with ECS × VII also slightly enhanced the apomorphine induced suppression of prolactin secretion in rats administered reserpine (10 mg/kg) 4 h before injection of the DA agonist (Fig. 5) (Balldin, 1981). ECT thus also appears to affect the responsiveness of pituitary DA receptors.

In vitro experiments

DA-receptor binding sites in the striatum have been investigated in rats from one to four days after administration of repeated ECS. In none of several independent investigations have changes in affinity or number of binding sites been found (Bergstrom & Kellar, 1979; Atterwill, 1980; Deakin et al., 1981; Lerer et al., 1982). One must therefore assume that ECT affects structures connected to the DA receptors rather than the receptors themselves. In view of the observations in the behavioural studies, an alternative explanation for the unchanged DA receptor binding in ECS-pretreated animals may be that an increase in the number of post-synaptic binding sites is balanced by a reduction in presynaptic binding sites.

Studies on the dopaminergic adenylate cyclase system (Green *et al.*, 1977) reveal no long-lasting effects of ECS-pretreatment. This system appears, however, not to be linked to the physiologically important DA receptors (Costal & Naylor, 1981).

Development of the receptor changes

Increase in responsiveness of DA receptors develops equally effectively after convulsions induced by fluorothyl (Green, 1978) or bicuculline (Nutt *et al.*, 1980) as after repeated ECS. The phenomenon is thus dependent on the convulsions rather than on the electric current, as is the antidepressant effect of ECT (Cronholm & Ottosson, 1960; Ottosson, 1962). How it develops however, remains unknown. Lesioning of the DA neurons (Green *et al.*, 1977) or pretreatment before each ECS with the DA-receptor antagonist haloperidol (Green *et al.*, 1980) does not inhibit the phenomenon. Hence it is neither a denervation supersensitivity nor a kindling phenomenon (cf. Stevens & Livermore, 1978). The ECS-induced increase in DA receptor responsiveness is, however, blocked by the destruction of the NA terminals in the forebrain (Green & Deakin, 1980) indicating that the increased release of NA after ECS (cf. Modigh, 1976) triggers the change in DA receptor responsiveness (see also Green *et al.*, 1980). Interesting in this respect is the report by Green *et al.* (1978) of a reduced GABA turnover in the nucleus accumbens after repeated ECS, since GABA has a DA antagonistic function in this area.

Endorphins have modulatory effects on both pre- and postsynaptic DA mechanisms (Scheel-Krüger *et al.*, 1977; Pert, 1978; Volavka *et al.*, 1979) and there is evidence for a considerable release of endorphins after ECS (Katz & Siebel, 1981; Emrich & Höllt, 1982). This has prompted us to investigate whether the release of endorphins play a part in the development of receptor changes after repeated ECS, using the behavioural model illustrated in Fig. 1. Pretreatment with naloxone, 10 mg/kg, 10 min before each ECS did not counteract the potentiating effect of ECS × VII on apomorphine stimulated behaviour but counteracted the effect of ECS × VII on psychomotor stimulation induced by combined treatment with apomorphine + clonidine (Fig. 6). A tentative explanation for the latter result is that the ECS-induced release of NA is enhanced by pretreatment with naloxone, leading to enhancement also of a down-regulation of postsynaptic α-receptors. An enhanced release of NA resulting from the administration of naloxone has previously been demonstrated during stress (Tanaka *et al.*, 1982). If the assumption, that the activation of NA neurons is important in the antidepressant effect of ECT and triggers the changes in postsynaptic receptor responsiveness, is correct, then further studies on the interactions between naloxone and ECT seem warranted.

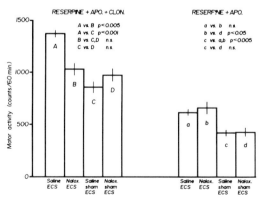

Fig. 6. *Motor activity in mice treated at day 1 with reserpine (10 mg/kg i.p.) followed by apomorphine (APO) (0.5 mg/kg i.p.) or apomorphine (0.5 mg/kg i.p.) plus clonidine (CLON) (0.5 mg/kg i.p.). The animals were pretreated with 7 daily injections of naloxone (10 mg/kg i.p.) or saline each given prior to ECS or sham shocks. Each bar represents the mean of 6–8 determinations ± s.e.m. (Hellstrand, K., Eriksson, E., and Modigh, K., unpublished observation.)*

Neuroendocrine experiments

The prerequisites for investigations of GH secretion in humans (hGH) differ from those in rats in that the normal hGH secretion is minute during day-time. Moreover, DA agonists are effective stimulants of the hGH secretion, when given alone (Lal *et al.*, 1973). The PRL secretion is inhibited by DA agonists equally effectively in humans (Lal *et al.*, 1973) as in rats. Clinical studies (Balldin *et al.*, 1982) have therefore investigated apomorphine (0.18–0.24 mg/kg, i.v.) induced stimulation of hGH secretion and suppression of PRL secretion before and after ECT, in both depressed patients (n = 12) and therapy resistant parkinsonian patients with on–off-phenomena (n = 9) (*vide infra*). Apomorphine-stimulated hGH secretion was not significantly affected by ECT whereas apomorphine induced suppression of PRL, expressed as percentage of baseline PRL levels, was enhanced after ECT. The enhancement reached statistical significance in the group of Parkinsonian patients (Fig. 7(a)) and in calculations based on the total number of patients (Fig. 7c). A similar tendency, not reaching statistical significance, was found when calculating results from the depressed patients (Fig. 7b). Meco *et al.* (1981) in contemporary investigations on depressed and schizophrenic patients reached almost identical results. They found no effect of ECT on either L-DOPA or apomorphine-stimulated hGH secretion. Apomorphine-induced suppression of PRL secretion however, appeared more pronounced after than before ECT. When using L-DOPA as the DA agonist, a similar difference in PRL secretion suppression, reaching statistical significance was observed. On the other hand, Christie *et al.* (1982) studying 12 depressed patients, found no significant differences in either apomorphine-induced stimulation of hGH secretion or suppression of PRL secretion following ECT. Recently Costain *et al.* (1982) reported enhanced apomorphine-stimulated hGH secretion in depressed patients following ECT.

The enhanced hormonal responses to apomorphine after ECT, observed in three of four clinical studies, are likely to reflect increased responsiveness of the DA receptors involved in

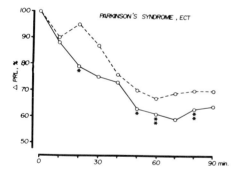

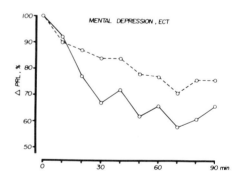

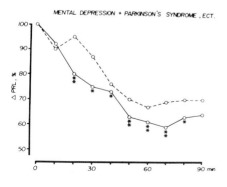

Fig. 7. *Apomorphine induced suppression of serum prolactin expressed as percentage of base line levels (Δ PRL, per cent in (a) parkinsonian, (b) depressed, (c) both together, patients before (————) and after (————) ECT.* Base-line levels of PRL before and after ECT were not significantly different. Apomorphine HCl was administered i.v. at 0 min. The points represent median values. Differences between determinations before and after ECT were evaluated statistically at each time interval by means of Wilcoxon signed rank test: *$P > 0.05$; **$P > 0.01$ (from Balldin *et al.*, 1982)

hormonal regulation. The lack of significant effect of ECT on apomorphine-induced hGH secretion found in three of the four experiments, however, indicates that this model for reflecting the sensitivity in DA receptors has limited validity. For instance, the involvement of α_2-receptors in DA-stimulated GH secretion (Edén & Modigh, 1977; Balldin *et al.*, 1980*a*) may invalidate the model when studying effects of ECT, since, according to animal experiments (Heal *et al.*, 1981) the treatment induces sub-sensitivity of α_2-receptors.

ECT in Parkinson's disease
The question whether clinically administered ECT changes DA receptor responsiveness to DA agonists can also be investigated by studying the interaction between ECT and L-DOPA in the treatment of patients with Parkinson's disease. ECT has, in fact, been reported to alleviate extrapyramidal symptoms in patients suffering concomitantly from Parkinson's disease and depression (Lebensohn & Jenkins, 1975; Asnis, 1977). The efficacy of L-DOPA therapy in patients with Parkinson's disease diminishes with time. Within seven years of treatment around 50 per cent of the patients develop on–off-phenomena characterized by frequent and abrupt shifts between periods with fairly good motor function and periods with severe extrapyramidal symptoms (Granérus, 1978; Rinne, 1978). The on–off-phenomenon is considered to be at least partially caused by the chronic L-DOPA treatment. Changes in postsynaptic DA receptor sensitivity may be involved, since chronic L-DOPA treatment has been shown to reduce the number of striatal DA binding sites in post-mortem studies of parkinsonian patients (Lee *et al.*, 1978; Quik *et al.*, 1979) and the activity of the dopaminergic adenylate cyclase system (Shibuya, 1979).

We have offered ECT to parkinsonian patients with on–off-phenomenon and up to now 12 patients have been treated. ECT is given according to the routines for treatment of depression, ie a total of three to eight ECS are given with a maximal frequency of three treatments weekly. The patients are maintained on earlier adjusted doses of L-DOPA during and after the ECT. The outcome in the first nine patients has been reported in detail (Balldin *et al.*, 1980*bb*; Balldin *et al.*, 1981). Marked improvement of parkinsonian symptoms was seen in five of the nine patients and a further two patients showed slight improvement. The effect persisted for 2–41 weeks. A positive correlation was found between improvement after ECT and age at the time of treatment with duration of L-DOPA therapy as well as the estimated life dose of L-DOPA. No correlation was found between improvement of parkinsonian symptoms and severity of depression, as measured by rating scale.

Ward *et al.* (1980) reported that ECT was ineffective when administered to five parkinsonian patients with on–off symptoms. Interestingly the means for age at the time of treatment and duration of L-DOPA therapy closely resembled those of our non-responders (Fig. 8). The mechanism underlying the anti-parkinsonian effect of ECT is in all probability identical with the DA-receptor-linked effect observed in the animal experiments, especially in view of the finding that duration of L-DOPA therapy is a predictor of improvement. Hence it seems likely

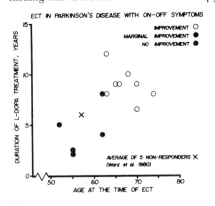

Fig. 8. *Predictors for improvement after ECT in Parkinson's disease with on–off symptoms*

that sub-sensitivity in postsynaptic DA receptors is a major mechanism for the therapy resistance in the highly distinguishable group of responders to ECT. The therapy resistance in the non-responders to ECT may largely be caused by other mechanisms, eg pronounced presynaptic degeneration. In this context it is interesting to note that a predictor for improvement of on–off symptoms during treatment with the DA receptor agonist bromocriptine is the opposite to that for ECT — young age (Glantz *et al.*, 1981).

Conclusions

There is evidence from numerous animal *in vivo* experiments that repeated ECS increases the responsiveness in mesolimbic, striatal, pituitary and hypothalamic postsynaptic DA receptors, whereas the responsiveness in presynaptic DA receptors appears to decrease. The mechanisms underlying these effects remain unknown. Since no effects of ECS has been reported in binding studies, it seems likely that the changes occur 'beyond' rather than at the receptor level. Further experiments studying separately pre- and postsynaptic binding sites are, however, needed before a definite conclusion can be made.

Evidence from neuroendocrine experiments in humans and from trials with ECT in Parkinson's Disease with on–off symptoms, indicate that an increased responsiveness in DA receptors also develops when ECT is administered under clinical conditions.

To what extent the ECT induced changes in postsynaptic DA structures are responsible for the antidepressant effect of the treatment remains to be clarified. It is reasonable to assume that they are of importance in alleviating psychomotor inhibition in depression (cf. van Praag & Korf, 1975). The possibility that they have more general significance in the treatment of depression should also be considered in view of the proposed role of DA in depression (see eg Randrup & Braestrup, 1977; Post, 1978).

Acknowledgements — This work was supported by grants from the Swedish Medical Research Council.

References

Asnis, G. (1977): Parkinson's disease, depression, and ECT: A review and case study. *Am. J. Psychiat.* **134**, 191–195.

Atterwill, C. K. (1980): Lack of effect of repeated electroconvulsive shock on (^{3}H) spiroperidol and (^{3}H) 5-hydroxy-tryptamine binding and cholinergic parameters in rat brain. *J. Neurochem.* **35**, 729–734.

Balldin, J. (1981): Experimental and clinical studies on neuroendocrine and behavioural effects of electroconvulsive therapy. (Thesis). ISBN 91-7222-410-X.

Balldin, J., Bolles, P., Edén, S., Eriksson, E. & Modigh, K. (1980*a*): Effects of electroconvulsive treatment on growth hormone secretion induced by monoamine receptor agonists in reserpine-pretreated rats. *Psychoneuroendocrinology* **5**, 329–337.

Balldin, J., Edén, S., Granérus, A.-K., Modigh, K., Svanborg, A., Wålinder, J. & Wallin, L. (1980*b*): Electroconvulsive therapy in Parkinson's syndrome with "on–off" phenomenon. *J. Neural Transm.* **47**, 11–21.

Balldin, J., Granérus, A.-K., Lindstedt, G., Modigh, K. & Wålinder, J. (1981): Predictors for improvement after electroconvulsive therapy in parkinsonian patients with on-off symptoms. *J. Neural Transm.* **52**, 199–211.

Balldin, J., Granérus, A.-K., Lindstedt, G., Modigh, K. & Wålinder, J. (1982): Neuroendocrine evidence for increased responsiveness of dopamine receptors in humans following electroconvulsive therapy. *Psychopharmacology* **76**, 371–376.

Bergstrom, D. A. & Kellar, K. J. (1979): Effect of electroconvulsive shock on monoaminergic receptor binding sites in rat brain. *Nature* **278**, 464–466.

Bhavsar, V. H., Dhumal, V. R. & Kelkar, V. V. (1981): The effect of some anti-epilepsy drugs on enhancement of the monoamine-mediated behavioural responses following the administration of electroconvulsive shocks to rats. *Eur. J. Pharmacol.* **74**, 243–247.

Bolwig, T. G., Bertz, M. M. & Holm-Jensen, J. (1977): Blood-brain barrier permeability during electroshock seizures in the rat. *Eur. J. Clin. Invest.* **7**, 95–100.

Charney, D. S., Menkes, D. B., Phil, M. & Heninger, G. R. (1981): Receptor sensitivity and the mechanism of action of antidepressant treatment. Implications for the etiology and therapy of depression. *Arch. Gen. Psychiatry* **38**, 1160–1180.

Chiodo, L. A. & Antelman, S. M. (1980): Electroconvulsive shock: Progressive dopamine autoreceptor subsensitivity independent of repeated treatment. *Science* **210**, 799–801.

Christie, J. E., Whalley, L. J., Brown, N. S. & Dick, H. (1982): Effect of ECT on the neuroendocrine response to apomorphine in severely depressed patients. *Br. J. Psychiat.* **140**, 268–273.

Costain, D. W., Cowen, P. J., Gelder, M. G. & Grahame-Smith, D. G. (1982): Electroconvulsive therapy and the brain: Evidence for increased dopamine-mediated responses. *Lancet* **ii**, 400–404.

Costall, B. & Naylor, R. J. (1981): The hypotheses of different dopamine receptor mechanisms. *Life Sci.* **28**, 216-228.

Cronholm, B. & Ottosson, J.-O. (1960): Experimental studies of the therapeutic action of electroconvulsive therapy in endogenous depression. *Acta Psychiatr. Scand.* (suppl. 145) **35**, 69-101.

Deakin, J. F. W., Owen, F., Cross, A. J. & Dashwood, M. J. (1981): Studies on possible mechanisms of action of electroconvulsive therapy; effects of repeated electrically induced seizures on rat brain receptors for monoamines and other neurotransmitters. *Psychopharmacology* **73**, 345-349.

Edén, S. & Modigh, K. (1977). Effects of apomorphine and clonidine on rat plasma growth hormone after pretreatment with reserpine and electroconvulsive shocks. *Brain Res.* **129**, 379-384.

Emrich, H. M. & Höllt, V. (1982): The influence of electroconvulsion upon endorphinergic systems. Abstract. 13th C.I.N.P. Congress in Jerusalem, Israel, June 20-25, 1982.

Eriksson, E., Edén, S. & Modigh, K. (1982): Up- and down-regulation of central postsynaptic α_2-receptors reflected in the growth hormone response to clonidine in reserpine pretreated rats. *Psychopharmacology* **77**, 327-331.

Evans, J. P. M., Grahame-Smith, D. G., Green, A. R. & Tordoff, A. F. C. (1976): Electroconvulsive shock increases the behavioural responses of rats to brain 5-hydroxytryptamine accumulation and central nervous system stimulant drugs. *Br. J. Pharmac.* **56**, 193-199.

Fibiger, H. C., Fibiger, H. P. & Zis, A. P. (1973): Attenuation of amphetamine induced motor stimulation and stereotypy by 6-hydroxydopamine in the rat. *Br. J. Pharmac.* **47**, 683-692.

Glantz, R., Goetz, C. G., Nausieda, P. A., Weiner, W. J. & Klawans, H. L. (1981): The effect of bromocriptine (BCT) on the on-off phenomenon. *J. Neural Transm.* **52**, 41-47.

Globus, M., Lerer, B., Hamburger, R. & Belmaker, R. H. (1981): Chronic electroconvulsive shock and chronic haloperidol are not additive in effects on dopamine receptors. *Neuropharmacology* **20**, 1125-1128.

Granérus, A.-K. (1978): Factors influencing the occurrence of "on-off" symptoms during long-term treatment with L-DOPA. *Acta Med. Scand.* **203**, 75-85.

Green, A. R. (1978): Repeated exposure of rats to the convulsant agent flurothyl enhanced 5-hydroxytryptamine- and dopamine-mediated behavioural responses. *Br. J. Pharmac.* **62**, 325-331.

Green, A. R., Heal, D. J. & Grahame-Smith, D. G. (1977): Further observations on the effect of repeated electroconvulsive shock on the behavioural responses of rats produced by increases in the functional activity of brain 5-hydroxytryptamine and dopamine. *Psychopharmacology* **52**, 195-200.

Green, A. R., Peralta, E., Hong, J. S., Mao, C. C., Atterwill, C. K. & Costa, E. (1978): Alterations in GABA metabolism and met-enkephalin content in rat brain following repeated electroconvulsive shocks. *J. Neurochem.* **31**, 607-611.

Green, A. R., Costain, D. W. & Deakin, J. F. W. (1980): Enhanced 5-hydroxytryptamine and dopamine-mediated behavioural responses following convulsions — III the effects of monoamine antagonists and synthesis inhibitors on the ability of electroconvulsive shock to enhance responses. *Neuropharmacology* **19**, 907-914.

Green, A. R. & Deakin, J. F. W. (1980): Brain noradrenaline depletion prevents ECS-induced enhancement of serotonin- and dopamine-mediated behaviour. *Nature* **285**, 232-233.

Heal, D. J. & Green, A. R. (1978): Repeated electroconvulsive shock increases the behavioural responses of rats to injection of both dopamine and dibutyryl cyclic AMP into the nucleus accumbens. *Neuropharmacology* **17**, 1085-1087.

Heal, D. J., Akagi, H., Bowdler, J. M. & Green, A. R. (1981): Repeated electroconvulsive shock attenuates clonidine-induced hypoactivity in rodents. *Eur. J. Pharmacol.* **75**, 231-237.

Hornykiewicz, O. (1973). Parkinson's Disease: from brain homogenate to treatment. *Fedn. Proc. Fedn. Am. Socs. exp. Biol.* **32**, 183-190.

Katz, R. J. & Siebel, M. (in press): Endogenous opiates and the psychobiological mode of action of electroconvulsive shock therapy. *Psychiat. Res.*

Kelly, P. H., Seviour, P. W. & Iversen, S. D. (1975): Amphetamine and apomorphine responses in the rat following 6-OHDA lesions of the nucleus accumbens septi and corpus striatum. *Brain Res.* **94**, 507-522.

Lal, S., de la Vega, C. E., Sourkes, T. L. & Friesen, H. G. (1973): Effect of apomorphine on growth hormone, prolactin, luteinizing hormone and follicle-stimulating hormone levels in human serum. *J. Clin. Endocrinol. Metab.* **37**, 719-724.

Lebensohn, Z. M. & Jenkins, R. B. (1975). Improvement of Parkinsonism in depressed patients treated with ECT. *Am. J. Psychiat.* **132**, 283-285.

Lee, T., Seeman, P., Rajput, A., Farley, I. J., and Hornykiewicz, O. (1978): Receptor basis for dopaminergic supersensitivity in Parkinson's Disease. *Nature* **273**, 59-60.

Lerer, B., Jabotinsky-Rubin, K., Bannet, J., Ebstein, R. P. & Belmaker, R. H. (1982): Electroconvulsive shock prevents dopamine receptor supersensitivity. *Eur. J. Pharmacol.* **80**, 131-134.

Meco, G., Casacchia, M., Boni, B., Falaschi, P. & Rocco, A. (1981): Prolactin and GH response to DA-agonist drugs before and after ECT. Third World Congress of Biological Psychiatry, Stockholm. Abstract No: F301.

Modigh, K. (1975): Electroconvulsive shock and postsynaptic catecholamine effects: increased psychomotor stimulant action of apomorphine and clonidine in reserpine pre-treated mice by repeated ECS. *J. Neural Transm.* **36**, 19-32.

Modigh, K. (1976): Long-term effects of electroconvulsive shock therapy on synthesis, turnover and uptake of brain monoamines. *Psychopharmacology* **49**, 179-185.

Modigh, K. (1979): Long lasting effects of ECT on monoaminergic mechanisms. In *Neuro-Psychopharmacology*, ed B. Saletu *et al.* Oxford & New York: Pergamon Press.

Modigh, K. & Jackson, D. M. (1975): Evidence for sustained effect of ECS on neuronal structures connected to brain catecholamines neurons. In 6th Int. Congr. Pharmacology, *Finnish pharmacol. Soc. Abstract* 394.

Nutt, D. J., Green, A. R. & Grahame-Smith, D. G. (1980). Enhanced 5-hydroxytryptamine and dopamine-mediated behavioural responses following convulsions — I the effects of single and repeated bicuculline-induced seizures. *Neuropharmacology* **19**,. 897–900.

Ottosson, J.-O. (1962): Seizure characteristics and therapeutic efficiency in electroconvulsive therapy: an analysis of the antidepressive efficiency of grand mal and lidocaine-modified seizures. *J. Nerv. Ment. Dis.* **135**, 239–251.

Pert, A. (1978): The effects of opiates on nigrostriatal dopaminergic activity. In *Characteristics and function of opioids*, ed J. M. Van Ree & L. Terenius. Amsterdam: Elsevier/North-Holland Biomedical Press.

Post, R. M. (1978): Frontiers in affective disorder research: new pharmacological agents and new methodologies. In *Psychopharmacology: a generation of progress*, ed M. A. Lipton, A. DiMascio & K. F. Killam. New York: Raven Press.

Praag, H. M. van & Korf, J. (1975): Zur diskussion: Central monoamine deficiency in depressions: Causative or secondary phenomenon? *Pharmacopsych.* **8**, 322–326.

Quik, M., Spokes, E. G., Mackay, A. V. P. & Bannister, R. (1979): Alterations in (³H)spiperone binding in human caudate nucleus, substantia nigra and frontal cortex in the Shy-Drager syndrome and Parkinson's disease. *J. Neurol. Sci.* **43**, 429–437.

Randrup, A. & Braestrup, C. (1977): Uptake inhibition of biogenic amines by newer antidepressant drugs: Relevance to the dopamine hypothesis of depression. *Psychopharmacology* **53**, 309–314.

Rinne, U. K. (1978): Recent advances in research on Parkinsonism. *Acta Neurol. Scand.* **57** (suppl. 67), 77–113.

Roberts, D. C. S., Zis, A. P. & Fibiger, H. C. (1975): Ascending catecholamine pathways and amphetamine induced locomotor activity: importance of dopamine and apparent non-involvement of norepinephrine. *Brain Res.* **93**, 441–454.

Serra, G., Argiolas, A., Fadda, F., Melis, M. R. & Gessa, G. L. (1981): Repeated electroconvulsive shock prevents the sedative effect of small doses of apomorphine. *Psychopharmacology* **73**, 194–196.

Scheel-Krüger, J., Golembiowska, K. & Mogilnicka, E. (1977): Evidence for increased apomorphine-sensitive dopaminergic effects after acute treatment with morphine. *Psychopharmacology* **53**, 55.

Shibuya, M. (1979). Dopamine-sensitive adenylate cyclase activity in the striatum in Parkinson's disease. *J. Neural Transm.* **44**, 287–295.

Stevens, J. R. & Livermore, Jr., A. (1978): Kindling of the mesolimbic dopamine system: animal model of psychosis. *Neurology* **28**, 36–46.

Strömbom, U. (1976): Catecholamine receptor agonists. Effects on motor activity and rate of tyrosine hydroxylation in mouse brain. *Naunyn-Schmiedeberg's Arch. Pharmacol.* **292**, 167–174.

Tanaka, M., Kohno, Y., Nakagawa, R., Ida, Y., Iimori, K., Hoaki, Y., Tsuda, A. & Nagasaki, N. (1982): Naloxone enhanced stress-induced increases in noradrenaline turnover in specific brain regions in rats. *Life Sci.* **30**, 1663–1669.

Ward, C., Stern, G. M., Pratt, R. T. C. & McKenna, P. (1980): Electroconvulsive therapy in parkinsonian patients with the 'on-off' syndrome. *J. Neural Transm.* **49**, 133–135.

Vetulani, J. & Sulser, F. (1975): Action of various antidepressant treatments reduces reactivity of noradrenergic cyclic AMP-generating system in limbic forebrain. *Nature* **257**, 495.

Wielosz, M. (1981): Increased sensitivity to dopaminergic agonists after repeated electroconvulsive shock (ECS) in rats. *Neuropharmacology* **20**, 941–945.

White, D. K. & Barrett, R. J. (1981): The effects of electroconvulsive shock on the discriminative stimulus properties of d-amphetamine and apomorphine: evidence for dopamine receptor alteration subsequent to ECS. *Psychopharmacology* **73**, 211–214.

Volavka, J., Davis, L. G. & Ehrlich, Y. H. (1979): Endorphins, dopamine, and schizophrenia. *Schizophrenia Bull.* **5**, 227–239.

Zis, A. P. & Goodwin, F. K. (1979): Novel antidepressants and the biogenic amine hypothesis of depression. *Arch. Gen. Psychiat.* **36**, 1097–1107.

3.
Stress-induced sensitization: a framework for viewing the effects of ECS and other antidepressants

S. M. ANTELMAN and L. A. CHIODO

Department of Psychiatry, School of Medicine, Western Psychiatric Institute & Clinic, 402 Langley Hall, University of Pittsburgh, Pittsburgh, PA 15260, USA; Neuropsychopharmacology Research Unit, Yale University School of Medicine, 333 Cedar Street, P.O. Box 3333, New Haven, Connecticut 06510, USA — LAC: current address.

Introduction

The therapeutic effects of ECS, like those of pharmacological antidepressants are not seen immediately, but rather develop gradually — and increase ie, *sensitize*, with repeated treatment. This almost invariable delay in clinical efficacy has never been understood and, until recent receptor hypotheses of antidepressant function, received little attention. We believe that important insights can be gained into the nature of the therapeutic delay and perhaps ultimately into the basic mode of action of ECS and other antidepressants when these are viewed from the framework of a sensitization perspective.

In this chapter, we would like briefly to discuss some of the characteristics governing sensitization with the aim of determining the extent to which they are applicable to the effects of ECS and other antidepressants.

Sensitization is a response to stress

Behavioral sensitization reflects the development of a cellular process of fundamental importance by which organisms at all phylogenetic levels adapt to periodic exposure to activating and stressful stimuli (Groves & Thompson, 1970; Kandel, 1976, 1979; Antelman & Eichler, 1979; Antelman *et al.*, 1980). The evolutionary significance to the organism of stress-induced sensitization is readily apparent. In the wild, the stress associated with the sight, sound and/or smell of a predator is sufficient to permanently sensitize an animal to the risks to survival associated with such stimuli.

How might such a process relate to the treatment of depression? Since the gradual development of clinical efficacy in depression following ECT and other antidepressants appears (by definition) to reflect a sensitization process, and since sensitization is a response to periodic presentation of stressful stimuli, there are two questions of relevance to us here. First, is depression the type of disorder to benefit from stress? Second, do ECS and other anti-depressants mimic the influence of stressors in their actions on physiological processes?

Several points may be made with regard to the question of whether stressors are likely to be beneficial in treating depression. Of particular theoretical interest is the finding that during the 'naturally-occurring' (as opposed to drug-induced) switch from depression to mania, which is thought to be associated with stressful situations, patients pass through an interim period of normalcy (Bunney *et al.*, 1972; Bunney & Murphy, 1974). This transitional stage can either be very brief or persist for several days, depending on whether the switch is rapid or gradual in onset. In other words, stressors can result in at least a temporary recovery period in bipolar depressives. Therapeutic effects, albeit brief, are also well known to occur following sleep deprivation (Vogel *et al.*, 1975) an obvious stressor, and amphetamine (Silberman *et al.*, 1981), which we have shown to be interchangeable with non-pharmacological stressors in inducing sensitization (Antelman & Chiodo, 1983). In addition, it is known that in the earlier stages of depression, the lowering of mood can be reversed during activating circumstances such as those provided by the demands of employment or social exposure (Hamilton, 1979). Finally, there is a suggestion that strenuous physical exercise, such as running, may be effective in the treatment of moderate depressions (Glasser, 1976; Greist *et al.*, 1979).

The second question raised at the beginning of this section is whether ECS and other antidepressants mimic the influence of stressors in their physiological actions? A growing body of evidence suggests that this is indeed the case. Repeated administration of ECS and virtually all other antidepressants examined indicates that these agents decrease the responsiveness of cortical and limbic cyclic AMP to norepinephrine (Sulser, 1979) and most, including ECS (Pandey *et al.*, 1979), also reduce the sensitivity of postsynaptic β-adrenergic receptors. Each of these effects have now been demonstrated using repeated administration of experimental stressors rather than antidepressants. Thus, decreased density of β-adrenergic receptors in rat cortex and other regions has been observed following 72 hours (but not less) of REM sleep deprivation (Mogilnicka *et al.*, 1980), repeated immobilization (U'Prichard & Kvetnansky, 1980; Stone & Platt, 1982), repeated footshock (Nomura *et al.*, 1981) and isolation (Kraeuchi *et al.*, 1981). ACTH, one of the principal hormones associated with stressful situations, has also been shown to speed the influence of an antidepressant on β-receptor sensitivity (Kendall *et al.*, 1982). Also, the stress of strenuous exercise has recently been shown to be associated with a decrease in the responsivity of peripheral β-adrenergic receptors (MacKenzie *et al.*, 1980). In addition, some of the same stressors noted above have been shown to reduce the formation of cyclic AMP in response to norepinephrine (NE) stimulation of rat brain slices after repeated treatment (Stone, 1979; Kraeuchi *et al.*, 1981).

The similarities among the effects of ECS and other antidepressants on the one hand and stressors on the other are not limited to postsynaptic NE responses as originally proposed by Stone (1979) but have also been observed using indices of dopamine (DA) autoreceptor function. Earley & Leonard (1982) recently reported that repeated administration of ORG 2766, an ACTH 4–9 analogue, reduced the hypokinetic effect of an autoreceptor-stimulating dose of apomorphine, just as Serra *et al.* (1981) had found after daily ECS. These investigators also found that ORG 2766 'like all known antidepressant agents, reversed the hyperactivity of the bulbectomized rat. . . .' Moreover, using single-unit electrophysiological recording procedures (Lucik & Antelman, in preparation), we have recently found that immobilization stress induces the same time-dependent sub-sensitivity of substantia nigra DA autoreceptors as we had earlier reported following ECS (Chiodo & Antelman, 1980a). The data reviewed are consistent with the hypothesis that ECS (which of course, is a stressor), may be inducing neuronal and behavioral effects potentially relevant to its antidepressant efficacy, by acting as a stressor. This is in keeping with the view of this manuscript that the clinical effects of ECS may be understood from the standpoint of sensitization, a stress-dependent phenomenon.

Sensitization is a time-dependent phenomenon

Temporal factors play a key role in sensitization. Intermittent stimulus presentation appears to be necessary in order to demonstrate sensitization, while more massed or continuous exposure favors the development of tolerance (Post, 1980). This factor is particularly well-illustrated in experiments by Nelson & Ellison (1978), where continuous exposure to implanted pellets of amphetamine resulted in decreased stereotypy ratings while once-daily injections led to sensitization. The evolutionary significance of temporal distribution as a determinant of sensitization or tolerance can readily be guessed at. In the wild, social animals are most likely to be more or less continuously exposed to members of the same species, with predators and prey (ie, stressful stimuli) appearing more intermittently. Tolerance to the former makes for harmonious societal relations while sensitization to the latter increases the likelihood of survival.

29

The importance of intermittency in the development of sensitization in response to stress is not limited to mammals but is also evident in mollusks such as *Aplysia Californica* (Kandel, 1979).

If we are right in arguing that successful treatment of depression with ECT represents an instance of stressor-induced sensitization, then one might expect intermittent treatment to be at least equal to, if not superior to more regular therapy. This indeed appears to be the case. ECT is typically administered no more than two to three times a week with intervals between treatments ranging from 48–96 hours (Fink, 1979; Johnstone *et al.*, 1980). More frequent treatment has only occasionally been shown to decrease the interval required for a therapeutic response (see Fink, 1979).

Animal data also clearly indicate that daily ECS or pharmacological antidepressant administration is not necessary to induce the receptor changes typically associated with such a regime. In fact, our own work pioneered in demonstrating that a single ECS was sufficient to trigger a progressive sub-sensitivity of midbrain DA autoreceptors (indexed electrophysio-logically) that was actually 32 per cent greater than that seen two days following six, daily administrations of ECS (Chiodo & Antelman, 1980*a*). We have also reported similar findings after acute administration of a tricyclic antidepressant (Chiodo & Antelman, 1980*b*) and a monoamine oxidase inhibitor (Antelman *et al.*, 1982). More recently, we have extended this work to other neurotransmitter systems. We have shown that desmethylimipramine (DMI) administration on day 1 and day 17 induces sub-sensitivity of cortical β-adrenergic receptors in the rat, not significantly different from that seen after 17 days of treatment (Lace & Antelman, submitted). Using head-twitch, a behavioral response associated with serotonin, we have also demonstrated that a single day of treatment with amitriptyline (two injections) was sufficient to significantly sensitize the head-twitch response to the serotonin precursor, 5-hydroxytryptophan, 11 days later (Antelman *et al.*, submitted).

Collectively, our data suggest that many (if not all) neuronal effects of ECS and other antidepressants are seen not only after regular, though intermittent (eg, daily) treatment, but in fact, once triggered, grow merely with the passage of time (up to a point), independent of further treatment. Such time-dependency is characteristic of sensitization phenomena. Thus, we have repeatedly demonstrated that acute or short-term administration of a variety of experimental stressors or amphetamine induces sensitization which is evident weeks later (Antelman & Eichler, 1979; Antelman *et al.*, 1980; Antelman & Chiodo, 1983).

Our finding that one week after its administration, the effect of a single ECS on DA autoreceptor sensitivity is as great as if it were given daily for 6 days (Chiodo & Antelman, 1980*a*), has now been replicated by Groves and co-workers (Tepper *et al.*, 1982). Moreover, this group has extended our finding to α_2-receptors in the locus coeruleus by showing a substantial decrement (ie, sub-sensitivity) in the ability of the α_2-agonist, clonidine, to inhibit NE neuronal firing in this region 7 days after a single ECS (Tepper *et al.*, 1982). Additional support for our notion that ECS induces sensitization dependent on the passage of time rather than repeated treatment comes from the very recent work of Vetulani (see Ch. 4). This investigator, using behavioral and biochemical indices of NE and 5-HT function, reports that the effects of ECS given every third day 'are similarly, or sometimes even more prominent than those observed after daily treatment'.

Sensitization is a state-dependent phenomenon

The final aspect of sensitization which we wish to discuss is its apparent state-dependent nature. Between challenges or provocations an already-sensitized system gives little or no hint that a change in either behavioral or neuronal responsiveness has taken place. This is true whether sensitization is the result of treatment with stimulants, non-pharmacological stressors (Antelman & Chiodo, 1983), ECS (Chiodo & Antelman, 1980*a*; Tepper *et al.*, 1982) or tricyclics (Chiodo & Antelman, 1980*b*). For example, although we have shown that each of these stimuli can induce a sub-sensitivity of DA autoreceptors as indexed by noting changes in neuronal firing rate after presynaptic doses of apomorphine, we have never observed a significant change in *basal* DA neuronal firing. Tepper *et al.* (1982) in their replication of our ECS study also failed to find a significant alteration of basal DA neuronal discharge. In other words, even though a system may already be sensitized, it may nevertheless require an additional challenge in order to manifest that sensitization. This may have important implications for designing new regimes for clinical treatment.

When we first discovered that the effects of antidepressants on DA autoreceptors were dependent on the passage of time rather than repeated treatment (Chiodo & Antelman, 1980a,b), we proposed that clinical efficacy might gradually appear as a function of time after acute or short-term treatment with such agents. We continue to believe that the time-dependent neuronal changes which underlie the therapeutic influence of ECS and other antidepressants may be triggered by a single or very brief treatment. However, just as apomorphine (Chiodo & Antelman, 1980a,b) or DA itself (Antelman et al., 1982) were necessary to reveal DA autoreceptor changes, a second treatment a week or two after the first, may be necessary in order to reveal therapeutic effects as well. On the other hand, if the clinical efficacy of ECS and other antidepressants are related to their stressful properties, it is not unlikely that in some individuals the activating or stressful influence of everyday environmental events may be sufficient to reveal and sustain the influence of the trigger effect provided by an initial ECS or pharmacological antidepressant.

Conclusion

We have proposed that the longer-term neuronal and clinical effects of ECS and other antidepressants can be better understood when viewed within a framework of sensitization. Consistent with this, our review has provided evidence that three major principles governing sensitization phenomena, ie, stress, time and state-dependency, are all applicable to antidepressant treatments. The potential value of our approach derives from the fact that it places ECS and pharmacological approaches to depression within the context of other agents which — to a greater or lesser degree — also mimic the time-dependent, sensitizing influence of stressors, eg, amphetamine. The study of mechanisms which underlie sensitization may provide us with a better understanding of how ECS and other antidepressants exert their clinical effects.

Acknowledgement — Supported by MH-32306 and RSDA-00239 to SMA.

References
Antelman, S. M. & Chiodo, L. A. (1983): Amphetamine as a stressor. In *Stimulants: neurochemical, behavioral and clinical perspectives*, ed I. Creese, New York: Raven Press.
Antelman, S. M., Chiodo, L. A. & DeGiovanni, L. A. (1982): Antidepressants and dopamine autoreceptors: Implications for both a novel means of treating depression and understanding bipolar illness. In *Typical and atypical antidepressants: molecular mechanisms*, ed E. Costa & G. Racagni. pp. 121-132. New York: Raven Press.
Antelman, S. M. & Eichler, A. J. (1979). Persistent effects of stress on dopamine-related behaviors: clinical implications. In *Catecholamines: basic and clinical frontiers*, ed E. Usdin, I. J. Kopin & J. Barchas. Pp. 1759-1761. New York: Pergamon Press.
Antelman, S. M., Eichler, A. J., Black, C. A. & Kocan, D. (1980): Interchangeability of stress and amphetamine in sensitization. *Science* **207**, 329-331.
Bunney, W. E., Jr. and Murphy, D. L. (1974): Switch processes in psychiatric illness. In *Factors in depression*, ed N. S. Kline. Pp. 139-158. New York: Raven Press.
Bunney, W. E. Jr., Murphy, D. L., Goodwin, F. K. & Borge, G. F. (1972): The 'Switch process' in manic depressive illness. A systematic study of sequential behavioral changes. *Archs Gen. Psychiat.* **27**, 295-302.
Chiodo, L. A. & Antelman, S. M. (1980a). Electroconvulsive shock: Progressive dopamine autoreceptor subsensitivity independent of repeated treatment. *Science* **210**, 799-801.
Chiodo, L. A. & Antelman, S. M. (1980b). Repeated tricyclics induce a progressive dopamine autoreceptor subsensitivity independent of daily drug treatment. *Nature* **287**, 451-454.
Earley, B. & Leonard, B. E. (1982). The effect of an ACTH$_{4-9}$ analogue (ORG 2766) on some rodent models of depression. Abstracts, Vol. 1, 13th C.I.N.P. Congress, Jerusalem, Israel, p. 186.
Fink, M. (1979). *Convulsive therapy*. New York: Raven Press.
Glasser, W. (1976). *Positive addiction*. New York: Harper & Sons.
Greist, J. H., Klein, M. H., Eischens, R. R., Faris, J., Gurman, A. S. & Morgan, W. P. (1979). Running as treatment for depression. *Comp. Psychiat.* **20**, 41-54.
Groves, P. M. & Thompson, R. F. (1970): Habituation: a dual-process. *Psychol. Rev.* **77**, 419-450.

Hamilton, M. (1979): Mania and depression: classification, description and course. In *Psychopharmacology of affective disorders*, ed E. S. Paykel & A. Coppen. Pp. 1-13. New York: Oxford University Press.

Johnstone, E. C., Lawler, P., Stevens, M., Deakin, J. F. W., Frith, C. D., McPherson, K. & Crow, T. J. (1980): The Northwick Park electroconvulsive therapy trial. *Lancet* **2**, 1317-1320.

Kandel, E. R. (1976): *Cellular basis of behavior, an introduction to behavioral neurobiology*. San Francisco: W. H. Freeman and Company.

Kandel, E. R. (1979). *Behavioral biology of aplysia*. Pp. 351-358. San Francisco: W. H. Freeman and Company.

Kendall, D. A., Duman, R., Slopis, J. & Enna, S. J. (1982): Influence of adrenocorticotropin hormone and yohimbine on antidepressant-induced declines in rat brain neurotransmitter receptor binding and function. *J. Pharm. Exper. Ther.* **22**, 566-571.

Kraeuchi, K., Gentsch, C. & Feer, H. (1981): Individually reared rats: alteration in noradrenergic brain functions. *J. Neural Transmission* **50**, 103-112.

MacKenzie, T. B., Popkin, M. K., Sheppard, J. R., Stillner, V., Davis, C. M. & Fenimore, D. C. (1980): Changes in beta-adrenergic receptor sensitivity associated with stress. *Lancet* **1**, 322.

Mogilnicka, E., Arbilla, S., DePoortere, H. & Langer, S. Z. (1980): Rapid-eye-movement sleep deprivation decreases the density of [^{3}H]-dihydroalprenolol and [^{3}H]-imipramine binding sites in the rat cerebral cortex. *Eur. J. Pharm.* **65**, 289-292.

Nelson, L. R. & Ellison, G. (1978): Enhanced stereotypies after repeated injections but not continuous amphetamines. *Neuropharmacol.* **17**, 1081-1084.

Nomura, S., Watanabe, M., Ukei, N. & Nakazawa, T. (1981): Stress and β-adrenergic receptor binding in the rat's brain. *Brain Res.* **224**, 199-203.

Pandey, G. N., Heinze, W. J., Brown, B. D. & Davis, J. M. (1979): Electroconvulsive shock treatment decreases β-adrenergic receptor sensitivity in rat brain. *Nature* **280**, 234-235.

Post, R. M. (1980): Intermittent versus continuous stimulation: effect of time interval on the development of sensitization or tolerance. *Life Sci.* **26**, 1275-1282.

Serra, G., Argiolas, A., Fadda, F., Melis, M. R. & Gessa, G. L. (1981): Repeated electroconvulsive shock prevents the sedative effect of small doses of apomorphine. *Psychopharmacol.* **73**, 194-196.

Silberman, E. K., Reus, V. I., Jimerson, D. C., Lynott, A. M. & Post, R. M. (1981): Heterogeneity of amphetamine response in depressed patients. *Am. J. Psychiat.* **138**, 1302-1307.

Stone, E. A. (1979): Subsensitivity to norepinephrine as a link between adaptation to stress and antidepressant therapy: An hypothesis. *Res. Comm. Psychol. Psychiat. Behav.* **4**, 241-255.

Stone, E. A. & Platt, J. E. (1982). Brain adrenergic receptors and resistance to stress. *Brain Res.* **237**, 405-414.

Sulser, F. (1979): New perspectives on the mode of action of antidepressant drugs. *Trends in Pharmacological Sci.* **1**, 92-94.

Tepper, J. M., Nakamura, S., Spanis, C., Squire, L. R., Young, S. J. & Groves, P. M. (1982): Subsensitivity of catecholaminergic neurons to direct acting agonists after single or repeated electroconvulsive shock. *Biol. Psychiat.* **17**, 1059-1070.

U'Prichard, D. C. & Kvetnansky, R. (1980): Central and peripheral adrenergic receptors in acute and repeated immobilization stress. In *Catecholamines and stress: recent advances*, ed E. Usdin, R. Kvetnansky & J. J. Kopin. Pp. 299-308. New York: Elsevier/North-Holland.

Vogel, F. W., Thurmond, A. & Gibbons, P. (1975): REM sleep reduction effects on depression syndromes. *Archs. Gen. Psychiat.* **32**, 765.

4.
Changes in responsiveness of central aminergic structures after chronic ECS

JERZY VETULANI

Institute of Pharmacology, Polish Academy of Sciences, Smetna 12, 31-343 Kraków, Poland.

Introduction

Electroconvulsive shock (ECS), in addition to being an efficient method for the treatment of endogenous depression, is a convenient tool for students investigating the biological basis of the action of antidepressant treatments and of depression itself. An advantage over the chronic administration of antidepressant drugs is that with ECS one does not encounter any pharmaco-kinetic complications. This is particularly important if one studies the effects of antidepressant treatments on the central receptors for neurotransmitters. After chronic administration, tricyclic and other antidepressant drugs are present in the brain in large quantities for a considerable period of time (see eg, Daniel *et al.*, 1981; Vetulani *et al.*, 1976*a*). It has been established that antidepressants may interact directly with some populations of cerebral receptors, for instance with α-adrenergic or 5-HT$_2$ receptors (U'Prichard *et al.*, 1978; Peroutka & Snyder, 1980*a,b*) and therefore, their presence in the investigated material may seriously affect the receptor studies. The changes in receptor populations brought about by ECS are unlikely to be produced by persistent occupancy of receptors by agents interfering with the receptor binding assay.

ECS may thus be used to verify conclusions on the mode of action of antidepressant treatments drawn from drug studies. Such an approach was used for the first time by Dr Sulser and myself when we proposed that reduction of reactivity of the noradrenergic cyclic AMP generating system is the common effect of various antidepressant treatments (Vetulani & Sulser, 1975). These findings formed the basis of the hypothesis that the mode of action of antidepressant treatments consists of the down-regulation of central β-adrenoceptors (Sulser, 1982).

It has been well established that eight to ten daily ECS depress the response of noradrenergic cyclic AMP in brain slices to noradrenaline (Vetulani & Sulser, 1975; Vetulani *et al.*, 1976*a*) and cause a decrease in the density of specific binding sites for [^{3}H]-dihydroalprenolol, a response indicating down-regulation of β-adrenoceptors in the cerebral cortex (Bergstrom & Kellar, 1979; Pandey *et al.*, 1979). In this chapter I would like to present data indicating that ECS also affects other monoaminergic mechanisms. These were investigated both functionally and biochemically:

(i) The α_2-adrenergic system was tested by recording postdecapitation convulsions (PDC) and specific [^{3}H]-prazosin binding;

(ii) the α_2-adrenergic system by testing clonidine hypothermia and specific [^{3}H]-clonidine binding; (iii) the serotonergic system by recording the frequency of head twitches produced by serotoninomimetics, hyperthermia brought about by serotoninomimetics in heat-adapted rats, and specific binding of [^{3}H]-spiroperidol to 5-HT$_2$ receptor sites and of

33

[^{3}H]-serotonin to 5-HT$_1$ receptor sites. In addition a preliminary investigation was carried out on the effect of ECS on the central histamine system, using the hypothermia induced by a specific histamine H$_2$ receptor stimulant, impromidine (Durant *et al.*, 1978);

(iv) the effect of ECS applied less frequently than on a daily basis was tested, since clinical ECT is administered at two to three day intervals rather than daily as in most laboratory studies.

The present results suggest that ECS produces up-regulation of α_1-adrenoceptors and 5-HT$_2$ receptors, down-regulation of α_2-adrenoceptors, and hyposensitivity of histamine H$_2$ receptors. ECT given 3–5 times at 72 h intervals produces effects similar to although usually slightly less prominent than those brought about by daily treatment.

Methods and materials

Male Wistar rats, 160–230 g, were used throughout. They were kept ten to a cage, with free access to laboratory food and water. ECS (150 mA, 50 Hz, 400 ms) was delivered through ear clip electrodes. The current invariably produced tonic seizures. Unless stated to the contrary, ECS was administered once daily for ten consecutive days and the tests or decapitation were carried out 24 h after the last electroshock. In one experiment the duration of the effect of ECS was tested and rats were investigated at various intervals after the last ECT. The effect of various schedules of ECS administration was also investigated. ECS were spaced 24–216 h and the tests were carried out 24 h after the last shock. Control rats were handled similarly to ECS rats and had the electrodes attached without passage of current.

Intracerebroventricular injections (ivtr). Injections were given to nonanesthetized, previously prepared animals with a free-hand, direct puncture technique as described earlier (Vetulani *et al.*, 1972). Other injections were always given intraperitoneally (i.p.), in a volume of 4 ml/kg.

Postdecapitation convulsions (PDC). Rats were decapitated and the carcasses immediately placed in a plastic box standing on the top of a motility meter operating on the same principle as the Animex apparatus. Movements of the body were counted for as long as they lasted.

Temperature measurement. Temperature was measured in the esophagus with an Ellab electric thermometer. The first measurement, taken before drug administration, yielded the reference temperature and the results were expressed as the differences from it. In some instances the difference between the initial temperature and that at a specified time interval was used as the measure of the effect (clonidine and impromidine hypothermia), while in others thermal response index (TRI) was calculated. TRI represents the area under (or over) the time curve per hour and was calculated as follows: the temperature measurements were taken every 30 min and results expressed as differences from the reference temperature. The results were added, divided by 2 and divided by the time of experiment in hours. For each rat TRI was calculated separately.

Clonidine hypothermia. Rats kept at a room temperature of approximately 21 °C were injected with clonidine, 100 μg/kg. The maximum temperature depression, which occurred one hour after the injection (Pilc & Vetulani, 1982a) was regarded as the measure of the hypothermic effect.

Impromidine hypothermia. Rats kept at a room temperature of approximately 21 °C were injected ivtr with 20 or 50 μg impromidine dissolved in 20 μl of saline. The controls received the solvent. The temperature was measured 30 min after the injection.

3-Chlorophenylpiperazine (CPP) hypothermia. Rats kept at room temperature of approximately 20°C were injected with 10 mg/kg CPP; the temperature was measured every 30 min for 2 h, and TRI was calculated as the measure of the hypothermic effect.

Hyperthermia induced by serotoninomimetics in heat-adapted rats. Rats were transferred to the hot room (28 °C) and kept there for 3 h before measurement of initial temperature. After that they were injected with quipazine, 5 mg/kg, or with various doses of CPP. The temperature measurements were taken for 3 h; TRI was calculated as the measure of the hyperthermic effect.

Head-twitch responses to serotoninomimetics. Head twitches were evoked (1) by ivtr injections of 25 μg 5-HT, or 250 μg 5-HTP to rats pretreated 30 min earlier with 20 mg/kg tranylcypromine, (2) by intraperitoneal injection of 5-HTP, 10 mg/kg, to tranylcypromine-pretreated rats, or (3) by intraperitoneal injection of 5 or 10 mg/kg quipazine, to non-pretreated animals. Head twitches were counted six times for 4 min, at 10 min intervals (Corne *et al.*, 1963), and the average frequency of response per hour was calculated.

Radioligand binding studies. Membranes were prepared from the frontal or total cerebral cortex of rats killed 24 h after the last ECT. [^{3}H]-Clonidine, [^{3}H]-spiroperidol and [^{3}H]-serotonin binding were measured as previously described (Pilc & Vetulani 1982*a,b*; Vetulani *et al.*, 1981). For measurement of [^{3}H]-prazosin binding, membrane preparations (0.7 mg protein in 450 μl of Tris-HCl buffer pH 7.6) were incubated for 30 min at 30 °C with six concentrations (0.05–8 nM in final sample) of [^{3}H]-prazosin (dissolved in 50 μl) in the presence or absence of 10 μM phentolamine, used as a blank. The total sample volume was 550 μl. The rest of the procedure was identical as for the other radioligands.

In studying [^{3}H]-serotonin binding, two radioligand concentrations (5 and 10 nmol/liter) were used. [^{3}H]-prazosin binding to membranes of rats receiving spaced ECS was tested using a single concentration of 4 nmol/liter. For the remaining experiments Scatchard plots were constructed based on assays with at least six concentrations of ligands. The B_{max} and K_D values were calculated from the plots. If the plots were curvilinear they were graphically resolved into two rectilinear components (Rosenthal, 1967). The B_{max} and K_D values reported here are means ± s.e.m. of at least three independent experiments (with the exception of [^{3}H]-prazosin binding sites, which were obtained in a single experiment).

The significance of differences among groups was tested using a one-way analysis of variance. If appropriate, specific comparisons were carried out with the Newman–Keuls test (Linton & Gallo, 1975).

Results
(1) The effect of ECS on the α_1-adrenergic system (Table 1)
Rats subjects to chronic ECS displayed more PDC than the controls. The density of [^{3}H]-prazosin binding sites, presumably identical with α_1-adrenoceptors (Greengrass & Bremner, 1979), was significantly increased with no change in receptor affinity.

Table 1. *The effect of ECS on PDC and [^{3}H]-prazosin binding to the membranes from the frontal cortex of rats.* The data are means ± s.e.m. B_{max} and K_D values were calculated from six separate linear Scatchard plots

Group	PDC number	B_{max} (fmol/mg protein)	K_D (nM)
Control	48.0 ± 5.1 (10)	218.6 ± 8.84 (6)	0.49 ± 0.043 (6)
ECS	71.2 ± 4.4 (9)	261.3 ± 9.78 (6)	0.67 ± 0.200 (6)
Per cent control	148*	120†	105

*$P < 0.05$; †$P < 0.01$ (F-test).

(2) The effect of ECS on the α_2-adrenergic system (Table 2)
Rats subjected to chronic ECS displayed reduced hypothermic response to clonidine. Scatchard analysis of [^{3}H]-clonidine-binding data revealed that in these rats the high affinity sub-population of α_2 receptors which was present in the controls, disappeared. The single receptor

population in the ECS group had a density similar to that of the low affinity subpopulation in the control group while its K_D value was significantly lower.

Table 2. *The effect of ECS on clonidine hypothermia and [³H]-clonidine binding to the membranes from the cerebral cortex of rats.* The difference between the initial and postclonidine body temperature was measured 60 min after clonidine (100 µg/kg). The Scatchard plot for [³H]-clonidine binding was concave in the controls but rectilinear in the ECS group

Parameter	Control	ECS	Per cent control
Degree of hypothermia (Δt; °C)	-1.24 ± 0.26 (10)	-0.52 ± 0.14 (10)	42*
High affinity B_{max} (fmol/mg protein)	13 ± 3 (4)	none	
High affinity K_D (nM)	0.31 ± 0.10 (4)	none	
Low affinity B_{max} (fmol/mg protein)	61 ± 3 (4)	69 ± 7 (4)	103
Low affinity K_D (nM)	7.6 ± 0.19 (4)	3.9 ± 0.51 (4)	51†

*$P < 0.05$; †$P < 0.01$ (F-test)

(3) The effect of ECS on the serotonergic system
There was approximately a twofold increase in the head-twitch response to various serotonino-mimetics after chronic ECS (Table 3). The hyperthermic response to quipazine and CPP was also significantly elevated in ECS-treated, heat-adapted rats; the effect was most conspicuous in the group receiving a low dose of CPP, producing only slight effect in the controls (Table 4).

Table 3. *The effect of ECS on head twitch response to serotoninomimetics.* The head twitch response was measured for 60 min after injection of a serotoninomimetic; the data (means ± s.e.m.) are presented as a number of twitches per h

	Head twitches (h^{-1})		Per cent control
Treatment	Control	ECS	
5-HT (25 µg ivtr)*	131 ± 14 (10)	272 ± 20 (10)	208§
5-HTP (10 mg/kg i.p.)	50 ± 11 (10)	108 ± 13 (10)	216†
Quipazine (5 mg/kg i.p.)	61 ± 10 (10)	125 ± 16 (10)	205†

*Administered 30 min after tranylcypromine (20 mg/kg); †$P < 0.01$; §$P < 0.001$ (F-test)

Table 4. *The effect of ECS on hyperthermic response to serotoninomimetics in heat-adapted rats.* The hyperthermic response is presented as the thermal response index, calculated from results of measurements taken every 30 min for 3 h after injection of a serotoninomimetic. The data are means ± s.e.m.

	TRI (°C.h)		Per cent control
Treatment	Control	ECS	
Quipazine (5 mg/kg i.p.)	4.36 ± 0.36 (10)	6.72 ± 0.50 (10)	154†
CPP (0.6 mg/kg i.p.)	0.46 ± 0.18 (10)	1.55 ± 0.45 (10)	330*
CPP (1.25 mg/kg i.p.)	1.69 ± 0.24 (10)	2.98 ± 0.37 (10)	176†
CPP (2.5 mg/kg i.p.)	2.59 ± 0.24 (10)	3.98 ± 0.59 (10)	154*

*$P < 0.05$; †$P < 0.01$ (F-test).

The hyperthermic response to CPP did not appear 1 h after the last shock, but was maintained up to five days after the completion of the ECS; the effect was most noticeable on the second day (Table 5).

The study on [³H]-spiroperidol-specific binding displaceable by LSD which labels 5-HT$_2$ receptors (Peroutka & Snyder, 1979), revealed a significant increase in the B_{max} value of a high affinity site population; the K_D value also increased but the result did not reach a level of statistical significance. No significant changes in the parameters of low affinity subpopulation were observed (Table 6).

Table 5. *The persistence of the effect of ECS on the hyperthermic response of heat-adapted rats to CPP.* The hyperthermic response was presented as the thermal response index, calculated from results of measurements taken every 30 min for 3 h after injection of 2.5 mg/kg i.p. CPP. The data are means ± s.e.m.

	TRI (°C.h)		Per cent
Days after the last ECT	Control	ECS	control
0[a]	1.80 ± 0.38 (10)	2.05 ± 0.41 (10)	114
1	1.56 ± 0.37 (10)	3.50 ± 0.54 (10)	224†
2	1.05 ± 0.31 (10)	3.20 ± 0.28 (10)	305§
5	2.55 ± 0.34 (10)	3.98 ± 0.58 (10)	156*
8	2.04 ± 0.31 (10)	2.21 ± 0.42 (10)	108

[a]1 h after the last ECS. *$P < 0.05$; †$P < 0.01$; §$P < 0.001$ (F-test)

Table 6. *The effect of ECS on [³H]-spiroperidol binding to the membranes from the frontal cortex of the rat (Vetulani et al., 1981).* The parameters of [³H]-spiroperidol binding sites were calculated from concave Scatchard plots, resolved graphically in two linear components (Rosenthal, 1967)

Parameter	Control	ECS	Per cent control
High affinity B_{max} (fmol/mg protein)	57 ± 7 (3)	79 ± 7 (3)	139*
High affinity K_D (nM)	0.68 ± 0.06 (3)	0.92 ± 0.15	135
Low affinity B_{max} (fmol/mg protein)	118 ± 8 (3)	134 ± 12 (3)	114
Low affinity K_D (nM)	6.22 ± 1.21 (3)	5.73 ± 0.34 (3)	92

*$P < 0.05$ (F-test).

No significant change in the degree of hypothermia produced by CPP at ambient temperature was observed in rats subjected to chronic ECS in comparison with the control group; if anything a slight tendency to attenuate the response was observed. The [³H]-serotonin binding which labels 5-HT receptors (Peroutka & Snyder, 1979) was also unchanged (Table 7).

Table 7. *The lack of effect of ECS on CPP-induced hypothermia and [³H]-serotonin binding to the frontal cortex of the rat.* CPP hypothermia was measured every 30 min for 2 h after injection of 10 mg/kg i.p. CPP. The data are means ± s.e.m.

Parameter	Control	ECS	Per cent control
CPP hypothermia (TRI, °C.h)	-1.19 ± 0.18 (10)	-0.98 ± 0.15 (10)	82
[³H]-5-HT binding at 5 nM (fmol/mg protein)	30.2 ± 2.8 (6)	28.8 ± 1.8 (6)	95
[³H]-5-HT binding at 10 nM (fmol/mg protein)	61.1 ± 7.0 (6)	59.0 ± 7.5 (6)	97

(4) The effect of ECT on histamine H_2 receptors
Impromidine, a very potent agonist of histamine H_2 receptor (Durant *et al.*, 1978) produced hypothermia that was much less prominent in ECS than in control rats (Table 8).

(5) The effects of spaced ECS
ECS given at intervals of two to five days produced a significant increase in PDC when compared with the group receiving a single ECS, this increase being statistically significant only in the group receiving ECS every third day. On the other hand, the frequency of PDC in groups receiving ECS every second, third, fourth and fifth day did not differ significantly from that in the group receiving daily ECS (Table 9).

Clonidine hypothermia was attenuated in several groups receiving ECS less frequently than at 24 h intervals; the effect of clonidine was particularly weak in the group receiving ECS at three days intervals (Table 10).

Table 8. *The effect of ECS on impromidine-induced hypothermia in rat.* The difference between initial and postimpromidine body temperature was measured 30 min after the intraventricular injection of impromidine. The mean hypothermia induced by impromidine, 20 μg, in rats receiving a single ECS 24 h before the test was -0.45 ± 0.14 ($n = 8$), virtually the same as in the control rats. The data are means ± s.e.m.

| Treatment | Degree of hypothermia (t, °C) | |
	Control	ECS
Impromidine (20 μg)	-0.46 ± 0.12 (9)	-0.08 ± 0.10 (13)*
Impromidine (50 μg)	-1.11 ± 0.15 (10)	-0.46 ± 0.24 (10)*

*$P < 0.05$ (F-test).

Table 9. *The effect of various ECS dosages on PDC in rats.* The rats were sacrificed 24 h after the last ECS. The data are means ± s.e.m. The mean PDC in naive group, 48.0 ± 5.1 (10), did not differ significantly from 'single ECS' group

ECS spacing (h)	ECS number	PDC number	Per cent 'single ECS' group	Per cent '10 ECS' group
24	10	72.2 ± 4.4 (10)	159†	100
48	5	58.9 ± 5.8 (10)	129	82
72	4	64.9 ± 5.2 (10)	143*	90
96	3	62.4 ± 4.2 (10)	137	86
120	3	61.1 ± 2.0 (10)	134	85
216	2	45.1 ± 5.3 (10)	99	62†
	1	45.5 ± 5.8 (10)	100	63†

$F = 4.80$, d.g. 6/63 ($P < 0.001$). *$P < 0.05$; †$P < 0.01$ (Newman–Keuls test)

Table 10. *The effect of various ECS dosages on clonidine hypothermia in the rat.* The rats received clonidine, 100 μg/kg i.p., 24 h after the last ECS. Hypothermia was presented as the difference in oral temperature before the injection and 60 min after it. The data are means ± s.e.m. The mean hypothermia in the naive group, -3.23 ± 0.12 °C ($n = 10$) did not differ significantly from that in 'single ECS' group

ECS spacing (h)	ECS number	Hypothermia (°C)	Per cent 'single ECS' group	Per cent '10 ECS' group
24	10	-1.97 ± 0.16 (10)	67	100
48	5	-1.65 ± 0.39 (9)	56*	84
72	4	-0.89 ± 0.51 (10)	30†	45
96	3	-3.29 ± 0.15 (10)	112	167*
120	3	-2.63 ± 0.19 (9)	90	133
216	2	-1.45 ± 0.20 (11)	49†	79
	1	-2.93 ± 0.21 (10)	100	148

$F = 9.33$, d.f. 6/62 ($P < 0.001$). *$P < 0.05$; †$P < 0.01$ (Newman–Keuls test)

The augmentation of the head-twitch response to serotoninomimetics was observed not only after daily ECS treatment, but also in rats receiving ECS every second, third and fourth day. This was true for the response evoked both by 5-HTP (Table 11) and quipazine (Table 12).

Preliminary measurements of specific binding of radioligands of α_1- and α_2-adrenergic and 5-HT$_2$ receptors have revealed that a series of five ECS given at three-day intervals produced an effect similar to that observed after ten daily treatments.

The most thoroughly investigated biochemical effect common to the chronic administration of various antidepressant drugs and ECS is the down-regulation of adenylate cyclase linked to the β-adrenergic receptor (see Sulser, 1982). In the present study the effects of ECS on other receptor systems were investigated, and it was demonstrated that receptor effects common to antidepressant drugs and ECS are not limited to the β-adrenergic system.

Table 11. *The effect of various ECS dosages on head twitches induced by 5-HTP in the rat.* Head twitches were induced by intraventricular injection of 250 µg of L-5-HTP 30 min after 20 mg/kg i.p. tranylcypromine, 24 h after the last ECS. The data are means ± s.e.m.

ECS spacing (h)	ECS number	Frequency of head twitches (h⁻¹)	Per cent 'single ECS' group	Per cent '10 ECS' group
24	10	238.2 ± 6.5 (7)	175*	100
48	5	192.0 ± 5.7 (7)	141*	81*
72	4	167.7 ± 5.4 (8)	123*	70*
96	3	168.0 ± 4.7 (7)	123*	71*
120	3	135.0 ± 3.0 (8)	99	57*
216	2	132.5 ± 5.0 (9)	97	56*
	1	136.2 ± 5.4 (7)	100	57*

$F = 54.20$, $d.f.$ 6/46 ($P < 0.001$). *$P < 0.01$ (Newman-Keuls test).

Table 12. *The effect of various ECS dosages on head twitches induced by quipazine in the rat.* Head twitches were induced by quipazine (10 mg/kg i.p.) given 24 h after the last ECS. The data are means ± s.e.m.

ECS spacing (h)	ECS number	Frequency of head twitches (h⁻¹)	Per cent 'single ECS' group	Per cent '10 ECS' group
24	10	169.2 ± 4.2 (8)	131*	100
48	5	169.5 ± 4.2 (7)	131*	100
72	4	161.3 ± 5.7 (8)	125*	95
96	3	162.0 ± 6.0 (8)	125*	96
120	3	137.3 ± 3.3 (7)	106	81*
216	2	134.3 ± 5.3 (7)	104	79*
	1	129.2 ± 3.8 (9)	100	76*

$F = 13.76$, $d.f.$ 6/47 ($P < 0.001$). *$P < 0.01$ (Newman-Keuls test)

α_1-adrenoceptor and responses mediated by it

As a specific functional test for α_1-adrenoceptors we have proposed quantification of post-decapitation convulsions (PDC) (Vetulani & Pilc, 1982). PDC are inhabited only by α_1-adrenoceptor antagonists, while β-adrenoceptor antagonists do not affect them (Eichbaum *et al.*, 1975; Mason & Fibiger, 1979; Pappas *et al.*, 1980). It has been found (Vetulani & Pilc, 1982) that α_2-adrenoceptor antagonists, yohimbine and piperoxan, also leave PDC unaffected. The method presented for measuring PDC with an Animex type activity meter permits an easy and objective assessment of the phenomenon.

If the assumption that the number of PDC reflect the functional state of α_1-adrenoceptors is correct, the present results would suggest that ECS produces up-regulation of α_1-adrenoceptors. This functional change is paralleled by a change in the characteristics of [³H]-prazosin-binding sites which may be identified with α_1-adrenergic receptors (Greengrass & Bremner, 1979); an increase in density with no change in affinity.

In subsequent experiments (Vetulani & Pilc, unpublished) we have observed that the chronic administration of imipramine for two weeks also brings about an increase in PDC and [³H]-prazosin binding, which suggests that these effects may be common to both antidepressant drugs and ECS. In fact, several behavioral and electrophysiological studies have suggested facilitation rather than depression of adrenergic transmission by the chronic administration of antidepressant drugs (Maj *et al.*, 1979; 1980; Menkes & Aghajanian, 1981; Modigh, 1975). Nevertheless, most of the data in the literature, regarding the behavior of the α_1-adrenoceptor population suggests no changes in its characteristics after prolonged treatment with anti-depressants (Peroutka & Snyder, 1980a) or ECT (Bergstrom & Kellar, 1979). However, in these studies [³H]-WB4101 was used as the radioligand and its specificity as an α_1-adrenoceptor ligand has recently been questioned (Hoffman & Lefkowitz, 1980), while prazosin was found to be much more selective than [³H]-WB4101 (Braunwalder *et al.*, 1981; Greengrass & Bremner, 1979; Hoffman & Lefkowitz, 1980; Miach *et al.*, 1980). If, as shown here and in previous studies (Pilc & Vetulani, 1982*a,b*), the α_2-adrenoceptor subpopulation is concomitantly depressed, the binding studies employing [³H]-WB4101 may yield equivocal results. In spite of this, at least one report outside this department (Rehavi *et al.*, 1980) demonstrated a slowly developing increase in [³H]-WB4101 binding sites after the chronic administration of high doses of amitriptyline. The effect occurred only in superhigh-affinity sites.

α_2-adrenoceptor and its reactivity
In contrast to α_1-adrenoceptors, α_2-adrenoceptors appear to be down-regulated by chronic ECS, as indicated by both a decreased specific binding of [³H]-clonidine and the attenuation of clonidine-induced hypothermia. The behavioral data presented here are in agreement with the findings of Heal *et al.* (1981) that repeated ECS abolishes clonidine-induced hypoactivity in mice and rats. The Scatchard plot, presented elsewhere (Pilc & Vetulani, 1982*b*) indicates that in rats subjected to ECS the small high-affinity subpopulation of [³H]-clonidine-binding sites seem to disappear completely.

The presence of more than one [³H]-clonidine-binding site population was described previously (U'Prichard *et al.*, 1979; Vetulani *et al.*, 1979*b*). Recently, Braunwalder *et al.* (1981) have reported that catecholamines display a higher affinity to high- than to low-affinity sites, while antidepressant drugs and several α_1 and α_2-adrenoceptor antagonists that displace [³H]-clonidine specifically, have a higher preference to low- than to high-affinity sites. It seems, therefore, that chronic ECT depresses the agonistic α_2-adrenoceptor population, that possibly control noradrenaline release (Langer, 1974).

With respect to its effects on responsiveness to clonidine, ECS resembles chronic treatment with antidepressant drugs which have repeatedly been demonstrated to inhibit electrophysiological, biochemical and behavioral effects of clonidine (Andén *et al.*, 1976; Górka & Zacny, 1981; Pilc & Vetulani, 1982*a*; Spyraki & Fibiger, 1980; Svensson & Usdin, 1978; Vetulani *et al.*, 1982; Von Voigtlander *et al.*, 1978). In fact, antagonism of clonidine hypothermia was proposed by von Voigtlander *et al.* (1978) as a test for the potential antidepressant properties of a drug. Moreover, it has been recently found that in depressive patients in whom clonidine produced an evident hypotension during the placebo period, the action of the drug was greatly attenuated after treatment with antidepressant drugs lasting long enough to bring about clinical improvement (Siever *et al.*, 1981).

On the other hand, the data on the effect of long-term treatment with antidepressant drugs on radioligand binding to α_2-adrenoceptors are apparently contradictory. In our group, a decrease in [³H]-clonidine binding after chronic administration of imipramine to normal and chemo-sympathectomized rats was observed (Pilc & Vetulani, 1982*a*; Vetulani *et al.*, 1980; 1982), and a similar effect after prolonged amitriptyline administration was reported by Smith *et al.* (1981). Other authors (Asakura *et al.*, 1982; Johnson *et al.*, 1980) have found an increase in the density of α_2-adrenoceptors. However, scrutiny of their data reveals that 'long-term treatment' in the paper of Asakura *et al.* (1982) meant one week's treatment, and Johnson *et al.* (1980) administered desipramine for four days only. A considerable period of treatment seems to be necessary for α_2-adrenoceptor subsensitivity; we have shown that attenuation of clonidine inhibitory effect on noradrenaline utilization does not develop after one or two weeks of treatment, but only after four weeks (Vetulani *et al.*, 1982). It is most probable, therefore, that the results of Asakura *et al.* (1982) and Johnson *et al.* (1980) reflect only early adaptatory changes but are not relevant to the effect of chronic treatment.

Recently, Sugrue (1981) reported that ECS given similarly to the presence experiments (but the rats were killed 6.5 instead of 24 h after the last shock) did not change the characteristics of [³H]-clonidine binding to rat cerebral membranes. However, a single, rectilinear Scatchard plot of [³H]-clonidine binding was observed in his experiments. It is thus possible that in those experiments only a large low-affinity subpopulation of α_2-adrenoceptors was observed. This subpopulation did not change its density in the experiments presented here either.

Serotonergic systems

Serotonergic stimulation produces several effects, some of them stimulatory, others inhibitory. Following the discovery of two types of serotonin receptors, 5-HT$_1$ and 5-HT$_2$ (Peroutka & Snyder, 1979), it has been suggested that most of the stimulatory serotonergic effects, such as head twitches (Corne *et al.*, 1963), are mediated via 5-HT$_2$ receptors (Peroutka *et al.*, 1981). The present results, published in part before (Vetulani *et al.*, 1981), indicate that the responsiveness of serotonergic receptors involved in such behavioral effects as head twitch or hyperthermia in heat-adapted rats (Sulpizio *et al.*, 1978) increases after chronic ECT, and in parallel the density of 5-HT$_2$ receptors is elevated. These data confirm behavioral and biochemical findings of others (Evans *et al.*, 1976; Green *et al.*, 1977; Kellar *et al.*, 1981; Lebrecht & Nowak, 1980) and suggest up-regulation of 5-HT$_2$ receptor by ECS. Similarly to Bergstrom & Kellar (1979) no effect of ECS on [^{3}H]-serotonin binding was observed; and treatment did not influence the hypothermia produced at room temperature by the serotonino-mimetic agent, CPP. The hypothermic response to serotoninomimetics is generated in brain centers that are different from those involved in hyperthermic response (Crawshaw, 1972) and is resistant to cyproheptadine-like serotoninolytics (Reichenberg *et al.*, 1975). Possibly, this, apparently inhibitory effect is mediated by 5-HT$_1$ receptors.

While ECS seems to act in a manner similar to antidepressant drugs on α- and β-adrenoceptors, its effect on 5-HT$_2$ receptors seems to be opposite. It has been reported that several anti-depressants bind preferentially to 5-HT$_2$ receptors and that after prolonged treatment with these drugs the density of 5-HT$_2$ receptors decreases (Peroutka & Snyder, 1980*a,b*; Kellar *et al.*, 1981). However, the response of 5-HT$_2$ receptor density to antidepressant treatment is not paralleled by functional inhibition. Facilitation of serotonergic responses, similar to that observed after chronic ECS, was reported after prolonged antidepressant treatments, particularly if tests were carried out after a period greater than 24 h after the last dose (De Montigny & Aghajanian, 1978; Friedman & Dallob, 1979; Gallager & Bunney, 1979; Mogilnicka & Klimek, 1979). One possible reason for this discrepancy between the results for receptor binding and functional studies is that the molecules of antidepressant may still occupy the 5-HT$_2$ receptors in membrane preparations obtained from chronically treated animals, and interfere with the assay. In behavioral or electrophysiological tests the serotoninomimetics are usually given in doses producing high cerebral concentrations that may displace the anti-depressant molecules from the receptor sites.

Histamine H$_2$ receptors

The results presented here are preliminary ones based on one test only: the impromidine-induced hypothermia, a response mediated by the central histamine H$_2$ receptor (Pilc *et al.*, 1980). The attenuation of impromidine hypothermia by chronic ECS may, therefore, suggest a hyposensitivity of H$_2$ receptors, particularly as the ECS effect is rather specific. Another kind of hypothermia, induced by a serotoninomimetic, CPP, was not altered by the treatment.

The involvement of histamine H$_2$ receptors in the action of antidepressant drugs has been postulated. These drugs antagonize the central histamine H$_2$ receptor and the effects of H$_2$ receptor agonists (Green & Maayani, 1977; Kanof & Greengard, 1978; Nowak *et al.*, 1979; Palmer *et al.*, 1977). The difference between ECS and antidepressant drugs lies in the fact that even a single dose of an antidepressant produces antagonistic effect, while hyposensitivity of H$_2$ receptors develops only after repeated ECT.

Spaced ECT

Early studies on the mode of action of antidepressant drugs suffered from the fact that pharmacological experiments did not follow the schedule of clinical administration, and many conclusions about the mechanism of the action of antidepressant treatments were based on single-dose experiments. Many current preclinical studies on ECT do not take into account the fact that in the clinic ECT is almost never administered on a daily basis, but the electro-shocks are spaced by a few days. A study of the effects of spaced ECT seems to be warranted, particularly as one report claims that some effects of ECT do not depend on the number of shocks, but develop even after a single treatment, and it is only the passage of time that determines the effect (Chiodo & Antelman, 1980). On the other hand, there is a possibility that some effects observed after daily treatment will not appear if the shocks are given at longer intervals.

The present results with spaced ECS not only confirmed the effects of ECS on adrenergic and serotonergic systems described in the first part of the paper, but have also showed that these effects are brought about by electro-shocks administered less frequently. The effects of daily treatment were only rarely significantly stronger than these observed after ECS given every second, third, or even fourth day.

These results indicate that the effects observed after daily treatment with ECS may be relevant to the clinical action of ECT, in spite of higher frequency. Moreover, as the effects of ECS given every third day are similar, or sometimes even more prominent than those observed after daily treatment, it is proposed that such spaced treatment replace the daily ECS schedule commonly used in preclinical studies. The spaced treatment also reduces the number of rats injured during the treatment, which seems to be proportional to the number of shocks.

Our results also indicate that the effects investigated in this study require not only time, but also a certain number of ECS to develop. In the experiments in which two shocks were applied, at nine days' interval, the effect was similar to that observed after a single shock given 24 h before the test or in non-shocked animals. Thus, in contrast to the effect of ECS on dopamine autoreceptors, which was independent of repeated treatment (Chiodo & Antelman, 1980), the effects on adrenergic and serotonergic systems require multiple ECT.

Possible functional meaning of receptor changes induced by ECT
The general picture resulting from the data presented here suggests that the action of ECT on monoaminergic system in the brain is a complex one, and that the down-regulation of β-adrenoceptors cannot be regarded as the only important factor in the action of anti-depressants. The similarities in the action of chronic antidepressant drug treatment and spaced ECT on α-adrenergic and serotonergic systems strongly suggest that these actions may be relevant for the clinical effect.

In the light of the present results it seems that the two apparently contradictory hypotheses on the mechanism of antidepressant action and, consequently, etiology of endogenous depression may be reconciled. The hypothesis of Schildkraut & Kety (1967) assumed that depression is caused by a deficit in noradrenergic transmission and that the antidepressants act by increasing the availability of noradrenaline at the receptor site. This was challenged by the adrenoceptor down-regulation theory of the action of antidepressant drugs (Sulser, 1982; Vetulani & Sulser, 1975; Vetulani *et al.*, 1976a,b), mainly on the grounds that the former hypothesis was based on the results of acute experiments and could not explain the mechanism of action of atypical antidepressants, such as iprindole, that do not affect noradrenaline uptake or metabolism. The down-regulation hypothesis was based on an evident functional biochemical effect (hypo-sensitivity of the cyclic AMP generating system) appearing only in the course of prolonged treatment and exerted by all known efficient antidepressant treatments (Sulser, 1982). Moreover, this hypothesis was corroborated by the results of receptor-binding studies (Banarjee *et al.*, 1977; Bergstrom & Kellar, 1979; Pandey *et al.*, 1979; Wolfe *et al.*, 1977) showing a reduction in the number of β-adrenergic receptors. This was observed even after such antidepressant treatments as rapid eye movement sleep deprivation (Mogilnicka *et al.*, 1980).

The present results suggest that ECS, and possibly other antidepressant treatments as well, produce concomitantly with down-regulation of β-adrenoceptor, up-regulation of α_1-adrenoceptors and facilitation of adrenergic transmission, caused by depression of α_2-adrenoceptors. The hyposensitivity of α_2-adrenoceptors leads to an increased release of noradrenaline from the adrenergic nerve terminals (Langer, 1974). Possibly α_1- and β-adrenoceptors differ between themselves in their response to the increased availability of noradrenaline at the receptor sites. While β-adrenoceptors undergo compensatory down-regulation (Vetulani et al., 1976b), the α_1-adrenoceptors retain their responsiveness or even develop hypersensitivity. If this is correct the action of ECT (and other antidepressant treatments) will lead to a specific facilitation of neurotransmission mediated via α_2-adrenoceptors, without increasing the metabolic, β-adrenoceptor mediated effects of catecholamines.

In addition, depression of α_2-adrenoceptors may lead to enhanced responses to serotoninomimetics. The α_2-adrenoceptors are also located presynaptically on the serotonin nerve terminals and control serotonin release (Göthert et al., 1981). Their hyposensitivity will increase the responses to several serotoninomimetics: integrity of presynaptic serotonin neurons is essential for serotoninomimetic action of quipazine, LSD and 5-HTP (Costall & Naylor, 1975; Vetulani et al., 1979a).

It is still uncertain what role the serotonin system may play in the etiology of endogenous depression. In a recent paper Kety (1978) proposes that: 'Behavioral studies in animals as well as clinical findings are compatible with the thesis that norepinephrine pathways are involved in mood, with deficiency producing depression and overactivity resulting in euphoria, hypomania, or mania. Similar types of observations with serotonin suggest that its role may be to exert a reciprocal or, more likely, a stabilizing or dampening effect on the synapses the activity of which may be associated with mood'. Kety (1978) further suggests that a deficiency of serotonin at central synapses may be an important factor in the development of affective disorders. If this is correct, the facilitation of serotonergic transmission may contribute to the beneficial action of antidepressant treatments. ECS seems to display more potent serotonin facilitating properties than drug treatments, and this possibly may be relevant to ECT clinical efficacy surpassing that of drug treatments.

References

Andén, N.-E., Grabowska, M. & Strömbom, U. (1976): Different alpha-adrenoceptors in the central nervous system mediating biochemical and functional effects of clonidine and receptor blocking agents. *Naunyn-Schmiedeberg's Arch. Pharmacol.* **292**, 43–52.

Asakura, M., Tsukamoto, T. & Hasegawa, K. (1982): Modulation of rat brain α_2 and β-adrenergic receptor sensitivity following long-term treatment with antidepressants. *Brain Res.* **235**, 192–197.

Banarjee, S. P., Kung, L. S., Riggi, S. J. & Chanda, S. K. (1977): Development of β-adrenergic receptor subsensitivity by antidepressants. *Nature* **268**, 455–456.

Bergstrom, D. A. & Kellar, K. J. (1979): Effect of electroconvulsive shock on monoaminergic receptor binding sites in rat brain. *Nature* **278**, 464–466.

Braunwalder, A., Stone, G. & Lovell, R. A. (1981): Characterization of [^{3}H]-clonidine binding to two sites in calf brain membranes. *J. Neurochem.* **37**, 70–78.

Chiodo, L. A. & Antelman, S. M. (1980): Electroconvulsive shock: progressive dopamine autoreceptor subsensitivity independent of repeated treatments. *Science* **210**, 799–801.

Corne, S. J., Pickering, R. W. & Warner, B. T. (1963): A method for assessing the effects of drugs on the central action of 5-hydroxytryptamine. *Br. J. Pharmacol.* **20**, 106–120.

Costall, B. & Naylor, R. J. (1975): The role of the raphe and the extrapyramidal nuclei in the stereotyped and circling response to quipazine. *J. Pharm. Pharmacol.* **27**, 368–371.

Crawshaw, L. I. (1972): Effects of intracerebral 5-hydroxytryptamine injection on thermoregulation in rat. *Physiol. Behav.* **9**, 133–140.

Daniel, W., Adamus, A., Melzacka, M., Szymura, J. & Vetulani, J. (1981): Cerebral pharmacokinetics of imipramine in rats after a single and multiple dosage. *Naunyn-Schmiedeberg's Arch. Pharmacol.* **317**, 209–213.

De Montigny, C. & Aghajanian, G. K. (1978): Tricyclic antidepressants: long-term treatment increases responsivity of rat forebrain neurons to serotonin. *Science* **202**, 1303–1306.

Durant, C. J., Duncan, N. A. M., Gannelin, C. R., Parsons, M. E., Blakemore, R. & Rasmussen, A. (1978): Impromidine (SK&F-92676) is a very potent and specific agonist for histamine H_2 receptors. *Nature* **276**, 403–405.

Eichbaum, F. W., Slemer, O. & Yasaka, W. J. (1975): Postdecapitation convulsions and their inhibition by drugs. *Exptl. Neurol.* **49**, 802–812.

Evans, J. P. M., Grahame-Smith, D. G., Green, A. R. & Tordoff, A. F. C. (1976): Electroconvulsive shock increases the behavioural responses of rats to brain 5-hydroxytryptamine accumulation and central nervous system stimulant drugs. *Br. J. Pharmacol.* **56**, 193–199.

Friedman, E. & Dallob, A. (1979): Enhanced serotonin receptor activity after chronic treatment with imipramine or amitriptyline. *Commun. Psychopharmacol.* **3**, 89–92.

Gallager, D. W. & Bunney, W. R., Jr. (1979). Failure of chronic lithium treatment to block tricyclic antidepressant-induced 5-HT supersensitivity. *Naunyn-Schmiedeberg's Arch. Pharmacol.* **307**, 129-133.

Górka, Z. & Zacny, E. (1981): The effect of single and chronic administration of imipramine on clonidine-induced hypothermia in the rat. *Life Sci.* **28**, 2847-2854.

Göthert, M., Huth, H. & Schlicker, E. (1981): Characterization of receptor subtype involved in alpha-adrenergic-mediated modulation of serotonin release from rat brain cortex slices. *Naunyn-Schmiedeberg's Arch. Pharmacol.* **317**, 199-203.

Green, A. R., Heal, D. J. & Grahame-Smith, D. G. (1977): Further observations on the effect of repeated electro-convulsive shock on the behavioural responses of rats produced by increases in the functional activity of brain 5-hydroxytrayptamine and dopamine. *Psychopharmacology* **52**, 195-200.

Green, J. P. & Maayani, S. (1977). Tricyclic antidepressant drugs block histamine H_2 receptor in brain. *Nature* **269**, 162-165.

Greengrass, P. & Bremner, R. (1979): Binding characteristics of [^{3}H]-prazosin to rat brain α-adrenergic receptors. *Eur. J. Pharmacol.* **55**, 323-326.

Heal, D. J., Akagi, H., Bowdler, J. M. & Green, A. R. (1981): Repeated electroconvulsive shock attenuates clonidine-induced hypoactivity in rodents. *Eur. J. Pharmacol.* **75**, 231-237.

Hoffman, B. B. & Lefkowitz, R. J. (1980): [^{3}H]-WB4101 — caution about its role as an alpha-adrenergic subtype selective radioligand. *Biochem. Pharmacol.* **29**, 1537-1541.

Johnson, R. W., Reisine, T., Spotnitz, S., Wiech, N., Ursillo, R. & Yamamura, H. I. (1980): Effects of desipramine and yohimbine on α_2- and β-adrenoceptor. *Eur. J. Pharmacol.* **67**, 123-127.

Kanof, P. D. & Greengard, P. (1978): Brain histamine as target for antidepressant drugs. *Nature* **272**, 329-333.

Kellar, K. J., Cascio, C. S., Butler, J. A. & Kurtzke, R. N. (1981): Differential effects of electroconvulsive shock and antidepressant drugs on serotonin-2 receptors in rat brain. *Eur. J. Pharmacol.* **69**, 515-518.

Kety, S. S. (1978): Biochemistry of the central nervous system and behavior. In *Transmethylations and the central nervous system*, ed V. M. Andreoli, A. Agnoli and C. Fazio. Pp. 4-16. Berlin, Heidelberg, New York: Springer-Verlag.

Langer, S. Z. (1974): Presynaptic regulation of catecholamine release. *Biochem. Pharmacol.* **23**, 1793-1800.

Lebrecht, U. & Nowak, J. Z. (1980): Effect of single and repeated electroconvulsive shock on serotonergic system in rat brain. II. Behavioural studies. *Neuropharmacology* **19**, 1055-1061.

Linton, M. & Gallo, P. S., Jr. (1975): *The Practical statistician. Simplified handbook of statistics.* Monterey, California: Brooks/Cole Publishing Co.

Maj, J., Mogilnicka, E. & Kordecka, A. (1979): Chronic treatment with antidepressant drugs: potentiation of apomorphine-induced aggressive behaviour in rats. *Neurosci. Lett.* **13**, 337-341.

Maj, J., Mogilnicka, E. & Kordecka-Magiera, A. (1980): Effect of chronic administration of antidepressant drugs on aggressive behavior induced by clonidine in mice. *Pharmacol. Biochem. Behav.* **13**, 153-154.

Mason, S. T. & Fibiger, H. C. (1979): Physiological function of descending noradrenaline projections to the spinal cord: role in postdecapitative convulsions. *Eur. J. Pharmacol.* **75**, 29-34.

Menkes, D. B. & Aghajanian, G. K. (1981): α_1-Adrenoceptor mediated responses in the lateral geniculate nucleus are enhanced by chronic antidepressant treatment. *Eur. J. Pharmacol.* **74**, 27-35.

Miach, P. J., Dausse, J. P., Cardot, A. & Meyer, P. (1980): [^{3}H]-Prazosin binds specifically to 'α_1'-adrenoceptors in rat brain. *Naunyn-Schmiedeberg's Arch. Pharmacol.* **312**, 23-26.

Modigh, K. (1975): Electroconvulsive shock and postsynaptic catecholamine effects: increased psychomotor stimulant action of apomorphine and clonidine in reserpine pretreated mice by repeated ECS. *J. Neural Transm.* **36**, 19-32.

Mogilnicka, E., Arbilla, S., Depoortere, H. & Langer, S. Z. (1980): Rapid-eye-movement sleep deprivation decreases the density of [^{3}H]-dihydroalprenolol and [^{3}H]-imipramine binding sites in the rat cerebral cortex. *Eur. J. Pharmacol.* **65**, 289-292.

Mogilnicka, E. & Klimek, V. (1979): Mianserin, danitracen and amitriptyline withdrawal increases the behavioural responses of rats to L-5-HTP. *J. Pharm. Pharmacol.* **31**, 704-705.

Nowak, J. Z., Bielkiewicz, B. & Lebrecht, U. (1979): Dimaprit-induced hypothermia in normal rats: its attenuation by cimetidine and by tricyclic antidepressant drugs. *Neuropharmacology* **18**, 787-789.

Palmer, G. C., Wagner, H. R., Palmer, S. J. & Manian, A. A. (1977): Histamine-stimulated adenylate cyclase: blockade by imipramine and its analogues. *Comm. Psychopharmacol.* **1**, 61-69.

Pandey, G. N., Heinze, W. J., Brown, B. D. & Davis, J. M. (1979): Electroconvulsive shock treatment decreases β-adrenergic receptor sensitivity in rat brain. *Nature* **280**, 234-235.

Pappas, B. A., Breese, G. R., Mailman, R. B. & Mueller, R. A. (1980): Importance of the locus coeruleus and involvement of α-adrenergic receptors in the postdecapitation reflex in the rat. *Psychopharmacology* **69**, 163-171.

Peroutka, S. J., Lebovitz, R. M. & Snyder, S. H. (1981): Two distinct central serotonin receptors with different physiological functions. *Science* **212**, 827-829.

Peroutka, S. J. & Snyder, S. H. (1979): Multiple serotonin receptors: differential binding of [^{3}H]-5-hydroxytryptamine, [^{3}H]-lysergic acid diethylamide and [^{3}H]-spiroperidol. *Mol. Pharmacol.* **16**, 687-699.

Peroutka, S. J. & Snyder, S. H. (1980a): Long-term antidepressant treatment decreases spiroperidol-labeled serotonin receptor binding. *Science* **210**, 88-90.

Peroutka, S. J. & Snyder, S. H. (1980b): Regulation of serotonin (5-HT$_2$) receptors labeled with [^{3}H]-spiroperidol by chronic treatment with the antidepressant amitriptyline. *J. Pharmacol. Exptl. Ther.* **215**, 582-587.

Pilc, A., Rogóz, Z. & Byrska, B. (1980): Some central effects of impromidine, a potent agonist of histamine H_2 receptor. *Neuropharmacology* **19**, 947-950.

44

Pilc, A. & Vetulani, J. (1982a). Attenuation by chronic imipramine treatment of [^{3}H]-clonidine-induced hypothermia: the influence of central chemosympathectomy. *Brain Res.* **238**, 499–504.

Pilc, A. & Vetulani, J. (1982b): Depression by chronic electroconvulsive treatment of clonidine hypothermia and [^{3}H]-clonidine binding to rat cortical membranes. *Eur. J. Pharmacol.* **80**, 109–113.

Rehavi, M., Ramot, O., Yavetz, B. & Sokolovsky, M. (1980): Amitriptyline: long-term treatment elevates α-adrenergic and muscarinic receptor binding in mouse brain. *Brain Res.* **194**, 443–453.

Reichenberg, K., Wiszniowska, G. & Marchaj, J. (1975): The influence of 5-hydroxytryptophan (5-HTP) administered into the lateral brain ventricle on the behavior and body temperature in rats. *Pol. J. Pharmacol. Pharm.* **27** Suppl., 217–222.

Rosenthal, H. E. (1967): A graphic method for the determination and presentation of binding parameters in a complex system. *Analyt. Biochem.* **20**, 525–532.

Schildkraut, J. J. & Kety, S. S. (1967). Biogenic amines and emotion. *Science* **156**, 21–30.

Siever, L. J., Cohen, R. M. & Murphy, D. L. (1981): Antidepressant and α_2-adrenergic autoreceptor desensitization. *Am. J. Psychiat.* **138**, 681–682.

Smith, C. B., Garcia-Sevilla, J. A. & Hollinworth, P. J. (1981): α_2-Adrenoceptors in rat brain are decreased after long-term tricyclic antidepressant treatment. *Brain. Res.* **210**, 413–418.

Spyraki, C. & Fibiger, H. C. (1980): Functional evidence for subsensitivity of noradrenergic alpha$_2$ receptors after chronic desipramine treatment. *Life Sci.* **27**, 1863–1867.

Sugrue, M. F. (1981): Effect of chronic antidepressant administration on rat frontal cortex α_2 and β-adrenoceptor binding. *Br. J. Pharmacol.* **74**, 761P–762P.

Sulpizio, A., Fowler, P. J. & Macko, A. (1978): Antagonism of fenfluramine-induced hyperthermia: a measure of central serotonin inhibition. *Life Sci.* **22**, 1439–1446.

Sulser, F. (1982): Antidepressant drug research: its impact on neurobiology and psychobiology. *Adv. Biochem. Psychopharmacol.* **31**, 1–20.

Svensson, T. H. & Usdin, T. (1978): Feedback inhibition of brain noradrenaline neurons by tricyclic antidepressants: α receptor mediation. *Science* **202**, 1089–1091.

U'Prichard, D. C., Bechtel, W. D., Rout, B. M. & Snyder, S. H. (1979): Multiple apparent alpha-noradrenergic receptor binding sites in rat brain: effect of 6-hydroxydopamine. *Mol. Pharmacol.* **16**, 47–60.

U'Prichard, D. C., Greenberg, D. A., Sheehan, P. P. & Snyder, S. H. (1978): Tricyclic antidepressants: therapeutic properties and affinity for α-noradrenergic binding sites in the brain. *Science* **199**, 197–198.

Vetulani, J., Antkiewicz-Michaluk, L., Golembiowska-Nikitin, K., Michaluk, J., Pilc, A. & Rokosz, A. (1980): The effect of multiple imipramine administration on monoaminergic systems of the rat brain. *Pol. J. Pharmacol. Pharm.* **32**, 523–530.

Vetulani, J., Byrska, B. & Reichenberg, K. (1979a): Head twitches produced by serotonergic drugs and opiates after lesion of the mesostriatal serotonergic system of the rat. *Pol. J. Pharmacol. Pharm.* **31**, 413–423.

Vetulani, J., Lebrecht, U. & Pilc, A. (1981). Enhancement of responsiveness of the central serotonergic system and serotonin-2 receptor density in rat frontal cortex by electroconvulsive treatment. *Eur. J. Pharmacol.* **76**, 81–85.

Vetulani, J., Nielsen, M., Pilc, A. & Golembiowska-Nikitin, K. (1979b). Two possible binding sites for [^{3}H]-clonidine in the rat cerebral cortex. *Eur. J. Pharmacol.* **58**, 95–96.

Vetulani, J. & Pilc, A. (1982). Postdecapitation convulsions in the rat measured with an Animex motility meter: relation to central α adrenoceptors. *Eur. J. Pharmacol.* **85**, 269–275.

Vetulani, J., Pilc, A., Antkiewicz-Michaluk, L., Golembiowska-Nikitin, K., Lebrecht, U. & Rokosz, A. (1982): Adaptive changes of monoaminergic systems in rats treated chronically with imipramine, electroshock, or serotoninomimetics. In *Neuronal Plasticity and Memory Formation*, ed C. Ajmone Marsan and H. Matties. Pp. 405–425. New York: Raven Press.

Vetulani, J., Reichenberg, K. & Wiszniowska, G. (1972): Asymmetric behavioral and biochemical effects of unilateral injections of 6-hydroxydopamine into the lateral brain ventricle of the rat. *Eur. J. Pharmacol.* **19**, 231–238.

Vetulani, J., Stawarz, R. J., Dingell, J. V. & Sulser, F. (1976a): A possible common mechanism of action of antidepressant treatments. Reduction in the sensitivity of noradrenergic cyclic AMP generating system in the rat limbic forebrain. *Naunyn-Schmiedeberg's Arch. Pharmacol.* **293**, 109–114.

Vetulani, J., Stawarz, R. J. & Sulser, F. (1976b): Adaptive mechanisms of the noradrenergic cyclic AMP generating system in the limbic forebrain of the rat: adaptation to persistent changes in the availability of norepinephrine (NE). *J. Neurochem.* **27**, 661–666.

Vetulani, J. & Sulser, F. (1975): Action of various antidepressant treatments reduces reactivity of noradrenergic cyclic AMP generating system in limbic forebrain. *Nature* **257**, 495–496.

Von Voigtlander, P. F., Triezenberg, H. J. & Losey, E. G. (1978): Interaction between clonidine and antidepressant drugs: a method for identifying antidepressant-like agents. *Neuropharmacology* **17**, 375–381.

Wolfe, B. B., Harden, T. K., Sporn, J. R. & Molinoff, P. B. (1977): Presynaptic modulation of β-adrenergic receptors in rat cerebral cortex after treatment with antidepressants. *J. Pharmacol. Exptl. Ther.* **207**, 446–457.

5.
ECS: effects on serotonergic and β-adrenergic receptor binding sites in brain

K. J. KELLAR

Department of Pharmacology, Georgetown University Schools of Medicine and Dentistry, 3900 Reservoir Road, N. W., Washington, DC 20007, USA.

Introduction

Electroconvulsive therapy (ECT) has been used in the treatment of depressions for more than 40 years. It is the oldest form of somatic antidepressant therapy still used — predating the antidepressant drugs in use today by almost 20 years. The efficacy of ECT in the treatment of depression has been demonstrated in controlled clinical trials (Freeman *et al.*, 1978; Medical Research Council, 1965), and it is considered to be at least the equal of antidepressant drugs in treating most depressions. In fact, it appears to be more effective than drugs in treating the most severe forms of these illnesses. Despite a history of use which is longer than that of anti-depressant drugs, the neural mechanisms affected by ECT which are relevant to its therapeutic effects, are not known.

A large volume of evidence has accumulated during the past 20 years which suggests that the tricyclic antidepressants and monoamine oxidase inhibitors, the major drugs used in treating depression, alter catecholamine and/or serotonin (5-HT) neurotransmission in the brain by increasing the amount of transmitter available to act at the postsynaptic receptors. The tricyclic antidepressants inhibit the transport of norepinephrine (NE) and 5-HT back into presynaptic neurons after release. These re-uptake processes are major mechanisms for ending the actions of NE and 5-HT in the synapse; therefore, inhibition of these processes results in increased stimulation of postsynaptic receptors. In general, the tricyclic antidepressants in use today are much less potent inhibitors of dopamine (DA) re-uptake than of NE or 5-HT re-uptake. The monoamine oxidase inhibitors decrease enzymatic degradation of catecholamines and 5-HT and increase the intraneuronal concentrations of these neurotransmitters. This presumably allows more neurotransmitter to be released from vesicular pools with each impulse and could also result in increased diffusion of catecholamines and 5-HT into the synaptic cleft from nonvesicular pools.

The potentiation of NE and 5-HT neurotransmission produced in animals by the acute actions of the two major classes of antidepressant drugs focused attention on, and led to theories of, the involvement of these two neurotransmitter systems in depression (Bunney & Davis, 1965; Schildkraut, 1965; Coppen, 1967). It was therefore important to determine whether electroconvulsive shock (ECS) in animals resulted in alterations of catecholamine and/or 5-HT neurotransmission, and if so, to determine whether the changes were consistent with the actions of antidepressant drugs.

In searching for neurochemical changes related to the antidepressant efficacy of ECT, two approaches have been taken. One is the measurement of metabolite changes in cerebrospinal fluid of depressed patients undergoing ECT. This approach has the advantage of studying changes under the most relevant conditions — that is, in depressed patients before and after therapy. It is, however, difficult to determine whether changes of metabolites in the cerebrospinal fluid of patients are related to the therapeutic aspects of ECT or to nonspecific processes. Furthermore, it is not yet possible to study the mechanisms which could account for cerebrospinal fluid metabolite changes originating in the brain.

A second approach is to study the neurochemical effects of ECS in animals (usually rats). Here the effects of brain seizures on synaptic processes can be studied more directly. This approach has the potential advantage of being able to separate and compare neurochemical changes due to nonspecific aspects of ECS, such as stress or anesthesia, from changes related primarily to seizure activity. In addition, animal studies facilitate controlled comparisons between the neurochemical effects of ECS and antidepressant drugs. Such comparisons have proved useful in identifying molecular mechanisms and effects common to or unique to both forms of treatment, and may also prove useful in identifying common neuronal structures and pathways affected by antidepressant drugs and ECS. A serious drawback to the use of animals in studying antidepressant related mechanisms of ECS (or drugs) is that extrapolations must be made from effects on presumably normal animal neurophysiology to human pathophysiologies.

Since mood disorders corresponding to human depressive illnesses are not known to exist in sub-primate species, and animal models generally applicable to the study of human depression have not been established, it is useful to compare the effects of ECS with those of antidepressant drugs in animals. By doing this, correlations across different types of antidepressant treatments can be made and isolated from effects produced by non-antidepressant drugs and procedures.

Since the observations that repeated administration of antidepressant drugs or ECS reduces β-adrenergic receptor stimulated cyclic AMP production in rat brain (Vetulani & Sulser, 1975; Vetulani et al., 1976a; Vetulani et al., 1976b; Frazer et al., 1974) the focus of many studies of the mechanisms involved in antidepressant action has shifted from presynaptic effects to postsynaptic effects. Several laboratories have demonstrated that repeated administration of antidepressant drugs decreases the density of β-adrenergic receptors in rat brain (Banerjee et al., 1977; Wolfe et al., 1978; Sarai et al., 1978; Bergstrom & Kellar, 1979a). This decrease in β-adrenergic receptor number (down-regulation) appears to be specific to antidepressant drugs (Sellinger-Barnette et al., 1980).

The effects of antidepressant drugs on receptor-binding sites in brain are relatively selective. Repeated administration of most antidepressant drugs does not alter the density of cerebral cortical α_1-adrenergic receptors (Bergstrom & Kellar, 1979a; Peroutka & Snyder, 1980a) or muscarinic cholinergic receptors (Maggi et al., 1980; Peroutka & Snyder, 1980a) or striatal dopamine receptors (Peroutka & Snyder, 1980a). Serotonin-1 (5-HT$_1$) receptor-binding sites labeled by [^{3}H]-5-HT are not altered by most tricyclic antidepressant drugs (Wirtz-Justice et al., 1978; Bergstrom & Kellar, 1979a; Peroutka & Snyder, 1980a). However, 5-HT$_2$ receptor-binding sites, which in rat cerebral cortex can be labeled with [^{3}H]-spiperone, are down-regulated by repeated administration of antidepressant drugs (Peroutka & Snyder, 1980a; Kellar et al., 1981a).

Repeated ECS shares with antidepressant drugs the capacity to decrease the number of β-adrenergic receptors in rat brain (Bergstrom & Kellar, 1979b; Pandey et al., 1979; Gillespie et al., 1979). We have compared the changes in receptor-binding sites induced by ECS to those induced by antidepressant drugs. In particular, we have compared the brain region specificity of β-adrenergic receptor changes and the selectivity of receptor-binding site changes induced by ECS and antidepressant drugs. In several respects antidepressant drugs and ECS produce similar effects on β-adrenergic receptor-binding sites, but these two treatments appear to produce opposite effects on 5-HT$_2$ binding sites.

Methods

Animals. Male Sprague-Dawley rats weighing 220–300 g were housed in groups in a light- and temperature-controlled room (12 h light cycle, lights on 7:00 a.m.; 22 °C) and had free access to food and water.

47

Electroconvulsive shock. ECS was administered through saline-moistened corneal electrodes once daily for 1–14 d. Current (150 mA, 0.2–0.3 s, 60 Hz) was delivered by a Wahlquist electroshock generator. All stimulated rats experienced generalized tonic-clonic seizures that lasted approximately 30 s. Control rats were exposed to the electrodes but no current was passed (handled controls). Rats were sacrificed between 9:00 a.m. and 12:00 noon either 1, 3, or 7 d after the last treatment.

Footshock stress. Rats were placed in a test chamber containing a grid floor connected to a constant current shock source and a shock scrambler. The rats received footshocks of 2 mA intensity and 1.0 s duration delivered on a variable time schedule with a mean interval of 15 s. The rats were shocked daily for 12 min for 14 consecutive days. Control rats were placed in the test chamber, but no current was delivered. Rats were sacrificed 1 day following the last session.

Drug treatment. Drugs were injected (i.p.) either once or twice a day for 14–30 d, as indicated in figure legends. Controls received vehicle injections. The rats were sacrificed at least 1 d after the last injection.

Receptor binding assays. Brain areas were dissected on ice and stored at $-80\,°C$ until assayed. Binding assays were carried out as described previously (Kellar *et al.*, 1981*a*; Kellar *et al.*, 1981*b*).

5-HT uptake assays. Brains were dissected on ice and fresh cortex was gently homogenized in 0.32 M sucrose. The homogenate was centrifuged at 1000 g for 10 min, and the supernatant containing synaptosomes was used for [^{3}H]-5-HT uptake studies. The uptake assays were carried out as previously described (Bergstrom & Kellar, 1979*a*). Kinetic constants were calculated from Lineweaver–Burk plots.

Results and discussion

ECS reduces the density of β-adrenergic receptor-binding sites in rat cerebral cortex without altering the affinity of the sites (Bergstrom & Kellar, 1979*b*; Pandey *et al.*, 1979). Studies of the time course of the change in β-adrenergic receptors indicate that the effect is progressive. No significant change was seen after one or two days of ECS, but by four days the binding was reduced by approximately 17 per cent and by 14 days the binding had decreased by nearly 40 per cent (Fig. 1). In rats given seven days of ECS, the decrease in β-adrenergic receptors was still evident one week after the last ECS (Fig. 2).

The change in β-adrenergic receptors is brain region specific. Among five areas of rat brain, binding was reduced only in the cortex and hippocampus (Table 1). No significant changes were seen in the striatum, hypothalamus or cerebellum (Table 1).

It was important to know whether ECS could affect altered states of the β-adrenergic receptor. Reserpine depletes the brain of norepinephrine (Holzbauer & Vogt, 1956; Brodie *et al.*, 1957). After chronic administration of reserpine, both the norepinephrine-stimulated production of cyclic AMP and the density of β-adrenergic receptors in rat brain is increased (Dismukes & Daly, 1974; U'Prichard & Snyder, 1978; Kellar *et al.*, 1981*b*). Vetulani & Sulser (1975) found that ECS administered concurrently with reserpine significantly attenuated the marked increase in brain norepinephrine-stimulated cyclic AMP production seen in rats treated with reserpine alone. It was of interest to know whether ECS administered *after* a series of reserpine injections could affect β-adrenergic receptors. In the cerebral cortex from rats chronically treated with reserpine for 30 days, the increase in β-adrenergic receptors was still evident 11 days after the last reserpine injection (Fig. 3). However, in cortex from rats which received reserpine for 30 days followed by ECS during the period between the last injection and sacrifice, the β-adrenergic receptors had returned to control values (Fig. 3). Thus, ECS accelerates the return of β-adrenergic receptors to normal levels after reserpine treatment.

Previous studies have indicated that the effects of ECS on receptor-binding sites are relatively

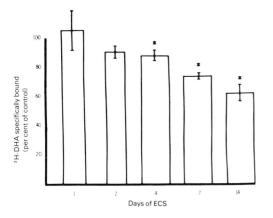

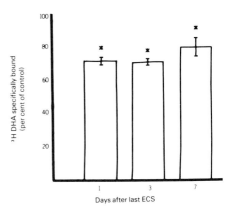

Fig. 1. *Time course of the effect of ECS on β-adrenergic receptors in rat cerebral cortex.* Rats received ECS once daily for the indicated number of days and were sacrificed 1 d later. Values are the mean ± s.e.m. of 4–9 rats assayed using 4.0 nM [3H]-dihydroalprenolol. In all experiments, control groups and treated groups were assayed in parallel. Control value = 7.1 ± 0.3 pmol/g tissue. (From Kellar *et al.*, 1981*b*.)

*$P < 0.05$ compared to controls.

Fig. 2. *Duration of effect of ECS on beta-adrenergic receptor-binding sites in rat cerebral cortex.* Rats received ECS once daily for 7 d and were sacrificed on the day indicated after the last ECS. Values are the mean ± s.e.m. of 4–8 rats assayed using 4.0 nM [3H]-dihydroalprenolol. Control value was 6.5 ± 0.3 pmol/g tissue. (From Kellar *et al.*, 1981*b*.)

*$P < 0.05$ compared to controls.

Table 1. *Effect of repeated ECS (once a day, 12–14 days) on β-adrenergic receptors in different rat brain regions.* Rats were sacrificed 1 day after last ECS. Values are mean ± s.e.m. of 5–9 rats. β-Adrenergic receptor binding was measured using 3.5–4.5 nM [3H]-dihydroalprenolol ([3H]-DHA). (From Kellar *et al.*, 1981*b*.)

| | Ligand specifically bound (pmol/g tissue) | |
Brain region	Control	ECS
Cortex	6.2 ± 0.4	3.9 ± 0.4*
Hippocampus	5.9 ± 0.3	4.5 ± 0.3*
Striatum	10.1 ± 0.8	9.1 ± 0.1
Hypothalamus	6.2 ± 0.6	5.7 ± 0.6
Cerebellum	5.5 ± 0.4	4.8 ± 0.2

*$P < 0.01$ compared to control.

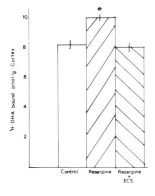

Fig. 3. *Effect of chronic ECS following reserpine-induced increases in β-adrenergic receptor-binding sites in rat cerebral cortex.* Rats were treated with reserpine (0.25 mg/kg, i.p.) for 30 d, following which they were divided into two groups. One group received ECS for 10 d and the other group was handled for 10 d. The control group received vehicle injections and was handled. All rats were sacrificed 1 d after the last ECS or handling. β-Adrenergic receptors in cortical membranes were assayed using [3H]-DHA at a concentration of 4.5 nM. Values are the mean ± s.e.m. of 8 animals per group each assayed in triplicate. (From Kellar *et al.*, 1981*b*.)

*Significantly different from control group and reserpine + ECS group, $P < 0.001$.

selective. Among adrenergic, dopaminergic, serotonergic, cholinergic, GABA and opiate receptors in rat brain, only the β-adrenergic receptor was decreased by 7–10 days of ECS (Bergstrom & Kellar, 1979b; Deakin et al., 1981). These observations were extended by examining several receptor types in the cortex and the hippocampus after 14 days of ECS. Again, in the cortex, we observed no change in α-adrenergic, cholinergic or 5-HT$_1$ receptor binding; and in the hippocampus, 5-HT$_1$ and muscarinic cholinergic receptor binding appeared to be unchanged (Table 2). This regional specificity and selectivity of receptor-binding site changes following ECS is similar to that found after the chronic administration of tricyclic antidepressant drugs. For example, repeated administration of either desipramine or chlorimipramine decreased β-adrenergic receptor binding in the cortex and hippocampus, but not in the striatum (Table 3), and neither drug altered α_1-adrenergic or 5-HT$_1$ binding sites in the cortex, 5-HT$_1$ binding sites in the hippocampus, or dopaminergic binding sites in the striatum (Table 3).

Although ECS apparently does not directly affect 5-HT$_1$ or DA receptor-binding sites, both serotonergic- and dopaminergic-mediated behaviors are enhanced by ECS (Evans et al., 1976;

Table 2. *Effects of repeated ECS (once a day for 14 days) on adrenergic, serotonergic and cholinergic receptor-binding sites in rat cortex and hippocampus.* Rats were sacrificed 1 d after last ECS. β-adrenergic, α_1-adrenergic and α_2-adrenergic receptor-binding sites were measured using [3H]-DHA (3.5 nM), [3H]-WB-4101 (0.8 nM) and [3H]-clonidine (2.0 nM), respectively. Muscarinic cholinergic, nicotinic cholinergic and serotonergic-1 receptor-binding sites were measured using [3H]-quinuclidinyl benzilate (0.2 nM), [3H]-acetylcholine (10 nM) and [3H]-5-HT
(10 nM, respectively. Values are mean $\pm$ s.e.m. of 4–9 rats. (Adapted from Kellar et al., 1981b.)

| | Ligand specifically bound (pmol/g tissue) | | | |
| | Cortex | | Hippocampus | |
Receptor-binding site	Control	ECS	Control	ECS
β-Adrenergic	6.2 $\pm$ 0.2	3.9 $\pm$ 0.4*	5.9 $\pm$ 0.3	4.5 $\pm$ 0.3*
α_1-Adrenergic	4.7 $\pm$ 0.2	4.8 $\pm$ 0.2	—	—
α_2-Adrenergic	4.8 $\pm$ 0.3	4.6 $\pm$ 0.2	—	—
Muscarinic cholinergic	32.4 $\pm$ 2.2	29.5 $\pm$ 3.1	24.3 $\pm$ 2.3	22.7 $\pm$ 2.3
Nicotinic cholinergic	2.1 $\pm$ 0.02	2.1 $\pm$ 0.1	—	—
Serotonergic-1	11.9 $\pm$ 0.6	11.4 $\pm$ 0.5	18.4 $\pm$ 1.3	19.8 $\pm$ 1.1

*$P < 0.01$ compared to control.

Table 3. *Effects of long-term administration of desipramine and chlorimipramine on adrenergic, 5-HT$_1$ and dopaminergic receptor-binding sites in 3 areas of rat brain.* Rats were sacrificed 1 day after the last injection of desipramine (6 mg/kg once a day for 2–4 weeks), chlorimipramine (10 mg/kg twice a day for 2 weeks) or vehicle. β-Adrenergic, α_1-adrenergic, 5-HT$_1$ and dopaminergic receptors were measured using [3H]-DHA (4.0 nM), [3H]-WB-4101 (1.2 nM), [3H]-5-HT (6.0 nM) and [3H]-spiperone (0.9 nM), respectively. Values are mean $\pm$ s.e.m. of 4–7 rats

| Brain area and | Ligand specifically bound (pmol/g tissue) | | |
Receptor-binding site	Control	Desipramine	Chlorimipramine
Cortex			
β-Adrenergic	5.6 $\pm$ 0.4	4.3 $\pm$ 0.3*	4.4 $\pm$ 0.4*
α_1-Adrenergic	6.3 $\pm$ 0.2	6.3 $\pm$ 0.3	6.7 $\pm$ 0.2
5-HT$_1$	6.5 $\pm$ 0.5	6.8 $\pm$ 0.6	6.5 $\pm$ 1.3
Hippocampus			
β-Adrenergic	5.8 $\pm$ 0.2	4.6 $\pm$ 0.3*	4.2 $\pm$ 0.2*
5-HT$_1$	8.2 $\pm$ 1.0	8.2 $\pm$ 1.2	8.2 $\pm$ 0.9
Striatum			
β-Adrenergic	8.0 $\pm$ 1.1	8.4 $\pm$ 1.1	—
Dopaminergic	23.3 $\pm$ 0.7	24.1 $\pm$ 0.9	25.3 $\pm$ 0.8

*$P < 0.05$ compared to control.

Green *et al.*, 1977; Modigh, 1975; Green & Deakin, 1980). Interestingly, Green & Deakin (1980) found that the ECS-induced increase in behavioral responses to both 5-HT and DA agonists was prevented by prior lesioning of noradrenergic pathways. These investigators suggested that the enhanced 5-HT- and DA-mediated behaviors may be a result of ECS-induced changes in noradrenergic systems. Another effect of ECS on dopaminergic receptor systems, possibly indirect, was suggested by Lerer *et al.* (1982) who reported that ECS administered concurrently with haloperidol diminished the behavioral supersensitivity and the increase in dopamine receptor density seen with haloperidol alone.

The reported effects of antidepressant drugs and ECS on α_2-adrenergic receptors are inconsistent. Repeated administration of tricyclic antidepressant drugs to rats has been reported to decrease brain α_2-adrenergic receptor-binding sites (Vetulani *et al.*, 1980; Smith *et al.*, 1981), to increase these binding sites (Johnson *et al.*, 1980), and to result in no change in these sites (Peroutka & Snyder, 1980*b*). Similarly, ECS has been reported to decrease α_2-adrenergic receptor-binding sites (Stanford & Nutt, 1982; Pilc & Vetulani, 1982), to increase these binding sites (Garcia *et al.*, 1982), and to result in no change in these sites (Table 2, and Kellar *et al.*, 1981*b*; Deakin *et al.*, 1981). There appears to be more than one type of α_2-adrenergic receptor-binding site in rat brain (U'Prichard *et al.*, 1979), and the inconsistencies in results from different laboratories may reflect differences in the population of binding sites being measured as well as differences in the lengths of drug or ECS treatment. If α_2-adrenergic receptor-binding sites in brain represent, in part, a population of receptors which participate in the regulation of NE release, then changes in these receptors could be important to the down-regulation of β-adrenergic receptors and to the therapeutic mechanisms of action of antidepressant drugs and ECS. Obviously, further studies are needed to clarify this point.

In addition to their effects on β-adrenergic receptors, antidepressant drugs reduce the density of putative 5-HT$_2$ receptor-binding sites labeled by [^{3}H]-spiperone in the cerebral cortex (Peroutka & Snyder, 1980*a,b*; Kellar *et al.*, 1981*a*; Blackshear & Sanders-Bush, 1982). It was therefore of interest to know whether ECS produced similar effects on this binding site. Chronic administration of three different types of antidepressant drugs (a tricyclic uptake inhibitor, a monoamine oxidase inhibitor and an 'atypical tricyclic') markedly reduced the binding of [^{3}H]-spiperone in rat cerebral cortex (Table 4). In contrast, chronic administration of ECS increased the binding of [^{3}H]-spiperone (Table 4). The increase in binding sites was not seen after 1 or 2 days of ECS, but became evident after 3 days and reached a maximum increase after 12–14 days of ECS (Fig. 4). The change in 5-HT$_2$ binding sites was due to an increase in the density of the sites with no significant change in the binding affinity (Table 5). The increase is reversible and binding returned to control values within 7 days after the last ECS (Fig. 4).

Table 4. *Effects of chronic treatment with antidepressant drugs (21 days) or ECS (12 days) on 5-HT$_2$ receptor-binding sites in rat cerebral cortex. Rats were sacrificed 1 day after last treatment, and 5-HT$_2$ binding sites were measured using 1.0 nM [^{3}H]-spiperone. Each value is the mean ± s.e.m. of 5–6 rats. (From Kellar et al., 1981a.)*

Treatment	[^{3}H]-spiperone specifically bound (pmol/g tissue)
Control (vehicle injection)	11.3 ± 1.3
Amitriptyline (10 mg/kg)	7.0 ± 0.9*
Iprindole (10 mg/kg)	6.8 ± 1.1*
Tranylcypromine (5 mg/kg)	6.2 ± 1.1*
Control (handled)	11.2 ± 0.5
ECS (12 days)	15.6 ± 0.2†

*$P < 0.05$; †$P < 0.01$ compared to control.

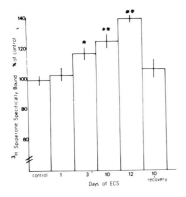

Fig. 4. *Time course of the effects of ECS on [³H]-spiperone binding to 5-HT₂ receptors in cerebral cortex.* Rats received ECS once daily for 1-12 d and were sacrificed 1 d later, except rats in the recovery group which were sacrificed 7 d later. Values are the mean ± s.e.m. of 5-10 rats each assayed at a [³H]-spiperone concentration of 1.0 nM. In all experiments, control groups and treated groups were assayed in parallel. Control value = 10.8 ± 0.3 pmol/g tissue. (From Kellar et al., 1981a.)

*$P < 0.05$; **$P < 0.01$ compared to controls.

Table 5. *ECS-induced changes in 5-HT₂ receptor-binding site kinetic constants in rat cerebral cortex.* Rats received ECS once a day for 14 days and were sacrificed 1 day later. Values are mean ± s.e.m. from 6 Scatchard analyses of [³H]-spiperone binding in each group

	Control	ECS
B_{max} (pmol/g tissue)	26.8 ± 1.4	36.6 ± 2.1*
K_D (nM)	0.8 ± 0.07	1.0 ± 0.05

*$P < 0.01$ compared to control.

ECS increases the behavioral responses of rats to 5-HT agonists (Evans *et al.*, 1976; Green *et al.*, 1977; Green & Deakin, 1980), and these behavioral responses appear to be mediated by 5-HT₂ receptors (Peroutka *et al.*, 1981). The increase in [³H]-spiperone binding sites, which in the cerebral cortex appear to represent 5-HT₂ receptors predominantly, may contribute to the enhanced behavioral response of rats to 5-HT agonists following ECS. In addition, Vetulani *et al.* (1981) reported that ECS augmented the hyperthermic response to 3-chlorophenylpiperazine, a serotonin agonist, at a time when the 5-HT₂ receptor-binding site was increased. Interestingly, although biochemical studies indicate that chronic treatments with antidepressant drugs result in a decreased number of 5-HT₂ receptor-binding sites, electrophysiological studies (de Montigny & Aghajanian, 1978) and behavioral studies (Freidman & Dallob, 1979) indicate that chronic treatment of rats with antidepressant drugs increases the response of serotonin systems. Thus, while ECS and antidepressant drugs appear to produce opposite effects on 5-HT₂ receptor-binding sites, both treatments result in an increase in the response of the serotonin system to agonists. An explanation for the apparent disparity between the effects of antidepressant drugs on 5-HT₂ receptor-binding sites and the responsivity of serotonin neurons *in vivo* is not yet available.

The mechanisms responsible for the ECS-induced changes in β-adrenergic and 5-HT₂ receptors are not clear. Stress alone does not account for the changes, since 14 days of footshock stress did not alter either β-adrenergic or serotonergic receptors (Table 6).

Table 6. *Effect of chronic footshock stress (14 days) on β-adrenergic and serotonergic receptor-binding sites in rat cortex.* Rats were given footshock stress once a day (4 shocks per min for a 12-min period) for 14 days and sacrificed 1 day later. Values are means ± s.e.m. of 5 control and 6 footshock rats

Receptor-binding site	Ligand specifically bound (pmol/g tissue)	
	Control	Footshock
β-Adrenergic	8.1 ± 0.4	8.0 ± 0.4
5-HT₂	12.9 ± 0.5	13.8 ± 0.3
5-HT₁	8.0 ± 0.9	8.1 ± 0.4

It is not known whether the changes in β-adrenergic and 5-HT$_2$ receptor-binding sites following ECS are primary effects or are adaptations to changes in presynaptic neuro-transmission processes. Repeated ECS alters NE uptake into rat brain (Hendley, 1976; Modigh, 1976), and these presynaptic effects could be related to the down-regulation of β-adrenergic receptors. Modigh (1976) examined the *in vivo* effects of repeated ECS on the uptake systems for NE and 5-HT in rat brain using a method in which the depletion of NE and 5-HT by tyramine analogs was used as an index of the state of the transport systems. This method, though indirect, is sensitive to the inhibitory effects of tricyclic antidepressants on NE and 5-HT uptake (Carlsson *et al.*, 1969a,b). Three days after the last of seven ECS treatments, the NE-uptake system appeared to be slightly, but significantly, inhibited. At the same time, there was no apparent effect on the 5-HT-uptake system (Modigh, 1976). We examined the 5-HT-uptake system in rat cerebral cortical synaptosomes 1 day after the last of 10 ECS and found no change in the kinetic constants for [^{3}H]-5-HT uptake (Table 7). However, Green (this volume) reports a decrease in V_{max} for [^{3}H]-5-HT uptake in rat cortical slices following ECS.

Table 7. *Effect of ECS (10 days) on [^{3}H]-5-HT uptake into rat cortex synaptosomes.* Rats were sacrificed 24 h after the last ECS. Uptake was measured over a [3H]-5-HT concentration range of 20–400 nM. Kinetic constants were determined by Lineweaver–Burk plots. Values are the mean ± s.e.m. of 4 control and 4 ECS treated rats

	Control	ECS
K_m (nM)	66.6 ± 8.0	69.9 ± 7.7
V_{max} (pmol/5 mg tissue/4 min)	2.2 ± 0.14	2.2 ± 0.07

A possible explanation for this apparent discrepancy is that ECS induces a short-lived change in 5-HT uptake which might not be detected 24 h after the last ECS. In this regard, it is relevant to note that the effects of tricyclic antidepressants on NE uptake are relatively short-lived. For example, 30 min after the last of a series of chronic injections of desipramine (6 mg/kg/day for 10 weeks), NE uptake was inhibited but 24 h after the last injection there was no longer evidence of uptake inhibition (Bergstrom & Kellar, 1979a). Thus, 24 h may be too long to wait to examine ECS effects on 5-HT uptake. Clearly, more work is necessary for a better under-standing of the mechanisms responsible for receptor changes following ECS.

Among the 10 or more different receptor-binding sites which have been measured in several areas of rat brain following ECS, β-adrenergic receptors in the cortex and hippocampus are decreased and 5-HT$_2$ receptor binding sites in the cortex are increased. The effects of ECS (as well as those of antidepressant drugs) on α_2-adrenergic receptors have been inconsistent, and further studies are needed to resolve the conflict in results among different laboratories. In general, however, the relative selectivity of receptor binding site changes following ECS is consistent with the effects of tricyclic antidepressant drugs.

The cerebral cortex and hippocampus were the only two brain regions examined in which β-adrenergic receptor binding sites were decreased by ECS. Similar results have recently been reported by Stanford & Nutt (1982). This pattern of brain regional decreases in β-adrenergic receptors following ECS is similar to that seen following repeated administration of desipramine and chlorimipramine. In both the rat cortex and hippocampus the β-adrenergic receptors are predominantly of the β_1 subtype; whereas in the cerebellum, β-adrenergic receptors are predominantly of the β_2 subtype (Minneman *et al.*, 1979a). The β-adrenergic receptors in the striatum and hypothalamus are predominantly of the β_1 subtype (Minneman *et al.*, 1979a), but ECS does not appear to activate the catecholamine axons which innervate these structures (Musacchio *et al.*, 1969; Masserano *et al.*, 1981). These brain region specific effects on β-adrenergic receptors suggest that decreases in these receptors following ECS are restricted to the β_1 subtype of receptor and are dependent on presynaptic activation of noradrenergic innervation. A decrease in β-adrenergic receptors restricted to the β_1 subtype following ECS would be consistent with the demonstration that chronic desipramine administration decreases the density of the β_1 subtype of adrenergic receptor in rat cerebral cortex, but has no effect on the density of the β_2 subtype of receptor (Minneman *et al.*, 1979b).

The capacity of ECS to accelerate the return of β-adrenergic receptors to control levels after up-regulation by chronic reserpine treatment may be a reflection of the actions of ECS on presynaptic processes. Chronic ECS has previously been found to increase tyrosine hydroxylase activity in certain brain areas (Musacchio et al., 1969; Modigh, 1976; Masserano et al., 1981), increase NE turnover in brain (Kety et al., 1967) and alter NE re-uptake (Hendley, 1976; Modigh, 1976), all of which could accelerate the return of normal synaptic concentrations of NE after reserpine treatment.

Thus, at the receptor level in rat brain, the effects of ECS appear to be relatively selective and specific. The reduction in β-adrenergic receptors develops gradually during two weeks of ECS administration, lasts at least one week after the last ECS, occurs in specific brain areas in which the β_1 subtype of receptor predominates and appears to be dependent on presynaptic activation of noradrenergic innervation. The effects of ECS on β-adrenergic receptors are functional and lead to decreased NE-stimulated cyclic AMP production in rat brain (Vetulani et al., 1976b; Gillespie et al., 1979). These effects of ECS are consistent with those of tricyclic antidepressant drugs on β-adrenergic receptors.

In contrast, the increase in 5-HT$_2$ receptor-binding sites following ECS is opposite to the effect produced by antidepressant drugs. This effect of ECS could be related to disorders other than depression in which ECS is effective, such as manic states or catatonia (Fink, 1979; Freedman et al., 1976). However, it is also possible that the different effects of ECS and antidepressant drugs on 5-HT$_2$ receptor-binding sites relate to different types of depression with fundamentally different underlying pathologies. For example, some depressions may involve hypersensitivity at β-adrenergic synapses, and a reduction of β-adrenergic receptors by either antidepressant drugs or ECS would be expected to be beneficial. Other depressions may involve hypersensitivity at 5-HT$_2$ synapses, and a reduction of 5-HT$_2$ receptors by antidepressant drugs would be expected to be beneficial. Still other types of depression (perhaps the most severe types) might result from decreased neurotransmission through 5-HT$_2$ synapses in certain brain areas. In this case, a reduction of 5-HT$_2$ receptors by antidepressant drugs might actually exacerbate the depression, but an increase of 5-HT$_2$ receptors by ECS could be of great benefit. These examples are speculative, of course, and it is difficult to extrapolate the effects of drugs or ECS on normal animal physiology to the effects on human pathophysiologies. Nevertheless, with regard to the last example, it is interesting to note that a recent report indicated that the density of [³H]-imipramine binding sites, which may be a presynaptic index for serotonergic innervation in brain (Sette et al., 1981), was reduced in the brains of suicide victims (Stanley et al., 1982).

ECS is an important treatment for depression. During the past decade information derived from animal studies in many laboratories has formed a base for a better understanding of the molecular mechanisms of action and potential consequences of this mode of antidepressant treatment. In addition, this information has begun to provide neurochemical bases for the effectiveness of ECT, and in many ways these bases appear to be similar to those of anti-depressant drug therapy. In doing so these studies have, perhaps, removed part of the mystique from ECT.

Acknowledgement — I thank Drs Debra A. Bergstrom, Judith A. Butler and Caren S. Cascio with whom studies in our laboratory were carried out. (Supported by USPHS grants NS12566 and DA 02540.)

References

Banerjee, L. P., Kung, L. S., Riggi, S. T. & Chanda, S. K. (1977): Development of beta-adrenergic receptor subsensitivity by antidepressants. *Nature* **268**, 455–456.

Bergstrom, D. A. & Kellar, K. J. (1979a): Adrenergic and serotonergic receptor binding in rat brain after chronic desmethylimipramine treatment. *J. Pharmacol. Exp. Ther.* **209**, 256–261.

Bergstrom, D. A. & Kellar, K. J. (1979b): Effect of electroconvulsive shock on monoaminergic receptor binding sites in rat brain. *Nature* **278**, 464–466.

Blackshear, M. A. & Sanders-Bush, E. (1982): Serotonin receptor sensitivity after acute and chronic treatment with mianserin. *J. Pharmacol. Exp. Ther.* **221**, 303–308.

Bunney, W. E., Jr., & Davis, J. M. (1965): Norepinephrine in depressive reactions. *Arch. Gen. Psychiatr.* **13**, 483–494.

Brodie, B. B., Olin, J. S., Kuntzman, R. G. & Shore, P. A. (1957): Possible interrelationship between release of brain norepinephrine and serotonin by reserpine. *Science* **125**, 1293-1294.

Carlsson, A., Corrodi, H., Fuxe, K. & Hokfelt, T. (1969a): Effects of some antidepressant drugs on the depletion of catecholamine stores caused by 4,alpha-dimethyl-metatyramine. *Eur. J. Pharmacol.* **5**, 367-373.

Carlsson, A., Corrodi, H., Fuxe, K. and Hokfelt, T. (1969b): Effect of antidepressant drugs on the depletion of intraneuronal brain 5-hydroxytryptamine stores caused by 4-methyl-α-ethyl-metartyramine. *Eur. J. Pharmacol.* **5**, 357-366.

Coppen, A. (1967): The biochemistry of affective disorders. *Br. J. Psychiat.* **113**, 1237-1264.

Deakin, J. F. W., Owen, F., Cross, A. J. & Dashwood, M. J. (1981): Studies on the possible mechanisms of action of electroconvulsive therapy; effects of repeated electrically induced seizures on rat brain receptors for monoamines and other neurotransmitters. *Psychopharmacology* **73**, 345-349.

Dismukes, R. J. & Daly, J. W. (1974): Norepinephrine sensitive systems generating adenosine $3',5'$-monophosphate: increased responses in cerebral cortical slices from reserpine-treated rats. *Mol. Pharmacol.* **10**, 933-940.

Evans, J. P. M., Grahame-Smith, D. G., Green, A. R. & Tordoff, A. F. C. (1976): Electroconvulsive shock increases the behavioral responses of rats to brain 5-hydroxytryptamine accumulation and central nervous system stimulant drugs. *Br. J. Pharmacol.* **56**, 193-199.

Fink, M. (1979): *Convulsive therapy: theory and practice*. Pp. 182-183. New York: Raven Press.

Frazer, A., Pandey, G., Mendels, J., Neeley, S., Kane, M. & Hess, M. E. (1974): The effect of tri-iodothyronine in combination with imipramine on [^{3}H]-cyclic AMP production in slices of rat cerebral cortex. *Neuropharmacology* **13**, 1131-1140.

Freeman, C. P. L., Basson, J. V. & Crighton, A. (1978): Double blind controlled trial of electroconvulsive therapy (ECT) and simulated ECT in depressive illness. *Lancet* **1**, 738-740.

Freedman, A. M., Kaplan, H. I. & Sadock, B. J. (1976): *Comprehensive textbook of psychiatry*, 2nd edition. Pp. 992-993. Baltimore: Williams & Wilkens Co.

Friedman, E. & Dallob, A. (1979): Enhanced serotonin receptor activity after chronic treatment with imipramine or amitriptyline. *Commun. Psychopharmacol.* **3**, 89-92.

Garcia, A., Wang, C. H., Salama, A. I. & U'Prichard, D. C. (1982): Regulation of rat cerebral cortex $α_2$ receptor affinity states after electroconvulsive shock and antidepressant treatment. *Soc. Neurosci. Abstr.* **8**, 525.

Gillespie, D. D., Manier, D. H. & Sulser, F. (1979): Electroconvulsive treatment: rapid subsensitivity of the norepinephrine receptor coupled adenylate cyclase system in brain linked to down-regulation of β-adrenergic receptors. *Commun. Psychopharmacol.* **3**, 191-195.

Green, A. R., Heal, D. J. & Grahame-Smith, D. G. (1977): Further observations on the effect of repeated electro-convulsive shock on the behavioral responses of rats produced by increases in the functional activity of brain 5-hydroxy-tryptamine and dopamine. *Psychopharmacology* **52**, 195-200.

Green, A. R. & Deakin, J. F. W. (1980): Depletion of brain noradrenaline prevents electroconvulsive shock induced enhancement of 5-hydroxytryptamine and dopamine mediate behavior. *Nature* **285**, 232-233.

Hendley, E. D. (1976): Electroconvulsive shock and norepinephrine uptake kinetics in the rat brain. *Commun. Psychopharmacol.* **2**, 17-25.

Holzbauer, M. & Vogt, M. (1956): Depression by reserpine of the noradrenalin concentration in hypothalamus of the cat. *J. Neurochem.* **1**, 8-11.

Johnson, R. W., Reisine, T., Spotnitz, S., Wiech, N., Ursillo, R. & Yamamura, H. I. (1980): Effects of desipramine and yohimbine on alpha-2 and beta-adrenoreceptor sensitivity. *Eur. J. Pharmacol.* **67**, 123-127.

Kellar, K. J., Cascio, C. S., Butler, J. A. & Kurtzke, R. N. (1981a): Differential effects of electroconvulsive shock and antidepressant drugs on serotonin-2 receptors in rat brain. *Eur. J. Pharmacol.* **69**, 515-518.

Kellar, K. J., Cascio, C. S., Bergstrom, D. A., Butler, J. A. & Iadarola, P. (1981b): Electroconvulsive shock and reserpine: effects on beta-adrenergic receptors in rat brain. *J. Neurochem.* **37**, 830-836.

Kety, S. S., Javoy, F., Thierry, A.-M., Julou, L. & Glowinski, J. (1967): A sustained effect of electroconvulsive shock on the turnover of norepinephrine in the central nervous system of rat. *Proc. Natl. Acad. Sci. USA* **58**, 1949-1954.

Lerer, B., Jabotinsky-Rubin, K., Bannet, J., Ebstein, R. P. & Belmaker, R. H. (1982): Electroconvulsive shock prevents dopamine receptor supersensitivity. *Eur. J. Pharmacol.* **80**, 131-134.

Maggi, A., U'Pritchard, D. C. & Enna, S. J. (1980): Differential effects of antidepressant treatment on brain monoaminergic receptors. *Eur. J. Pharmacol.* **61**, 91-98.

Masserano, J. M., Takimoto, G. S. & Weiner, N. (1981): Electroconvulsive shock increases tyrosine hydroxylase activity in the brain and adrenal gland of the rat. *Science* **214**, 662-664.

Medical Research Council (1965): Clinical trial of the treatment of depressive illness. *Brit. Med. J.* **1**, 881-886.

Minneman, K. P., Hegstrand, L. R. & Molinoff, P. B. (1979a): Simultaneous determination of $β_1$ and $β_2$ adrenergic receptors in tissues containing both receptor subtypes. *Mol. Pharmacol.* **16**, 34-46.

Minneman, K. P., Dibner, M. D., Wolfe, B. B. & Molinoff, P. B. (1979b): $β_1$- and $β_2$-adrenergic receptors in rat cerebral cortex are independently regulated. *Science* **204**, 866-868.

Modigh, K. (1975): Electroconvulsive shock and postsynaptic catecholamine effects: increased psychomotor stimulant action of apomorphine and clonidine in reserpine pretreated mice by repeated ECS. *J. Neural Transm.* **36**, 19-32.

Modigh, K. (1976): Long-term effects of electroconvulsive shock therapy on synthesis turnover and uptake of brain monoamines. *Psychopharmacology* **49**, 179-185.

de Montigny, C. & Aghajanian, G. K. (1978): Tricyclic antidepressants: long-term treatment increases responsivity of rat forebrain neurons to serotonin. *Science* **202**, 1303-1306.

55

Musacchio, J. M., Julou, L., Kety, S. S. & Glowinski, J. (1969): Increase in rat brain tyrosine hydroxylase activity produced by electroconvulsive shock. *Proc. Natl. Acad. Sci. USA* **63**, 1117–1119.

Pandey, G. N., Heinze, W. J., Brown, B. D. & Davis, J. M. (1979): Electroconvulsive shock treatment decreases beta-adrenergic receptor sensitivity in rat brain. *Nature* **280**, 234–235.

Peroutka, S. J. & Snyder, S. H. (1980*a*): Long-term antidepressant treatment decreases spiroperidol-labeled serotonin receptor binding. *Science* **210**, 88–90.

Peroutka, S. J. & Snyder, S. H. (1980*b*): Regulation of serotonin-2 (5-HT$_2$) receptors labeled with [^{3}H]-spiroperidol by chronic treatment with the antidepressant amitriptyline. *J. Pharmacol. Exp. Ther.* **215**, 582–587.

Peroutka, S. J., Lebovitz, R. M. & Snyder, S. H. (1981): Two distinct central serotonin receptors with different physiological functions. *Science* **212**, 827–829.

Pilc, A. & Vetulani, J. (1982): Depression by chronic electroconvulsive treatment of clonidine hypothermia and [^{3}H]-clonidine binding to rat cortical membranes. *Eur. J. Pharmacol.* **80**, 109–113.

Sarai, K., Frazer, A., Brunswick, D. & Mendels, J. (1978): Desmethylimipramine-induced decrease in β-adrenergic receptor binding in rat cerebral cortex. *Biochem. Pharmacol.* **27**, 2179–2181.

Schildkraut, J. J. (1965): The catecholamine hypothesis of affective disorders: a review of supporting evidence. *Am. J. Psychiat.* **122**, 509–522.

Sellinger-Barnette, M. M., Mendels, J. & Frazer, A. (1980): The effect of psychoactive drugs on beta-adrenergic receptor binding sites in rat brain. *Neuropharmacology* **19**, 447–454.

Sette, M., Raisman, R., Briley, M. & Langer, S. Z. (1981): Localization of tricyclic antidepressant binding sites on serotonin nerve terminals. *J. Neurochem.* **37**, 40–42.

Smith, C. B., Garcia-Sevilla, J. A. & Hollingsworth, P. J. (1981): α_2-adrenoreceptors in rat brain are decreased after long-term tricyclic antidepressant drug treatment. *Brain Res.* **210**, 413–418.

Stanford, S. C. & Nutt, D. J. (1982): Comparison of the effects of repeated electroconvulsive shock on α_2- and β-adrenoceptors in different regions of rat brain. *Neuroscience* **7**, 1753–1757.

Stanley, M., Virgilio, J. & Gershon, S. (1982): Tritiated imipramine binding sites are decreased in the frontal cortex of suicides. *Science* **216**, 1337–1339.

U'Prichard, D. C., Bechtel, W. D., Rouot, B. M. & Snyder, S. H. (1979): Multiple apparent alpha-noradrenergic receptor binding sites in rat brain. Effect of 6-hydroxydopamine. *Mol. Pharmacol.* **16**, 47–60.

U'Prichard, D. C. & Snyder, S. H. (1978): [^{3}H]-Catecholamine binding to α-receptors in rat brain: Enhancement by reserpine. *Eur. J. Pharmacol.* **51**, 145–155.

Vetulani, J. & Sulser, F. (1975): Action of various antidepressant treatments reduces reactivity of noradrenergic cyclic AMP-generating system in limbic forebrain. *Nature* **257**, 495–496.

Vetulani, J., Stawarz, R. J., Dingell, J. V. & Sulser, F. (1976*a*): A possible common mechanism of action of anti-depressant treatments. *Naunyn-Schmeideberg's Arch. Pharmacol.* **293**, 109–114.

Vetulani, J., Stawarz, R. J. & Sulser, F. (1976*b*): Adaptive mechanisms of the noradrenergic cyclic AMP generating systems in the limbic forebrain of the rat: Adaptations to persistent changes in the availability of norepinephrine. *J. Neurochem.* **27**, 661–666.

Vetulani, J., Antkiewicz-Michaluk, L., Golembiowska-Nikitin, K., Michaluk, J., Pilc, A. & Rokosz, A. (1980): The effect of multiple imipramine administration on monoaminergic systems in the rat brain. *Pol. J. Pharmacol. Pharm.* **32**, 523–528.

Vetulani, J., Lebrecht, U. & Pilc, A. (1981): Enhancement of responsiveness of the central serotonergic system and serotonin-2 receptor density in rat frontal cortex by electroconvulsive treatment. *Eur. J. Pharmacol.* **76**, 81–85.

Wirz-Justice, A., Krauchi, K., Lichtsteiner, M. & Freer, H. (1978): Is it possible to modify serotonin receptor sensitivity? *Life Sci.* **23**, 1249–1254.

Wolfe, B. B., Harden, T. K., Sporn, J. R. & Molinoff, P. B. (1978): Presynaptic modulation of beta-adrenergic receptors in rat cerebral cortex after treatment with antidepressants. *J. Pharmacol. Exp. Ther.* **207**, 446–457.

6.

Effects of ECS on adenosine receptor systems in the brain

M. NEWMAN, J. ZOHAR, M. KALIAN and R. H. BELMAKER

Jerusalem Mental Health Center, Ezrath Nashim Hospital, P.O.B. 140, Jerusalem, Israel.

Introduction

A relationship between adenosine and the mechanisms involved in electroconvulsive shock (ECS) was first suggested by the work of Kakiuchi *et al.* (1969), who applied electrical pulses to slices of guinea-pig cerebral cortex, and observed a tenfold increase in tissue cyclic AMP levels. This effect was inhibited by 0.5 mM theophylline, which until then had only been characterized as a phosphodiesterase inhibitor and would therefore be expected to potentiate any increase in cyclic AMP. The endogenous substance responsible for the cyclic AMP rise on electrical excitation was subsequently identified as adenosine by Sattin & Rall (1970), and an adenosine-sensitive adenylate cyclase, with theophylline acting as a specific antagonist, has now been demonstrated in many systems including brain slices (Huang *et al.*, 1971) and homogenates prepared from rat caudate nucleus (Premont *et al.*, 1977).

Sattin (1971) showed that electrical seizures produced significant rises in the *in vivo* content of cyclic AMP in mouse forebrain, and that these were significantly reduced when the mice were previously injected with theophylline or caffeine. He proposed, as the mechanism of the effect, that the seizures produced asphyxia in the mouse forebrain which, though dephosphorylation of adenine nucleotides, led to the liberation of free adenosine which then activated its adenylate cyclase-linked receptor. The increase in adenosine content by ischemia or hypoxia is well documented in both guinea-pig (Newman & McIlwain, 1977) and rat (Winn *et al.*, 1981) brain and has been shown to occur within 5 s.

The above studies used single electrical pulses or seizures, while repeated seizures are necessary for the therapeutic effect of ECT in humans.

The relationship between the adenosine-releasing effect of ECS and the well-known diminuition of the cyclic AMP response to noradrenaline after chronic ECS treatment, first shown in rat limbic forebrain by Vetulani *et al.* (1976), was studied by Sattin (1981). Chopped cortex from rats which had received ECS daily for 8 days sacrificed 2 days after the last treatment, showed the expected reduction in the cyclic AMP response to 10 μM noradrenaline and a significantly increased response to 1 μM *N*-ethyl carboxamide adenosine (NECA) after treatment with adenosine deaminase to remove endogenous brain adenosine. The response to a combination of noradrenaline and NECA was also increased, indicating a functional super-sensitivity of the adenosine receptors and possibly also the adenosine-dependent α-adrenergic component of the noradrenaline receptor. However, in the absence of adenosine deaminase, a series of five ECS given every other day had no effect on either the response to 100 μM noradrenaline or basal cyclic AMP levels (which would have been expected to be raised as a result of endogenous adenosine generated by the seizures) although the response to 200 μM adenosine added either alone or in combination with 100 μM noradrenaline, was increased. It would therefore appear that the increase in adenosine concentrations is strictly an acute phenomenon and any effect of chronic ECS must be sought at the receptor rather than the effector level. Sattin (1981) proposed that chronic ECS causes an increase in sensitivity of A_2 receptors and that this may be important to the mechanism of therapeutic action of ECT. While adenosine antagonists such as caffeine are usually thought of as only mild stimulants, acute delirious reactions to these drugs have been reported (McManamy & Schube, 1936; Stillner *et al.*, 1978) and the relationship of adenosine to affective disorders is an unexplored area.

Direct measurements of adenosine receptors linked to cyclic AMP production, named A_2 (Van Calker *et al.*, 1979) or R_a (Londos *et al.*, 1980) receptors, has been hampered by the lack of a labelled ligand suitable for binding studies. Moreover, binding studies with the ligands [^{3}H]-cyclohexyladenosine (Bruns *et al.*, 1980), [^{3}H]-chloroadenosine (Williams & Risley, 1980) and [^{3}H]-phenylisopropyladenosine (Schwabe & Trost, 1980) have revealed the presence of another adenosine receptor site in cortical membranes with nanomolar affinity and specificity different to that shown by adenosine analogs in stimulation of cyclic AMP production in brain slices. This site, named the A_1 (Van Calker *et al.*, 1979), or R_i (Londos *et al.*, 1980) receptor, is associated with the inhibition of adenylate cyclase in cortical membranes (Cooper *et al.*, 1980) and also with a variety of behavioural and electrophysiological effects of adenosine (Snyder *et al.*, 1981; Reddington *et al.*, 1982). Amongst these, of greatest interest are its actions in producing behavioural depression and reducing locomotor activity in mice (Snyder *et al.*, 1981) and in antagonising seizures elicited by a variety of convulsants with different mechanisms of action (Dunwiddie & Worth, 1982). The sedative and anticonvulsant actions of adenosine were first shown by Maitre *et al.* (1974) by direct injection into the cerebral ventricles of mice susceptible to audiogenic seizures. The effects of the convulsant pentylenetetrazol (Metrazol), one of the first compounds used to induce convulsions as a form of therapy for schizophrenia before the advent of ECT (Kalinowsky, 1982), were antagonised 20 times more potently by the L-isomer of phenylisopropyladenosine than by the D-isomer (Dunwiddie & Worth, 1982), a difference in potency characteristic of A_1 rather than A_2 receptors. A further indication of the relationship between anticonvulsant efficacy and A_1 receptor activity was provided by the findings of Wybenga *et al.* (1982) of a 21 per cent decrease in the number of A_1 receptor sites, measured by binding of the labelled ligand [^{3}H]-cyclohexyladenosine, in the cerebellum of rats convulsed by a single injection of pentylenetetrazol, although there was no effect in the cerebral cortex. This acute effect could, however, be related to the increase in adenosine levels in the brain following the hypoxia due to the seizure (Winn *et al.*, 1981; Schrader *et al.*, 1980) resulting in the down-regulation of receptor number, although the differential effect on cortex and cerebellum argues against this. In this chapter the effects of a series of chronic ECS on A_2 receptors are reported. Studies on the effects of chronic ECS on A_1 receptors, as determined by [^{3}H]-cyclohexyladenosine binding to cortical membranes, are in progress.

Experimental analysis of A_2 receptors

Male rats of the sabra strain, 150–200 g were housed with a reversed lighting cycle and *ad lib* food and water. Sham ECS or ECS, 150 volts for 1 s was administered daily for 10 days through earclip electrodes, and all animals receiving ECS displayed seizures characterized by tonic followed by clonic convulsive movements. For the first group of experiments, animals were housed so that two rats which received ECS shared the same cage with a control rat which received a series of sham ECS's beginning at the same time. All three rats were then sacrificed on the same day, 2 days after the last treatment, and slices cut from the neocortex using a McIlwain tissue chopper set at 0.5 mm. The slices were pre-incubated in Krebs Ringer bicarbonate buffer containing 1.29 mM $CaCl_2$ for 30 min at 37 °C with gassing with 95% O_2: 5% CO_2, collected in a Buchner funnel and distributed among vials containing 5 ml Krebs Ringer, with additions, for a further 20 min incubation. The slices were then transferred to test tubes and centrifuged, the supernatant decanted and the pellets homogenised in 1 ml 95% ethanol, for determination of cyclic AMP by a protein-binding method based on that of Brown *et al.* (1971), using a kit supplied by the Radiochemical Centre, Amersham, UK.

Results obtained from these animals are shown in Table 1 and indicate a reduced response to

Table 1. *Effects of noradrenaline, 2-chloradenosine, and a combination of these agents, on cyclic AMP accumulation in chopped cerebral cortex from sham- and ECS-treated rats.* Results are mean ± s.e.m. of the number of observations in parentheses

	Cyclic AMP (pmol/mg protein)	
	Control	ECT
Basal	18.7 ± 5.2 (6)	16.3 ± 3.2 (10)
10 μM noradrenaline	48.9 ± 5.9 (6)	38.5 ± 5.2 (10)
50 μM noradrenaline	57.1 ± 9.7 (5)	41.7 ± 6.6 (10)
100 μM noradrenaline	66.1 ± 23.2 (6)	43.0 ± 8.4 (10)
10 μM 2-Cl-adenosine	37.9 ± 4.5 (6)	27.0 ± 4.5 (10)
50 μM 2-Cl-adenosine	49.2 ± 5.0 (6)	40.3 ± 7.1 (10)
100 μM 2-Cl-adenosine	57.7 ± 9.1 (6)	37.6 ± 7.1 (10)
100 μM NA + 10 μM 2-Cl-adenosine	90.0 ± 12.8 (4)	69.4 ± 6.3 (10)
100 μM NA + 50 μM 2-Cl-adenosine	121.2 ± 9.9 (6)	60.1 ± 10.4 (9)*
100 μM NA + 100 μM 2-Cl-adenosine	120.6 ± 11.8 (5)	87.6 ± 10.4 (10)*

*Significantly different from control ($P < 0.05$) by Student's t-test.

both noradrenaline and the adenosine deaminase resistant adenosine analog 2-chloroadenosine, at all concentrations tested, in slices obtained from the ECS as compared to control rats. Simultaneous incubation of the slices with noradrenaline and 2-chloroadenosine resulted in an additive response to the two agents, and the total cyclic AMP levels under these conditions were very significantly reduced in slices derived from ECS-treated animals.

These results differ considerably from those of Sattin (1981), although the methodology employed was similar, so the experiment was repeated with slightly older rats, 200–250 g. This time the rats were segregated so that ECS-treated rats did not share cages with sham-treated rats. This was done in order to avoid placing the sham-treated animals under stress due to the aggressive behaviour displayed by animals which had just received ECT. However, in this group a significantly higher fraction of the animals receiving ECT developed paralysis and were excluded from the study.

Results with these animals are given in Table 2 and show no difference in response to noradrenaline but a significantly higher response to 50 μM 2-chloroadenosine in the ECS-treated rats. This result, which parallels the findings of Sattin (1981) was however not reproduced when various concentrations of 2-chloroadenosine were examined in the presence of 100 μM noradrenaline, conditions under which Sattin (1981) observed a large augmentation of the cyclic AMP response in ECS-treated rats. The failure to observe sub-sensitivity to noradrenaline in this group, which incidently parallels Sattin (1981)'s findings when he used

Table 2. *Effects of noradrenaline, 2-chloradenosine, and a combination of these agents, on cyclic AMP accumulation in chopped cerebral cortex from sham- and ECS-treated rats housed as described in the text.* Results are mean ± s.e.m. of 4 observations in each group

	Cyclic AMP (pmol/mg protein)	
	Control	ECT
Basal	10.0 ± 2.2	15.3 ± 2.6
10 μM noradrenaline	29.8 ± 10.0	37.6 ± 10.4
50 μM noradrenaline	23.8 ± 9.9	42.0 ± 10.2
100 μM noradrenaline	38.5 ± 7.3	45.0 ± 10.5
10 μM 2-Cl-adenosine	22.4 ± 3.4	36.1 ± 7.5
50 μM 2-Cl-adenosine	22.7 ± 4.9	46.6 ± 5.4*
100 μM 2-Cl-adenosine	39.4 ± 10.9	66.4 ± 19.1
100 μM NA + 10 μM 2-Cl-adenosine	71.3 ± 15.4	85.0 ± 15.7
100 μM NA + 50 μM 2-Cl-adenosine	79.1 ± 18.5	79.5 ± 20.4
100 μM NA + 100 μM 2-Cl-adenosine	54.8 ± 10.4	71.9 ± 15.4

*Significantly different from control ($P < 0.01$) by paired t-test.

a schedule of five ECS given every alternate day and measured the response to 100 μM noradrenaline, suggest that the animals which survived the treatment may not have fully responded to the ECS, despite the fact that no differences in the duration or nature of the tonic-clonic convulsions were noted. It is also of interest that Sattin (1983) obtained no differences in response to adenosine between sham- and ECS-treated rats when incubations of the slices were performed beginning at 4:00 pm rather than earlier in the day.

Conclusions

It would therefore appear that strain differences, age differences and variations in the handling of the animals may contribute to the effects of ECS on the noradrenergic and adenosine sensitive cyclic AMP generating systems. A reciprocal relationship between the activities of these systems, as found by Sattin (1981) after chronic ECS, would indeed be expected if the mechanisms of coupling of the two receptors to adenylate cyclase were different, as postulated by Tolkovsky & Levitzki (1978). According to this theory β-adrenergic agonists activate adenylate cyclase by a diffusion-dependent 'collision coupling' mechanism while adenosine receptors are permanently coupled to the enzyme, so that the activity attained with a β-adrenergic agonist depends on the degree to which adenosine or its analogs occupy their receptors which are covalently linked to adenylate cyclase. Indeed a rise in adrenaline-dependent enzyme activity was observed in rat kidney fibroblast membranes after *in vitro* desensitisation with an adenosine analog (Newman & Levitzki, 1983) indicative of a reciprocal relationship between the activity of the two receptors. However, no such relationship has been demonstrated for brain tissue, and in the slice system where many factors interact to produce the final effect on cyclic AMP, a simple reciprocal relationship would not be expected. The present results, however show that chronic ECS does affect the adenosine-sensitive as well as the noradrenergic cyclic AMP system in cerebral tissue, although the nature of the interaction between them remains to be clarified.

References

Brown, B. L., Albano, J. D. M., Ekins, R. P., Sghergi, A. M. & Tampion, W. (1971): A simple and sensitive saturation assay method for the measurement of adenosine 3':5'-cyclic monophosphate. *Biochem. J.* **121**, 561–562.

Bruns, R. F., Daly, J. W. & Snyder, S. H. (1980): Adenosine receptors in brain membranes: Binding of N⁶-cyclohexyl [³H] adenosine and 1,3-diethyl-8-[³H] phenylxanthine. *Proc. Natl. Acad. Sci. USA* **77**, 5547–5551.

Cooper, D. M. F., Londos, C. & Rodbell, M. (1980): Adenosine receptor-mediated inhibition of rat cerebral cortical adenylate cyclase by a GTP-dependent process. *Mol. Pharmacol.* **18**, 598–601.

Dunwiddie, T. V. & Worth, T. (1982): Sedative and anticonvulsant effects of adenosine analogs in mouse and rat. *J. Pharm. Exp. Ther.* **220**, 70–76.

Huang, M., Shimizu, H. & Daly, J. W. (1971): Regulation of adenosine cyclic 3',5'-phosphate formation in cerebral cortical slices. *Mol. Pharmacol.* **7**, 155–162.

Kakiuchi, S., Rall, T. W. & McIlwain, H. (1969): The effect of electrical stimulation upon the accumulation of adenosine 3',5'-phosphate in isolated cerebral tissue. *J. Neurochem.* **16**, 485–491.

Kalinowsky, L. B. (1982): History of electroconvulsive therapy, in *Electroconvulsive therapy*, ed R. Abrams and W. B. Essman. Pp. 1–5. New York: SP Medical & Scientific Books.

Londos, C., Cooper, D. M. F. & Wolff, J. (1980): Subclasses of external adenosine receptors. *Proc. Natl. Acad. Sci. USA* **77**, 2551–2554.

Maitre, M. L., Ciesielski, A., Lehmann, A., Kempf, E. & Mandel, P. (1974): Protective effect of adenosine and nicotinamide against audiogenic seizure. *Biochem. Pharmacol.* **23**, 2807–2816.

McManamy, M. C. & Schube, P. G. (1936): Caffeine intoxication: Report of a case the symptoms of which amounted to a psychosis. *N. Eng. J. Med.* **215**, 616–620.

Newman, M. E. & Levitzki, A. (1983): Desensitization of normal rat kidney cells to adenosine. *Biochem. Pharmacol.*, **32**, 137–140.

Newman, M. E. & McIlwain, H. (1977): Adenosine as a constituent of the brain and of isolated cerebral tissues, and its relationship to the generation of adenosine 3',5'-cyclic monophosphate. *Biochem. J.* **164**, 131–137.

Premont, J., Perez, M. & Bockaert, J. (1977): Adenosine-sensitive adenylate cyclase in rat striatal homogenates and its relationship to dopamine and Ca²⁺-sensitive adenylate cyclases. *Mol. Pharmacol.* **13**, 662–670.

Reddington, M., Lee, K. S. & Schubert, P. (1982): An A₁-adenosine receptor, characterized by [³H] cyclohexyl-adenosine binding, mediates the depression of evoked potentials in a rat hippocampal slice preparation. *Neurosci. Lett.* **28**, 275–279.

Sattin, A. (1971): Increase in the content of adenosine 3′,5′-monophosphate in mouse forebrain during seizures and prevention of the increase by methylxanthines. *J. Neurochem.* **18**, 1087–1096.

Sattin, A. (1981): Adenosine as a mediator of antidepressant treatment. In *Chemisms of the brain*, ed R. Rodnight, H. S. Bachelard and W. L. Stahl. Pp.265–275. Edinburgh: Churchill Livingstone.

Sattin, A. (1983): Behavioural correlates of adenosine stimulated (A_2) cyclase activity in rat cerebral cortex. In *The regulatory function of adenosine.* ed R. M. Berne, F. W. Roll & R. Rubio. Boston: Martinus Nijhoff.

Sattin, A. & Rall, T. W. (1970): The effect of adenosine and adenine nucleotides on the adenosine 3′,5′-phosphate content of guinea pig cerebral cortex slices. *Mol. Pharmacol.* **6**, 13–23.

Schrader, J., Wahl, M., Kutschinsky, W. & Kreutzberg, G. W. (1980): Increase of adenosine content in cerebral cortex of the cat during bicuculline-induced seizures. *Pfluger's Arch.* **387**, 245–251.

Schwabe, U. & Trost, T. (1980): Characterization of adenosine receptors in rat brain by ($-$) [^{3}H] N^6-phenyliso-propyladenosine. *N.S. Arch. Pharmacol.* **313**, 179–187.

Snyder, S. H., Katims, J. J., Annau, Z., Bruns, R. F. & Daly, J. W. (1981): Adenosine receptors and behavioural actions of methylxanthines. *Proc. Natl. Acad. Sci. USA* **78**, 3260–3264.

Stillner, V., Popkin, M. K. & Pierce, C. M. (1978): Caffeine-induced delerium during prolonged competitive stress. *Am. J. Psych.* **135**, 855–856.

Tolkovsky, A. M. & Levitzki, A. (1978). Coupling of a single adenylate cyclase to two receptors; adenosine and catecholamine. *Biochemistry* **17**, 3811–3817.

Van Calker, D., Müller, M. & Hamprecht, B. (1979): Adenosine regulates via two different types of receptors, the accumulation of cyclic AMP in cultured brain cells. *J. Neurochem.* **33**, 999–1005.

Vetulani, J., Stawartz, R. J., Dingell, J. V. & Sulser, F. (1976): Possible common mechanism of action of anti-depressant treatments; reduction in the sensitivity of the noradrenergic cyclic AMP generating system in the rat limbic forebrain. *N.S. Arch. Pharmacol.* **293**, 109–114.

Williams, M. & Risley, E. A. (1980). Biochemical characterization of putative central purinergic receptors by using 2-chloro[^{3}H]adenosine, a stable analog of adenosine. *Proc. Natl. Acad. Sci. USA* **77**, 6892–6896.

Winn, H. R., Rubio, R. & Berne, R. M. (1981): Brain adenosine concentration during hypoxia in rats. *Am. J. Physiol.* **241**, H235–H242.

Wybenga, M. P., Murphy, M. G. & Robertson, H. A. (1981): Rapid changes in cerebellar adenosine receptors following experimental seizures. *Eur. J. Pharmacol.* **75**, 79–80.

7.
ECS and noradrenaline release

R. P. EBSTEIN, B. LERER, M. SHLAUFMAN and R. H. BELMAKER

Jerusalem Mental Health Center, P.O. Box 140, Jerusalem, Israel; Department of Psychiatry, Wayne State University and Lafayette Clinic, Detroit, Michigan, USA — BL, present address.

Introduction

Although electroconvulsive therapy (ECT) is an efficacious treatment in depression and mania (Fink, 1979) the molecular substrate of ECT action in the brain is unknown. Chronic electro-convulsive shock (ECS) has been consistently shown to reduce the number of β-adrenergic receptors in rat cerebral cortex (Bergstrom & Kellar, 1979; Pandey *et al.*, 1979) and the sensitivity of the noradrenaline-sensitive cyclic AMP generating system in rat limbic forebrain (Vetulani & Sulser, 1975). These findings of noradrenergic sub-sensitivity after chronic treatment also put ECT in common with other chronically-administered antidepressant treatments such as the tricyclic antidepressants and monoamine oxidase inhibitors (Vetulani & Sulser, 1975; Pandey *et al.*, 1979).

Experimental evidence

The role of presynaptic mechanisms in the development of postsynaptic sub-sensitivity following chronic administration of ECS and other antidepressant treatments, remains to be clearly elucidated (Wolfe *et al.*, 1978; Vetulani *et al.*, 1976). Kety *et al.* (1967) examined the effects of two-daily ECS for seven days on NA turnover in rat brain using intracisternally injected [^{3}H]-NA. Kety *et al.* (1967) found a 19–22 per cent increase in endogenous NA levels and a 15–28 per cent reduction over control in [^{3}H]-NA levels 5 h after intracisternal injection of [^{3}H]-NA and inferred an increase in both synthesis and utilization of NA. Modigh (1976) calculated the synthesis rate of NA from the accumulation of dihydroxyphenylalanine 30 min after administration of decarboxylase inhibitor. He found a 20 per cent increase up to day 7 after the last of series of seven daily ECS. Modigh (1976) found no significant increase in NA turnover estimated by the rate of NA depletion 2.5 h after the administration of a synthesis inhibitor.

Effects of chronically administered ECS on catecholamine enzymes have also been reported. Musacchio *et al.* (1969) found a 15 per cent increase in the whole brain activity of tyrosine hydroxylase 24 h after the last of a series of two daily ECS for seven days. Pryor (1974) reported a less than 10 per cent increase in brain monoamine oxidase (MAO) activity after daily ECS for 14 days. MAO activity increased to 20 per cent above control after daily ECS for 42 consecutive days. However, such small changes in a rather nonspecific catabolic enzyme such as MAO after an excessively lengthy series of ECS are probably not clinically relevant.

Small effects of ECS on uptake of NA into presynaptic terminals were also reported by Modigh (1976). Using a displacement model to measure uptake mechanisms, he found a 20 per cent reduction in uptake after seven daily ECS. Hendley & Welch (1975) examined the effect of nine daily ECS on the uptake kinetics of [^{3}H]-NA in crude synaptosome-rich homogenates from the cerebral cortex of chronically reserpinized mice. ECS was found to be associated with a

63 per cent increase in apparent K_m for [³H]-NA and a 55 per cent increase in V_{max}. These findings were interpreted as indicating a decreased affinity for NA uptake in the presence of an increased uptake capacity. Such a biphasic effect would be neatly consistent with the usefulness of ECT in mania as well as depression (McCabe, 1976). The use by Hendley & Welch (1975) of an 'abnormal' model of reserpinized mice also gives weight to their effects which are larger than other reported NA effects in 'normal' animals. Hendley (1976) subsequently demonstrated similar effects of two daily ECS for seven days on NA uptake kinetics in 'normal' rats (24 h after the last shock). However, three days after the last shock K_m and V_{max} were significantly decreased, and a week later were no different from control. Hendley (1976) interprets this time-course as indicative of compensatory mechanisms in the normal rats. Minchin *et al.* (1983) have replicated these findings with regard to changes in both K_m and V_{max} after chronic ECS.

Heal *et al.* (1981) have demonstrated an attenuated sedative response to clonidine in mice and rats following 10 daily ECS. The decrease in brain MOPEG-SO$_4$ concentration that occurs after clonidine administration was also attenuated by repeated ECS (Heal *et al.*, 1981). Clonidine-induced sedation and clonidine-induced decreases in brain MOPEG-SO$_4$ were also attenuated by chronic desmethylimipramine administration (Sugrue, 1981). Pilc & Vetulani (1982) have demonstrated attenuation of clonidine induced hypothermia following both ECS and chronic imipramine administration. These findings are interpreted as indicating sub-sensitivity of inhibitory presynaptic receptors subserving NA release (Langer, 1979) following repeated ECS or chronic antidepressant administration.

Kellar *et al.* (1981) found no change in [³H]-clonidine labeled cortical receptors following repeated ECS. However, Stanford & Nutt (1982) and Pilc & Vetulani (1982) have demonstrated down-regulation of [³H]-clonidine labeled α_2-adrenoceptors in rat cortex, following repeated ECS. These discrepancies may be related to labeling [³H]-clonidine binding sites of different affinities (Vetulani, this volume) and/or different locations (ie, pre- or post-synaptic α_2-receptor sites). Down-regulation of cortical [³H]-clonidine binding may represent the biochemical correlate of attenuated sensitivity to the behavioral and hypothermic effects of clonidine (Heal *et al.*, 1981; Pilc & Vetulani, 1982) and reflect presynaptic α_2-adrenoceptor sub-sensitivity induced by repeated ECS. On the other hand it is difficult to be certain whether [³H]-clonidine labels pre- or post-synaptic sites.

In order to further elucidate the role of presynaptic mechanisms in the β-adrenergic receptor changes induced by chronic ECS, it was of interest to examine the effects of single and repeated ECS on the presynaptic release of NA. Release of NA from rat brain cortical vesicular preparation was studied in the presence and absence of clonidine (Ebstein *et al.*, 1983).

Recently, chronic monoamine oxidase inhibition with clorgyline has been shown to increase NA release from rat brain cortical vesicular preparation and markedly decrease the inhibition of NA release (Cohen *et al.*, 1983) caused by the selective agonist, clonidine. [³H]-NA release from brain vesicular preparation was studied using a recently described gravity-flow perfusion technique (Ebstein *et al.*, 1982; Ebstein & Daly, 1982*a,b*).

The effect of a single ECS on [³H]-NA release from cerebral cortical vesicular preparations is shown in Table 1. Animals were sacrificed 24 h after a single ECS and K⁺-evoked [³H]-norepinephrine release was determined in the presence and absence of clonidine which activates inhibitory presynaptic α_2-receptors (De Potter *et al.*, 1971; Starke, 1971; Langer, 1979). There is no difference at either 0.1 mM or 0.2 mM CaCl$_2$ in K⁺-evoked [³H]-NA release between a cortical vesicular preparation obtained from ECS and sham-treated animals. At 0.1 mM and 0.2 mM CaCl$_2$, clonidine significantly inhibits K⁺-evoked release of [³H]-NA. The magnitude of clonidine inhibition is similar in cortical vesicles obtained from ECS and sham-treated animals.

The effect of 10 daily ECS on K⁺-evoked [³H]-NA release from cerebral cortical vesicular preparations is shown in Table 2. At 0.1 mM CaCl$_2$ there is a small but significant increase in K⁺-evoked release of [³H]-NA in vesicles obtained from ECS-treated animals. In vesicles obtained from sham-treated animals, 50 and 250 nM clonidine significantly inhibits [³H]-NA release whereas in vesicles obtained from ECS-treated animals significant inhibition by clonidine is observed only at 250 mM clonidine.

Table 1. *The effect of a single ECS treatment on K^+-evoked [^3H]efflux from rat cerebral cortical vesicular preparations.* The KCl concentration was 18.4 mM. The values are means ± s.e.m. $*P < 0.05$; $\dagger P < 0.02$; $\ddagger P < 0.01$; $\S P < 0.001$, comparing control release with release in the presence of clonidine. The numbers in parentheses are the number of separate columns measuring release in vesicles obtained from ECS and sham-treated animals. ECS was administered (150 V for 1.5 s) through earclip electrodes. No anesthetic was used and the current used was always observed to cause a typical tonic–clonic seizure with recovery within a few minutes. Untreated animals were handled identically and earclipped without any current being applied. Animals were sacrificed 24 hours after a single ECS or 24 h after the last of a series of 10 daily ECS

	[^3H]efflux (cpm) ECS				[^3H]efflux (cpm) SHAM			
		Clonidine (nM)				Clonidine (nM)		
CaCl$_2$ (mM)	Control	50	250	1000	Control	50	250	1000
0.1	887±80 (15)	538±59‡ (15)	634±68* (15)	574±74† (14)	831±87 (12)	617±87 (11)	467±50‡ (12)	444±83‡ (12)
0.2	3593±195 (15)	2371±174§ (15)	2292±181§ (15)	2603±178‡ (13)	3308±276 (15)	2551±221* (15)	2412±246* (15)	2193±214‡ (15)

Table 2. *The effect of 10 daily ECS treatments on K^+-evoked [^3H]efflux from rat cerebral cortical vesicular preparations.* The KCl concentration was 18.4 mM. The values are means ± s.e.m. [a]ECS control release compared to SHAM-treated control release, $P < 0.02$; [b]ECS release in the presence of 50 nM clonidine compared to SHAM-treated release in the presence of 50 nM clonidine, $P < 0.05$; [c]ECS release in the presence of 250 nM clonidine compared to ECS control release, $P < 0.05$; ECS release in the presence of 250 nM clonidine compared to SHAM release in the presence of 250 nM clonidine, $P < 0.05$; [d]SHAM release in the presence of 50 nM clonidine compared to SHAM control, $P < 0.01$; [e]SHAM release in the presence of 250 nM clonidine compared to SHAM control, $P < 0.01$; [f]SHAM release in the presence of 250 nM clonidine compared to ECS release in the presence of 250 nM clonidine, $P < 0.05$. $*P < 0.05$, $\dagger P < 0.02$, $\ddagger P < 0.01$, $\S P < 0.001$ comparing control release with release in the presence of clonidine in either ECS or SHAM-treated groups. The numbers in parentheses are the number of separate columns measuring release in vesicles obtained from ECS-treated and SHAM-treated animals

	[^3H]efflux (cpm) ECS				[^3H]efflux (cpm) SHAM			
		Clonidine (nM)				Clonidine (nM)		
CaCl$_2$ (mM)	Control	25	50	250	Control	25	50	250
0.1	1350±85[a] (54)	1234±177 (16)	1071±125[b] (18)	973±157[c] (18)	1076±70 (54)	1025±143 (17)	710±108[d] (18)	564±113[e] (17)
			50	250	1000		50	250	1000
0.2	1614±170 (17)	1190±110* (18)	1433±121 (18) n.s.	1001±147† (16)	1368±177 (12)	865±165* (12)	983±82[f] (12) n.s.	847±121* (12)
1.0	4554±227 (18)	3256±176§ (18)	3353±207§ (18)	3387±234§ (17)	4252±336 (17)	2978±287‡ (18)	2778±327‡ (18)	2723±283‡ (16)

At 0.2 mM and 1.0 mM CaCl$_2$ K^+ evoked [^3H]-NA release is slightly greater in vesicles obtained from ECS-treated animals but this small difference is not significant (except at 0.2 mM CaCl$_2$ and 250 mM clonidine concentration). The magnitude of clonidine inhibition is similar in vesicles obtained from ECS and sham-treated animals.

The effect of multiple ECS treatments on presynaptic release of [^3H]-NA from rat cortical vesicular preparation is small. Release of NA in the presence and absence of clonidine was measured at low and high CaCl$_2$ concentrations since the inhibitory effect of this α-agonist is most easily demonstrated at low CaCl$_2$ concentrations (De Langen & Mulder, 1980; Ebstein *et al.*, 1982). At low concentration of CaCl$_2$ there is a small (25 per cent) but significant increase of NA release in vesicles obtained from chronically ECS-treated animals. On the other hand, after a single ECS no effect on NA release was observed.

Increased release of [^3H]-NA observed in vesicles obtained from chronically ECS-treated rats could be due to a reduction in α^2-adrenergic binding sites reported by some investigators to be reduced after repeated ECS treatment (Pilc & Vetulani, 1982; Stanford & Nutt, 1982). At 0.2 mM CaCl$_2$, 250 nM clonidine in the perfusion buffer reduces release of [^3H]-NA by

48 per cent in vesicles obtained from sham-treated rats whereas a similar concentration of clonidine reduces $[^3H]$-NA release in vesicles obtained from ECS-treated rats by 28 per cent. Nevertheless, in both groups 250 nM clonidine significantly inhibits $[^3H]$-NA release, although the magnitude of the inhibition is somewhat reduced in vesicles obtained from ECS-treated rats. At both 50 and 250 nM clonidine there is significantly greater release of $[^3H]$-NA in vesicles obtained from ECS-treated animals. However, at 0.2 and 1.0 mM $CaCl_2$ there is no longer any significant difference in release of $[^3H]$-NA in vesicles obtained from ECS or sham-treated animals. Minchin *et al.* (1983) reported no effect of repeated ECS treatment on release of NA from rat cortical slices. The experiments of Minchin *et al.* (1983) were carried out in the presence of 1.2 mM $CaCl_2$ and 40 mM KCl, conditions which have been shown to reduce the effectiveness of presynaptic α_2-receptors in inhibiting release of NA (De Langen & Mulder, 1980; Ebstein *et al.*, 1982). However, the results obtained in the current study at high external medium $CaCl_2$ concentration are in agreement with those reported by Minchin *et al.* (1983).

Conclusion

In comparison to experiments where clorgyline (Cohen *et al.*, 1983), a specific A type MAO inhibitor, was administered to rats, the effect of ECS reported in the current study on release of $[^3H]$-NA from rat cortical vesicles, is minimal. Cortical vesicles obtained from clorgyline-treated rats showed markedly enhanced release of NA (approximately 160 per cent). Moreover, the enhanced release of NA was observed over a range of $CaCl_2$ concentrations (0.05–1.0 mM). In addition there was a near total escape from clonidine suppression in vesicles obtained from clorgyline-treated animals whereas in chronically ECS-treated rats there was only a partial reduction in clonidine inhibition.

Although chronic MAO inhibition and ECS both induce increased NA release, possibly through a mechanism involving presynaptic α_2-adrenergic receptors, the effect of repeated ECS treatment on these specific presynaptic mechanisms is much weaker than that observed after chronic clorgyline administration. The weak effect of ECS on the release of NA from rat cortical vesicles suggests that a common mechanism of action of these two antidepressant treatments on presynaptic mechanisms is not involved. The presynaptic mechanisms involved in the post-synaptic β-adrenergic receptor sub-sensitivity induced by chronic ECS remain to be definitively established.

References

Bergstrom, D. A. & Kellar, K. J. (1979): Effect of electroconvulsive shock on monoaminergic receptor binding sites in rat brain. *Nature* **278**, 464–466.

Cohen, R. M., Ebstein, R. P., Daly, J. W. & Murphy, D. L. (1983): Chronic effects of a monoamine oxidase inhibiting antidepressant: decreases in functional α-adrenergic autoreceptors precede the decrease in norepinephrine stimulated cyclic AMP systems in rat brain. *J. Neuroscience*, in press.

De Langen, C. D. J. & Mulder, A. H. (1980): On the role of calcium ions in the presynaptic alpha-receptor mediated inhibition of $[^3H]$-noradrenaline release from rat brain cortex synaptosomes. *Brain Res.* **185**, 389–408.

De Potter, W. P., Chubb, W., Put, A. & De Schaepdryver, A. F. (1971): Facilitation of the release of noradrenaline and dopamine-β-hydroxylase at low stimulation frequencies by α-blocking agents. *Arch. Int. Pharmacodyn. Ther.* **193**, 191–197.

Ebstein, R. P. & Daly, J. W. (1982a). Release of norepinephrine and dopamine from brain vesicular preparations: Effects of adenosine analogues. *Cell. Molec. Neurobiol.* **2**, 193–204.

Ebstein, R. P. & Daly, J. W. (1982b): Release of norepinephrine and dopamine from brain vesicular preparations: effects of calcium antagonists. *Cell. Molec. Neurobiol.* **2**, 205–213.

Ebstein, R. P., Seamon, K., Creveling, C. R. & Daly, J. W. (1982): Release of norepinephrine from brain vesicular preparations: effects of an adenylate cyclase activator, forskolin, and a phosphodiesterase inhibitor. *Cell. Molec. Neurobiol.* **2**, 179–192.

Ebstein, R. P., Lerer, B., Shlaufman, M. & Belmaker, R. H. (1983): The effect of repeated electroconvulsive shock treatment and chronic lithium feeding on the release of $[^3H]$ norepinephrine from rat cortical vesicular preparations. Submitted for publication.

Fink, M. (1979): *Convulsive therapy: theory and practice.* New York: Raven Press.

Heal, D. J., Akagi, H., Bowdler, J. M. & Green, A. R. (1981): Repeated electroconvulsive shock attenuates clonidine-induced hypoactivity in rodents. *Eur. J. Pharmacol.* **75**, 231.

Hendley, E. D. & Welch, B. L. (1975): Electroconvulsive shock: Sustained decrease in norepinephrine uptake affinity in a reserpine model of depression. *Life Sci.* **16**, 45–54.

Hendley, E. D. (1976): Electroconvulsive shock and norepinephrine uptake kinetics in rat brain. *Psychopharmacol. Comm.* **2**, 17-25.

Kellar, K. J., Cascio, C. S., Bergstrom, D. A., Butler, J. A. & Iadorola, P. (1981): Electroconvulsive shock and reserpine: effects on β-adrenergic receptors in rat brain. *J. Neurochem.* **37**, 830-836.

Kety, S. S., Javoy, F., Thierry, A. M., Julon, L. & Glowinski, J. (1967): A sustained effect of electroconvulsive shock on the turnover of norepinephrine in the central nervous system of the rat. *Proc. Natl. Acad. Sci. USA* **58**, 1249-1254.

Langer, S. Z. (1979): Physiological and pharmacological role of presynaptic receptor systems in neurotransmission. In *Advances in the Biosciences*, Vol. 18, ed S. Z. Langer, K. Starke and M. L. Dubrocovich. Pp. 13-22. New York: Pergamon Press.

McCabe, M. S. (1976): ECT in the treatment of mania: a controlled study. *Amer. J. Psychiat.* **33**, 688-690.

Minchin, M. C. W., Williams, J., Bowdler, J. M. & Green, A. R. (1983): The effect of electroconvulsive shock on the uptake and release of noradrenaline and 5-hydroxytryptamine in rat brain slices. *J. Neurochem.*, In press.

Modigh, K. (1976): Long-term effects of electroconvulsive shock therapy on synthesis, turnover and uptake of brain monoamines. *Psychopharmacology* **49**, 179-185.

Musacchio, J. M., Julon, L., Kety, S. S. & Glowinski, J. (1969): Increase in rat brain tyrosine hydroxylase activity produced by electroconvulsive shock. *Proc. Natl. Acad. Sci. USA* **63**, 1117-1119.

Pandey, G. N., Heinze, W. J., Brown, B. D. & Davis, J. M. (1979): Electroconvulsive shock treatment decreases β-adrenergic receptor sensitivity in rat brain. *Nature* **280**, 234-235.

Pilc, A. and Vetulani, J. (1982): Depression by chronic electroconvulsive treatment of clonidine hypothermia and [^{3}H]-clonidine binding to rat cortical membranes. *Eur. J. Pharmacol.* **80**, 109-113.

Pryor, G. T. (1974): Effect of repeated ECS on brain weight and brain enzymes. In *Psychobiology of convulsive therapy*, ed M. Fink, S. S. Kety, S. McGaugh and T. A. Williams. Pp. 171-184. Washington, D.C.: H. V. Winston & Sons.

Stanford, S. C. & Nutt, D. J. (1982): Comparison of the effects of repeated electroconvulsive shock on α_2- and β-adrenoceptors in different regions of rat brain. *Neuroscience* **7**, 1753-1757.

Starke, K. (1971): Influence of α-receptor stimulants on noradrenaline release. *Naturwissenschafften* **58**, 420.

Sugrue, M. F. (1981): Effect of chronic antidepressant administration on rat frontal cortex α_2- and β-adrenoceptor binding. *Br. J. Pharmacol.* **74**, 761P-762P.

Vetulani, J. & Sulser, F. (1975): Action of various antidepressant treatments reduces reactivity of noradrenergic cyclic AMP-generating system in limbic forebrain. *Nature* **257**, 495-496.

Vetulani, J., Stawarz, R. J., Dingell, J. V. & Sulser, F. (1976): Possible common mechanism of action of antidepressant treatments: reduction in the sensitivity of the noradrenergic cyclic AMP generating system in the rat limbic forebrain. *Naunyn-Schmiedebergs Arch. Pharmacol.* **293**, 109-114.

Wolfe, B. W., Harden, T. K., Sporn, J. R. & Molinoff, P. B. (1978): Presynaptic modulation of β-adrenergic receptors in rat cerebral cortex after treatment with antidepressants. *J. Pharmacol. Exptl. Therap.* **307**, 446-457.

8.
ECT and lithium: parallels and contrasts in receptor mechanisms

B. LERER, M. STANLEY and R. H. BELMAKER

Jerusalem Mental Health Center, P.O.B. 140, Jerusalem, Israel (BL, RHB); Departments of Psychiatry and Pharmacology, Lafayette Clinic and Wayne State University School of Medicine, 951 E. Lafayette, Detroit, MI 48207 (MS and BL, present address).

Introduction

ECT and lithium (Li) share a similar therapeutic profile characterized by a unique bidirectional clinical efficacy in affective disorder. ECT is a treatment of choice for severe depressions (Kendell, 1981), is effective in mania (McCabe, 1976) and may have prophylactic efficacy for recurrent affective episodes (Stevenson & Geoghegan, 1951; Karliner & Werheim, 1965). Li is uniquely antimanic (Shopsin *et al.*, 1975), possibly antidepressant (Mendels, 1976) and highly effective in preventing affective decompensation in bipolar and probably unipolar patients (Prien *et al.*, 1974).

The parallels between the clinical profiles of these two very different treatments clearly justify a search for mechanisms of action which they may have in common. The contrasts which do exist in the clinical spectra of ECT and Li should, however, be noted in this context. An important example is the clear antidepressant efficacy of ECT as opposed to the less conclusive results for Li. Also, available data on prophylaxis of affective episodes by maintenance ECT are by no means definitive. A further intriguing observation is that, although effective in treating mania, ECT may itself induce a switch to mania or hypomania in depressed subjects, an effect not characteristic of Li. Thus while basic mechanisms common to both ECT and Li may be postulated to exist, differences in the neurochemical actions of the two treatments should also be expected. Finally, clinical experience has documented possible deleterious interactions between ECT and Li, with neurotoxic effects (Weiner *et al.*, 1980; Small *et al.*, 1980). The basis underlying this interaction is not known. Nor is it entirely clear whether the therapeutic efficacy of ECT is impeded by concurrent Li administration or whether the interaction is one of toxicity only.

The present chapter will review and compare the effects of ECT and Li on neurotransmitter receptors for dopamine (DA) noradrenaline (NA) and acetylcholine (ACh). Roles have been postulated for all three neurotransmitters in the pathogenesis of affective disorders and in mediating treatments effective in these disorders (Schildkraut, 1965; Janowsky *et al.*, 1972; Post *et al.*, 1980). The findings reviewed are derived primarily from studies on rodents, with the focus on effects induced by clinically relevant, 'chronic' rather than single dose administration of electroconvulsive shock (ECS) and Li. Findings which may be relevant to the interaction between concurrently administered ECT and Li will also be discussed on the basis of the effect of the two treatments, administered separately and concurrently, on rat brain β-adrenergic receptors.

ECT, lithium and dopamine receptors

Presynaptic effects

ECS, administered to rats daily for 7–10 d, induces no significant change in DA concentration nor in turnover of the neurotransmitter in the different brain regions studied (Evans *et al.*, 1976;

Modigh, 1976). This contrasts with increased DA synthesis reported following a single ECS (Engel *et al.*, 1968). Reports of Li effects on DA metabolism in rat brain have yielded conflicting results with some authors reporting decreases in DA synthesis by subacute or chronic Li administration (Friedman & Gershon, 1973), some increases (Hesketh *et al.*, 1978) and some no change (Schubert, 1973). Ahluwalia & Singhal (1980) found significant decreases in DA concentration in the pons-medulla and midbrain following 12 d of 2 meq/kg per day Li with striatal DA concentration unchanged, although striatal DA and HVA were both significantly elevated two days following Li withdrawal. The absence of presynaptic effects of chronic ECS on DA metabolism and the conflicting findings regarding Li effects make it seem unlikely that the therapeutic action of either treatment is mediated via presynaptic alterations in DA metabolism.

Dopamine-mediated behaviors
The effects of both ECT and Li on DA receptors have been studied by the use, in animal models, of behavioral responses to pharmacological manipulations which stimulate DA systems and by direct radioligand binding to DA receptor sites. Studies on the effect of ECS on DA-mediated behaviors show that motor activity following tranylcypromine/L-DOPA and methamphetamine (Evans *et al.*, 1976; Green *et al.*, 1977), methamphetamine and apomorphine-induced circling in rats with unilateral nigro-striatal lesions (Green *et al.*, 1977) and apomorphine induced stereotypies (Modigh, 1979) were all increased by 7–10 daily ECS. When ECS was administered according to a more clinically equivalent schedule (three ECS per week for four weeks), increased apomorphine-induced stereotypies could not be demonstrated (Lerer *et al.*, 1982). Apomorphine stereotypies were increased in the same laboratory following a regimen of seven daily ECS (Globus *et al.*, 1981). Green & Deakin (1980) have, however, been able to demonstrate enhancement of apomorphine-induced total activity scores following a regimen of five ECS over 10 days. The slightly more frequent ECS dosage regimen of Green & Deakin (1980) compared to Lerer *et al.* (1982), may be sufficient to explain the discrepant observations. It should also be noted, that Green & Deakin (1980) measured total motor activity unlike Lerer *et al.* (1982) who rated stereotyped behavior. Apomorphine-induced motor activity is thought to be mediated via the nucleus accumbens — versus striatal mediation for apomorphine-induced stereotypy (Kelly *et al.*, 1975). The apparent discrepancy between the findings of Green & Deakin (1980) and those of Lerer *et al.* (1982) may therefore reflect differences in site of mediation of the DA behaviors tested.

The effect of Li on DA-mediated behaviors has been extensively studied with inconsistent results. Ebstein *et al.* (1980*a*) studied the effect of 21–28 d chronic oral Li, achieving blood levels of 0.56–1.54 meq/l, on responses to 5–15 mg/kg amphetamine. A small but significant potentiation of amphetamine-induced stereotypy and hypothermia was observed, extending previous reports that acute- or short-term Li has a synergistic effect on amphetamine-induced stereotypy (Lal & Sourkes, 1972; Matussek & Linsmayer, 1968; Ozawa & Miyauchi, 1977). Methodological considerations may explain the differences between these results and those of Smith (1976), Cox *et al.* (1971), Segal *et al.* (1975) and Flemenbaum (1977) who found no effect or inhibition by Li of amphetamine-induced hyperactivity and stereotypy. Methodological factors include the length of Li treatment (acute- or short-term v chronic), Li blood levels achieved and dosage of amphetamine used (see: Ebstein *et al.*, 1980*b*). The importance of amphetamine dosage is further highlighted by a recent finding (Lerer *et al.*, 1983*a*) that 21 days of chronic oral Li (blood levels 1.01 meq/l) inhibits open-field locomotor activity induced by low (0.5 mg/kg) dose amphetamine. Locomotor activity induced by low dose amphetamine may be noradrenergically mediated while the stereotypy responses induced by higher amphetamine doses may be dopaminergic in nature (Snyder & Taylor, 1971).

While some dopaminergically-mediated behavioral responses may thus be potentiated by chronic Li, the evidence is clearly inconclusive and the findings can best be summarized as contradictory. Repeated ECS (daily for 7–10 d) clearly potentiated DA responses (see above) but reports disagree as to whether less frequent, more clinically equivalent ECS schedules

68

induce behavioral DA super-sensitivity (Green & Deakin, 1980; Lerer *et al.*, 1982). The possible relevance of the increased DA responses following daily ECS to ECT mechanisms, is not known.

Dopamine receptors
Behavioral DA super-sensitivity following daily ECS is not matched by parallel changes in DA receptor number, as measured by striatal [³H]-spiperone binding (Bergstrom & Kellar, 1979; Atterwill, 1980; Lerer *et al.*, 1982). Chronic Li has also been reported to induce no change in striatal DA receptor number (Pert *et al.*, 1978). However, Pert *et al.* (1978) reported that chronic pretreatment with Li prevented increases in apomorphine induced stereotypy and striatal [³H]-spiperone binding induced by chronic haloperidol administration, extending a previous report by Klawans *et al.* (1977). Pert *et al.* (1978) suggested that Li may act therapeutically in affective disorders by stabilizing receptor sensitivity. In view of the similarities between the therapeutic spectra of ECT and Li, Lerer *et al.* (1982) tested the effect of concurrent ECS administration on haloperidol-induced DA receptor super-sensitivity.

Male albino rats were divided into four treatment groups receiving haloperidol, haloperidol + ECS, ECS only, or no treatment. Haloperidol was administered in finely ground rat pellets (0.01 per cent by weight) for four weeks. Control animals received identical, drug-free ground food. ECS was administered (150 V for 1.5 s) through earclip electrodes three times a week during the four-week haloperidol feeding, giving a total of 12 treatments. No anesthetic was used and the current was always observed to cause a typical tonic–clonic seizure with recovery within a few minutes. Untreated animals were handled identically and earclipped without any current being applied. Behavioral observations and sacrifice for biochemical studies were performed after a four-day washout period in which neither haloperidol nor ECS was administered.

A parallel group of animals in each treatment group was sacrificed by decapitation and the brains removed rapidly. Caudate nuclei were removed by dissection and immediately frozen at $-70\,°C$. [³H]-Spiperone binding was determined by the method of Burt *et al.* (1977). The number of receptor sites (B_{max}) and the affinity constant (K_D) were determined from Scatchard analysis for each individual rat striatum.

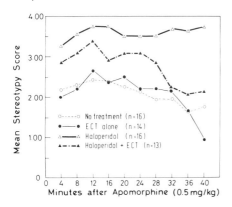

Fig. 1. *Effect of ECS, haloperidol and haloperidol + ECS on stereotyped behavior*. Each point represents the mean stereotypy score for the animals in the treatment group at that time point. Behavioral observations were conducted in a darkened room by an observer blind as to the pharmacological status of the animals. Apomorphine 0.5 mg/kg was injected i.p. to animals, 4 at a time (one from each treatment group), who were then placed in identical wire observation cages. Stereotyped movements were observed and rated every 4 min for 1 min over a period of 40 min. Total stereotypy scores were the sum of the 10 scores so obtained for each animal, using the scale of Kelly & Iversen (1976)

Figure 1 illustrates the results of the behavioral observations. ECS alone did not significantly alter stereotypy scores at any point in the time course. Haloperidol pretreatment induced a consistent and highly significant increase in apomorphine-induced stereotypy which was present through the 40-min observation period. Administration of ECS concurrently with haloperidol attenuated the haloperidol-induced increase in apomorphine stereotypies, this attenuation becoming more prominent in the last 12 min of the 40-min observation period. Total stereotypy scores (sum of all 10 observations) for haloperidol plus ECS were 48 per cent lower than for haloperidol alone ($P < 0.01$).

Table 1 illustrates the results of the [³H]-spiperone binding studies. A haloperidol-induced increase in DA receptor number is clearly evident. Concurrent ECS ameliorated the haloperidol-induced super-sensitivity as it did in the behavioral experiment. ECS alone induced no changes in dopamine receptor number. There was no difference in the K_D for spiperone (mean K_D = 0.75 nM) for the four groups.

Table 1. *Effect of ECS on haloperidol-induced biochemical DA supersensitivity.* Effect of ECS, haloperidol and haloperidol plus ECS on [³H]-spiperone binding in the rat caudate nucleus. B_{max} and K_D values represent mean ± s.e.m. derived from 5-point Scatchard plot analysis of [³H]-spiperone binding (NEN) in an individual rat using concentrations from 0.1–1.0 nM. Blanks contained 10 μM dopamine. Plots were fitted by a computer program

	Control	ECS	Haloperidol	Haloperidol + ECS
n	13	13	12	11
B_{max}	43.5 ± 2.0	45.7 ± 2.4	67.5 ± 3.1†	58.9 ± 3.8*
K_D	0.67 ± 0.05	0.71 ± 0.05	0.84 ± 0.06	0.73 ± 0.07

*$P < 0.001$ haloperidol vs. no treatment (Student's t-test, two-tailed); †$P < 0.05$ haloperidol + ECS vs. haloperidol (Student's t-test, one-tailed used because the biochemical hypothesis was defined after the behavioral results had been obtained).

These findings show ECS effects on changes in DA receptor sensitivity induced by haloperidol rather than direct effects of ECS on baseline DA receptor function and yield parallel results with biochemical and behavioral methods. Chronic haloperidol induced a 72 per cent super-sensitivity of DA receptors as measured behaviorally, 48 per cent of which was prevented by ECS. The biochemical super-sensitivity was 55 per cent, 36 per cent of which was prevented by ECS. Although the biochemical effect was significant only at $P < 0.05$ (one-tailed), it is in the direction of the behavioral findings and is derived from full Scatchard analysis for each of the animals. ECS did not significantly affect weight gain in the haloperidol-treated animals so that the ECS prevention of haloperidol-induced super-sensitivity was unlikely to be due to reduced haloperidol intake.

These findings suggest that ECS may, as reported for Li, prevent antagonist induced increases in apomorphine-induced stereotypy and [³H]-spiperone-labeled DA receptor number. Rosenblatt *et al.* (1980) have suggested that Li may in fact induce a down-regulation of striatal DA receptor which is demonstrable in the course of Li administration and one day following Li withdrawal. Other authors have also reported that chronic Li decreases [³H]-spiperone binding (Wajda *et al.*, 1981), although Staunton *et al.* (1982) found no effect. An effect of Li to down-regulate [³H]-spiperone-labeled striatal DA receptors might be the mechanism of stabilization by Li of DA receptors. This would not, however, explain the ECS effect reported above, since ECS alone has no reported effect on [³H]-spiperone binding.

The finding that chronically administered Li prevents behavioral super-sensitivity of DA receptors, has been more consistently replicated (see Bunney & Garland, 1983) than the reported prevention of parallel biochemical super-sensitivity (Staunton *et al.*, 1982; Reches *et al.*, 1982). Prevention of receptor super-sensitivity by Li nevertheless remains an heuristically attractive explanation for the prophylactic efficacy of Li in affective disorders. A prophylactic effect of maintenance ECT is also clinically well recognized but remains to be conclusively investigated (Stevenson & Geoghegan, 1951; Karliner & Werheim, 1965). It is possible that prevention of DA receptor super-sensitivity may be a basic mechanism common to the prophylactic action of both Li and ECS. Neither Li nor ECS has been shown to reverse existing DA receptor super-sensitivity (Klawans *et al.*, 1977; Globus *et al.*, 1981) so that a prophylactic role for this mechanism is the most plausible. It remains, however, to be definitively determined whether stabilization of DA receptors by Li (and ECT) is a robustly replicable finding or an inconsistently observed, artefactual interference with receptor proliferation common to both treatments.

Presynaptic effects

The effects of ECS on presynaptic noradrenergic functions, have been extensively investigated. Repeated ECS has been found to increase synthesis and utilization of NA (Kety *et al.*, 1967; Modigh, 1976), decrease uptake of NA into synaptosomal preparations (Hendley, 1976; Minchin *et al.*, 1983) and increase the activity of the rate-limiting enzyme, tyrosine hydroxylase (Mussachio *et al.*, 1969). Studies on rodents employing the sedative response and decrease in brain MOPEG-SO$_4$ induced by clonidine (Heal *et al.*, 1981), suggest that chronic ECS may induce sub-sensitivity of inhibitory presynaptic receptors subserving NA release (Langer, 1974). Data from NA release studies reported by Ebstein *et al.* (this volume), support moderately increased release of NA by ECS. Taken together, these findings indicate that repeated ECS increases presynaptic availability of NA.

Findings relevant to the effects of Li on NA turnover, uptake and release are, for the most part, based on the use of acute- or short-term Li administration. While acute Li injections increase NA turnover in rat brain, Li administration over 14–28 d does not appear to change brain NA concentrations (Schildkraut, 1975; Goodnick & Gershon, 1983). Li has been reported to increase neuronal uptake of NA (Colburn *et al.*, 1968) and to inhibit the electrically-induced release of NA from superfused rat brain slices (Katz *et al.*, 1968). Chronically administered Li, however, clearly increased the potassium-evoked release of NA from cortical vesicular preparations (Ebstein *et al.*, this volume). The presynaptic Li data is thus less convincing than for ECS and contrasts with the more consistent effect of ECS to increase NA availability.

β—Adrenergic receptors

Effects of ECS on cortical β-adrenergic receptors are extensively reviewed by Kellar (this volume). Daily ECS for seven days down-regulates cortical [^{3}H]-DHA binding by 20–25 per cent (Bergstrom & Kellar, 1979; Pandey *et al.*, 1979); this effect is also demonstrable when ECS is administered at a clinically equivalent schedule of three ECS per week for four weeks (Belmaker *et al.*, 1982). Vetulani & Sulser (1975) have demonstrated sub-sensitivity of noradrenaline-sensitive adenylate cyclase in rat limbic forebrain following chronic ECS administration. Down-regulation of β-adrenergic receptor sensitivity has also been shown to be an effect common to chronically administered tricyclic antidepressants, monoamine oxidase inhibitors and ECS, and represents a highly plausible mechanism of antidepressant action for all three treatments (Vetulani & Sulser, 1975). In contrast to ECS, Li does not appear to alter β-receptor binding in rat cortex (Maggi & Enna, 1980; Birmaher *et al.*, 1982) although small decreases have been reported (Treiser & Keller, 1979; Rosenblatt *et al.*, 1979). The clearly replicable down-regulation of β-adrenergic receptors by ECS and the apparent lack of effect of Li on these receptors, may be consistent with the contrasting antidepressant effects of the two treatments. While the antidepressant efficacy of ECT is well established, that of Li remains questionable and a differential effect on β-receptors may underlie this clinical difference.

It should be noted, however, that Li has been shown to directly inhibit NA-sensitive adenylate cyclase in rat brain, both *in vitro* and *in vivo*, at therapeutic serum Li concentrations (Ebstein *et al.*, 1980c; Belmaker, 1981). This effect is dependent on the continued presence of Li in the tissues and is not demonstrable after the cessation of Li administration. Sub-sensitivity of NA-sensitive adenylate cyclase induced by ECS (Vetulani & Sulser, 1975) and inhibition of NA-sensitive adenylate cyclase by Li may both represent a functional reduction of β-adrenergic receptor activity and of neurotransmission via the NA synapse. This direct effect of Li to inhibit NA-sensitive adenylate cyclase may thus functionally parallel the effect of ECS to reduce β-adrenoceptor number and β-adrenoceptor-linked adenylate cyclase activity.

While Li does not appear to directly affect β-adrenergic receptor binding, findings suggesting receptor stabilization by Li in the DA system (Pert *et al.*, 1978), have been extended to the NA system. Treiser & Kellar (1979) found that chronic Li pretreatment prevented reserpine-induced increases in β-adrenergic receptor number. Hermoni *et al.* (1980) found that chronic Li prevented reserpine-induced super-sensitivity of β-adrenoceptor-linked NA-sensitive adenylate cyclase. ECS has also been shown to prevent reserpine-induced super-sensitivity of NA-sensitive adenylate cyclase (Vetulani & Sulser, 1975) and to reverse reserpine induced increases in β-adrenergic receptor number (Kellar et al., 1981). Both Li and ECT have been shown to prevent hypoactivity induced in rodents by concurrently administered reserpine (Lerer et al., 1980; Hendley & Welch, 1975). Li and ECT are both effective in preventing depressive relapses and prevention of β-adrenergic super-sensitivity may be the basic mechanism underlying this common therapeutic effect. Differences in the direct effect of ECS and Li on β-adrenergic receptor binding discussed above may explain the differences in direct therapeutic action in an existing depressive episode.

Concurrent ECT and Li administration

Deleterious interactions between concurrently administered Li and ECT have been reported by a number of authors (Small et al., 1980; Weiner et al., 1980). Small et al. (1980) observed that patients on Li experienced more severe memory loss, atypical neurological findings and impairment in neuropsychological test performance during and after ECT. Therapeutic outcome following ECT appeared to be less satisfactory in Li-treated patients. Weiner (1980) reported a prolonged confusional state and EEG seizure activity following concurrent ECT and Li use in a patient who had previously been treated with both Li or ECT alone and subsequently again received Li without untoward effects. The mechanism which may underlie these reported negative interactions is not known.

As noted above, chronic ECS has been reported to cause a 20–25 per cent reduction in rat cortical β-adrenoceptor number (Bergstrom & Kellar, 1979; Pandey et al., 1979). Chronic Li pretreatment prevented reserpine induced increases in [^{3}H]-DHA binding and reserpine-induced super-sensitivity of noradrenaline-sensitive adenylate cyclase (Treiser & Kellar, 1979; Hermoni et al., 1980). If antidepressant treatments reduce β-adrenergic receptor number and Li prevents changes in receptor number, it may be asked whether the reported clinical incompatibility of ECT and Li may be related to the prevention by Li of ECS-induced β-adrenoceptor down-regulation. We (Birmaher et al., 1982) addressed this question by studying the effect of concurrent administration of Li and ECS on β-adrenoceptor number in rat cortex as measured by [^{3}H]-DHA binding.

Male albino rats were fed ground rat pellets containing 0.2% LiCl. The Li-treated rats were maintained on this diet for three weeks and then received a series of 10 daily ECS (150 V for 1 s), while continuing on Li feeding. Control animals were fed ground pellets without added Li and then received 10 daily ECS. Parallel groups of Li-fed and control-fed animals received ear-clipping without current. Twenty-four hours after the last ECS, animals were sacrificed and cortex dissected and stored at $-70\,°C$ until assay. Carotid blood obtained at sacrifice was assayed for Li by flame photometry and serum Li meaned 0.51 meq/l. Cortices were assayed for β-receptor number using [^{3}H]-DHA according to the method of Bylund & Snyder (1976). Concentrations of 3 and 6 nM were used for each individual cortex. One cortex in each of the four treatment groups was assayed on each assay day.

The results, (Table 2) show that Li does not prevent ECS-induced down-regulation of β-adrenergic binding sites. Li alone has no effect on DHA binding. The per cent decline in DHA

Table 2. *DHA binding in rat cortex after ECS plus Li (pmol/g wet weight).* Two-way analysis of variance revealed $F = 6.5$, $P < 0.05$ at 3 nM for an ECS effect, with no significant effect on Li and no interaction. At 6 nM $F = 15.1$, $P < 0.01$ for ECS effect, no Li effect and no significant interaction

	3 nM	6 nM
Control	4.5 ± 0.6 ($\times \pm$ s.e.m.)	7.2 ± 0.6
ECS only	3.4 ± 0.3*	5.1 ± 0.4*
Lithium only	4.6 ± 0.5	7.6 ± 0.7
ECS + Li	3.3 ± 0.3†	5.4 ± 0.5†

*$P < 0.05$ ECS only vs control, paired *t*-test; †$P < 0.01$ ECS + Li vs Li only, paired *t*-test; $n = 10$ in each of the four groups at 3 nM, $n = 9$ in each of the four groups at 6 nM.

binding is the same in the presence of Li (27 per cent at 3 nM, 25 per cent at 6 nM) as in its absence (25 per cent at 3 nM, 29 per cent at 6 nM). There was no difference in DHA binding in those rats in the Li + ECS group with Li levels above 0.65 (3.2 pmol/g at 3 nM, 5.3 pmol/g at 6 nM) and those with Li levels below 0.65 (3.3 pmol/g at 3 nM, 5.5 pmol/g at 6 nM). K_D for DHA, calculated from Scatchard analysis, was similar in the four treatment groups ($\cong$ 5 nM).

These results confirm reports that ECS induces a reduction in β-adrenergic receptor binding without a change in K_D for DHA (Bergstrom & Kellar, 1979; Pandey et al., 1979). Lithium has no effect in preventing ECS-induced decreases in DHA binding. This is consistent with the lack of Li effect in preventing agonist-induced sub-sensitivity in other systems (Zohar et al., 1982; Levy et al., 1983). If Li and ECS are indeed clinically incompatible, this incompatibility does not appear to be mediated by conflicting effects at the level of the β-adrenergic receptor.

ECT, lithium and acetylcholine receptors

Presynaptic effects

Relatively few studies have examined the effects of repeated ECS on central cholinergic systems. Studies performed to date, yield little evidence for persistent changes in presynaptic cholinergic mechanisms following repeated ECS. Atterwill (1980; this volume) found no persistent effect of repeated ECS on high-affinity choline uptake and on choline acetyl-transferase (ChAT) activity. ECS- and drug-induced seizures acutely increased ChAT activity in several brain areas (including the striatum hippocampus and cortex) but these effects were transient.

Studies on the effect of chronic Li administration on acetylcholine metabolism in rodent brain have yielded complex results. Decreases in acetylcholine levels in rat whole brain were found by Ho & Tsai (1975); Krell & Goldberg (1973) found no change in mouse whole brain and Miyauchi et al. (1980) reported increases in ACh levels in four of five brain regions and in choline levels for three of five regions. Miyauchi et al. (1980) also found that chronic Li increased ACh turnover in four of five cortical brain regions by 63 per cent. A recent review of Li mechanisms (Goodnick & Gershon, 1983) concludes that Li, when given chronically, may increase high affinity transport of choline into brain cells, increase ACh synthesis and release and cause elevation of ACh and choline brain content. While the complex effects of Li on brain acetylcholine are difficult to interpret in terms of mechanism of action, they clearly differ from those of repeated ECS which are minimal.

Acetylcholine receptors

Effects of both ECS and Li on muscarinic cholinergic receptors have not been extensively studied. Maggi & Enna (1980) studied the effect of chronic oral Li, yielding blood levels of 0.8–1.0 meq/l, on muscarinic receptors in rat brain. [^{3}H]-QNB binding in the cortex, hippocampus and striatum was unchanged by Li pretreatment. Pestronk & Drachman (1980) examined the effects of Li on denervated soleus muscle in rats. Li attenuated the denervation-induced increase in extrajunctional ACh receptors by 61 per cent. Li decreased ACh receptor number in innervated muscle by 35 per cent. Tollefson et al. (1981) studied microsomal preparations from human caudate nucleus and found that 1 mmol Li reduced the affinity of QNB for muscarinic receptors (K_D increased 35.9 to 72.4) and reduced specific QNB binding by 23 per cent. Levy et al. (1982) found that chronic oral Li induced a small but significant 6 per cent increase in [^{3}H]-QNB binding in rat whole brain minus cerebellum. Concurrent Li nevertheless completely blocked the significant 23 per cent rise in [^{3}H]-QNB binding caused by atropine 3 mg/kg per day for 5 d. Li did not prevent the significant 16 per cent decline in [^{3}H]-QNB binding found 24 hours after administration of the cholinesterase inhibitor di-isopropyl fluorophosphate (DFP) 1.2 mg/kg. These findings extend those of Pestronk & Drachman (1980) and suggest that Li may stabilize muscarinic receptor sensitivity in rat brain. Only antagonist induced up-regulation of the receptor appears to be blocked while agonist induced down-regulation is unaffected. The direct effect of Li on brain muscarinic receptors is still unclear since small increases (Levy et al., 1983) and no change (Maggi & Enna, 1980) have been reported in rat brain, reduction of binding and affinity in *in vitro* human brain preparations (Tollefsen *et al.*, 1981) and reduction in junctional acetylcholine receptors on peripheral muscle (Pestronck & Drachman, 1980).

The effects of ECS on rat brain muscarinic cholinergic receptors have been studied by four groups. Kellar *et al.* (1981) found a slight but nonsignificant reduction in [^{3}H]-QNB binding in rat cortex and hippocampus 24 h after daily ECS for 14 d. Deakin *et al.*, (1981) found minimal effects in rat cortex after daily ECS over 10 d. Dashieff *et al.* (1982) administered 4 ECS daily for 4 d and found a highly significant 19–25 per cent decline in [^{3}H]-QNB binding in the dentate and hippocampal gyri respectively. Scatchard analysis confirmed a decline in B_{max} without alteration of K_D.

Lerer *et al.* (1983*b*) studied the effect of seven consecutive daily ECS (130 volts for 0.75 s administered via earclip electrodes) on [^{3}H]-ONB binding in rat cerebral cortex and hippocampus. The animals were sacrificed 24 h after the last ECS and the brains rapidly dissected and frozen at $-70°C$ until assay. All non-ECS treated animals had earclip electrodes applied without current being passed (sham-ECS). Binding of [^{3}H]-QNB was determined in accordance with the methods described by Fields *et al.* (1978) at 25 pM [^{3}H]-QNB concentration. Protein was determined according to Lowry *et al.* (1951). Specific binding was defined as that which was displaced by 5 μM atropine sulfate and represented approximately 87 per cent of total binding at the concentration used in this experiment.

Table 3. *Effect of ECS on muscarinic cholinergic receptors in rat cerebral cortex and hippocampus.* Figures represent percentage of control [^{3}H]-QNB binding at 25 pM QNB. Each value is the mean ± s.e.m. for binding data from 8–12 separate animals. Two-tailed *t*-test were used for statistical comparisons which were done on raw data before conversion into percentages

	24 h after ECS × 1 (per cent of control)	7 d after ECS × 1 (per cent of control)	24 h after ECS × 7 (per cent of control)
Cortex	95 ± 5.8	108 ± 6.9	85 ± 4.4*
Hippocampus	103 ± 4.1	96 ± 10.0	87 ± 4.7*

*ECS vs control, $P < 0.05$

ECS induced a significant 15 per cent decline in [^{3}H]-QNB binding in rat cortex (Table 3). In the hippocampus too a significant reduction in [^{3}H]-QNB binding of similar magnitude, was found. Scatchard analysis confirmed a change in B_{max} with no alteration of K_D. These reductions were not present 24 h after a single ECS nor 7 d after a single ECS. The latter time frame was studied in view of reports (Chiodo & Antelman, 1980) that a single ECS plus a delay may induced as significant a reduction in electrophysiologically measured DA autoreceptor sensitivity, as a series of consecutive ECS given over the same time interval.

In order to study the effect of concurrent ECS on atropine-induced changes in [^{3}H]-QNB binding in the cortex, two additional groups of rats were studied in a subsequent experiment. One received atropine 10 mg/kg day for 5 d and was sacrificed 48 h after the last atropine injection. A second group received, in addition to the atropine regimen, seven consecutive ECS; atropine was administered to this group from day 2 to day 6 of the ECS schedule. Atropine induced a small but significant increase in [^{3}H]-QNB binding in the cortex which was completely blocked by concurrent ECS administration (Fig. 2).

The finding of ECS-induced reduction in [^{3}H]-QNB binding supports the results reported by Dashieff *et al.* (1982) in the hippocampal formation. The results also demonstrate muscarinic receptor down-regulation by ECS at a somewhat more clinically equivalent regimen than the four ECS per day for four days schedule used by Dashieff *et al.* (1982). In view of the similar magnitudes of the atropine induced increase in [^{3}H]-QNB binding and the ECS-induced attenuation thereof, one cannot speak of a 'stabilization' effect of ECS on the muscarinic

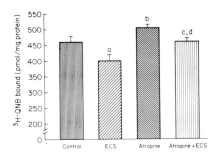

Fig. 2. *Effects of ECS, atropine and ECS + atropine on muscarinic cholinergic receptors in rat cerebral cortex.* For methods, see text. Two-tailed t-test used for statistical comparisons. (a) ECS vs control, $P < 0.04$; (b) Atropine vs control, $P < 0.05$; (c) Atropine + ECS vs atropine, $P < 0.02$; (d) Atropine + ECS vs ECS, $P < 0.04$

receptor as reported by Levy *et al.* (1982) for Li. Functionally, however, both treatments may be seen as preventing antagonist-induced super-sensitivity of muscarinic cholinergic receptors.

The clinical implications of these findings are currently not clear and definitive interpretation should await studies involving other brain areas and even less frequent, more clinically equivalent ECS schedules. It may be noted, however, that cholinergic predominance has been implicated in the pathogenesis of depression (Janowsky *et al.*, 1972) and more recent findings show accelerated REM sleep induction by arecoline (Sitaram & Gillin, 1980) and increased fibroblast muscarinic receptors in depressed subjects (Nadi *et al.*, unpublished). Both ECS and Li have been shown to prevent super-sensitivity of muscarinic receptors and this common mechanism may be relevant in the context of cholinergic theories of depression.

ECS-induced down-regulation of brain muscarinic receptors may, however, have relevance to the mechanism of ECT-induced amnesia rather than to the therapeutic mechanisms of ECT. Anticholinergics have been shown to impair memory functions which are enhanced by cholinomimetics (Crow & Grove-White, 1971; Sitaram *et al.*, 1978). Cholinergic hypoactivity may be associated with the cognitive deficit of Alzheimer's disease (Bartus *et al.*, 1982) which may be alleviated by cholinergic agonists (Christie *et al.*, 1981). The possibility that ECT-induced amnesia may be related to muscarinic receptor sub-sensitivity is currently being investigated.

Conclusions

The clinical profiles of ECT and Li share a greater similarity than might be expected on the basis of the very different nature of the two treatments. With these similarities in mind, parallels and contrasts between the effects of ECS and Li on neurotransmitter-receptor systems for DA, NA and acetylcholine, have been reviewed. The neurochemical effects of ECS and Li are obviously not limited to these three neurotransmitters. Effects of ECS and Li on serotonergic, GABA and opiate receptor systems fall outside the scope of this review but lend themselves to a similarly heuristic comparison. With regard to the neurotransmitters discussed in this chapter, the following general conclusions are suggested.

(1) In the DA system the most striking parallel between the effects of ECS and Li is the effect of both treatments to prevent antagonist-induced DA receptor super-sensitivity as measured by behavioral and possibly biochemical indices. The possible relevance of these effects is to the prophylactic action of both treatments and this remains to be further studied.

(2) In the NA system, down-regulation of β-adrenergic receptor sensitivity by ECS may represent a mechanism of action common to ECT and other antidepressant treatments. This effect is not shared by Li and this difference may underlie the contrasting antidepressant profile of the two treatments. Both ECS and Li prevent induced super-sensitivity of β-adrenergic receptors and this action may be the basis of the efficacy of both treatments in preventing recurrent depressions.

(3) Concurrently administered Li does not prevent the down-regulation of β-adrenergic receptors induced by ECS. The reported clinical incompatibility between ECT and Li is thus unlikely to be linked to attenuation by Li of this putative antidepressant mechanism of ECT.

(4) In the cholinergic system, Li has inconsistent direct effects on muscarinic receptors number while ECS is reported to reduce muscarinic-cholinergic binding in cerebral cortex and hippocampus. Both treatments prevent atropine induced supersensitivity of muscarinic cholinergic receptors. These findings may have relevance in the context of theories linking depression to central cholinergic supersensitivity. Subsensitivity of muscarinic-cholinergic receptors induced by ECS may, however, be related to the causation of ECT-induced amnesia rather than to therapeutic mechanisms.

Acknowledgements — Karni Jabotinsky-Rubin, Boris Birmaher, Mordechai Globus and Jacob Bannet collaborated on some of these studies. We thank Sandra Demetriou and Franz Fucek for valuable technical assistance and Mary Ratza for typing the manuscript.

References

Ahluwalia, P. & Singhal, P. L. (1980): Effect of low-dose lithium administration and subsequent withdrawal of biogenic amines in rat brain. *Br. J. Pharmac.* **71**, 601–607.

Atterwill, C. K. (1980): Lack of effect of repeated electroconvulsive shock on [^{3}H]-spiroperidol and [^{3}H]-5HT binding and cholinergic parameters in rat brain. *J. Neurochem.* **35**, 729–734.

Bartus, R. T., Dean, R. L., Beer, B. & Lippa, A. S. (1982): The cholinergic hypothesis of geriatric memory dysfunction. *Science* **217**, 407–417.

Belmaker, R. H. (1981): Receptors, adenylate cyclase, depression and lithium. *Biol. Psychiat.* **16**, 333–350.

Belmaker, R. H., Lerer, B., Bannet, J. & Birmaher, B. (1982): The effect of repeated electroconvulsive shock at a clinically equivalent schedule on rat cortical adrenoceptors. *J. Pharm. Pharmacol.* **34**, 275.

Bergstrom, D. A. & Kellar, K. J. (1979): Effect of electroconvulsive shock on monoaminergic receptor binding sites in rat brain. *Nature* **278**, 464–466.

Birmaher, B., Lerer, B. & Belmaker, R. H. (1982): Lithium does not prevent ECS-induced decreases in β-adrenergic receptors. *Psychopharmacology* **78**, 190–191.

Bunney, W. E., Jr. & Garland, B. L. (1983): Possible receptor effect of chronic lithium administration. *Neuropharmacology*, In press.

Burt, D. R., Creese, I. & Snyder, S. H. (1977): Antischizophrenic drugs: Chronic treatment elevates dopamine receptor binding in brain. *Science* **196**, 326.

Bylund, D. B. & Snyder, S. H. (1976): Beta-adrenergic receptor binding in membrane preparations from mammalian brain. *Mol. Pharmacol.* **12**, 568–580.

Chiodo, L. A. & Antelman, S. M. (1980): Electroconvulsive shock: Progressive dopamine autoreceptor subsensitivity independent of repeated treatment. *Science* **210**, 799–801.

Christie, J. E., Shering, A., Ferguson, J. & Glen, A. I. M. (1981): Physiotigmine and arecoline: Effects of intravenous infusion in Alzheimer presenile dementia. *Br. J. Psychiat.* **138**, 46–50.

Colburn, R. W., Goodwin, F. K. & Bunney, W. E., Jr. (1968): Effect of lithium on the uptake of noradrenaline by synaptosomes. *Nature* **215**, 1395–1397.

Cox, C., Harrison-Read, P. E., Steinberg, H. & Tomkiemicz, M. (1971): Lithium attenuates drug-induced hyperactivity in rats. *Nature* **232**, 336.

Crow, T. J. & Grove-White, I. G. (1971): Differential effects of atropine and hyoscine on human learning capacity. *Br. J. Pharmacol.* **43**, 464.

Dashieff, R. M., Savage, D. D. & McNamara, J. O. (1982): Seizures down-regulate muscarinic cholinergic receptors in hippocampal formation. *Brain Res.* **235**, 327–334.

Deakin, J. F. W., Owen, F., Cross, A. J. & Dashwood, M. J. (1981): Studies on possible mechanisms of action of electroconvulsive therapy: Effects of repeated electrically induced seizures on rat brain receptors for monoamines and other neurotransmitters. *Psychopharmacology* **73**, 345–349.

Ebstein, R. P., Eliashar, R. H., Belmaker, R., Ben-Uriah, S. & Yehuda, S. (1980*a*). Chronic lithium treatment and dopamine-mediated behavior. *Biol. Psychiat.* **15**, 495–496.

Ebstein, R. P., Eliashar, S. & Belmaker, R. H. (1980*b*): The effect of chronic lithium on adenylate cyclase and dopamine-mediated animal behaviors. In *Enzymes and neurotransmitters in mental disease*, ed E. Usdin, T. L. Sourkes and M. B. H. Youdim. Pp. 395–409. Oxford: John Wiley.

Ebstein, R. P., Hermoni, M. & Belmaker, R. H. (1980*c*). The effect of lithium on noradrenaline-induced cyclic AMP accumulation in rat brain: Inhibition after chronic treatment and absence of super-sensitivity. *J. Pharmacol. Exp. Ther.* **213**, 161–167.

Engel, J., Hanson, L. C. F., Roos, B. E. & Strombergsson, L. E. (1968): Effect of electroshock on dopamine metabolism in rat brain. *Psychopharmacologia* **13**, 140–144.

Evans, J. P. M., Grahame-Smith, D. G., Green, A. R. & Tordoff, A. F. C. (1976): Electroconvulsive shock increases the behavioral responses of rats to brain 5-hydroxytryptamine stimulation and central nervous system stimulant drugs. *Br. J. Pharmacol.* **56**, 193–199.

Fields, J. Z., Roeske, W. R., Morkine, E. & Yamamura, H. I. (1978): Cardiac muscarinic cholinergic receptors: Biochemical identification and characteristics. *J. Biol. Chem.* **253**, 3251–3258.

Flemenbaum, A. (1977). Lithium inhibition of norepinephrine and dopamine receptors. *Biol. Psychiat.* **12**, 563.

76

Friedman, E. & Gershon, S. (1973): Effect of lithium on brain dopamine. *Nature* **243**, 520–521.

Globus, M., Lerer, B., Hamburger, R. & Belmaker, R. H. (1981): Chronic electroconvulsive shock and chronic haloperidol are not additive in effects on dopamine receptors. *Neuropharmacology* **20**, 1125–1128.

Goodnick, P. & Gershon, S. (1983): Lithium. In *Handbook of Neurochemistry*, Vol. 9, (in press) ed A. Lajtha. New York: Plenum.

Green, A. R. & Deakin, J. F. W. (1980): Brain noradrenaline depletion prevents ECS-induced enhancement of serotonin- and dopamine-mediated behavior. *Nature* **285**, 232–233.

Green, A. R., Heal, D. J. & Grahame-Smith, D. G. (1977): Further observations on the effect of repeated electro-convulsive shock on behavioral responses of rats produced by increases in the functional activity of brain 5-hydroxy-tryptamine and dopamine. *Psychopharmacology* **52**, 195–200.

Heal, D. J., Akagi, H., Bowdler, J. M. & Green, A. R. (1981): Repeated electroconvulsive shock attenuates clonidine-induced hypoactivity in rodents. *Eur. J. Pharmacol.* **75**, 231–237.

Hendley, E. D. (1976): Electroconvulsive shock and norepinephrine uptake kinetics in rat brain. *Psychopharmacol. Commun.* **2**, 17–25.

Hendley, E. D. & Welch, B. L. (1975): Electroconvulsive shock: sustained decrease in norepinephrine uptake affinity in a reserpine model of depression. *Life Sci.* **16**, 45–54.

Hermoni, M., Lerer, B., Ebstein, R. P. & Belmaker, R. H. (1980): Chronic lithium prevents reserpine induced supersensitivity of adenylate cyclase. *J. Pharm. Pharmacol.* **32**, 510–511.

Hesketh, J. E., Nicolaou, N. M., Arbuthnott, G. W. & Wright, A. K. (1978): The effect of chronic lithium administration on dopamine metabolism in rat striatum. *Psychopharmac.* **56**, 163–166.

Ho, K. S. & Tsai, S. C. S. (1975): Lithium and ethanol preference. *J. Pharm. Pharmac.* **27**, 58–60.

Janowsky, D. S., El-Yousef, M. K., Kavis, J. M. & Sekerk, H. J. (1972): A cholinergic-adrenergic hypothesis of mania and depression. *Lancet* 632–635.

Karliner, W. & Werheim, H. K. (1965): Maintenance convulsive treatment. *Am. J. Psychiat.* **121**, 113–115.

Katz, R. I., Chase, T. N. & Kopin, I. J. (1968): Evoked release of norepinephrine and serotonin from brain slices: Inhibition by lithium. *Science* (Wash. DC) **162**, 466–467.

Kellar, K. J., Cascio, C. S., Bergstrom, D. A., Butler, J. A. & Iadorola, P. (1981). Electroconvulsive shock and reserpine: Effects on β-adrenergic receptors in rat brain. *J. Neurochem.* **37**, 830–836.

Kelly, P. H. & Iversen, S. D. (1976): Selective 6-OHDA-induced destruction of mesolimbic dopamine neurons: Abolition of psychostimulant-induced locomotor activity in rats. *Eur. J. Pharmacol.* **40**, 45.

Kelly, P. H., Seviour, P. W. & Iversen, S. D. (1975). Amphetamine and apomorphine responses in the rat following 6-OHDA lesions of the nucleus accumbens septi and corpus striatum. *Brain Res.* **94**, 507–522.

Kendell, R. E. (1981): The present status of electroconvulsive therapy. *Br. J. Psychiat.* **189**, 265–283.

Kety, S. S., Javoy, F., Thierry, A. M., Julou, L. & Glowinski, J. (1967): A sustained effect of electroconvulsive shock on the turnover of norepinephrine in the central nervous system of the rat. *Proc. Natl. Acad. Sci.* USA **58**, 1249–1254.

Klawans, H. L., Weiner, W. J. & Nausieda, P. A. (1977): The effect of lithium on an animal model of tardive dyskinesia. *Prog. Neuropsychopharmac.* **1**, 53–60.

Krell, R. D. & Goldberg, A. M. (1973): Affect of acute and chronic administration of lithium on steady state levels of mouse brain choline and acetylcholine. *Biochem. Pharmacol.* **22**, 3289–3291.

Lal, S. & Sourkes, T. L. (1972): Potentiation and inhibition of the amphetamine-induced stereotypy in rats by neuroleptics and other agents. *Arch. Int. Pharmacodyn.* **199**, 289.

Langer, S. Z. (1974): Presynaptic regulation of catecholamine release. *Biochem. Pharmacol.* **23**, 1793–1800.

Lerer, B., Ebstein, R. P., Felix, A. & Belmaker, R. H. (1980): Lithium amelioration of reserpine-induced hypoactivity in rats. *Int. Pharmacopsychiat.* **15**, 338–343.

Lerer, B., Jabotinsky-Rubin, K., Bannet, J., Ebstein, R. P. & Belmaker, R. H. (1982): Electroconvulsive shock prevents dopamine receptor supersensitivity. *Eur. J. Pharmacol.* **80**, 131–134.

Lerer, B., Globus, M., Brik, E., Hamburger, R. & Belmaker, R. H. (1983a): Effect of treatment and withdrawal from chronic lithium in rats on stimulant induced responses. *Neuropsychobiology*, in press.

Lerer, B., Stanley, M., Demetriou, S. & Gershon, S. (1983b): Effect of electroconvulsive shock on [^{3}H]-QNB binding in rat cerebral cortex and hippocampus, *J. Neurochem.*, in press.

Levy, A., Zohar, J. & Belmaker, R. H. (1982): The effect of chronic lithium pretreatment on rat brain muscarinic receptor regulation. *Neuropharmacology*, **21**, 1199–1201.

Lowry, O. H., Rosebrough, N. J., Farr, A. L. & Randall, R. J. (1951): Protein measurement with the Folin phenol reagent. *J. Biol. Chem.* **193**, 265–275.

Maggi, A. & Enna, S. J. (1980): Regional alterations in rat brain neurotransmitter systems following chronic lithium treatment. *J. Neurochem.* **34**, 888–892.

Matussek, N. & Linsmayer, M. (1968): The effect of lithium and amphetamine on desmethylimipramine-RO 5-1284 induced motor hyperactivity. *Life Sci.* **7**, 371.

McCabe, M. S. (1976): ECT in the treatment of mania: a controlled study. *Am. J. Psychiat.* **33**, 688–690.

Mendels, J. (1976). Lithium in the treatment of depression. *Am. J. Psychiat.* **133**, 373–377.

Minchin, M. C. W., Williams, J., Bowdler, J. M. & Green, A. R. (1983): The effect of electroconvulsive shock on the uptake and release of noradrenaline and 5-hydroxytryptamine in rat brain slices. *J. Neurochem.*, in press.

Miyauchi, T., Oikawa, S. & Kitada, Y. (1980): Effects of lithium chloride on the cholinergic system in different brain regions in mice. *Biochem. Pharmacol.* **15**, 654–657.

77

Modigh, K. (1976): Long-term effects of electroconvulsive shock therapy on synthesis turnover and uptake of brain monoamines. *Psychopharmacology* 49, 179–185.

Modigh, K. (1979): Long-lasting effects of ECT on monoaminergic mechanisms. In *Neuropsychopharmacology*, ed P. Saletu, P. Berner and L. Hollister. Pp. 11–20. Oxford: Pergamon Press.

Musacchio, J. M., Julou, L., Kety, S. S. & Glowinski, J. (1969): Increase in rat brain tyrosine hydroxylase activity produced by electroconvulsive shock. *Proc. Natl. Acad. Sci. US* 63, 1117–1119.

Ozawa, H. & Miyauchi, T. (1977): Potentiating effect of lithium chloride on methamphetamine-induced stereotypy in mice. *Eur. J. Pharmacol.* 41, 213.

Pandey, G. N., Heinze, W. J., Brown, B. D. & Davis, J. M. (1979): Electroconvulsive shock treatment decreases β-adrenergic receptor sensitivity in rat brain. *Nature* 280, 234–235.

Pert, A., Rosenblatt, J., Sivit, C., Pert, C. B. & Bunney, W. E. Jr. (1978): Long-term treatment with lithium prevents the development of dopamine receptor super-sensitivity. *Science* 201, 171–173.

Pestronck, A. & Drachman, D. B. (1980): Lithium reduces the number of acetylcholine receptors in skeletal muscle. *Science* 210, 342–343.

Post, R. M., Jimerson, D. C., Bunney, W. E. Jr. & Goodwin, F. K. (1980): Dopamine and mania: behavioral and biochemical effects of the dopamine blocker pimozide. *Psychopharmacology* 67, 297–305.

Prien, R. F., Klett, C. J. & Caffey, E. M. (1974): Lithium prophylaxis in recurrent affective illness. *Am. J. Psychiat.* 131, 198–203.

Reches, A., Wagner, H. R., Jackson, V. & Fahn, S. (1982): Prophylactic treatment with lithium does not prevent haloperidol-induced supersensitivity of dopamine in the rat. *Soc. Neurosci. Abstr.* 6, 546.

Rosenblatt, J. E., Pert, A., Bunney, W. E. Jr. (1980): Chronic lithium reduced [^{3}H]-spiroperidol binding in rat striatum. *Eur. J. Pharmac.* 67, 321–322.

Rosenblatt, J. E., Pert, C. B., Tallman, J. F., Pert, A. & Bunney, W. E. Jr. (1979): The effect of imipramine and lithium on α- and β-receptor binding in rat brain. *Brain Res.* 160, 186–191.

Schildkraut, J. J. (1975): In *Lithium: its role in psychiatric research and treatment*, ed S. Gershon and B. Shopsin. Pp. 51–73. New York: Plenum.

Schildkraut, J. J. (1965): The catecholamine hypothesis of affective disorders: A review of supporting evidence. *Am. J. Psychiat.* 122, 509–522.

Schubert, J. (1973): Effect of chronic lithium treatment on monoamine metabolism in the rat brain. *Psychopharmacologia* 32, 301–311.

Segal, D. S., Callaghan, M. & Mandell, A. J. (1975): Alterations in behavior and catecholamine biosynthesis induced by lithium. *Nature* 254, 58.

Shopsin, B., Gershon, S., Thompson, H. & Collin, P. (1975): Psychoactive drugs in mania. A controlled comparison of lithium carbonate, chlorpromazine and haloperidol. *Arch. Gen. Psychiat.* 32, 34–42.

Sitaram, N. & Gillin, J. C. (1980): Development and use of pharmacological probes of the CNS in man: Evidence of cholinergic abnormality in primary affective illness. *Biol. Psychiat.* 15, 925–955.

Sitaram, N., Weingartner, H. & Gillin, J. C. (1978): Human serial learning: Enhancement with arecoline and choline and impairment with scopolaine. *Science* 201, 274–276.

Small, J. G., Kellamy, J. J. & Melstein, V. (1980): Complications with electroconvulsive treatment combined with lithium. *Biol. Psychiat.* 15, 103–112.

Smith, D. F. (1976): Antagonistic effect of lithium chloride on L-DOPA-induced locomotor activity in rats. *Pharmac. Res. Comm.* 8, 575.

Snyder, S. and Taylor, K. M. (1971): Differential effects of D- and L-amphetamine on behavior and on catecholamine disposition in dopamine and norepinephrine containing neurons of rats brain. *Brain Res.* 28, 295–309.

Staunton, D. A., Magistretti, P. J., Shoemaker, W. J., Deyo, S. & Bloom, F. E. (1982): Effect of chronic lithium treatment on dopamine receptors in the rat corpus striatum II. No effect on denervation or neuroleptic-induced supersensitivity. *Brain Res.* 232, 401–412.

Stevenson, G. H. & Geoghegan, J. J. (1951): Prophylactic electroshock. *Am. J. Psychiat.* 107, 743–748.

Tollefson, G., Senogles, S. & Frey, W. (1981): *Abstracts of Society of Biological Psychiatry*, 35.

Treiser, S. & Kellar, J. (1979): Lithium: effects of adrenergic receptor supersensitivity in rat brain. *Eur. J. Pharmacol.* 58, 85–86.

Vetulani, J. & Sulser, F. (1975): Action of various antidepressant treatments reduces reactivity of noradrenergic cyclic AMP-generating system in limbic forebrain. *Nature* 257, 495–496.

Wajda, I. J., Banay-Schwartz, M., Manigault, I. & Lajtha, A. (1981): Effect of lithium and sodium ions on opiate and dopamine receptor binding. *Neurochem. Res.* 6, 321–331.

Weiner, R. D., Whanger, A. D., Erwin, C. W. & Wilson, W. P. (1980): Prolonged confusional state and EEG seizure activity following concurrent ECT and lithium use. *Am. J. Psychiat.* 137, 1452–1453.

Zohar, J., Lerer, B., Ebstein, R. P. & Belmaker, R. H. (1982): Lithium does not prevent agonist-induced sub-sensitivity of human adenylate cyclase. *Biol. Psychiat.* 17, 343–350.

9.
The effects of ECS on central cholinergic and interrelated neurotransmitter systems

C. K. ATTERWILL

MRC Developmental Neurobiology Unit, Institute of Neurology, 33 John's Mews, London WC1N 2NS, England.

Introduction

There have been relatively few recent studies on central cholinergic changes following electro-convulsive shock (ECS), compared with other neurotransmitter systems. Table 1 summarises the findings from a selection of studies carried out between 1949 and 1982. This is rather surprising in view of the evident involvement of cholinergic neurones in both the seizure mechanism and the adaptive changes which follow induced convulsions in both the human and animal CNS, which may be relevant to the antidepressant mechanism of ECT. For example, Fink (see 1966, 1974) noted that ECT elicits high degrees of EEG slow-wave activity (hyper-synchrony) in patients showing clinical improvement together with increases in cerebrospinal

Table 1. *Summary of brain cholinergic changes induced by seizures*

Parameter	Direction of change	Mechanism of seizure	Post-ictal time	Brain region/ species	Further details	Reference
ACh levels and turnover						
[ACh]	Reduced	ECS × 1	During convulsion	Rat whole brain	Transient	Richter & Crossland (1949)
[ACh]	Reduced	ECS × 1	During tonic flexion phase	Mouse brain		Takahishi et al. (1961)
Bound and free ACh	Reduced	ECS × 1	10 min-2 h	Mouse cerebral cortex	Synaptosomal ACh remained reduced	Essman (1972, 1973)
[ACh]	Reduced	PTZ × 1	During convulsion	Rat cerebral cortex caudate and hippocampus	Cerebral cortex and caudate same magnitude	Longoni et al. (1974)
[ACh]	Reduced	ECS × 1 ECS × 13	30 s	Rat cerebral cortex	Hippocampus, caudate unaffected	Longoni et al. (1976)
	Unchanged	ECS × 1 ECS × 13	5 min			
Bound & free ACh	Increased Reduced	ECS × 1	During seizure 10-30 min after	Mouse brain	ACh turnover increases in parallel post-ictally	Karczmar (1974)
[ACh]	Increased	Anticholinesterase (DFP)	0-3 h	Rat brain Mouse brain	Seizure reversed by small dose atropine	Holmstedt et al. (1966) Karczmar et al. (1973)
ACh and choline	Increased	PTZ/epilepsy	Post-ictally	CSF		Fink (1966)
Cholinergic enzymes						
AChE	Increased	ECS × 1	Within 10 s or 4-96 h	Rat brain	Transient	Adams et al. (1969)
ChAT	Reduced	ECS × 1	10-30 min	Mouse brain	Transient	Essman (1973)
AChE	Unchanged	Repeated ECS		Rat brain		Pryor (1974)
ChAT	Increased Unchanged	ECS × 1 ECS × 13	30 s-5 min 30 s-24 h	Rat cerebral cortex	No changes in caudate or hippocampus	Longoni et al. (1976)
Cholinergic receptor						
Muscarinic Receptor ([3H]QNB)	Reduced	ECS 4 × daily for 4 days	Approximately 24 h	Rat hippocampal formation		Dashieff et al. (1982)
Muscarinic Receptor ([3H]QNB)	Unchanged	ECS 1 × daily for 14 days	24 h	Rat hippocampus and cerebral cortex		Kellar et al. (1981)

acetylcholine (ACh) levels. Anticholinergic drugs such as atropine appear to reduce the slow-wave activity and reverse the clinical improvement. That the release of ACh into the synapse may be one of the primary mechanisms underlying a seizure is drawn from the information showing that anticholinesterases, such as the organophosphorous compounds, which increase synaptic ACh, both induce seizures and affect the parameters of electrically induced seizures (see Karczmar, 1974). These changes disappear after a few hours and are also susceptible to reversal by anticholinergic drugs. There are also some rather conflicting reports correlating brain ACh with seizure susceptibility in convulsive mice strains (see Karczmar 1974). Certain studies have concluded that a high brain ACh level predisposed animals to seizures (Kurokawa et al., 1963; Takahishi et al., 1961; Pryor, 1974). Others, in a comparative study of non-convulsive strains, found ECS latency to be longer and seizures of shorter duration in types characterized by higher brain ACh levels (Karczmar et al., 1973; Karczmar, 1974).

It is important, however, not to confuse or co-interpret the changes occurring during cholinergic drug-induced convulsions with the events occurring in cholinergic neurones after ECS, which may reflect part of the overall neurochemical response of the brain to ECT. Here, in general, ECS appears to increase brain ACh turnover post-ictally with decreases in brain ACh concentrations and an increase in release (see Table 1) together with adaptations in certain of the cholinergic enzymes acetylcholinesterase (AChE) and choline acetyl transferase (ChAT) and in cholinergic receptor properties (see Table 1) which will be discussed later in this chapter. Increases in cerebrospinal ACh levels also occur following seizures (see Fink, 1966) which may reflect an increase in intercellular free ACh liberated from its synaptic bound form because of the increase in cholinergic activity. These events must, therefore, be considered alongside changes occurring in interrelated neurotransmitter systems which may be related to the efficacy of ECT in treating depression.

It is known that repeated ECS can alter central dopaminergic (and serotonergic) function as assessed largely by behavioural techniques (Modigh, 1975; Atterwill & Green, 1980; Evans et al., 1976; Heal & Green, 1978). There has, however, been a paucity of information on neuro-chemical changes. In this chapter the striatum has been chosen as a 'model' study system because of its relatively well-defined pathways and connections. With respect to the nigro-striatal dopamine pathway the cataleptogenic effect of haloperidol in the rat is diminished by ECS, suggesting increased striatal dopamine-receptor function or altered cholinergic function in the striatum. Since nigro-striatal dopaminergic nerve terminals innervate cholinergic inter-neurones in the striatum (via an inhibitory receptor) (see Fig. 1 and Ladinsky et al., 1978) the effects of ECS on the striatal dopamine receptor ([^{3}H]-spiroperidol binding) and cholinergic function were determined 24 h after repeated ECS administration, a time at which the dopaminergic responses are enhanced. In the case of the cholinergic system the ACh-synthesising enzyme choline acetyltransferase (ChAT) and sodium-dependent high-affinity choline uptake (HAUC) were measured. HAUC has been shown to be regulatory and rate limiting in the control of ACh synthesis (Atweh et al., 1976) and can thus be utilised as a measure of presynaptic cholinergic activity and ACh turnover in vivo. In general, drug treatments which alter the in vivo activity of cholinergic neurones cause a parallel change in in vitro HAUC. With respect to the dopaminergic–cholinergic link, acute and chronic administration of neuroleptics alter HAUC and ACh release (Atweh et al., 1976; Sherman et al., 1978a; Stadler et al., 1973) as does chronic administration of reserpine or lithium (Burgess et al., 1978; Jope, 1979). Possible postsynaptic cholinergic changes were investigated in a joint study with Dr A. R. Green by studying the effects of ECS on the cataleptic effect of the cholino-mimetic agonist arecoline (see Fig. 1). Using the striatal model, the effects of ECS on certain GABA parameters were also studied. Striatal cholinergic neurones may connect with striato-nigral GABAergic neurones (Fig. 1). GABAergic inhibitory interneurones are also present in the striatum where repeated ECS has been shown to decrease GABA turnover (Green et al., 1978). GABA Receptor function following ECS was studied by investigating [^{3}H]-muscimol binding and presynaptic GABA activity by measuring the GABA-synthetic enzyme glutamate decarboxylase (GAD). For comparison with the striatum, certain other brain areas such as the

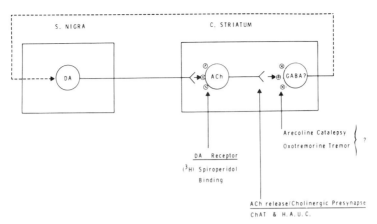

Fig. 1. *Simplified scheme of nigro-striatal pathways relevant to the present studies.* The points which the various measured parameters are thought to represent are indicated. It is likely that the function of dopaminergic nigro-striatal fibres is to exert a tonic depressant effect on a significant percentage of caudate neurons which are believed to be cholinergic interneurones. Drugs that stimulate DA receptors (eg apomorphine, piribedil, bromocriptine) inhibit cholinergic activity, decrease the release and turnover of ACh and increase its intraneuronal level. The converse applies to DA blockers (eg pimozide, haloperidol, chlorpromazine) which disinhibit the cholinergic cells. It is still uncertain whether the striato-nigral GABAergic feedback pathway is mono or polysynaptic (the GABA neurones may synapse in globus pallidus). Furthermore, there may also be descending excitatory substance-P containing neurones. DA-innervated GABA interneurones are also probably present in the striatum. It should also be noted that serotonergic projections from the brain stem raphe nuclei may modulate striatal neuronal activity as may noradrenergic projections and also glutamate-ergic projections from cortical regions. In addition, it is relevant to this chapter that cholinergic receptors exist on dopaminergic nerve terminals which control DA release

hippocampus (cholinergic parameters) and the cerebral cortex (GABAergic parameters) were also examined.

Methods

Male Sprague–Dawley rats (150–200 g body weight) were used in these studies. Following halothane anaesthesia the rats were given a single ECS (150 V, 50 Hz sinusoidal, 1 s via earclip electrodes) daily or on alternate days for 10–12 days. Control animals were anaesthetised only.

[^{3}H]-Choline uptake
Sodium-dependent uptake of choline was measured essentially as described previously (Burgess *et al.*, 1978). To calculate HAUC, total uptake values were corrected for sodium-independent, low-affinity uptake.

Choline acetyltransferase (ChAT)
Rat brain regions from ECS or control animals were rapidly dissected and frozen on a solid CO_2-cooled surface. ChAT activity was assayed as previously described in detail (Burgess *et al.*, 1978) using [^{14}C]acetyl-CoA.

Measurements of arecoline-induced catalepsy
Twenty-four or more hours after the final ECS the rats were given arecoline (15 mg kg^{-1} i.p.) and the length of time the animal remained cataleptic over a horizontal bar was measured 5 min after the injection (see Green *et al.*, 1979).

[^{3}H]-Spiroperidol binding
Striata were homogenised in 50 mM Tris-HCl buffer (pH 7.4, 0–4 °C) and extensively washed and centrifuged membrane portions were assayed for specific [^{3}H]-spiroperidol binding as described previously (Atterwill, 1980).

[³H]-Muscimol binding and GAD activity
GAD activity was estimated radiometrically by monitoring $[^{14}C]CO_2$ evolution from [1–14C]glutamate as described by Atterwill *et al.* (1981). For [³H]-muscimol binding, fresh crude synaptic membranes (CSMs) from the striatum and cerebral cortex were prepared according to Atterwill *et al.* (1981) and binding measured using a filtration assay similar to that of Williams & Risley (1979).

Results and discussion

Striatal dopamine receptor
It has previously been demonstrated that both single and repeated ECS attenuate the cataleptic response of rats to the neuroleptic, haloperidol, which is thought to act primarily by blocking the striatal DA receptors (Green *et al.*, 1979). Other ECS-induced effects, such as enhancement of the stimulant effect of apomorphine on growth hormone secretion in reserpine-pretreated rats (Eden & Modigh, 1977), suggested possible changes at or beyond central postsynaptic DA receptors or in other neuronal systems which are postsynaptic to the DA neurones (eg cholinergic interneurones in the striatum). However, investigation of the effects of repeated ECS (five times over 10 days) on striatal specific [³H]-spiroperidol binding 24 h post-ictally, showed no differences in binding at either single ligand concentrations (Fig. 2(a)) or in a Scatchard kinetic analysis (Fig. 2(b)) compared to anaesthetised control animal tissue (Atterwill, 1980). The kinetic constants for the binding data are rather higher than some reported values for striatum (see Seeman, 1980) and we may have been labelling a specific population of DA receptors.

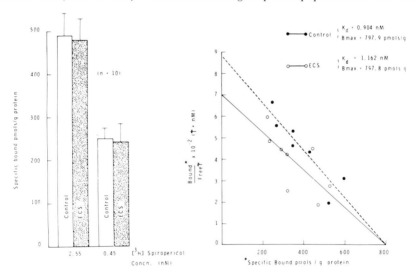

Fig. 2. *Effects of repeated ECS on rat striatal [³H]-spiroperidol binding 24 h post-ictally. (a, left) Specific binding at different spiroperidol concentrations. (b, right) Scatchard representation of data*

Studies of 'higher-affinity' receptors may yield different results. A reappraisal of some of the behavioural work does, however, support these findings. Repeated ECS not only enhanced the locomotor responses of dopamine injected directly into the nucleus accumbens but also enhanced the responses to dibutyryl cyclic AMP (Heal & Green, 1978) which appears to act 'beyond' the DA receptor. Furthermore, ECS does not alter the response of striatal adenylate cyclase to DA nor striatal cyclic AMP concentrations (Green *et al.*, 1977). With respect to the ECS-induced dopaminergic, mesolimbic changes (see above) it is interesting to note that neuroleptic-induced catalepsy may also involve these sites (Costall & Naylor, 1974) and it may thus be worthwhile examining DA receptor properties in these brain areas following ECS.

Cholinergic system

The striatal cholinergic system was examined in some detail for possible changes in those cells bearing the inhibitory DA receptors. The hippocampus, an area rich in cholinergic innervation, was examined for comparison in the choline uptake studies as were several other areas (cerebral cortex and hypothalamus) in the ChAT study. The hippocampus (and septum) is quite important in this respect because of its apparent involvement in a variety of emotional, motivational and associative processes. As well as single and repeated ECS, the effect of pentylenetetrazol (PTZ) convulsions on some of the parameters was investigated. This drug (Metrazol) has been used in certain situations for ECT (see Fink, 1979).

There were no differences between ECS and control (hippocampal or striatal) preparations in HAUC either 1 h following a single ECS or 24 h following repeated ECS (five over 10 days) (Table 2). However, halothane anaesthesia appeared to affect HAUC in both brain regions by reducing it some 20–30 per cent. This can be seen by comparing control HAUC 1 h post-halothane with control HAUC 24 h post-halothane exposure, and indicates the importance of an evaluation of anaesthetic effects in studies of ECS on cholinergic and other neurotransmitter systems.

Table 2. *Effect of ECS-induced or pentylenetetrazol (PTZ)-induced convulsions on [³H]-choline uptake by rat brain slices.* Rats were given either one ECS (150 V for 1 s) or halothane exposure (control) or PTZ (75 mg/kg i.p.), and uptake was tested 1 h or 1–2 min post-ictally respectively; or five ECS or halothane exposures (control) over 10 days, with uptake tested 24 h post-ictally. Results are expressed as mean uptake ± s.e.m. In each case, total uptake = uptake in Krebs/Tris medium plus sodium, LAUC = uptake in Krebs/Tris medium minus sodium, and HAUC = total uptake – LAUC

Experimental conditions	Brain region	Control (halothane) (pmol/min/g wet wt)		ECS or PTZ (pmol/min/g wet wt)		n	Statistical significance HAUC[a]
		LAUC	HAUC	LAUC	HAUC		
Tissue-'cooling' method A[b]							
1 × ECS (1 h)	striatum	117.5 ± 14.7	568.8 ± 42.3	117.7 ± 15.1	592.2 ± 42.0	9	n.s.
5 × ECS (24 h)	striatum	78.4 ± 2.8	720.5 ± 26.5[d]	83.8 ± 3.5	768.5 ± 42.1	9	n.s.
1 × ECS (1 h)	hippocampus	82.2 ± 6.0	83.6 ± 8.9	78.8 ± 6.2	70.7 ± 7.5	6	n.s.
5 × ECS (24 h)	hippocampus	44.2 ± 4.1	126.3 ± 12.4[d]	45.7 ± 3.8	118.7 ± 10.4	6	n.s.
1 × PTZ (2 min)	hippocampus	50.3 ± 6.1	120.5 ± 2.3[e]	46.6 ± 5.3	146.3 ± 7.5	6	P < 0.05
Tissue-'cooling' method B[c]							
5 × ECS (24 h)	striatum	102.7 ± 4.1	874.3 ± 46.8	106.3 ± 4.0	721.2 ± 64.9	11	n.s.
5 × ECS (24 h)	hippocampus	56.8 ± 2.3	156.6 ± 10.8	58.8 ± 3.8	147.5 ± 5.5	8	n.s.
1 × PTZ (2 min)	hippocampus	52.3 ± 2.1	150.8 ± 10.8[e]	47.8 ± 1.5	217.4 ± 13.3	9	P < 0.01

[a]Student's two-tailed *t*-test. [b]Glass Petri dish + 15 min preincubation. [c]Aluminium foil + 5 min preincubation. [d]Control striatal and hippocampal uptake 24 h post-halothane exposure significantly greater than control uptake 1 h post-exposure (P < 0.01, Student's two-tailed *t*-test). [e]Control hippocampal uptake cooling preincubation method (B) Significantly greater than control uptake cooling method (A) (P < 0.02, Student's two-tailed *t*-test). From Atterwill (1980).

In order to further validate the ECS study and to expand the study of convulsions on immediate HAUC changes, the effects of acute pentylenetetrazol administration on hippocampal HAUC were examined. This treatment has previously been shown to elevate HAUC in hippocampal synaptosomes (Sherman *et al.*, 1978*b*) thus further validating the use of HAUC for studying presynaptic cholinergic changes after ECS.

Groups of rats were given either saline or pentylenetetrazol (75 mg/kg i.p.) and sacrificed immediately (approximately 2 min post-ictal) following the elicited convulsions. Following brain extirpation the hippocampal tissue was either cooled on a glass Petri dish on ice prior to weighing and chopping (method A), or more efficiently cooled on aluminium foil placed on ice (method B). The preincubation time in the latter experiment (method B) was reduced from 15 to 5 min. It can be seen from the results in Table 2 that using both cooling methods, pentylenetetrazol induced significant increases in HAUC. However, using method A increases were 21 per cent, whereas in method B increases were 45 per cent. Furthermore, comparing control HAUC values by method A with method B, the improved cooling-preincubation procedure (aluminium foil — method B) gave overall 25 per cent higher HAUC values.

When HAUC was re-examined 24 h following repeated ECS in both striatum and hippocampus using method B (Table 2), apart from slightly higher rates of HAUC, there were still no

Table 3. *Effect of repeated ECS (× 10 over 10 days) on rat brain ChAT activity (24 h post-ictally.* Twelve brains per group were tested

	Specific -enzyme activity (pmols/min/mg wet wt tissue ± s.e.m.)		
Region	ECS		Control (Halothane only)
Corpus Striatum	332.5 ± 14.8	P< 0.05*	365.7 ± 21.7
Hypothalamus	40.9 ± 2.4	n.s.	39.7 ± 1.8
Hippocampus	74.3 ± 4.5	n.s.	78.6 ± 5.2
Cerebral Cortex	57.0 ± 3.4	n.s.	63.1 ± 5.3

*Significantly different from control group using two-way analysis of variance test on 2 sets of experimental data.

statistically, significant changes between ECS and control preparations. There was, however, a small (18 per cent) decrease in striatal HAUC after chronic ECS which parallels the change in striatal ChAT activity (see below).

The specific activity of the ACh synthesising enzyme, ChAT, was measured 24 h post-ictally in brain regions of rats pretreated with either 10 days ECS plus halothane or halothane alone (control); results are shown in Table 3. In this extension of the study described previously (Atterwill, 1980) it was found that repeated ECS caused a small but significant (10 per cent) reduction in rat striatal ChAT 24 h after the last ECS with no significant changes in the hypothalamus, hippocampus or cerebral cortex (Table 3). Thus, in this model repeated ECS can slightly alter presynaptic cholinergic function (as measured by ChAT) at a time after the last convulsion when dopaminergic behavioural parameters are enhanced. Perhaps an increase in striatal DA inhibitory tone leads to this small long-term reduction in cholinergic activity. Longoni *et al.* (1976; see Table 1) have demonstrated rapid post-ictal increases in cerebral cortical ChAT following both single and repeated ECS. This occurred at a time after the convulsion when cerebral ACh turnover and release are enhanced (Table 1) and no long-term changes were found to persist after repeated ECS.

The rapid post-ictally PTZ-induced increases in hippocampal HAUC are in agreement with the contention that convulsions rapidly increase central ACh turnover (Table 1) and similar findings have been reported for the striatal cholinergic system (Longoni *et al.*, 1974), where the single PTZ convulsion-induced reductions in striatal and cortical ACh were of similar magnitude.

Although cholinergic presynaptic function appears to be relatively refractory to repeated convulsions, the cholinergic receptors or connecting postsynaptic neurones do not. The cataleptogenic effect of arecoline, a central muscarinic agonist, in rats is attenuated 24 h following single and repeated ECS (see Table 4). This could perhaps be interpreted as meaning a compensatory increase in postsynaptic muscarinic receptor activity (see Fig. 1) due to a decreased presynaptic function. However, besides other transmitters being involved in the modulation of striatal cataleptic phenomena (see Green *et al.*, 1979 for discussion) brain regions other than the caudate nucleus may be involved — possibly the substantia nigra or globus

Table 4. *Effect of electroconvulsive shock (ECS) on arecoline-induced catalepsy.* Results show mean s.d. with number of observations in brackets. Significance calculated using Students *t*-test. (From Green, Bloomfield, Atterwill & Costain, 1979)

Treatment	Time after last ECS (h)	Total time of catalepsy (s)	Significance
Anaesthetic × 1	—	39 ± 21 (6)	—
ECS × 1	24	12 ± 5 (6)	P< 0.01
	48	26 ± 18 (5)	n.s.
Anaesthetic × 10	—	37 ± 12 (4)	—
ECS × 10	48	15 ± 14 (6)	P< 0.025
	120	17 ± 10 (5)	P< 0.025

pallidus (Costall & Olley, 1971). Furthermore, the receptors themselves may be unaltered and the neurones postsynaptic to the receptors may have changed in activity. It must also be considered that presynaptic muscarinic receptors are present on dopaminergic nerve terminals in the striatum (De Belleroche & Gardiner, 1982) and these could be both involved in cataleptic and other dopaminergic phenomena, and be altered by ECS. It is perhaps significant that the degree of striatally-mediated tremor induced in rats by oxotremorine (a muscarinic agonist) was not altered by repeated ECS (Atterwill & Green, unpublished observations).

Kellar *et al.* (1981) have shown that 14 days ECS produces no significant change in rat hippocampal muscarinic receptors using [^{3}H]-QNB binding. A recent and more detailed study has shown that repeated ECS given on a different time course (4 × daily for 4 days), entorhinal kindling and lesion-induced seizures caused a 20 per cent down-regulation of muscarinic receptors ([^{3}H]-QNB binding) in the rat hippocampal formation (Dashieff *et al.*, 1982). No change is seen in cholinergic presynaptic markers in the hippocampus after repeated ECS (this chapter). Phenobarbital blocked in parallel both the seizures and the receptor decline, thus causally linking the down-regulation to the seizures. It has been proposed that the intense neuronal depolarisation which accompanies the seizures is responsible for this down-regulation (and not ACh release) which represents an endogenous inhibitory response of the activated neurones (Dashieff *et al.*, 1982). It is also possible, however, to produce down-regulation of these receptors for example by chronic cholinesterase inhibition *in vivo* (Ehlert *et al.*, 1980) or with cholinergic agonists *in vitro* (Luqmani *et al.*, 1979). This does not seem to occur, however, in rat cerebral cortex where no change in cholinergic receptors seems to occur upon repeated ECS (Cross *et al.*, 1979; Kellar *et al.*, 1981). Evidently, a rigorous and detailed regional study of cholinergic receptors (both muscarinic and nicotinic) following single and repeated ECS protocols on different time courses, both with and without anaesthetic, and with parallel measurements of presynaptic markers would be extremely worthwhile.

GABA system

In the striatum GABA function may be intimately related to cholinergic function (see Fig. 1). Repeated ECS, administered alone, induces decreased GABA turnover rates and increased GABA concentrations in rat caudate nucleus and nucleus accumbens 24 h following the last convulsion (Green *et al.*, 1978). GABA concentrations in several brain regions including the striatum, rise 30 min following a single ECS or PTZ-induced convulsion (Bowdler & Green, 1982). GABA receptors in the striatum were therefore measured by [^{3}H]-muscimol binding to see whether the proposed decrease in GABA release from presynaptic terminals might lead to alterations in postsynaptic GABA receptors. GAD activity was similarly measured to see whether possible alterations in this rate-limiting enzyme might be causally related to the observed GABA metabolism change. Depolarization-induced changes in striatal GABAergic activity *in vitro* lead to increases in GAD activity in striatal GABAergic interneurones (Spehlmann *et al.*, 1977; Gold & Roth, 1979). Repeated ECS (× 10 days with anaesthetic) produced a significant 15 per cent increase in striatal GAD activity 24 h post-ictally (Table 5). This is not entirely consistent with a decreased GABA turnover following ECS without anaesthetic (Green *et al.*, 1978) which might be expected to result from a decreased enzyme activity. A more detailed comparison of the ECS effects with and without anaesthesia is thus required. A single ECS did not alter GAD activity, which contrasts with convulsants which cause GAD inhibition around the time of the convulsion by interfering with the enzyme co-factor, pyridoxal phosphate (Horton *et al.*, 1978; Loscher, 1979).

GABA receptor density was unaltered by repeated or single ECS or repeated injections of the GABA antagonist, bicuculline, in both the striatum and cerebral cortex. This was somewhat surprising as these receptors can alter their sensitivity after manipulation of the presynaptic input, as do central DA receptors (Campochiaro *et al.*, 1977; Kuriyama *et al.*, 1980; Waddington & Cross, 1978; Ferkany *et al.*, 1980). However it must again be considered that the ECS treatment was administered with halothane whereas in the previous study where striatal GABA turnover changes were observed it was not. Preliminary experiments have in fact shown

85

Table 5. *Effect of single and repeated ECS on rat brain GABA receptor and GAD activity*. Results given as mean ± s.e.m. (statistics by students two-tailed unpaired *t*-test). (Data from Atterwill, Batts & Bloomfield, 1981)

Convulsion	Test		Control
[³H]-muscimol specific binding			
(pmol g⁻¹ protein) (mean ± s.e.m.)			
ECS × 10 (24 h)* striatum	130.6 ± 7.9	(n.s.)	118.6 ± 4.1
Bicuculline × 10 (24 h)*† Cerebral cortex	154.3 ± 4.5	(n.s.)	163.9 ± 9.9
ECS × 10 (24 h)* Cerebral cortex	172.7 ± 7.9	(n.s.)	162.0 ± 8.9
GAD activity			
(μmol h⁻¹ g⁻¹ wet wt) (mean ± s.e.m.)			
ECS × 10 (24 h)* striatum	31.5 ± 1.2	(P < 0.02)	27.5 ± 0.9
ECS × 1 (2 min)*† striatum	27.2 ± 1.4	(n.s.)	28.6 ± 1.2

*Post-ictal time tested. †Convulsions elicited without halothane anaesthesia

that ECS plus anaesthetic produces no change in brain GABA concentration (Cross *et al.*, 1979; Atterwill, unpublished).

Conclusions

Since this chapter has focused on seizure-induced changes in central cholinergic mechanism I shall conclude by attempting to briefly summarise the present status of the research in this field. ACh is evidently involved in post-convulsive phenomena as shown by both experimental and clinical studies. However, the link between the cholinergic changes and neurochemical adaptions in other transmitter systems leading to the antidepressant action of ECT is still unknown.

ECS or drug-induced seizures increase ACh turnover and release, AChE activity, and ChAT activity in several brain areas including the striatum, hippocampus and cerebral cortex and these effects seem to disappear fairly quickly following a seizure. Long-term changes in cholinergic presynaptic terminals 24 h following repeated ECS appear to be absent in most areas except the striatum where the small decrease in ChAT activity may reflect an altered dopaminergic or GABA-ergic inhibitory tone in this region. However, the effects of anaesthetic administration on high-affinity choline uptake (HAUC) highlighted in the present study must be considered when evaluating such phenomena. It is tempting to speculate that the initial post-ictal changes in presynaptic cholinergic function may consolidate to produce long-term modifications of the postsynaptic receptors or neurones. For example, in the hippocampus down-regulation of postsynaptic muscarinic receptors has been reported following repeated ECS and in the nigro-striatal system the alteration of arecoline-induced catalepsy suggests a possible adaptation of cholinergic postsynaptic function. These changes in receptor function are obviously important in terms of controlling interrelated neurones, and a detailed regional study of effects of repeated ECS on both muscarinic and nicotinic receptors may prove to be fruitful.

Acknowledgements — I should like to thank Dr A. K. Prince (Department of Pharmacology, Kings College, London) for his collaboration in the ChAT assays, and Dr A. R. Green (MRC Clinical Pharmacology Unit, Oxford) with whom the catalepsy experiments were performed. My thanks also to Professor D. G. Grahame-Smith (MRC Clinical Pharmacology Unit, Oxford) who enabled this work to be carried out in his department.

References
Adams, H. E., Hoblit, P. R. & Sulker, P. D. (1969): Electroconvulsive shock, brain acetylcholinesterase activity and memory. *Physiol. Behav.* **4**, 113–116.

Atterwill, C. K. (1980): Lack of effect of repeated electroconvulsive shock (ECS) on [^{3}H]-spiroperidol and [^{3}H]-5-hydroxytryptamine binding and cholinergic parameters in rat brain.

Atterwill, C. K., Batts, C. & Bloomfield, M. R. (1981): Effect of single and repeated convulsions on glutamate decarboxylase (GAD) activity and [^{3}H]-muscimol binding in the rat brain. *J. Pharm. Pharmacol.* **33**, 329-331.

Atterwill, C. K. & Green, A. R. (1980): Responses of developing rats to L-tryptophan plus an MAOI — II: effects of repeated electroconvulsive shock. *Neuropharmacology* **19**, 337-341.

Atweh, S., Simon, J. R. & Kuhar, M. J. (1976): Utilization of sodium-dependent high affinity choline uptake *in vitro* as a measure of the activity of cholinergic neurons *in vivo*. *Life Sci.* **17**, 1535-1544.

Bowdler, J. & Green, A. R. (1981): Rat brain benzodiazepine receptor number and GABA concentration following a seizure. *Br. J. Pharmacol.* **74**, 814.

Burgess, E. J., Atterwill, C. K. & Prince, A. K. (1978): Choline acetyltransferase and the high affinity uptake of choline in corpus striatum of reserpinised rats. *J. Neurochem.* **31**, 1027-1033.

Campochiro, P., Schwarcz, R. & Coyle, J. T. (1977): GABA receptor binding in rat striatum: localization and effects of denervation. *Brain Res.* **136**, 501-511.

Costall, B. & Naylor, R. J. (1974): The importance of the ascending dopaminergic systems to the extrapyramidal and mesolimbic brain areas for the cataleptic action of the neuroleptic and cholinergic agents. *Neuropharmacology* **13**, 353-364.

Costall, B. & Olley, J. E. (1971): Cholinergic and neuroleptic-induced catalepsy: modification by lesions in the caudate-putamen. *Neuropharmacology* **10**, 297-306.

Cross, A. J., Deakin, J. F. W., Lofthouse, R., Longden, A., Owen, F. & Poulter, M. (1979): On the mechanism of action of electroconvulsive therapy: some behavioural and biochemical consequences of repeated electrically induced seizures in rats. *Br. J. Pharmacol.* **66**, 111P.

Dashieff, R. M., Savage, D. D. & McNamara, J. O. (1982): Seizures down-regulate muscarinic cholinergic receptors in hippocampal formation. *Brain Res.* **235**, 327-334.

De Belleroche, J. & Gardiner, I. M. (1982): Cholinergic action in the nucleus accumbens: modulation of dopamine and acetylcholine release. *Br. J. Pharmacol.* **75**, 359-365.

Eden, S. & Modigh, K. (1977): Effects of apomorphine and clonidine on rat plasma growth hormone after pre-treatment with reserpine and electroconvulsive shocks. *Brain Res.* **129**, 379-384.

Ehlert, F. J., Kokka, N. & Fairhurst, A. S. (1980): Altered [^{3}H]-quinuclidinyl benzilate binding in the striatum of rats following chronic cholinesterase inhibition with diiso propyl fluorophosphate. *Mol. Pharmacol.* **17**, 24-30.

Essman, W. B. (1972): Neurochemical changes in ECS and ECT. *Sem. Psychiat.* **4**, 67-79.

Essman, W. B. (1973): *Neurochemistry of cerebral electroshock.* New York: John Wiley.

Evans, P. M., Grahame-Smith, D. G., Green, A. R. & Tordoff, A. F. C. (1976): Electroconvulsive shock increases the behavioural responses of rats to brain 5-hydroxytryptamine accumulation and central nervous system stimulant drugs. *Br. J. Pharmacol.* **56**, 193-199.

Ferkany, J. W., Strong, R. & Enna, S. J. (1980): Dopamine receptor supersensitivity in the corpus striatum following chronic elevation of brain γ-aminobutyric acid. *J. Neurochem.* **34**, 247-249.

Fink, M. (1966): Cholinergic aspects of convulsive therapy. *J. Nervous Ment. Dis.* **142**, 475-484.

Fink, M. (1974): Induced seizures and human behaviour. In *Psychobiology of convulsive therapy*, ed M. Fink, S. Kety, J. McGaugh & T. Williams. Pp. 1-17. Washington D.C.: V. H. Winston and Sons.

Fink, M. (1979): Convulsive therapy: theory and practice. New York: Raven Press.

Gold, B. I. & Roth, H. (1979): Glutamate Decarbyxylase activity in striatal slices: characterization of the increase following depolarization. *J. Neurochem.* **32**, 883-888.

Green, A. R., Heal, D. J. & Grahame-Smith, D. G. (1977): Further observations on the effect of repeated electro-convulsive shock on the behavioural responses of rats produced by increases in the functional activity of brain 5-hydroxytryptamine and dopamine. *Psychopharmacology* **52**, 195-200.

Green, A. R., Peralta, E., Hong, J. S., Mao, C. C., Atterwill, C. K. & Costa, E. (1978): Alterations in GABA metabolism and met-enkephalin content in rat brain following repeated electroconvulsive shocks. *J. Neurochem.* **31**, 607-611.

Green, A. R., Bloomfield, M. R., Atterwill, C. K. & Costain, D. W. (1979): Electroconvulsive shock reduces the cataleptogenic effect of both haloperidol and arecoline in rats. *Neuropharmacology* **18**, 447-451.

Heal, D. J. & Green, A. R. (1978): Repeated electroconvulsive shock increases the behavioural responses of rats to in-jection of both dopamine and dibutyryl cyclic AMP into the nucleus accumbens. *Neuropharmacology* **17**, 1085-1087.

Holmstedt, B., Harkonen, M., Lundgren, J. & Sundvall, A. (1966): Relationship between acetylcholine content and cholinesterase activity in the brain following an organophosphorus inhibitor. *Biochem. Pharmacol.* **16**, 404-406.

Horton, R. W., Chapman, A. G. & Meldrum, B. S. (1978): Regional changes in cerebral GABA concentration and convulsions produced by D and by L-allylglycine. *J. Neurochem.* **30**, 1501-1504.

Jope, R. S. (1979): Effects of lithium treatment *in vitro* and *in vivo* on acetylcholine metabolism in rat brain. *J. Neurochem.* **33**, 487-495.

Karczmar, A. G. (1974): Brain acetylcholine and seizures. In *Psychobiology of convulsive therapy* ed G. Fink, S. Kety, J. McGaugh & T. Williams. Washington D.C.: V. H. Winston and Sons.

Karczmar, A. G., Scudder, C. L. & Richardson, D. (1973): Interdisciplinary approach to the study of behaviour in related mice-types. In *Neurosciences Research*, Vol. 5, ed I. Kopin. Pp. 159-244. New York: Academic Press.

Kellar, K. J., Cascio, C. S., Bergstrom, D. A., Butler, J. A. & Iadarola, P. (1981): Electroconvulsive shock and reserpine: effects on β-adrenergic receptors in rat brain. *J. Neurochem.* **37**, 830-836.

Kuriyama, K., Kurihara, E., Yoshihisa, I. & Yoneda, Y. (1980): Increase in striatal [^{3}H]-muscinol binding following intrastriatal injection of kainic acid: a denervation supersensitivity phenomenon. *J. Neurochem.* **35**, 343-348.

Kurokawa, M., Machiyama, Y. & Kato, M. (1963): Distribution of acetylcholine in the brain during various states of activity. *J. Neurochem.* **10**, 341-348.

Ladinsky, H., Consolo, S., Bianchi, S., Ghezzi, D. & Samamin, R. (1979): Link between dopaminergic and cholinergic neurons in the striatum as evidenced by pharmacological, biochemical, and lesion studies. In *Interactions between putative neurotransmitters in the brain*, ed S. Garattini, J. F. Pujol & R. Samamin. New York: Raven Press.

Longoni, R., Mulas, A., Oderfeld, B., Pepeu, I. M. & Pepeu, G. (1976): Effect of single and repeated electroshock applications on brain acetylcholine levels and choline acetyltransferase activity in the rat. *Neuropharmacology* **15**, 283-286.

Longoni, R., Mulas, A. & Pepeu, G. (1974): Drug effect on acetylcholine in discrete brain regions of rats killed by microwave irradiation. *Br. J. Pharmac.* **52**, 429-430.

Loscher, W. (1979): 3-Merceptopropionic acid: convulsant properties, effects on enzymes of the γ-aminobutyrate system in mouse brain and antagonism by certain anticonvulsant drugs, aminoxyacetic acid and GABAculine. *Biochem. Pharmacol.* **28**, 1397-1407.

Luqmani, Y. A., Bradford, H. F., Birdsall, N. J. M. & Hulme, E. C. (1979): Depolarization-induced changes in muscarinic cholinergic receptors in synaptosomes. *Nature* **277**, 481-483.

Modigh, K. (1975): Electroconvulsive shock and postsynaptic catecholamine effects: Increased psychomotor stimulant action of apomorphine and clonidine in reserpine pretreated mice by repeated ECS. *J. Neural Transm.* **36**, 19-32.

Pryor, G. T. (1974): Effect of repeated ECS on brain weight and enzymes. In *Psychobiology of convulsive therapy*, ed G. Fink, S. Kety, J. McGaugh & T. William. Pp. 171-184. Washington D.C.: V. H. Winston and Sons.

Richter, D. & Crossland, J. (1949): Variation in acetylcholine content of the brain with physiological state. *J. Physiol.* **159**, 247-255.

Seeman, P. (1980): Brain dopamine receptors. *Pharmacol. Rev.* **32**, 229.

Sherman, K. A., Hanin, I. & Zigmond, M. J. (1978a). The effect of neuroleptics on acetylcholine concentration and choline uptake in striatum: Implications for regulation of acetylcholine metabolism. *J. Pharmacol. Exp. Ther.* **206**, 677-686.

Sherman, K. A., Zigmond, M. J. & Hanin, I. (1978b): High affinity choline uptake in striatum and hippocampus: Differential effects of treatments which release acetylcholine. *Life Sci.* **23**, 1863-1870.

Spehlmann, R., Norcross, K. & Grimmer, E. J. (1977): GABA in the caudate nucleus: a possible synaptic transmitter of interneurones. *Experientia* **33**, 623-624.

Stadler, H., Lloyd, K. G., Gadia-Ciria, H. & Bartholini, G. (1973): Enhanced striatal acetylcholine release by chlorpromazine and its reversal by apomorphine. *Brain Res.* **55**, 476-480.

Takahashi, R., Nasu, T., Tamura, T. & Koriya, T. (1961): Relationship of ammonia and acetylcholine levels to brain excitability. *J. Neurochem.* **7**, 103-112.

Waddington, J. L. & Cross, A. J. (1978): Denervation supersensitivity in the striatonigral GABA pathway.

Williams, M. & Risley, E. A. (1979): Characterization of the binding of [^{3}H]-muscimol, a potent γ-aminobutyric acid agonist, to rat brain synaptosomal membranes using a filtration assay. *J. Neurochem.* **32**, 713-718.

10.
The role of endorphin systems in the effects of ECS

G. L. BELENKY, F. C. TORTELLA, R. J. HITZEMANN and J. W. HOLADAY

Department of Medical Neurosciences, Division of Neuropsychiatry, Walter Reed Army Institute of Research, Washington, D.C.; Department of Pharmacology, Temple University School of Medicine, Philadelphia, Pennsylvania (FCT); Department of Pharmacology, University of Cincinatti School of Medicine, Cincinatti, Ohio, USA (RJH).

Introduction

Electroconvulsive therapy (ECT), a technique which uses electroconvulsive shock (ECS) to induce a generalized seizure, is effective in treating severe depression, mania and some cases of schizophrenia (Salzman, 1978). In the treatment of depression, ECT is more effective and its therapeutic effects are more rapid in onset than is the case with the tricyclic antidepressants. From clinical studies, it appears that ECT works by inducing a generalized seizures. For the antidepressant effect to occur, this generalized seizure must be repeated four to six times over a period of several days. The locus of the antidepressant effect appears to be in the diencephalon since the presence of neurovegetative symptoms and signs such as insomnia, anorexia, and weight loss predicts a good therapeutic response to ECT (Salzman, 1978) and the antidepressant effect itself is positively correlated with the duration of the diencephalic component of the seizure (Ottoson, 1962). The mechanism by which this diencephalic seizure exerts its antidepressant effect is unknown.

Several years ago, we became interested in the possibility that endorphin systems (endorphins here defined as endogenous opiates) were involved in the antidepressant effects of ECT, and decided initially to approach this hypothesis by studying the behavioral and physiological effects of ECS in rats to determine if in fact they had an endorphin component.

Endorphin involvement in the acute behavioral and physiological effects of a single ECS

With the exception of the studies evaluating the electroencephalographic effects of ECS (described below), in all our studies reviewed in this chapter, we used anaesthetized male Sprague–Dawley rats and transauricular ECS with current parameters of 150 V, 60 Hz, for 2 s. Our studies began with our finding an opioid-like catalepsy in rats following a single ECS (see Fig. 1). We observed that the post-ECS catalepsy began immediately following the end of the tonic–clonic seizures and lasted 5–10 min. This catalepsy was indistinguishable from β-endorphin- or morphine-induced catalepsy as it was characterized by a loss of righting reflex and an inability to cling to a wire grid (Holaday *et al.*, 1978; Holaday & Belenky, 1980; Segal *et al.*, 1977). In these respects, the characteristic catalepsy induced by β-endorphin, morphine, and ECS differs from the catalepsy seen following neuroleptic administration (Segal *et al.*, 1977).

Since the post-ECS catalepsy appeared opioid-like, we next investigated if pretreatment with the opioid antagonist naloxone would alter its intensity or duration. Post-ECS, we measured catalepsy by assessing the duration of the absence of the righting reflex and, once the righting reflex returned, we measured the latency to step down from a horizontal bar. Combining these measurements into an integrated score, we found that naloxone pretreatment (10 mg/kg i.p.)

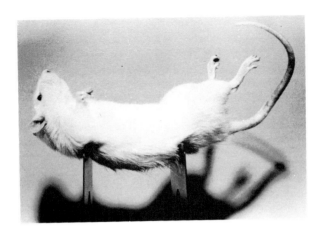

Fig. 1. *Following cessation of tonic–clonic seizures produced by ECS, rats became cataleptic with loss of righting reflexes*. The post-ictal loss of righting reflexes persisted for 3–5 min and resembled β-endorphine and morphine induced catalepsy

significantly attenuated the post-ECS catalepsy (Holaday *et al.*, 1978). In contrast, naloxone pretreatment had no effect on seizure intensity or duration (Holaday *et al.*, 1978; Holaday & Belenky, 1980). The finding of an ECS-induced naloxone-reversible opioid-like catalepsy suggested, to us, that ECS produced a functional release of endorphins.

In subsequent studies, we observed that ECS produced an opioid-like naloxone-reversible increase in tail-flick and hot-plate escape latencies (Holaday *et al.*, 1978; Holaday & Belenky, 1980). We initially measured tail-flick latencies for 30 min following ECS. Tail-flick latencies were elevated above sham-shock control values for a maximum of 25 min following ECS. The ECS-induced increase in tail-flick latency was attenuated by naloxone preinjection (10 mg/kg i.p.) (see Fig. 2), indicating endorphin involvement. In subsequent studies, this naloxone-reversibility was difficult to replicate. This could be a result of the direct antinociceptive effects of naloxone on the tail-flick response (Holaday & Belenky, 1980), or could indicate that nonopioid systems were also important components of the post-ECS elevation in tail-flick latencies (Lewis *et al.*, 1980). An alternative explanation is that the opioid-like effects of ECS are predominantly manifested at higher levels of neural integration. The tail-flick response is primarily a spinal reflex; higher levels of the central nervous system provide only modulating inhibitory influences. Either way, the tail-flick response may not be the best method by which to evaluate the opioid-like antinociceptive effects of ECS.

Recent work (Amir & Amit, 1978) suggested to us that a more appropriate nociceptive response in which to study endorphin involvement in the antinociceptive effects of ECS might be the hot-plate response. These investigators observed that restraint stress produced a naloxone-reversible increase in hot-plate escape latencies without affecting the more reflexive paw-lick latency. Therefore we extended our experiments to include measurements of hot-plate responses, and we observed that ECS reliably increased hot-plate escape latencies. The antinociceptive effects as measured by this procedure were of significantly longer duration than the post-ECS increases in tail-flick latency we had previously observed (Holaday *et al.*, 1978; Holaday & Belenky, 1980). Moreover, these post-ECS increases in hot-plate escape latency were significantly and reliably attenuated by both 3 mg/kg and 10 mg/kg i.p. naloxone preinjection (see Figs 3 and 4), again suggesting endorphin involvement in ECS-induced post-ictal phenomena (Holaday & Belenky, 1980). These observations provided further support for our hypothesis that ECS results in a functional activation of endorphin systems. Also, the robustness of our findings of ECS-induced naloxone-reversible antinociception when using the more highly integrated hot-plate escape response (as opposed to the more spinally-mediated

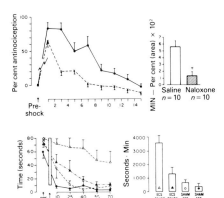

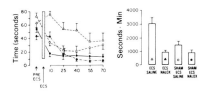

Fig. 2. *Tail-flick latencies (expressed as per cent antinociception) are elevated post-ECS in saline i.p. pretreated control rats (solid line), these elevations are attenuated when the rats are pretreated with the 10 mg/kg i.p. of the opioid antagonist naloxone (dashed line).* Area scores obtained by integrating the area under the time-response curves for each animal are depicted at right. Vertical bars represent s.e.m.

Fig. 3. *The effects of ECS or sham ECS in rats pretreated with 3.0 mg/kg naloxone or saline i.p. on hot-plate escape latencies.* ECS elevates hot-plate escape latencies, naloxone pretreatment attenuates this increase. Area scores are depicted at right. Vertical bars represent s.e.m.

Fig. 4. *The effect of ECS or sham ECS in rats pretreated with 10 mg/kg naloxone or saline i.p. on hot-plate escape latencies.* ECS elevates hot-plate escape latencies and naloxone attenuates this increase. Area scores are depicted at right. Vertical bars represent s.e.m.

tail-flick response) suggested that the apparent ECS-induced endorphin release may involve a component which is mediated at higher levels of the central nervous system.

In our initial studies, we noticed that respiratory rates were significantly lower post-ECS. As opiates and endorphins both depress respiration, we wondered if this could represent an endorphin-mediated respiratory depression. Since cardioregulatory centers lie close to respiratory centers within the brain stem, and injected opiates and endorphins can affect heart rate and blood pressure, we were also interested in evaluating the potential opiate-like effects of ECS upon cardiovascular variables. In conducting these studies, we used rats in which indwelling tail artery cannulae had been implanted 24 h earlier. These cannulae allowed continuous monitoring of heart rate and blood pressure in awake, freely moving rats. Post-ECS, control rats maintained normal respiratory rates, whereas naloxone-pretreated rats (1.0 or 10.0 mg/kg i.p.) had significantly higher respiratory rates for up to 15 min post-seizure (see Fig. 5) (Belenky & Holaday, 1979). These data provided further evidence for endorphin release during ECS, and also provided the first evidence of a role for the endorphins in the regulation of respiration.

Our results with respect to blood pressure and heart rate were more complex. Associated with the tonic–clonic seizure produced by ECS was a 250 per cent increase in mean arterial pressure which was unaffected by naloxone pretreatment (Belenky & Holaday, 1979). In the saline-pretreated rats, mean arterial pressure returned to normal within 20 s post-ECS and remained normal thereafter. By contrast, in rats pretreated with naloxone (3 and 10 mg/kg i.p.), there was an exaggerated hypotension and bradycardia following the ECS-induced hypertensive surge. This baroreceptor reflex overshoot was most evident 25–40 s post-ECS (see Fig. 6) (Belenky & Holaday, 1979). These cardiovascular data may indicate that the enormous increases in arterial pressure following ECS activates endorphin systems which then facilitate a return of cardiovascular function to homeostatic levels. When the rat is deprived of the endorphin component of baroreceptor responses by naloxone pretreatment, an overcompensation in heart rate and arterial pressure results. Our initial results have been reinforced by subsequent studies which have confirmed increased baroreceptor sensitivity in the presence of naloxone (Freye & Arndt, 1979; Petty & Reid, 1980).

Recent electroencephalographic (EEG) studies (Tortella *et al.*, 1978, 1981) have shown that intracerebroventricular (icv) injections of β-endorphin and other opioids result in an initial

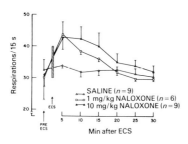

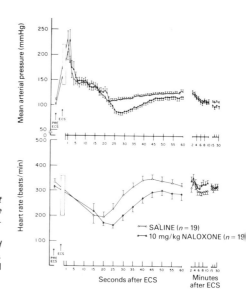

Fig. 5. (above). *The effects of ECS on respiratory rates of rat pretreated with 1.0 mg/kg naloxone (□), 10 mg/kg naloxone (▲), or saline i.p. (△). Naloxone pretreatment elevated respiratory rates post-ECS. Vertical bars represent s.e.m.*

Fig. 6 (right). *The effects of ECS on mean arterial pressure and heart rate in rats after 10 mg/kg naloxone (▲) or saline i.p. (△). The data indicate an exaggerated reflex hypotension and bradycardia. Vertical bars represent s.e.m.*

epileptiform activity followed by the onset of slow-wave cortical hypersynchrony (see Fig. 7). We wondered whether the EEG following ECS might show a similar EEG pattern. Following the electrically induced seizure, we observed a period of post-ictal depression characterized by high voltage cortical synchrony similar to that seen following icv β-endorphin (see Fig. 8, and compare with Fig. 7) (Tortella *et al.*, 1981). We further observed that the post-ECS cortical EEG hypersynchrony and increased voltage could be attenuated in a dose-dependent manner by intraperitoneal doses of naloxone ranging between 0.3–10.0 mg/kg. These data provided evidence that the post-ECS EEG slowing and hypersynchrony are mediated by an ECS-induced activation of endorphin systems (Tortella *et al.*, 1981). The time course of the post-ictal EEG slowing and hypersynchrony was similar to that of the post-ictal behavioral catalepsy, and the duration of EEG hypersynchrony and catalepsy were similarly attenuated by naloxone pretreatment (Tortella *et al.*, 1981). An important observation was that the duration of these acute EEG and cataleptic responses was enhanced by repeated ECS. However, after repeated ECS, naloxone pretreatment failed to significantly attenuate these effects (Tortella *et al.*, 1981).

Taken together, the above findings further strengthened our hypothesis that ECS produces a functional release of endorphins. More specifically, the activation of endogenous opiate responses by ECS appears to play a major role in those phenomena of post-ictal depression which are mediated by higher levels of the neuraxis. This was evidenced by the occurrence of

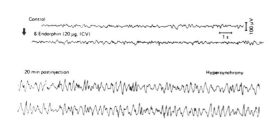

Fig. 7. *Control and β-endorphin-induced patterns of EEG activity.* Note high amplitude slow wave activity at 20 min post-injection

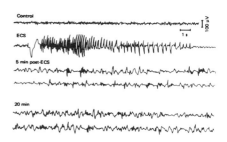

Fig. 8. *Control and ECS-induced EEG changes in the rat.* Note high amplitude slow wave activity at 20 min post-ECS

naloxone-reversible post-ECS catalepsy, analgesia, respiratory depression, and EEG slowing and hypersynchrony. In a similar manner, others workers have found that naloxone reverses the behavioral depression following seizures in amygdaloid-kindled rats (Frenk *et al.*, 1979). This seizure-induced endorphin release and consequent naloxone-reversible post-ictal depression may function to inhibit further seizures (Tortella *et al.*, 1981), a possibility which is supported by the findings of an anticonvulsant effect of certain opioid peptides (Tortella *et al.*, 1980).

Endorphin involvement in the behavioral and physiological effects of repeated ECS

Having established, to our satisfaction, an endorphin involvement in the acute effects of a single ECT, and bearing in mind that the therapeutic efficacy of ECT in humans requires several treatments usually spaced over several days, we turned our attention to repeated ECS. Specifically, we hypothesized that repeated ECS, by virtue of its repeated release of endorphins would induce a state of opioid tolerance. Conversely, we anticipated that the opioid-like effects of a single ECS would be attenuated in an animal made tolerant to morphine. We found exactly the opposite results.

In the repeated ECS study (Belenky & Holaday, 1981), we gave two groups of rats transauricular ECS or sham-ECS daily for nine consecutive days. Repeated ECS alone resulted in decreased body weight gain as well as elevated colonic temperatures which persisted for at least one day following the last ECS. Twenty-four hours after the last of the nine ECS or sham-ECS treatments, the rats were challenged with either 4 or 16 mg/kg of morphine sulfate. Instead of tolerance as we had expected, we found that the repeated ECS rats were more sensitive to the morphine challenge as indicated by their being more cataleptic and having longer tail-flick latencies when compared to the sham-ECS controls (see Fig. 9). Thus, repeated ECS sensitized rats to those opiate behaviors produced by challenging doses of morphine.

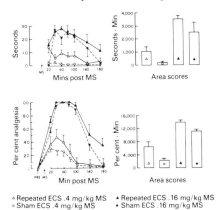

Fig. 9. *Repeated ECS study: group means over time pre- and post-morphine sulfate (4 or 16 mg/kg i.p.) and group mean area scores post-morphine sulfate for catalepsy (above) and tail-flick latency (below) for both ECS and sham ECS rats on the day after the last ECS or sham ECS.* Vertical bars represent s.e.m.

△ Repeated ECS .4 mg/kg MS   ▲ Repeated ECS .16 mg/kg MS
○ Sham ECS .4 mg/kg MS   ● Sham ECS .16 mg/kg MS

In the complementary study involving chronic morphine administration (Belenky & Holaday, 1981), two groups of rats were implanted for two consecutive days with two 75 mg morphine or placebo pellets. On the third day, the morphine pellet-implanted group was tolerant to the effects of morphine released by the pellets as indicated by their identical values for tail-flick latencies, hot-plate escape latencies, and respiratory rates when compared to the placebo pellet-implanted rats. Similar to our observations with the repeated ECS rats, the morphine tolerant rats were hyperthermic and had decreased body weight gain when compared to the placebo pellet-implanted rats. Following these premeasures, both morphine pellet- and placebo pellet- implanted rats were given a single transauricular ECS. We found that the chronically morphinized rats were significantly more sensitive to the opioid-like effects of ECS. Following ECS, the morphine pellet-implanted rats were more cataleptic, had higher tail-flick latencies, had lower respiratory rates, and were more hyperthermic than the placebo pellet-implanted rats (see Fig. 10). Thus chronic morphine administration sensitized rats to the opioid-like effects of a single ECS.

In summary, nine days of repeated daily ECS sensitized opiate naive rats to the acute effects of a single morphine injection and, conversely, the induction of morphine tolerance by morphine pellet implantation sensitized ECS naive rats to the acute opioid-like effects of a single ECS. This cross-sensitization suggested to us that the effects of repeated ECS and the effects of chronic morphine administration shared a common neurobiologic mechanism which may be unrelated to opiate tolerance phenomena *per se* (Belenky & Holaday, 1981).

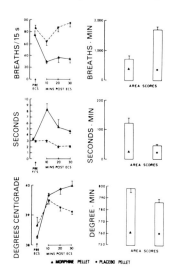

Fig. 10. *Morphine tolerance study: group means over time pre- and post-ECS and post-ECS group mean area scores for respiration (top panel), tail-flick latency (middle) and colonic temperature (below) for both morphine sulfate pellet (75 mg) and placebo pellet implanted rats 24 h after the second pellet implantation.* Vertical bars represent s.e.m.

The effect of repeated ECS and chronic morphine upon opioid receptors in brain

These findings of behavioral and physiological sensitivity following cross-challenge between repeated ECS and chronic morphine treatment indicated that the effect of these two treatments shared a common neurobiological mechanism (Belenky & Holaday, 1981). In order to determine if these two treatments produced functional alterations at the opioid receptor level that might serve to explain the cross-sensitivity we observed, we evaluated the effect of repeated ECS and chronic morphine administration on brain opioid receptor binding and affinity (Holaday *et al.*, 1983).

To analyze the effects of repeated ECS and chronic morphine administration on the opioid receptors in rat brain, binding studies were performed using tritiated D-ala2, D-leu5-enkephalin ([³H]-DADLE) as the ligand. Scatchard analysis of binding data was evaluated by varying concentrations of added [³H]-DADLE for individual rat brain synaptosomal membranes which allowed for comparison of relative affinities and numbers of opioid receptors across groups of rats. Five groups of six rats each received repeated ECS, repeated sham ECS, a single ECS, chronic morphine, or chronic placebo treatment. The repeated ECS group received trans-auricular ECS daily for nine days, the sham ECS group were handled in the same manner but received no current, the single ECS group received a single ECS, the chronic morphine group was implanted with two morphine pellets (75 mg each) and two days later implanted with four morphine pellets (75 mg each), and the chronic placebo group was implanted with placebo pellets on the same schedule as the morphine-pellet group.

On the day following the last ECS or pellet implantation, the rats were decapitated and their brains removed. Synaptosomes from the whole brains (minus cerebella) were prepared for the binding studies. Assays were conducted blind. The brains from each group were separately analyzed with 10–12 concentrations of [³H]-DADLE for each brain to obtain the Scatchard analysis data summarized in Table 1. This study demonstrated that repeated daily ECS for nine days produces a 31.3 per cent increase in the number of [³H]-DADLE binding sites as determined from brains removed the day following the last ECS. Likewise, chronic morphine administration produced a 17.4 per cent increase in the apparent number of binding sites for this opioid ligand. As the standard errors and the statistical probability figures in Table 1 indicate, these findings were highly significant. In fact, all six individual values for the repeated ECS and chronic morphine rats were above their respective control values. In contrast, a single ECS failed to alter the number of binding sites. Also, opioid receptor affinities were unaffected by repeated ECS, single ECS, or chronic morphine administration.

Our findings could represent an absolute increase in the number of opioid receptor-binding sites. Alternatively, as [³H]-DADLE is primarily a delta opioid receptor agonist, our data could indicate a shift from one or more of the other receptor subtypes to the delta subtype without an absolute increase in total opioid receptor number. Either way, these findings suggested that the common neurobiological mechanism underlying our prior findings of cross-sensitization may be a functional increase in available opioid receptors with which endogenously released or exogenously administered opioids could interact. Especially strong support came from the similarity in the timing of the cross-sensitivity and opioid receptor increase which were observed. We found both phenomena 24 h after the last ECS or pellet implantation.

In addition, our findings by virtue of their robustness, their presence at some interval after the last ECS, and their being associated with repeated but not single ECS were consistent with the working hypothesis that increases in opioid receptor number may be associated with the antidepressant effects of ECT in depressed humans. Other work (Green et al., 1978; Hong et al., 1979) indicates that repeated but not single ECS in rats raises met-enkephalin levels in the striatum and nucleus accumbens. These findings also support the possibility that endorphin-ergic systems may be involved in the neurobiological changes wrought by repeated ECS. As our results were for the whole brain, we are currently pursuing studies to determine the specific neuroanatomical localization within the brain of the changes that we observed. We are also pursuing similar studies using ligands specific for other opioid receptor subtypes. A strong correlation between pharmacological and biochemical effects following repeated ECS as well as their association with specific receptor subpopulations at precise neuroanatomical sites previously shown to undergo a repeated ECS-induced increase in met-enkephalin levels would provide additional strong support for our hypothesis that endorphinergic changes at the transmitter–receptor level may underlie the antidepressant effects of ECT.

Table 1. *Effects of repeated ECS, repeated sham ECS, single ECS, chronic morphine, and placebo treatments upon binding affinities (K_D) and receptor number (B_{max}) using the delta opioid receptor ligand [³H]-DADLE. Values are expressed as ± s.e.m.*

	Repeated ECS	Repeated sham-ECS	Single ECS	Chronic morphine	Chronic placebo
K_D (nM)	3.99 ± 0.63	3.29 ± 0.10	3.50 ± 0.22	3.38 ± 0.27	3.14 ± 0.18
B_{max} (fmol/mg)	231 ± 10*	176 ± 3	175 ± 8	196 ± 4*	167 ± 3

*Compared to controls, $P < 0.001$

Conclusions

Electroconvulsive therapy (ECT) is a dramatically effective treatment for human depression. Its mechanism of action remains unknown, although clinical studies indicate that ECT is effective by virtue of inducing a generalized seizure and that this seizure must be repeated 4–6 times for the antidepressant effect to occur. Workers in the field have long held that some central neuro-biological change associated with the induction of repeated generalized seizures underlies the antidepressant effect of ECT (Fink, 1974). To date, no such neurobiological change has been definitively associated with the antidepressant effects of ECT.

We have investigated the possibility that changes in endorphin systems might be involved in the mechanisms which mediate this neurobiological change. For any such change to be considered as mechanistically relevant to ECT in humans, it would have to be associated with repeated ECS. While bearing this in mind, we initially sought to demonstrate that endorphins were in fact released acutely during ECS. Through an indirect behavioral approach, using rats as an experimental model to test for endorphinergic involvement, we demonstrated that the post-ictal depression following ECS was attenuated by naloxone pretreatment. Specifically, we found that naloxone pretreatment attenuated the catalepsy, antinociception, respiratory depression, and EEG slowing and hypersynchrony produced by a single ECS treatment. This apparent endorphin mediation of post-ictal events led us to conclude that ECS induced a functional release of endorphins.

Turning our attention to repeated ECS, we then sought to determine if the repeated release of endorphins by daily ECS would have other functional consequences. We had expected that repeated ECS, by virtue of inducing repeated release of endorphins, would produce a tolerance to morphine challenge. Instead we found exactly the opposite results. Repeated ECS sensitized rats to the effects of morphine and, conversely, chronic morphine administration enhanced the opioid-like post-ictal events following a single ECS. In the light of these results, we suggested that repeated ECS and the chronic administration of morphine produced similar neuro-biological changes.

To investigate this possibility at the receptor level we compared Scatchard plots on individual brains in rats subjected to repeated ECS, single ECS, and chronic morphine administration, with the appropriate sham and placebo controls. As evidenced above, we found statistically significant increases in opiate receptor numbers in rats given repeated ECS or chronic morphine. A single ECS was without effect, and relative receptor affinities across groups were also unaffected. These findings may account for our observations of behavioral and physiological cross-sensitization between the two treatments. As the increase in receptor number is associated with repeated rather than a single ECS, and is statistically significant, we propose that alterations in endorphin release and receptor numbers may play an important role in the neurobiological changes underlying the antidepressant effects of ECT in man.

In conducting the research described in this report, the investigators adhered to the 'Guide for laboratory animal facilities and care', as promulgated by the Committee of the Guide for Laboratory Animal Resources, National Academy of Sciences, National Research Council.

References

Amir, S. & Amit, Z. (1978): Endogenous opioid ligands may mediate stress-induced changes in the affective properties of pain-related behavior in rats. *Life Sci.* **23**, 1143–1152.

Belenky, G. L. & Holaday, J. W. (1979): The opiate antagonist naloxone modifies the effects of electroconvulsive shock (ECS) on respiration, blood pressure and heart rate. *Brain Res.* **177**, 414–417.

Belenky, G. L. & Holaday, J. W. (1981): Repeated electroconvulsive shock (ECS) and morphine tolerance: demonstration of cross-sensitivity in the rat. *Life Sci.* **29**, 553–563.

Fink, M. (1974): Induced seizures and human behavior. In *Psychobiology of convulsive therapy*, ed M. Fink *et al.*. Pp. 1–19. Winston-Wiley.

Frenk, H., Engel, J., Ackermann, R. F., Shavit, Y. & Liebeskind, J. C. (1979): Endogenous opioids may mediate post-ictal behavioral depression in amygdaloid kindled rats. *Brain Res.* **167**, 435–440.

Freye, E. & Arndt, J. O. (1979): Perfusion of the fourth cerebral ventricle with fentanyl induces naloxone-reversible bradycardia, hypotension, and EEG synchronization in conscious dogs. *Arch. Pharmacol.* **307**, 123–128.

Green, A. R., Peralta, E., Hong, J. S., Mao, C. C., Atterwill, C. K. & Costa, E. (1978): Alterations in GABA metabolism and met-enkephalin content in rat brain following repeated electroconvulsive shocks. *J. Neurochem.* **31**, 607–611.

Holaday, J. W. & Belenky, G. L. (1980): Opiate-like effects of electroconvulsive shock in rats: a differential effect of naloxone on nociceptive measures. *Life Sci.* **27**, 1929–1938.

Holaday, J. W., Belenky, G. L., Loh, H. H. & Meyerhoff, J. L. (1978): Evidence for endorphin release during electroconvulsive shock. *Soc. Neurosci. Abstr.* **4**, 409.

Holaday, J. W., Hitzemann, J., Curell, J., Tortella, F. C. & Belenky, G. L. (1982): Repeated electroconvulsive shock or chronic morphine treatment increases the number of [^{3}H]-D-Ala2, D-Leu5-enkephalin binding sites in rat brain membranes. *Life Sci.* **31**, 2359–2362.

Hong, J. S., Gillin, J. C., Yang, H.-Y.T. & Costa, E. (1979): Repeated electroconvulsive shocks and the brain content of endorphins. *Brain Res.* **177**, 273–278.

Lewis, J. W., Cannon, J. T. & Liebeskind, J. C. (1980): Opioid and nonopioid mechanisms of stress analgesia. *Science* **208**, 623–625.

Ottosson, J.-O. (1962): Lidocaine modification of seizures in electroconvulsive therapy. *J. Nerv. Ment. Dis.* **135**, 239–251.

Petty, M. A. & Reid, J. L. (1981): Opiate analogs, substance P, and baroreceptor reflexes in the rabbit. *Hypertension* **3**, I142–I147.

Salzman, C. (1978): Electroconvulsive therapy. In *Harvard guide to modern psychiatry*, ed A. M. Nicholl. Pp. 471–479. Harvard: Harvard University Press.

Segal, D. S., Browne, R. G., Bloom, F., Ling, N. & Guillemin, R. (1977): Beta-endorphin: endogenous opiate or neuroleptic? *Science* **198**, 411–414.

Tortella, F. C., Cowan, A. & Adler, M. W. (1980): Comparison among opioid peptides using flurothyl seizures in rats. *Pharmacologist* **22**, 233.

Tortella, F. C., Cowan, A., Belenky, G. L. & Holaday, J. W. (1981): Opiate-like electroencephalographic and behavioral effects of electroconvulsive shock in rats. *Eur. J. Pharmacol.* **76**, 121–128.

Tortella, F. C., Moreton, J. E. & Khazan, N. (1978): Electroencephalographic and behavioral effects of D-ala2-methione-enkephalinamide and morphine in the rat. *J. Pharmac. Exp. Ther.* **206**, 636–642.

11.
Effect of ECT on endorphinergic systems: clinical aspects

H. M. EMRICH and V. HÖLLT

Max-Planck-Institut für Psychiatrie, Kraepelinstr. 10, D-8000 München 40, West Germany.

Introduction

In the search for significant progress in pharmacopsychiatric research one is invariably confronted with the highly pertinent question of what is the specific mode of action of drugs or other somatic treatments in clinical psychiatry. Neuroleptic drugs apparently exert their antipsychotic effect via a blockade of dopamine receptors. Compelling support for such an hypothesis is acquired by the systematic clinical investigation of the therapeutic activity of structurally modified analogues of such psychotropic agents and by the demonstration of a positive correlation between dopamine receptor blockade and clinical efficacy (Seeman *et al.*, 1975). On the other hand, in the case of thymoleptic drugs, one is far removed from an explanation of their specific mode of action. Nevertheless, in the case of thymoleptics, systematic research is possible due to the fact that the efficacy of various congeners of these drugs may systematically be examined. In the case of ECT, as with lithium (Emrich, 1982*a*), such an approach is currently not feasible; there exists no substitute for lithium and no mode of treatment comparable to ECT. Moreover, both therapies induce a *diversity* of effects on neurochemical systems so that it is necessary to establish which of these manifold effects is responsible for their therapeutic efficacy. As discussed recently, in the case of lithium (see Emrich, 1982*a*), the question of the specific mode of action of drugs may be clinically addressed by an analysis of their clinical spectrum of action and by a comparison with the effects of other types of therapies.

Regarding the mode of action of ECT a number of different mechanisms have been suggested, ranging from psychological mechanisms to the effects on the molecular biology of the brain (Fink, 1979; Palmer, 1981). The impact of ECT on the operation of brain monoamines is the focus of neurobiological research as to the clinical mode of action of ECT. According to these findings, ECT increases the response to brain monoamines (Grahame-Smith *et al.*, 1978), is effective via a noradrenergic mechanism of action in potentiating serotonin- and dopamine-mediated behaviors (Green & Deakin, 1980) and induces a down-regulation of β-adrenergic receptors (Pandey *et al.*, 1979). These findings may explain some of the antidepressant and anticatatonic effects of ECT. On the other hand, as reviewed by Fink (1979), the neuro-hormonal effects of ECT also demand consideration. Neuropeptides especially, may play an important role in the mediation of the beneficial effects of ECT.

Clinical profile of action of ECT and the effects of opioids in psychiatric patients

According to the results of controlled studies (cf. Fink, 1979; Palmer, 1981; Salzman, 1980), the therapeutic effect of ECT is much more pronounced in primary depression than in schizo-phrenia. However, in catatonia, ECT may be the therapy of choice and even in mania ECT is therapeutically efficacious, a finding which must be understood by taking into account the uni/bi-dimensionality problem of affective disorders (Emrich, 1982*a*).

A comparison of the profile of action of ECT with the observation of the effects of opioids in psychiatric patients reveals that, at least, a component of the clinical effects of ECT is analogous to those of these compounds. As summarized by Emrich (1981; 1982*b*), β-endorphin exerts only a marginal or very questionable antipsychotic effect (Berger *et al.*, 1980; Kline *et al.*, 1977; Pickar *et al.*, 1981) whereas its antidepressant properties are well characterized (Gerner *et al.*, 1980). In line with these findings are the observations of Emrich *et al.* (1982) that the partial opioid agonist buprenorphine exerts antidepressant effects in thymoleptic nonresponders. Regarding the possible therapeutic effect of β-endorphin or other opioids in catatonia and mania, no controlled investigation has, as yet, been performed. So, up to now, no valid statements can be made regarding this aspect of the clinical profile of action. However, in catatonic states, a very pronounced effect of the opiate antagonist naloxone has been reported (Schenk *et al.*, 1978). As discussed recently by Emrich (1982*c*), due to the very short half-life of naloxone, some of its actions may be due more to a counterbalancing-activation of endorphin-ergic systems, as recently shown by Reker *et al.*, (1983), than to opioid blockade. A similar explanation may hold true for the antipsychotic effects of naloxone in schizophrenic patients (Emrich *et al.*, 1977; 1979*b*; Pickar *et al.*, 1982; Watson *et al.*, 1978).

From the present state of knowledge one has to conclude that some components of the clinical mode of action of ECT exhibit similarities to that of opioids, but much critical information is still missing.

Influence of ECT on plasma β-endorphin immunoreactivity

Owing to the parallelism in the secretion of β-endorphin and ACTH (Guillemin *et al.*, 1977) and the finding that ECT induces an elevation of plasma ACTH (Allen *et al.*, 1974), an activating effect of ECT on plasma β-endorphin immunoreactivity may be anticipated. In line with this, Emrich *et al.* (1979*a*) observed an elevation of β-endorphin immunoreactivity in the plasma of patients suffering from endogenous depression 10 min subsequent to ECT. The determinations were performed by the use of a radioimmunoassay exhibiting a detection limit for β-endorphin of 35 pg/ml (Höllt *et al.*, 1978). Ten minutes after ECT β-endorphin immuno-reactivity increased from about 40 to more than 60 pg/ml. These findings have recently been confirmed by Inturrisi *et al.* (1982) who found a rise of plasma β-endorphin immunoreactivity from about 30 to 80–90 pg/ml. These findings are also in line with the animal work of Holaday and co-workers (this volume; 1981), pointing to an ECT-induced activation of central endorphinergic systems.

Emrich and co-workers (1979*a*) hypothesized that (at least some part of) the therapeutic action of ECT may be mediated via an endorphinergic type of mechanism. Evidence obtained from a comparison of the clinical profiles of ECT and of opioids is, at present, not sufficiently comprehensive to be really convincing. In this context, it should be pointed out that ACTH is, apparently, not the relevant therapeutic factor, since, as summarized by Fink (1979), it has no real antidepressant activity.

Conclusions

The hypothesis that ECT may, at least partially, be therapeutically effective via an endorphin-ergic mode of action, is based on (i) the similarities between the clinical profiles of action of ECT and of opioids and (ii) on the finding that ECT induces an increase in plasma levels of β-endorphin immunoreactivity in depressed patients. This is further supported by findings that electroconvulsion activates central opioids in animals. This hypothesis implies the possibility that at least some part of the beneficial effects of ECT could be mimicked chemically by the use of opioid substances. Attempts based on this supposition have been recently performed by the administration of buprenorphine to depressed patients. From the clinical profiles discussed above, it appears reasonable to also examine the possible effects of opioids in mania and in catatonia. An investigation of putative inhibition of the beneficial effects of ECT in depressed patients by the administration of opiate antagonists (eg naloxone), may be of heuristic value although ethically equivocal. A possible relationship between the endorphin hypothesis and the monoamine hypothesis of ECT action has to be considered.

Acknowledgement—This work was supported by a grant (Heisenberg-Programm) of the Deutsche Forschungsgemeinschaft to H.M.E.

References

Allen, M. J. P., Denney, D., Kendall, J. W. & Blachy, P. H. (1974): Corticoprotein release during ECT in man. *Am. J. Psychiat.* **131**, 1225-1228.

Berger, P. A., Watson, S. J., Huda, A., Elliott, G. R., Rubin, R. T., Pfefferbaum, A., Davis, K. L., Barchas, J. D. & Li, C. H. (1980): β-Endorphin and schizophrenia. *Arch. Gen. Psychiat.* **37**, 635-640.

Emrich, H. M. (ed) (1981): *The Role of endorphins in neuropsychiatry*, Mod. Probl. Pharmakopsychiat., Vol. 17. Basel: Karger.

Emrich, H. M. (1982a): Prophylactic therapies in affective disorders: Mode of action from a clinical point of view. In *Basic mechanisms in the action of lithium*, ed H. M. Emrich, J. B. Aldenhoff & H. D. Lux. Pp. 202-214. Amsterdam: Excerpta Medica.

Emrich, H. M. (1982b): Possible role of opioids in mental disorders: present state of knowledge. In *Psychoneuroendocrine dysfunction in psychiatric and neurological illnesses: influence of psychopharmacological agents*, ed N. S. Shah & A. G. Donald. New York: Plenum Press.

Emrich, H. M. (1982c): A possible role of endorphinergic systems in schizophrenia. In *Psychobiology of schizophrenia*, ed M. Namba & H. Kaiya. Pp. 291-297. Oxford: Pergamon Press.

Emrich, H. M., Cording, C., Pirée, S., Kölling, A., v. Zerssen, D. & Herz, A. (1977): Indication of an antipsychotic action of the opiate antagonist naloxone. *Pharmakopsychiat.* **10**, 265-270.

Emrich, H. M., Höllt, V., Kissling, W., Fischler, M., Laspe, H., Heinemann, H., v. Zerssen, D. & Herz, A. (1979a): β-Endorphin-like immunoreactivity in cerebrospinal fluid and plasma of patients with schizophrenia and other neuropsychiatric disorders. *Pharmakopsychiat.* **12**, 269-276.

Emrich, H. M., Möller, H.-J., Laspe, H., Meisel-Kosik, I., Dwinger, H., Oechsner, R., Kissling, W. & v. Zerssen, D. (1979b): On a possible role of endorphins in psychiatric disorders—Actions of naloxone in psychiatric patients. In *Biological psychiatry today*, ed J. Obiols, C. Ballús, E. González Monclús and J. Pujol. Pp. 798-805. Amsterdam: Elsevier/North-Holland Biomedical Press.

Emrich, H. M., Vogt, P., Kissling, W. & Herz, A. (1982): Possible antidepressive effects of opioids. Action of buprenorphine. *Ann. N. Y. Acad. Sci.* **398**, 108-112.

Fink, M. (1979). *Convulsive Therapy*. New York: Raven Press.

Gerner, R. H., Catlin, D. H., Gorelick, D. A., Hui, K. K. & Li, C. H. (1980): β-Endorphin. *Arch. Gen. Psychiat.* **37**, 642-647.

Grahame-Smith, D. G., Green, A. R. & Costain, D. W. (1978): Mechanism of the antidepressant action of electroconvulsive therapy. *Lancet* **1**, 254-256.

Green, A. R. & Deakin, J. F. W. (1980): Brain noradrenaline depletion prevents ECS-induced enhancement of serotonine- and dopamine-mediated behaviour. *Nature* **285**, 232-233.

Guillemin, R., Vargo, T., Rossier, J., Minick, S., Ling, N., Rivier, C., Vale, M. & Bloom, F. (1977): β-Endorphin and adrenocorticotropin are secreted concomitantly by the pituitary gland. *Science* **197**, 1367-1369.

Höllt, V., Przewlocki, R. & Herz, A. (1978): Radioimmunoassay of β-endorphin. Basal and stimulated levels in extracted rat plasma. *Naunyn-Schmiedeberg's Arch. Pharmacol.* **303**, 171-174.

Holaday, J. W., Tortella, F. C. & Belenky, G. L. (1981): Electroconvulsive shock results in a functional activation of endorphin systems. In *The role of endorphins in neuropsychiatry*, ed H. M. Emrich. Pp. 142-157. Basel: Karger.

Inturrisi, C. E., Alexopoulos, G., Lipman, R., Foley, K. & Rossier, J. (1982): β-Endorphin immunoreactivity in the plasma of psychiatric patients receiving electroconvulsive treatment. *Ann. N. Y. Acad. Sci.* **398**, 413-423.

Kline, N. S., Li, C. H., Lehmann, H. E., Lajtha, A., Laski, E. & Cooper, T. (1977): β-Endorphin-induced changes in schizophrenic and depressed patients. *Arch. Gen. Psychiat.* **34**, 1111-1113.

Palmer, R. L. (ed.) (1981): *Electroconvulsive therapy: an appraisal.* Oxford: Oxford University Press.

Pandey, G. N., Heinze, W. J., Brown, B. D. & Davis, J. M. (1979): Electroconvulsive shock treatment decreases β-adrenergic receptor sensitivity in rat brain. *Nature* **280**, 234-235.

Pickar, D., Davis, G. C., Schulz, C., Extein, I., Wagner, R., Naber, D., Gold, P. W., van Kammen, D. P., Goodwin, F. K., Wyatt, R. J., Li, C. H. & Bunney, W. E., Jr. (1981): Behavioral and biological effects of acute β-endorphin injection in schizophrenic and depressed patients. *Am. J. Psychiat.* **138**, 160-166.

Pickar, D., Vartanian, F., Bunney, W. E. Jr., Maier, H. P., Gastpar, M. T., Prakash, R., Sethi, B. B., Lideman, R., Belyaev, B. S., Tsutsulkovskaja, M. V. A., Jungkunz, G., Nedopil, N., Verhoeven, W. & van Praag, H. (1982): Short-term naloxone administration in schizophrenic and manic patients. *Arch. Gen. Psychiat.* **39**, 313-319.

Reker, D., Anderson, B., Yackulic, C., Cooper, T. B., Banay-Schwartz, M., Leon, C. & Volavka, J. (1983): Naloxone, tardive dyskinesia and endogenous beta-endorphin. *Psychiat. Res.* (in press).

Salzman, C. (1980): The use of ECT in the treatment of schizophrenia. *Am. J. Psychiat.* **137**, 1032-1041.

Schenk, G. K., Enders, P., Engelmeier, M.-P., Ewert, T., Herdemerten, S., Köhler, K.-H., Lodemann, E., Matz, D. & Pach, J. (1978): Application of the morphine antagonist naloxone in psychic disorders. *Arzneim.-Forsch./Drug Res.* **28**(II), 1274-1277.

Seeman, P., Chan-Wong, M., Tedesco, I. & Wong, K. (1975): Brain receptors for antipsychotic drugs and dopamine: direct binding assay. *Proc. Natl. Acad. Sci. USA* **72**, 4376-4380.

Watson, S. J., Berger, P. A., Akil, H., Mills, M. J. & Barchas, J. D. (1978): Effects of naloxone on schizophrenia: reduction in hallucinations in a subpopulation of subjects. *Science* **201**, 73-76.

12.
Mechanism of action of ECT: neuroendocrine studies

S. A. CHECKLEY, B. S. MELDRUM and J. R. McWILLIAM

Maudsley Hospital and Institute of Psychiatry, Denmark Hill, London SE5, England.

Introduction

Arguably neuroendocrine tests provide the best measures of central neuroreceptor status in man. For this reason they occupy a central role in clinical tests of the hypothesis that the antidepressant effect of ECT involves an increased responsiveness to the stimulation of monoamine receptors (Grahame-Smith *et al.*, 1978). In this chapter a brief account will be given of several neuroendocrine measures of α-adrenoceptor and dopamine receptor function and the effects upon these measures of electroconvulsive shock (ECS) in animals and electroconvulsive treatment (ECT) in patients.

Neuroendocrine markers of neuroreceptor function

Neuroendocrine measures of α-adrenoceptor function

In a wide variety of animal species the release of growth hormone (GH) is stimulated by drugs which stimulate α-adrenoceptors and inhibited by drugs which block α-adrenoceptors (Checkley, 1980). In general α_2-noradrenergic agonists and antagonists have greater effects upon GH release than do drugs which act at α_1-adrenoceptors, and in rats there is evidence that whereas α_2-noradrenergic agonists stimulate the release of GH, α_1 agonists have the opposite effect (Krulich *et al.*, 1982).

The GH response to the α_2-noradrenergic agonist clonidine has been investigated as a convenient measure of α_2-adrenoceptor function. Both in rhesus monkeys and baboons clonidine provokes the release of GH in a dose-dependent manner (Chambers & Brown, 1976; McWilliam & Meldrum, unpublished). In baboons this dose–response curve is parallel to that produced by a more selective α_2 agonist UK 14 304. The GH response to clonidine is blocked by the α_2 antagonists yohimbine and piperoxane but not by the α_1 antagonist prazosin (McWilliam & Meldrum, unpublished). For these and other reasons (Lovinger *et al.*, 1976; Gold *et al.*, 1978) the GH response to clonidine is likely to involve the stimulation of α_2-adrenoceptors.

Such receptors are likely to be within the forebrain. A pituitary site is most unlikely as noradrenaline does not release GH from isolated pituitaries (McLeod, 1969; Birge *et al.*, 1970). Another peripheral site is also unlikely as division of the cervical spinal cord leaves the GH response to clonidine unchanged even though the hypotensive effects of clonidine are abolished (Ganong *et al.*, 1978). A forebrain site of action is suggested by the finding that the GH response to clonidine is abolished by the administration of phenoxybenzamine into the third ventricle; administration into the fourth ventricle blocks the hypotensive effect of clonidine but not the GH response (Lovinger *et al.*, 1976). Similar conclusions can be drawn from experiments in which the circle of Willis is divided so that the territories of the cerebral and vertebral arteries do not communicate. Under these circumstances the GH response to clonidine is only produced by injection of clonidine into the cerebral artery, just as the hypotensive effect of clonidine is produced only by injecting clonidine into the vertebral artery (Rudolph *et al.*, 1980).

For the following reasons it is likely that these forebrain α_2-adrenoceptors have a postsynaptic rather than presynaptic location. In rats the GH response to clonidine resists depletion of presynaptic noradrenaline stores with reserpine (Eden & Modigh, 1977). Similar findings have been obtained in baboons in which a more complete depletion of noradrenaline stores was produced by the combined administration of reserpine with α-methyl-P-tyrosine (McWilliam & Meldrum, unpublished).

Thus there is good evidence for a centrally mediated excitatory α_2-adrenoceptor control over GH release which is activated by clonidine. The finding that the GH response to clonidine is not inhibited by somatostatin antibodies (Eden et al., 1981) suggests that the α_2-adrenoceptor influence upon GH release is mediated through growth hormone releasing factor and not through the inhibitory hypothalamic factor, somatostatin.

Neuroendocrine measures of dopamine-receptor function
In man the release of GH is stimulated by a wide variety of dopamine agonists including apomorphine (Lal et al., 1973), bromocryptine (Camanni et al., 1975), CV 154 (Dammacco et al., 1976), lergotrile (Thorner et al., 1978) and lisuride (Delitala et al., 1979). The GH response to apomorphine must depend upon the stimulation of dopamine receptors as it is inhibited by the dopamine-blocking drugs chlorpromazine (Lal et al., 1973), pimozide (Lal et al., 1977), clozapine (Nair et al., 1979) and haloperidol (Rotrosen et al., 1979) but not by drugs with other actions such as methysergide (Lal et al., 1979) and cyproheptadine (Rotrosen et al., 1979). Similarly the GH responses to CV 154 and lergotrile are inhibited by dopamine-blocking drugs (Dammacco et al., 1976; Thorner et al., 1978).

Although there is clear evidence for an excitatory dopaminergic control of GH release in man, such evidence is not found in some experimental animals. It is particularly surprising that apomorphine does not stimulate the release of GH in conscious rhesus monkeys (Chambers & Brown, 1976) and baboons (McWilliam et al., unpublished). For this reason it is not possible to investigate in animals the pharmacology of the dopamine receptors which regulate GH release. It has been suggested that at least some of the receptors must be outside the blood brain barrier as infusions of dopamine (which does not cross the blood brain barrier) stimulate the release of GH (Leebaw et al., 1978; Burrow et al., 1977; Langer et al., 1978). These findings are, however, disputed (Verde et al., 1976; Camanni et al., 1977).

Neuroendocrine studies of the effects of ECS upon neuroreceptor function in rodents
In reserpinized mice the neuroreceptor control of GH release is slightly different from that in man. In both species clonidine releases GH, but in reserpinized mice apomorphine and 5-HTP fail to release GH when given alone although each drug enhances the GH response to clonidine (Eden & Modigh, 1977; Balldin et al., 1980).

In rats an enhancement is seen in the hyperactivity produced by the combined administration of clonidine and apomorphine 24 h after a course of 7 daily ECS (Modigh, 1975). The GH response to the combined administration of the two drugs is also enhanced at each of three different doses of clonidine (Eden & Modigh, 1977; Balldin et al., 1980). However, the GH response to clonidine alone in reserpinized rats is not altered by ECS (Balldin et al., 1980) possibly because clonidine alone is a weak stimulus to the release of GH. GH response to the combined administration to reserpinized mice of clonidine, 5-HTP and a decarboxylase inhibitor is inhibited 24 h after a course of ECS (Balldin et al., 1980). This finding cannot be interpreted until this highly complex pharmacoendocrine test has been studied under other conditions. However it does demonstrate that at least one neuroendocrine response is inhibited by ECS and this is in contrast to the psychopharmacological models of postsynaptic monoamine function which almost universally are enhanced following ECS.

In rats with normal monoamine stores the release of GH is episodic and related to stress. Under these conditions the resting GH secretion is increased following a course of ECS (Steiner et al., 1982). The GH response to clonidine was not augmented by ECS in these animals although the changes in baseline hormone secretion complicated the interpretation of these findings. In the same study, Steiner & Grahame-Smith (1980a) have shown that a course of ECS enhances the corticosteroid responses to oxotremorine, 5-HTP and (after pretreatment with α-methyl-P-tyrosine), clonidine. The pharmacology of these neuroendocrine systems has been described (Steiner & Grahame-Smith, 1980b) but will not be discussed here as it is different from the neuroendocrine regulation of ACTH release in man, and hence, is not clinically relevant. However, it is clinically relevant to note that there are three neuroendocrine responses which are enhanced following a course of treatment with ECS.

Thus in some, but not all, of the pharmacoendocrine systems which have been investigated in rodents, ECS enhances the neuroendocrine responses to the stimulation of monoamine receptors. This complements the larger psychopharmacological literature which has shown that ECS enhances the behavioural responses to the stimulation of monoamine receptors. The particular interest of the neuroendocrine models is that many of them can be directly tested in patients.

Neuroendocrine studies of the mechanism of action of ECT in patients

The first clinical neuroendocrine study of the mechanism of action of ECT measured GH responses to clonidine in patients with endogenous depression, before and 24 h after a course of seven ECT (Slade & Checkley, 1980). Consistently impaired responses to clonidine were found in the depressed patients. ECT had no effect upon the GH response or the hypotensive and sedative effects of clonidine.

In the same clinical study the GH response to methylamphetamine in 12 patients was unaltered 24 h after a course of six ECT (Slade & Checkley, 1980). At this time the cortisol response to methylamphetamine was significantly enhanced. However, most of the patients had recovered by this time and recovery alone is accompanied by an increase in the cortisol response to methylamphetamine (Checkley & Crammer, 1977). Thus it is not proven that ECT directly affects any of the neuroendocrine or other measures made in this study. Nor did ECT enhance the effects of methylamphetamine upon mood (Checkley, 1979) as might have been expected from reports that ECS enhances the hypersensitivity due to methylamphetamine (Green *et al.*, 1977).

Similarly, two other groups have failed to find an enhancement of the GH response to apomorphine following a course of ECT. Christie *et al.* (1982) studied 12 drug-free depressives of whom 11 had depressive delusions. This group had a particularly high incidence of raised baseline GH concentrations both before and after ECT which invalidated some of the data. However, both the valid data and the pooled data showed no effect of ECT upon the GH response to apomorphine. Similarly Balldin *et al.* (1982) reported that the GH response to apomorphine was unaltered in 13 drug-free depressives and in seven patients with Parkinson's disease following a course of ECT. Balldin *et al.*'s (1982) study reported a significant enhancement of the prolactin response to apomorphine in the Parkinsonian patients and in the group as a whole. However, this finding was not replicated in Christie's (1982) study. The unconfirmed report of an enhanced prolactin response to apomorphine is particularly surprising as it is a pituitary response.

At present it would appear that whereas neuroendocrine responses can be enhanced in animals by ECS, ECT has no such effect in patients. Furthermore in rats ECS raises basal GH secretion (Steiner *et al.*, 1982) but this does not happen in patients. One possible explanation for these differing effects of ECS in animals and of ECT in patients is the use in patients but not in animals of a general anaesthetic with premedication and muscle relaxant. Several studies have suggested that the behavioural (Cowen *et al.*, 1981) and neuroendocrine (Steiner & Grahame-Smith, 1980a) effect of ECS are modified by the concomitant general anaesthetic. The following studies in baboons were planned to investigate the neuroendocrine effect of ECS under conditions which closely matched those used clinically and in which the same anaesthetic drugs were used.

Neuroendocrine studies of the mechanism of action of ECS in baboons

In the first study four baboons were given a course of seven ECS using the same electrical stimulus received by the patients. Like the patients the baboons received a methohexitone anaesthetic with atropine premedication and suxamethonium as muscle relaxant. Prior to receiving ECS the baboons were intubated and oxygenated as are patients receiving ECT. Under these conditions the GH response to clonidine was significantly enhanced two weeks after a course of seven ECS. However, 24 h after the course of ECS no significant change was detected (McWilliam *et al.*, 1981) possibly because of a delayed effect of the anaesthetic drugs.

To test this possibility baboons were given a course of seven seizures induced by photic stimulation. No anaesthetic drugs of any kind were given and no electrical current was used. Both the test and the control animals received DL-allylglycine, a GABA synthesis inhibitor to lower seizure threshold. The DL-allylglycine alone did not influence the GH response to clonidine. However the photically-induced convulsions did in fact have such an effect; 24 h hours after a course of seven photically-induced convulsions the GH response to clonidine was significantly enhanced. This effect had become attenuated two weeks later. Thus when seizures are induced without the use of a general anaesthetic (or electrical stimulation) an immediate enhancement of the GH response to clonidine is found. These findings suggest that the anaesthetic which is given with ECT delays the neuroendocrine effect of ECT which may only be apparent at 1–2 weeks after the course of ECT.

In this same study a selective β_2-antagonist (ICI 118, 551) stimulated the release of GH. This effect was reduced one and seven days after a course of seven ECS, given under the conditions used clinically (McWilliam *et al.*, 1981). This is the second report of a neuroendocrine system which is inhibited by a course of ECS: it complements the animal findings that ECS reduces the number of β-adrenoceptor-binding sites in rat brain (Bergstrom & Kellar, 1979; Pandey *et al.*, 1979; Deakin *et al.*, 1981; Kellar *et al.*, 1981).

Conclusions

Neuroendocrine tests provide markers of α-adrenoceptor and dopamine receptor function both in patients and experimental animals. In experimental animals ECS enhances the following neuroendocrine responses.
(i)   GH response to clonidine and apomorphine in reserpinized mice (Eden & Modigh, 1977; Balldin *et al.*, 1980).
(ii) GH response to clonidine in baboons (McWilliam *et al.*, 1981, 1982).
(iii) Corticosteroid responses to oxotremorine to 5-HTP and (after α-methyl-*P*-tyrosine pretreatment) to clonidine (Steiner & Grahame-Smith, 1980*a*).
     ECS inhibits
(i)   the GH response to the combined administration of clonidine and 5-HTP in reserpinized mice (Balldin *et al.*, 1980).
(ii) The GH response to a selective β_2-antagonist (McWilliam *et al.*, 1981).
Equivocal effects of ECS upon the GH response to clonidine have been found in reserpinized mice (Balldin *et al.*, 1980) and in rats (Steiner *et al.*, 1982).
     In clinical studies ECT has had no significant effect upon
(i)   the GH response to clonidine (Slade & Checkley, 1980)
(ii) the sedative and hypotensive effects of clonidine (Slade & Checkley, 1982)
(iii) the GH response to methylamphetamine (Slade & Checkley, 1980)
(iv) the euphoric and stimulant effects of methylamphetamine (Slade & Checkley, 1980)
(v)   the GH response to apomorphine (Christie *et al.*, 1982; Balldin *et al.*, 1982).
     Only the prolactin response to apomorphine has been reported to be enhanced by ECT (Balldin *et al.*, 1982) and this finding is disputed (Christie *et al.*, 1982).
     Many of these negative clinical findings may be due to the delayed effects of the anaesthetic given with ECT. In the light of the animal studies which have led to this conclusion further clinical studies should be undertaken at 1–2 weeks after a course of ECT when effects of the anaesthetic have ceased.

References

Balldin, J., Bolle, P., Eden, S. *et al.* (1980): Effects of electroconvulsive treatment on growth hormone secretion induced by monoamine receptor agonists in reserpine-pretreated rats. *Psychoneuroendocrinol.* **5**, 329-337.

Balldin, J., Granerus, A. K., Lindstedt, G., Modigh, K. & Walinder, J. (1982): Neuroendocrine evidence for increased responsiveness of dopamine receptors in humans following electroconvulsive therapy. *Psychopharmacology* **76**, 371-376.

Bergstrom, D. A. & Kellar, D. J. (1979): Effect of electroconvulsive shock in monoaminergic receptor binding sites in rat brain. *Nature* **278**, 464-466.

Birge, C. A., Jacobs, L. S., Hammer, C. T. *et al.* (1970): Catecholamine inhibition of prolactin secretion by isolated rat hypophyses. *Endocrinology* **86**, 120-130.

Burrow, G. N., May, P. B., Spaulding, S. W. *et al.* (1977): TRH and dopamine interactions affecting pituitary hormone secretion. *J. Clin. Endocrinol. Metab.* **45**, 65-72.

Camanni, F., Massara, F., Belforte, L. *et al.* (1975): Changes in plasma growth hormone levels in normal and acromegalic subjects following administration of bromoergotryptine. *J. Clin. Endocrinol. Metab.* **40**, 363-366.

Camanni, F., Massara, F., Belforte, L. *et al.* (1977): Effect of dopamine on growth hormone and prolactin levels in normal and acromegalic subjects. *J. Clin. Endocrinol. Metab.* **44**, 465-473.

Chambers, J. W. & Brown, G. M. (1976): Neurotransmitter regulation of growth hormone and ACTH in the rhesus monkey: effects of biogenic amines. *Endocrinology* **98**, 420-428.

Checkley, S. A. & Crammer, J. C. (1977): Hormone responses to methyl-amphetamine in depressive illness: a new approach to the noradrenaline depletion hypothesis. *Br. J. Psychiat.* **131**, 582-586.

Checkley, S. A. (1979): A new distinction between the antidepressant and the euphoric effects of methylamphetamine. *Br. J. Psychiat.* **133**, 416-423.

Checkley, S. A. (1980): Neuroendocrine tests of monoamine function: a review of basic theory and its application to the study of depressive illness. *Psychol. Med.* **10**, 35-53.

Christie, J. E., Whalley, L. J., Brown, N. S. *et al.* (1982): Effect of ECT on the neuroendocrine response to apomorphine in severely depressed patients. *Br. J. Psychiat.* **140**, 268-273.

Cowen, P. J., Nutt, D. J. & Green, A. R. (1981): Enhanced 5-hydroxytryptamine and dopamine mediated behavioural responses following convulsions. II. The effect of anaesthesia and current conditions on the appearance of enhanced responses following electroconvulsive shock. *Neuropharmacol.* **19**, 901-906.

Dammacco, F., Regillo, N. & Tafaro, E. (1976): Effects of bromoergocryptine and pimozide and growth hormone secretion in man. *Horm. Metab. Res.* **8**, 247-248.

Deakin, J. F. W., Owen, F., Cross, A. J. *et al.* (1981): Studies on possible mechanisms of action of electroconvulsive therapy: effects of repeated electroconvulsive shocks on rat brain receptors monoamines and other neuro-transmitters. *Psychopharmacology* **73**, 345-349.

Delitala, G., Wass, J. A. H., Stubbs, W. A. *et al.* (1979): The effect of lisuride maleate, an ergot derivative, on anterior pituitary hormone secretion in man. *Clin. Endocrinol.* **2**, 1-9.

Eden, S. & Modigh, K. (1977): Effects of apomorphine and clonidine on rat plasma growth hormone after pretreatment with reserpine and electroconvulsive shock. *Brain. Res.* **129**, 379-384.

Eden, S., Eriksson, E., Martin, J. B. *et al.* (1981): Evidence for a growth hormone releasing factor mediating alpha-adrenergic influence on growth hormone secretion in the rat. *Neuroendocrinol.* **33**, 24-27.

Ganong, W. F., Wise, B. L., Reid, I. A. *et al.* (1978): Effect of spinal cord transection in the endocrine and blood pressure responses to intravenous clonidine. *Neuroendocrinol.* **25**, 105-110.

Gold, M. S., Donabedian, R. K. & Redmond, J. R. (1978): Clonidine-induced increase in serum growth hormone: possible role of epinephrine-mediated synapses. *Psychoneuroendocrinol.* **3**, 187-194.

Grahame-Smith, D. G., Green, A. R. & Costain, D. W. (1978): Mechanism of the antidepressant action of ECT. *Lancet* **1**, 254-256.

Green, A. R., Heal, D. J. & Grahame-Smith, D. G. (1977): Further observations on the effect of repeated electroconvulsive shock on the behavioural responses in rats produced by increases in the functional activity of brain 5-hydroxytryptamine. *Psychopharmacology* **52**, 195-200.

Kellar, D. J., Cascio, C. S., Bergstrom, D. A. *et al.* (1981): Electroconvulsive shock and reserpine: effects on β-adrenoceptors in rat brain. *J. Neurochem.* **37**, 830-836.

Kruhlich, L., Mayfield, M. A., Steele, M. K. *et al.* (1982): Differential effects of pharmacological manipulations of central α_1- and α_2-adrenergic receptors on the selection of thyrotrophin and growth hormone secretions in male rats. *Endocrinology* **110**, 796-804.

Lal, S., de la Vega, C. E., Sourkes, T. L. *et al.* (1973): Effect of apomorphine on growth hormone, prolactin, luteinizing hormone and follicle stimulating hormone levels in human serum. *J. Clin. Endocrinol. Metab.* **37**, 719-724.

Lal, S., Guyda, H. & Bikadoroff, S. (1977): Effect of methysergide and pimozide on apomorphine induced growth hormone release in man. *J. Clin. Endocrinol. Metab.* **44**, 766.

Langer, G., Sachar, E. J. & Halpern, F. (1978): Effect of dopamine and neuroleptics on plasma growth hormone and prolactin in normal men. *Psychoneuroendocrinol.* **3**, 165-169.

Leebaw, W. F., Lee, L. A. & Woolf, P. D. (1978): Dopamine affects basal and augmented pituitary hormone secretion. *J. Clin. Endocrinol. Metab.* **47**, 480-487.

Lovinger, R., Holland, J., Kaplan, S. *et al.* (1976): Pharmacological evidence for stimulation of growth hormone secretion by a central noradrenergic system in the dog. *Neuroscience* **1**, 443-450.

Macleod, R. M. (1969): Influence of norepinephrine and catecholamine depleting agents on the synthesis and release of prolactin and growth hormone. *Endocrinology* **85**, 916–923.

McWilliam, J. R., Meldrum, B. S. & Checkley, S. A. (1981): Enhanced growth hormone response to clonidine after repeated electroconvulsive shock in a primate species. *Psychoneuroendocrinol.* **6**, 77–79.

McWilliam, J. R., Meldrum, B. S. & Checkley, S. A. (1982): Changes in noradrenergic neuroendocrine responses following repeated seizures and the mechanism of action of ECT. *Psychopharmacol.* **77**, 53–57.

Modigh, K. (1975): Electroconvulsive shock and post-synaptic catecholamine effects: increased psychomotor stimulant action of apomorphine and clonidine in reserpine pretreated mice by repeated ECS. *J. Neural. Transm.* **36**, 19–32.

Nair, N. P. V., Lals, S., Cervantes, P. *et al.* (1979): Effect of clozapine on apomorphine-induced growth hormone secretion and serum prolactin concentrations in schizophrenia. *Neuropsychobiology* **5**, 136–142.

Pandey, G. N., Heinze, W. J., Brown, B. D. *et al.* (1979): Electroconvulsive shock treatment decreases β adrenoceptor sensitivity in rat brain. *Nature* **280**, 234–235.

Rotrosen, J., Angrist, B., Gershon, S. *et al.* (1979): Neuroendocrine effects of apomorphine: characterization of response patterns and application to schizophrenia research. *Brit. J. Psychiat.* **135**, 444–456.

Rudolph, C., Kaplan, S. L. & Ganong, W. F. (1980): Sites at which clonidine acts to affect blood pressure and the secretion of renin, growth hormone and ACTH. *Neuroendocrinology* **31**, 121.

Slade, A. P. & Checkley, S. A. (1980): A neuroendocrine study of the mechanism of action of ECT. *Br. J. Psychiat.* **137**, 217–221.

Steiner, J. A. & Grahame-Smith, D. G. (1980a): The effect of repeated electroconvulsive shock on corticosterone responses to centrally acting pharmacological stimuli in the male rat. *Psychopharmacol.* **71**, 205–212.

Steiner, J. A. & Grahame-Smith, D. G. (1980b). Central pharmacological control of corticostee secretion in the intact rat. Demonstration of cholinergic and serotonergic facilitatory and α adrenergic inhibitory mechanisms. *Psychopharmacol.* **71**, 213–217.

Steiner, J. A., Evans, G. & Grahame-Smith, D. G. (1982): The effect of repeated electroconvulsive shocks on growth hormone secretion and growth hormone responses to clonidine in the intact rat. *Psychopharmacol.* **76**, 98–100.

Thorner, M. O., Ryan, S. M., Wass, J. A. H. *et al.* (1978): Effect of dopamine agonist lergotrile mesylate on circulating anterior pituitary hormones in man. *J. Clin. Endocrinol. Metab.* **47**, 372–378.

Verde, G., Oppizzi, G., Colussi, G. *et al.* (1976): Effect of dopamine infusion on plasma levels of growth hormone in normal subjects and in acromegalic patients. *Clin. Endocrinol.* **5**, 419–423.

13.
Neuroendocrine markers in the practice of ECT

A. A. ALBALA, R. F. HASKETT and J. F. GREDEN

Department of Psychiatry, University of Michigan, Ann Arbor, Michigan 48109, USA.

Introduction

Neuroendocrine laboratory markers are relatively recent additions to clinical psychiatry. Their development stemmed from the observation that endocrine function was often altered in patients with abnormal mental states. The rationale for using peripheral hormone measurement as biological markers of psychiatric illness was provided by the identification of functional links between the hypothalamus and anterior pituitary gland. These links presumably explain how limbic system dysfunction associated with psychiatric illness can directly interfere with neuroendocrine regulation. Similar to clinical endocrinologists, psychiatrists have found that, if only basal hormone levels are measured, this usually provides incomplete information. Neuroendocrine abnormalities are most precisely identified if dynamic or 'challenge' studies of endocrine function are used. Examples include stimulation or suppression tests.

A number of studies have demonstrated abnormalities of the hypothalamic-pituitary-adrenal (HPA) and hypothalamic-pituitary-thyroid (HPT) axes in patients with melancholia. Evidence is accumulating that two neuroendocrine 'challenge' tests, the dexamethasone suppression test (DST) and the thyrotropin releasing hormone stimulation test (TRH test) which examine the function of the HPA and HPT axes respectively, have clinical utility in the study and management of melancholia.

The dexamethasone suppression test (DST)

The DST evolved from a procedure described by Liddle (1960) for the evaluation of HPA axis dysfunction in Cushing's disease. When normal subjects receive a dose of 1 or 2 mg dexamethasone at midnight, plasma cortisol levels are suppressed for at least the next 24 h. During the 1960s, several investigators reported that some melancholic patients not only secrete excessive amounts of corticosteroids, but their HPA axis is abnormally resistant to suppression by dexamethasone. Subsequent studies confirmed this finding and refined the DST methodology to improve test performance for the diagnosis of melancholia (Carroll *et al.*, 1981). Specifically, the clinician administers 1 mg dexamethasone at 23:30 hours and cortisol levels are measured at 16:00 hours and 23:00 hours the following day. If plasma cortisol concentrations exceed 5 ug/dl using the competitive protein binding assay, or 4 ug/dl using a radioimmuno-assay (RIA) procedure, the test is abnormal. This standardized DST procedure identified the syndrome of melancholia with a sensitivity of 67 per cent and a specificity of 96 per cent when administered to psychiatric in-patients in a setting with an approximate 50 per cent prevalence of melancholia. In addition to aiding diagnosis, the DST has other clinical applications. The reader is referred to more detailed reviews by Carroll (1982) and Greden (1982).

The thyrotropin releasing hormone stimulation test (TRH Test)

The TRH test in psychiatry is identical to that devised by endocrinologists for the study of hypothalamic-pituitary-thyroid (HPT) disorder. The test is usually conducted during mid-morning hours, after an overnight fast, when spontaneous plasma TSH level is fluctuating the least. After taking one or two baseline blood samples, TRH is administered intravenously over a 30-s period. Most studies have used TRH doses of either 200 or 500 μg. Plasma samples are obtained 15, 30, 60, and 90 min after TRH administration. Plasma TSH concentrations are determined by RIA and the maximal change in TSH (ΔTSH) is obtained by subtracting the baseline TSH value from the maximum TSH level after TRH administration.

Initial reports suggested that a proportion of depressed patients have blunted TSH responses to TRH (Kastin *et al.*, 1972; Prange *et al.*, 1972). Later investigations replicated and extended this finding (Kirkegaard, 1981; Loosen & Prange, 1982). The situation is complicated, however, by the observation that only between 25–30 per cent of euthyroid depressed patients have blunted TSH responses to TRH, regardless of whether a dose of 200 or 500 μg TRH is used in the test. With such low sensitivity, the diagnostic utility of the TRH test is probably low. Despite this limitation, treatment-associated changes in the TRH test may serve as predictors of outcome after successful treatment of the acute episode.

Possible utility in ECT practice

The syndrome of melancholia is the best accepted clinical indication for ECT. Because the DST and TRH test have been predominantly used in patients with melancholia, we will examine the information obtained from using these two markers in such patients and discuss the relevance of the DST and TRH tests for inpatients receiving ECT. These and similar techniques may be helpful in the future in defining the therapeutic mechanism of ECT, but there have been few human studies on this subject thus far.

Neuroendocrine strategies may be used to examine three important questions:
(1) how can ECT-responsive patients be identified and in particular, for which patients is ECT the *most* effective treatment?
(2) Can the therapeutic action of ECT be monitored by changes in biological markers and will these markers indicate the optimal endpoint for a course of ECT?
(3) Is it possible to predict which patients require continuation therapy to prevent relapse after a successful course of ECT?

Selection of ECT-responsive patients

Although results are conflicting, several reports indicate that an abnormal DST may be a useful predictor of response to treatment. Pilot reports suggested, for example, that patients with melancholia and an abnormal DST result have a better response to antidepressant treatment than similar patients with normal DST result (Brown & Shuey, 1980; Greden *et al.*, 1981). Another study reported that the DST result was more effective than clinician's judgment in predicting response of depressed catatonics to thymoleptics (Carman *et al.*, 1980).

It is unclear whether the DST can identify particular melancholic patients who will respond better to ECT than antidepressant medication. It is reasonable to hypothesize, however, that the test may have special applicability to two subgroups of melancholics which generally have an excellent response to ECT and are more likely to be unresponsive to antidepressant medications. These include depressed patients with a catatonic syndrome and patients with an affective psychosis. Melancholic patients with affective delusions may have a higher frequency of abnormal DSTs than is generally present in nondelusional melancholics (Carroll *et al.*, 1980; Rudorfer *et al.*, 1982). Retrospective examination of DST results in patients referred for ECT by clinical criteria alone also shows a high frequency of nonsuppression (Papakostas *et al.*, 1981; Albala, unpublished data). Obviously, these observations only hint at a possible relationship between an abnormal DST result in melancholia and good response to ECT. Confirmation will require prospective examination with controls for the psychotic and catatonic subtypes of melancholia, and treatment comparisons with established, well-documented courses of antidepressant medications. Some attempts in this direction have been made. McIntyre *et al.* (1981) conducted DSTs in consecutively admitted depressed patients classified as either endogenous or reactive by the Newcastle scale. They observed that 22 of 33 patients with abnormal DSTs were unresponsive to antidepressant medication and had favorable responses to ECT whereas only 15 of 62 patients with normal DSTs eventually required ECT. The authors did not mention whether they controlled for plasma levels of antidepressants and length of treatment. Their results suggest that an abnormal DST result in a depressed patient is associated with better response to ECT than to antidepressant drugs. This does not, however, imply that patients with normal DSTs will not do well with ECT.

Coryell (1982) also studied pretreatment DST results as a response predictor to ECT in 42 depressed patients. Half of the patients had abnormal DSTs. Mean severity ratings did not differ between nonsuppressors and suppressors. Coryell's (1982) results showed that patients with initially abnormal DSTs had a better response to ECT according to global ratings than patients with normal pretreatment DSTs. Hamilton Rating Scale scores, however, did not show differences among the two groups. Coryell (1982) emphasized the importance of outcome measure variability to the study of prediction of response and suggested that, if his results were replicated, the DST might be one of several factors to consider in the decision to administer ECT.

Opposite findings were reported by Qualls & Brown (1982). They used ECT to treat 25 patients with diagnosis of Primary Major Depressive Disorder, endogenous subtype (Research Diagnostic Criteria, Spitzer et al., 1977). Forty-eight per cent of the patients had abnormal pretreatment DSTs. They found no pretreatment differences in severity among the two groups. After treatment, patients with normal pretreatment DSTs showed significantly greater improvement in three rating measures (Hamilton Depression Scale, Beck Depression Inventory, and Global Assessment Scale). Clinician's impressions categorized 100 per cent of all initially normal DST patients as ECT responders whereas only 50 per cent of the initially abnormal DST group were categorized as responders.

An explanation for these discrepancies is not readily apparent. Many factors, in addition to diagnosis, influence the decision to give ECT and these may not be specifically identified by ratings scales. Examples include presence and quality of psychosis, degree of suicidality, previous response to ECT, etc. Many methodological concerns such as treatment with medications, type of cortisol assay, number of plasma samples analyzed and dose of dexamethasone may also alter DST performance. Different centers also use different criteria as an indication for ECT and these were not controlled for in the studies mentioned above.

In summary, based upon a small number of patients, there is no unanimity that the DST will be a strong predictor of ECT response. In that sense, the DST is like many laboratory markers in medicine; it should be used as a helpful *complement* to clinical considerations.

No prospective studies have specifically evaluated the TRH test to predict response to ECT. However, if the data reported by Papakostas et al. (1981) are re-examined using the ΔTSH criterion of less than 7 uU/ml for considering the test abnormal, as suggested by Gold et al. (1981), it is evident that six of seven patients with an abnormal TRH test responded to ECT whereas only one out of four patients with normal TRH test had a good response. These data suggest that the TRH test deserves further examination as a possible predictor of ECT outcome.

Determination of endpoint for a course of ECT
An important problem faced by the clinician using ECT is to determine when a treatment course is complete. The number of treatments given to an individual must be limited because of concern that excessive ECT might produce impairment in cognitive functioning, but premature discontinuation of treatment might result in poor outcome or early relapse. The twofold object is full remission of the acute psychopathology *and* a low relapse rate. Lacking objective markers for the therapeutic effects of ECT, clinicians have adopted arbitrary guidelines to determine the 'optimal dosage' of ECT. These guidelines have not been adequately tested in appropriately-designed clinical studies. An inflexible number of treatments or duration of the course of ECT is sometimes prescribed without consideration of clinical response. Sometimes, the policy may be to simply give an additional two treatments after full remission of symptoms. Most

commonly, clinicians are advised to treat until the psychopathology has resolved with the proviso that a certain minimum and maximum number of treatments are advised (American Psychiatric Association Task Force Report No. 14, 1978). Certainly, any laboratory aid that would objectively help this clinical issue of 'how much ECT to give' would be quite valuable. There are indications that the DST can provide such objectivity and may assist in determining the appropriate length of a course of ECT.

Several investigators have reported the results of serial DSTs performed throughout a course of ECT. Dysken et al. (1979) treated a 56-year old man with a diagnosis of major depressive disorder, psychotic and endogenous subtype. He and his associates did weekly DSTs throughout treatment and found that the abnormal results observed prior to treatment steadily normalized in association with clinical recovery. Albala et al. (1980) similarly observed that abnormal pretreatment DST results normalized in a melancholic patient after the third ECT even though her depressive symptoms remained quite prominent. Further treatment resulted in good clinical recovery. More recently, Rothschild & Schatzberg (1982) reported the case of a 39-year old man with a psychotic depression in whom the DST was performed serially during two courses of ECT. Each time, the DST normalized prior to complete, yet short-lived, clinical recovery.

Albala et al. (1981) also selected a group of six unipolar endogenous depressives with abnormal pretreatment DST results and treated them with ECT. The DST was repeated every five to seven days throughout treatment. Five out of the six patients responded favorably to ECT. The DST result normalized early in treatment for all responders, despite only modest clinical improvement. Further ECT resulted in complete clinical recovery and a persistence of normal DST results. The single patient in whom DST normalization was not observed failed to respond to treatment. Similar results were reported by Schlesser & Rush (1981) in their study of twelve endogenous depressives with abnormal DST results. They found that at midtreatment, six of the eventual ten responders had normal DST results and by the end of treatment the DST was normal in all ten responders. In contrast, the two patients who did not respond to ECT continued to show abnormal DSTs.

These findings seem to indicate that during the ECT-induced clinical improvement, nonsuppressive post-dexamethasone cortisol levels gradually decrease and eventually normalize. This pattern is only observed among ECT responders, however, and does not occur in patients who have a poor outcome to the treatment. This suggests that the DST can be used as a biological monitor of clinical response to ECT. Another aspect of these studies is the timing of the DST normalization in relation to clinical improvement. DST normalization precedes complete clinical recovery and accurately identifies eventual ECT responders. This finding has important implications for the clinician who may be inclined to stop a course of ECT because of no apparent response. The presence of a normalized DST may indicate that continued treatment will result in eventual good clinical recovery. The figure illustrates the change of DST results and depression ratings during a course of ECT administered to a 69-year old unipolar patient with severe psychomotor retardation. This pattern is fairly representative of the changes observed in the majority of melancholic patients treated with ECT.

Serial TRH tests may also yield useful information in the clinical management of patients receiving ECT. This would particularly apply to those depressed patients who have a normal DST result and an abnormal TRH test result. The existence of such a patient population has been demonstrated by Extein et al. (1981) who conducted both DSTs and TRH tests on patients diagnosed as major depressive disorder, primary subtype. They found that 34 per cent of these patients had an abnormal TSH response to TRH in the presence of a normal DST result. Langer et al. (1980) performed serial TRH tests in a group of 21 unipolar patients treated with clomipramine. Their data suggested a significant statistical correlation between clinical improvement and increased TSH response to TRH. A similarly designed study with ECT-treated patients has not been reported and is necessary to evaluate the potential use of the TRH test as a monitor of clinical response to ECT.

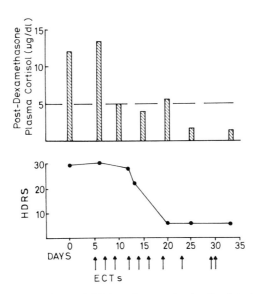

Fig. *Progressive normalization of abnormal DST results associated with clinical improvement in a unipolar depressed woman receiving ECT. (HDRS = Hamilton Depression Rating Scale scores).* Reprinted, with permission, from Albala *et al.* (1981), Biol. Psychiat. **16**, 551–560

Prediction of relapse after ECT

The incidence of relapse after successful treatment with ECT is reported to be high. Clinical indications for maintenance treatment are also confusing. A recent review shows that there is little consensus about risk of giving no continuation treatment, or the efficacy of specific medications or maintenance ECT in preventing relapse (Haskett, 1982). Some clinicians believe that the characteristics of the original course of ECT significantly influence the relapse rate, whereas others suggest that outcome depends upon the use of prophylactic treatment and the natural history of the disorder. It would be extremely valuable if laboratory tests could aid in identifying patients who are more likely to experience an early relapse. This would permit a clinician to prescribe continuation therapy for those patients who require prophylaxis after completion of a course of ECT. There are indications that the DST might be helpful for this clinical problem.

Several studies suggest that lack of DST normalization may predict early relapse despite apparent clinical remission of the depression (Greden *et al.*, 1980; Goldberg, 1980; Gold *et al.*, 1980; Papakostas *et al.*, 1981). In two of these studies, specific data regarding ECT-treated patients are available. Greden *et al.* (1980) reported 14 patients with abnormal pretreatment DST results. Four of these patients were treated with ECT and all responded to treatment. Three responders had a normal DST after ECT and remained asymptomatic for at least seven months. One patient clinically improved after the course of ECT but did not show normalization of the neuroendocrine disturbance. She was admitted six weeks later for treatment of a relapse with a second ECT course which resulted in both clinical recovery and DST normalization. She remained asymptomatic at the time of a one-year follow-up. Papakostas *et al.* (1981) presented a series of 14 unipolar depressed patients who were treated with ECT. Nine patients eventually responded to treatment and eight of these had pretreatment post-dexamethasone cortisol levels in excess of 5 µg/dl. At discharge, the DST result had normalized and all had good outcome for one to nine months. The three patients who responded clinically but still displayed abnormal DSTs had a poor outcome. Two were readmitted within two months and the third committed suicide four weeks after discharge.

These data suggest that persistently abnormal DST results after a course of ECT predict a high risk for relapse, even where clinical recovery appears adequate. Clinical recovery accompanied by DST normalization is usually but not always associated with good outcome. Rothschild & Schatzberg (1982), reported a patient who was successfully treated with ECT and normalization of the DST occurred. The patient quickly relapsed, however, and the DST again became abnormal. A second ECT course produced good clinical response and DST normalization. Still a second relapse occurred in association with an abnormal DST. Remission and DST normalization were eventually accomplished and maintained with the use of amoxapine. In this case, DST normalization failed to predict prolonged remission. An alternative explanation is that this patient may have been a 'rapid cycler' (Dunner et al., 1977) and every relapse could have represented a new episode rather than a re-emergence of the original episode. Greden et al. (1982) have shown that DST results can rapidly change in association with mood shifts in rapidly cycling bipolar patients.

Several studies reported repeat TRH findings after clinical recovery (Kirkegaard, 1981). Some patients do not show a normalized TRH test despite clinical recovery. Similar to data with the DST, this suggests that antidepressant treatment can produce symptomatic improvement in some patients without altering the pathophysiological process which presumably underlies the neuroendocrine disturbance. Kirkegaard (1981) reported that the persistence of abnormal TRH test responses after clinical recovery predicted early relapse. In their study of 66 'clinically cured' patients, antidepressant therapy was withdrawn after clinical recovery and the patients were followed for at least six months or until relapse. They showed that $\Delta\Delta$TSH values (ΔTSH at discharge $-$ ΔTSH on admission) clearly distinguished good prognosis from poor prognosis patients. The $\Delta\Delta$TSH cutoff value of 2.0 μU/ml predicted 'cure' in 27 of 29 patients and relapse in 33 of 37 patients. Most patients who had little treatment-associated improvement in their neuroendocrine disturbance relapsed within four months. In contrast, the patients with $\Delta\Delta$TSH $>$ 2.0 μU/ml had a good outcome during the first six months after discontinuation of antidepressant treatment. This group of patients includes a subset of 35 patients with endogenous depression who were treated with ECT. All 19 patients with $\Delta\Delta$TSH $\leq$ 2.0 uU/ml relapsed within six months of completing the ECT course. By comparison, only 3 out of 16 patients with $\Delta\Delta$TSH $>$ 2.0 uU/ml suffered a relapse. The relapse rates were similar among unipolars and bipolars (Kirkegaard & Bjorum, 1980). These results strongly suggest that normalization of the TRH test as defined by Kirkegaard (1981), may be a reliable indicator of 'cure' and identify patients who require maintenance antidepressant therapy to prevent relapse. Replications of this important finding are required.

In the series of patients presented by Papakostas et al. (1981), three of the nine ECT responders had blunted TRH test results ($\leq$ 5.0 μU/ml) prior to treatment. In two of these cases the TRH test was repeated and remained blunted (one with a $\Delta\Delta$TSH $>$ 2.0 μU/ml). Neither relapsed during a nine-month followup period. The third patient with a blunted response on admission committed suicide one month after discharge. No repeat TRH test was available in this case. The number of patients in this study is too small to draw any conclusions on the prognostic value of the TRH test.

Conclusion

There still are no definitive answers about the utility of neuroendocrine tests in ECT practice. There are, however, many suggestions that neuroendocrine laboratory markers are likely to be helpful to future clinicians using ECT.

It is unlikely that a single neuroendocrine test will select patients requiring ECT in preference to other antidepressant treatments. Combinations of neuroendocrine testing with other laboratory markers may perform somewhat better. The relationship of the normalization of neuroendocrine function to the therapeutic mechanism of ECT requires further examination. It may be possible to use these markers to determine more precisely the 'adequate dosage' of treatment of individuals receiving ECT. Finally, it appears that changes in neuroendocrine tests during ECT may be of great assistance in the identification of patients with a high likelihood of relapse. There is a need for prospective studies to clarify these questions. The clinician using

ECT may then be able to use objective criteria to support decisions on patient selection, duration of ECT course, and the need for maintenance treatment.

Acknowledgement — Supported in part by Public Health Grant MH 28294, by the University of Michigan Mental Health Research Institute, and by the State of Michigan Department of Mental Health.

References

Albala, A. A., Greden, J. F. & Carroll, B. J. (1980): Serial dexamethasone suppression tests in affective disorders. *Am. J. Psychiat.* **137**, 383.

Albala, A. A., Greden, J. F., Tarika, J. & Carroll, B. J. (1981): Changes in serial dexamethasone suppression tests among unipolar depressives receiving electroconvulsive treatment. *Biol. Psychiat.* **16**, 551-560.

American Psychiatric Association (1978): *Electroconvulsive therapy: Report of the Task Force on Electroconvulsive Therapy.* Washington, D.C.: American Psychiatric Association.

Brown, W. A. & Shuey, I. (1980): Response to dexamethasone and subtype of depression. *Arch. Gen. Psychiat.* **37**, 747-751.

Carman, J. S., Hall, K., Wyatt, E. S. & Crews, E. L. (1980): Dexamethasone non-suppression: Predictor of thymoleptic response in catatonic and schizo-affective patients. *Soc. Biol. Psychiat. Sci. Proc.*, Abstract no. **4**, 36.

Carroll, B. J., Greden, J. F., Feinberg, M., James, N. McI., Steiner, M., Haskett, R. F. & Tarika, J. (1980): Neuroendocrine dysfunction in genetic subtypes of primary unipolar depression. *Psychiat. Res.*, **2**, 251-258.

Carroll, B. J., Feinberg, M., Greden, J. F., Tarika, J., Albala, A. A., Haskett, R. F., James, N. McI., Kronfol, Z., Lohr, N., Steiner, M., DeVigne, J. P. & Young, E. (1981): A specific laboratory test for the diagnosis of melancholia. *Arch. Gen. Psychiat.* **38**, 15-22.

Carroll, B. J. (1982): The dexamethasone suppression test for melancholia. *Br. J. Psychiat.* **140**, 292-304.

Coryell, W. (1982): Hypothalamic-pituitary-adrenal axis abnormality and ECT response. *Psychiat. Res.* **61**, 283-291.

Dunner, D., Patrick, V. & Fieve, R. (1977): Rapid cycling manic depressive patients. *Comprehensive Psychiat.* **18**, 561-566.

Dysken, M. W., Pandey, G. N., Chang, S. S., Hicks, R. & Davis, J. M. (1979): Serial post-dexamethasone cortisol levels in a patient undergoing ECT. *Am. J. Psychiat.* **136**, 1328-1329.

Extein, I., Pottash, A. L. C. & Gold, M. S. (1981): Relationship of thyrotropin-releasing hormone test and dexamethasone suppression test abnormalities in unipolar depression. *Psychiat. Res.* **4**, 49-53.

Gold, M. S., Pottash, A. L. C., Extein, I. & Sweeney, D. R. (1980): Dexamethasone suppression tests in depression and response to treatment. *Lancet* **1**, 1190.

Gold, M. S., Pottash, A. L. C., Extein, I., Martin, D. M., Howard, E., Mueller, E. A. & Sweeney, D. R. (1981): The TRH test in the diagnosis of major and minor depression. *Psychoneuroendocrinology* **6**, 159-169.

Goldberg, I. K. (1980): Dexamethasone suppression test as indicator of safe withdrawal of antidepressant therapy. *Lancet* **1**, 376.

Greden, J. F., Albala, A. A., Haskett, R. F., James, McI., Goodman, L., Steiner, M. & Carroll, B. J. (1980): Normalization of dexamethasone suppression test: A laboratory index of recovery from endogenous depression. *Biol. Psychiat.* **15**, 449-458.

Greden, J. F., Kronfol, Z., Gardner, R., Feinberg, M., Mukhopadhyay, S., Albala, A. A. & Carroll, B. J. (1981): Dexamethasone suppression test and selection of antidepressant medications. *J. Affect. Dis.* **3**, 389-396.

Greden, J. F., DeVigne, J. P., Albala, A. A., Tarika, J., Buttenheim, M., Eiser, A. & Carroll, B. J. (1982): Serial dexamethasone suppression tests among rapidly cycling bipolar patients. *Biol. Psychiat.* **17**, 455-462.

Greden, J. F. (1982): The dexamethasone suppression test: An established biological marker of melancholia. In *Biological markers in psychiatry and neurology*, ed E. Usdin & I. Hanin. Pp. 229-240. Oxford: Pergamon Press.

Haskett, R. F. (1982): Factors affecting outcome after successful electroconvulsive therapy. *Psychopharmacol. Bull.* **18**, 75-78.

Kastin, A. J., Ehrensing, R. H., Schalch, D. S. & Anderson, M. S. (1972): Improvement in mental depression with decreased thyrotropin response after administration of thyrotropin-releasing hormone. *Lancet* **2**, 742.

Kirkegaard, C. (1981): Thyrotropin response to thyrotropin releasing hormone in endogenous depression. *Psychoneuroendocrinology* **6**, 189-212.

Kirgegaard, C. & Bjorum, N. (1980): TSH response to TRH in endogenous depression. *Lancet* **1**, 152.

Langer, G., Schonbeck, G., Koinig, G., Lesch, D., Schussler, M. & Waldhausl, W. (1980): Antidepressant drugs and the hypothalamic-pituitary-thyroid axis. *Lancet* **1**, 100-101.

Liddle, G. W. (1960): Tests of pituitary-adrenal suppressibility in the diagnosis of Cushing's syndrome. *J. Clin. Endocrinol. Metab.* **20**, 1539-1560.

Loosen, P. T. & Prange, A. J. (1982): Serum thyrotropin response to thyrotropin-releasing hormone in psychiatric patients: a review. *Am. J. Psychiat.* **139**, 405-416.

McIntyre, I. M., Norman, T. R., Burrows, G. D., Davies, B. & Maguire, P. (1981): Letter to the editor. *Br. Med. J.* **283**, 1609-1610.

Papakostas, Y., Fink, M., Lee, J., Irwin, P. & Johnson, L. (1981): Neuroendocrine measures in psychiatric patients: Course and outcome with ECT. *Psychiat. Res.* **4**, 55-64.

Prange, A. J., Wilson, I. C., Lara, P. P., Alltop, L. B. & Breese, G. R. (1972): Effects of thyrotropin-releasing hormone in depression. *Lancet* **2**, 999-1002.

Qualls, C. B. & Brown, W. A. (1982): Dexamethasone suppression test subgroups differ in ECT response. *New Research Proceedings*, Abstract no. NR 36, American Psychiatric Association Annual Meeting.

Rothschild, A. J. & Schatzberg, A. F. (1982): Fluctuating post-dexamethasone cortisol levels in a patient with melancholia. *Am. J. Psychiat.* **139**, 129–130.

Rudorfer, M. V., Hwu, H. & Clayton, P. (1982): Dexamethasone suppression test in primary depression: Significance of family history and psychosis. *Biol. Psychiat.* **17**, 41–48.

Schlesser, M. A. & Rush, A. J. (1981): Serial changes in hypothalamic-pituitary-adrenal axis activity among depressives receiving ECT. *Soc. Biol. Psychiat. Sci. Proc.*, Abstract no. 41, 69.

Spitzer, R. L., Endicott, J. & Robins, E. (1977): *Research diagnostic criteria (RDC) for a selected group of functional disorders*, 3rd edition. New York: New York State Psychiatric Institute.

14.
Theories of convulsive therapy:
a neuroendocrine hypothesis

M. FINK

Department of Psychiatry and Behavioral Science, School of Medicine, State University of New York at Stony Brook, Long Island, New York 11794; and the International Association for Psychiatric Research, Inc., P.O. Box 457, St James, New York 11780, USA.

Introduction

Convulsive therapy has been an important part of clinical psychiatry since 1934. In these 50 years, the efficacy of ECT in severe depression, mania and catatonia has been well documented (APA, 1978; Fink, 1979; Kendell, 1981; Palmer, 1981). To achieve clinical success, it seems necessary to subject patients to repeated grand mal seizures, spaced over two weeks. Severely depressed patients usually require eight seizures, given either twice or three times a week. At one time, the treatments were cumbersome, brutal and frightening. Missed seizures were common, so that patients often experienced pain, panic and fear. Complications were frequent, but modifications of the treatments were introduced which radically changed their character. As electrical inductions, anesthesia, muscle relaxation with succinylcholine, oxygenation, atropine, unilateral electrode placements, low threshold induction currents, and monitoring of seizures were accepted, complications became rare.

Throughout its history, the mechanism of the antidepressant action of ECT has been a challenge. Many hypotheses have been proposed, each derived from a different aspect of the treatment or from the research models which interested investigators at the time (Fink, 1979). The many hypotheses are reminiscent of the apocryphal story of the blind men and the elephant — as each man grasped a different part of the animal, each built a unique image from the details available to him. One thought the animal supple and maneuverable, like a snake; another, rough and rigid like a tree trunk; and a third, smooth and hard like polished stone. In like fashion in convulsive therapy, some authors emphasized the importance of panic, fear, amnesia, and forgetting, for these aspects were the most prominent. Others noted the changes in the blood brain barrier, in adrenal and pituitary functions, on stress mechanisms, and on salt and water metabolism. Some focussed their interest on electrophysiologic measures, some on biochemical aspects and many on psychological events (Fink *et al.*, 1974; Fink, 1979).

But as we learned more about the treatment, and as the process was modified without losing efficacy, the views changed. It is my aim to describe the hypotheses which have, from time to time, been useful to me, as well as the experiments and experiences which led us to discard one set of constructs and consider others. Our present picture of the antidepressant action of ECT is based on its neuroendocrine effects (Fink, 1979; Fink & Ottosson, 1980). Others are actively studying neurohumoral and receptor sensitivity models (Grahame-Smith *et al.*, 1978; Green, 1980; Modigh *et al.*, 1981; Lerer & Belmaker, 1982) or emphasizing the importance of the change in permeability of the blood brain barrier (Bolwig & Rafaelson, 1981).

Neurophysiologic–adaptive

The hypotheses which first interested me can be labeled neurophysiologic and neurophysiologic–adaptive. The neurophysiologic view was based on EEG studies of seizures (Fink & Kahn, 1957), and our views paralleled those proposed by Roth (1952) and Roth *et al.* (1957). In the first decades of ECT use, schizophrenic, depressed, and manic patients were treated with ECT. Among such a mixed population of subjects, there were many whose rapid improvement with ECT, was accompanied by a large neurophysiologic response, characterized by an early and rapid development of symmetric EEG slow wave activity. These patients were, for the most part, the older subjects in our sample, and many were severely depressed. Other patients required more treatments to develop a behavioral effect, and only occasionally did these patients show the same degree of enhanced EEG slow wave activity. These patients were usually younger and were often labeled as schizophrenic or manic patients. It was no wonder then, that we defined an association between the degree of EEG slow wave activity and clinical improvement, and believed that the development of EEG slow wave activity was necessary (though not sufficient) for improvement in the ECT process (Fink & Kahn, 1957). Later, when we examined more homogeneous samples of patients who were severely depressed, we found that the onset of EEG slowing was no longer a predictor of good clinical result, since all the patients showed the EEG changes, and most, but not all those with EEG slowing, showed the improved behavior (Volavka *et al.*, 1972; Volavka, 1974).

While the EEG changes were seen as necessary, they were clearly not sufficient for improvement and we sought another factor which would explain the differences in our observations. The psychologic and neurophysiologic views of E. A. Weinstein were helpful. He and his co-workers had reported that the administration of small doses of amobarbital to patients with structural brain disease (such as mass and vascular lesions) would elicit an organic mental syndrome, characterized by systematic changes in language (Weinstein & Kahn, 1955). They saw, in the language changes, a pattern of minimization and displacement which they identified as the 'language of denial'. The propensity to use this defense depended on personality characteristics, which they labeled the denial personality.

Within this framework, Weinstein *et al.* (1952) suggested that improvement in ECT resulted from the development of denial under the conditions of an induced organic mental syndrome. This 'neurophysiologic–adaptive hypothesis' was intriguing, and our early studies of the relation of improvement to denial personality, to psychological mechanisms and to the development of an organic mental syndrome were encouraging (Fink, 1979). But we found many exceptions. Some patients improved without demonstrating denial language or in whom we could not demonstrate a denial personality. Some patients improved without demonstrating an organic mental syndrome, although all improved patients did so under the influence of amobarbital. Perhaps our most difficult problem was to explain the persistence of behavioral improvement when the organic mental changes and denial language disappeared.

Cholinergic hypothesis

In assessing the EEG effects of seizures, our interest was stimulated by the early appearance and prominence of high voltage slow waves (expressed in bursts and runs) in those patients who improved. If EEG slow waves did not appear in some patients who did not improve, perhaps drugs which enhanced the amount of EEG slowing would be useful. We examined the effects of many substances on EEG patterns (and behavior) in patients undergoing ECT. We found none that usefully enhanced EEG slowing, but we did find many substances, particularly anti-cholinergics, that reduced EEG slowing, and did so rapidly, effectively, and transiently. Most striking was the re-appearance of the symptoms of psychosis—the delusions, depression, apathy and agitation—during the time when EEG slowing was reduced and replaced by pretreatment EEG patterns. The most active drugs in this series were the anticholinergic compounds, Ditran and diethazine, and the antiparkinson agent, procyclidine. Similar observations were made with atropine and scopolamine, but these compounds had systemic

116

effects which were unpleasant. This ability of anticholinergic drugs to reverse the behavioral and EEG effects of ECT was a compelling observation, indicating that some cholinergic aspect resulting from seizures encouraged the changes in mood and thought processes which were the basis of the improvement in the illness.

In examining the evidence for cholinergic effects of seizures, there was much that was supportive (Fink, 1966). Patients with severe epilepsy had elevated levels of acetylcholine and cholinesterases in the CSF. Following head trauma, animals and man had increased EEG slow wave activity accompanied by elevations of CSF cholinesterases. CSF examinations in patients during a course of ECT revealed elevations of CSF acetylcholine and cholinesterases after five or six treatments, at a time when the patients exhibited improvement in their behavior. We concluded that induced seizures were more like cerebral trauma than like spontaneous seizures; and that the increase in brain acetylcholine, permeability of the blood brain barrier, and vasodilatation were interrelated phenomena that were necessary to the therapeutic process in ECT.

We attempted to replicate the measurement of the CSF changes in acetylcholine in patients undergoing courses of ECT, but failed. In part, our failure resulted from the insensitivity and instability of the clam-heart preparations used in the biological assay of acetylcholine; and in part, to our failure to distinguish the measures in schizophrenic and depressed samples. The significance of acetylcholine and cholinergic mechanisms in depressive and manic disorders has lately become a focus of interest for some investigators, but none seem interested in applying their methods to assessments of the ECT process. The role of cholinergic mechanisms in ECT remains a viable inquiry and should be encouraged.

Present theories

Monoamine hypotheses

The prevailing theories of the antidepressant action of ECT were assessed in an NIMH sponsored meeting in 1972 (Fink *et al.*, 1974). Three principal themes were examined—the neurophysiologic, the amnestic (cognitive), and the biochemical. Both the neurophysiologic and the amnestic theories were seen to exhibit the characteristics of epiphenomena, associated more with the secondary effects of the treatments, than as part of the mainstream of the anti-depressant process. In biochemistry, the increased activity of adrenergic and catecholamine functions stimulated some interest. Pryor (1974) reported increases in brain monoamine oxidase activity with ECS, and Kety (1974) emphasized the increased turnover in brain catecholamines. These data encouraged the belief that the mechanism of action of ECT was similar to that of tricyclic and monoamine oxidase inhibiting drugs. In succeeding years, as the catecholamine hypotheses of drug action were found wanting, others examined different brain amines and changes in brain receptor sensitivity. The hypotheses focussed on changes in norepinephrine, dopamine, and serotonin receptors are under active study (Grahame-Smith *et al.*, 1978; Green, 1980; Modigh *et al.*, 1981; Checkley *et al.*, 1981; Grahame-Smith, 1981; Lerer & Belmaker, 1982).

But there are many objections to such constructs as explanations for the antidepressant efficacy of ECT (Kendell, 1981; Grahame-Smith, 1981; Checkley *et al.*, 1981). For the most part, the findings are limited to studies in 'normal' animals. When replication or logical derivatives are sought in man, the human assessments do not follow expectations. There is no assurance that the changes in ECT are not related to the altered pathophysiology which is the hallmark of the disease process, rather than to changed normal physiology. Further, observations in ECT are often made under conditions that do not simulate the ECT process, such as the defined repetition rate of seizures. Other observations seem to be species specific. The monoamine hypotheses suggest that both increases and decreases in monoamine functions or activity of receptor sites may result from repeated seizures—a difficult conclusion to support. Some hypotheses depend on alleged similarities between the activity of lithium and ECT in man, a view that is hardly consonant with clinical experience. Finally, even if the changes in receptor sensitivity are involved in the chain of antidepressant events in ECT, it is difficult to picture such changes as affecting behavior without the interpolation of an intervening variable, as yet undefined. The monoamine theories, therefore, leave many questions unanswered, even if the observations could be related to studies in man.

Neuroendocrine hypothesis

In reviewing the prevailing theories of ECT action for the American Psychiatric Association Task Force on Electroconvulsive Therapy, two new observations seemed significant — that brain tissues produced substances (hormones) with behavioral effects, and that neuroendocrine dysfunction characterized patients with severe endogenous depression (APA, 1978; Fink, 1979). These same observations also impressed Jan-Otto Ottosson, and in 1978 we began a collaboration which resulted in the expression of a neuroendocrine hypothesis of the anti-depressant activity of ECT (Fink & Ottosson, 1980).

Many observers have been interested in the effects of ECT on stress mechanisms, particularly changes in adrenal functions. With ECT, adrenal cortical steroid levels increase in plasma and urine, returning to pretreatment levels with more treatment. Plasma levels of 17 hydroxy-corticosteroids increase; an increase which is not reduced when the motor aspects of the convulsion are blocked by phenytoin and anesthesia (Bliss *et al.*, 1954). Patients without adrenal glands were successfully treated with ECT, making it unlikely that adrenal functions are central to the antidepressant process. There is also a functional hypertrophy of the adrenals in animals given ECS, with secondary changes in temperature control, appetite, weight and autonomic activity. These observations led to the belief that the hypothalamus, not the adrenal glands, was more directly involved in the ECT process.

Two recent case reports encourage this view. A patient with a catatonic psychosis developed a Cushing's syndrome. Transphenoidal surgery removed a basophil adenoma, leaving a persistent psychosis unresponsive to drug therapy, but which resolved with ECT (Reis & Bokan, 1979). In a case of drug-induced hypothalamic hypofunction defined as Cushing's syndrome of the CRF-ACTH type, ECT stimulated the hypothalamus to normal functioning when other therapies had failed (Pitts & Patterson, 1979).

ECT elicits a prompt, but temporary, release of ACTH and cortisol (Ashby, 1949; Clower & Migeon, 1967; Elithorn *et al.*, 1968). The possibility that the release of ACTH was central to the ECT therapeutic process was tested by direct ACTH administration, but the results were disappointing (Altshule *et al.*, 1950; Cleghorn *et al.*, 1950). Plasma prolactin levels increase with ECT and in patients with epilepsy after a spontaneous seizure, but not in patients with hysterical seizures (Öhman *et al.*, 1976; O'Dea *et al.*, 1978; Meco *et al.*, 1978; Trimble, 1978). ECT also elicits transient increases in plasma levels of β-endorphin-like immunoreactivity and vasopressin (Emrich *et al.*, 1979; Raskind *et al.*, 1979).

While these peptides are not demonstrated to be behaviorally active, there are other peptides which have behavioral effects in pharmacologic trials. ACTH fragments ($ACTH_{4-10}$, $ACTH_{4-9}$ analogue), vasopressin analogues (DDAVP, DGAVP), endorphins (des-tyr-γ-endorphin, β-endorphin, des-enkephalin-γ-endorphin), methionine enkephalin analogue (FK 33-824), and the peptides TRH and MIF_1 have each been reported to elicit behavioral effects when administered to animals and man (Nedophil & Rütter, 1979; Verhoeven *et al.*, 1979, 1982; Berger *et al.*, 1980; Gerner *et al.*, 1980; Pickar *et al.*, 1981). Infusions of β-endorphin elicited changes in depressive symptoms and not in symptoms of schizophrenia (Gerner *et al.*, 1980). In our clinical studies, we examined the activity of des-tyr-γ-endorphin in five severely depressed patients referred for ECT, and did not find antidepressant activity; each patient went on to a successful course of ECT. We also examined the effects of our preparation of des-tyr-γ-endorphin on pharmaco-EEG measures in normal volunteers, but were unable to demonstrate a direct CNS effect (Fink *et al.*, 1981). We are questioning whether these preparations penetrate the CNS when given by intramuscular or subcutaneous routes.

While the administration of none of these peptides has been associated with a sustained antidepressant effect, the possibility that brain stem products may be in the chain of feedback mechanisms governing mood and cognition remains a possibility. We are encouraged to seek similar substances, with a more specific and sustained effect on mood, which may be released in the ECT process (Fink & Ottosson, 1980).

ECT is most effective in cases of severe depression, where improvement rates approximate 90 per cent (Fink, 1979, 1981). In studies of predictors of outcome with ECT, many authors find that the more severe the depression and the more flagrant the vegetative symptoms (anorexia, loss of weight, decreased libido, insomnia, decreased secretions), the better the clinical result with ECT (Fink, 1979, 1982). These symptoms resolve early in the therapeutic process, and while the association is not always well defined (since ECT is sometimes effective in syndromes in which vegetative symptoms are not prominent), it is sufficiently reliable to suggest an intimate association between the functions of the hypothalamus and the anti-depressant effects of ECT.

Perhaps the most interesting data suggesting a neuroendocrine basis for the antidepressant effects of ECT are recent reports of abnormalities in cortisol and thyroid regulation in patients with severe melancholia (Carroll et al., 1980, 1981; Checkley, 1980; Garfinkel et al., 1979; Gold et al., 1980; Kirkegaard et al., 1978; Kirkegaard, 1981; Loosen & Prange, 1980). Depressed patients exhibit elevated levels of plasma cortisol, loss of its diurnal rhythmicity and failure of cortisol levels to be suppressed when exogenous steroids (such as dexamethasone) are administered. They exhibit a blunted release of TSH to the intravenous administration of TRH. Disturbances in the regulation of growth hormone, prolactin, and some sex steroids occur, but the data for these abnormalities are less compelling. Neuroendocrine measures are now used to classify more homogeneous subpopulations of severely depressed patients (Schlesser et al., 1979; Brown et al., 1979; Carroll et al., 1981; Kirkegaard, 1981).

In studies of patients with unipolar depression, we obtained cortisol measures before and after a course of ECT. Those patients who had elevated cortisol levels and whose cortisol levels failed to suppress with dexamethasone before treatment, responded well to ECT. As they improved clinically, the cortisol abnormalities resolved. Indeed, in those patients who were clinically improved, but in whom the cortisol abnormalities failed to resolve, the post-treatment course was stormy, with an early relapse (Papakostas et al., 1981). Similar findings have been also reported by others (Dysken et al., 1979; Albala et al., 1981).

The antidepressant efficacy of induced seizures is dependent on repeated, sustained, bilateral, grand mal cerebral epileptic activity. The principal neurophysiologic source for such synchronous and symmetric electrical discharges lies in the brain stem, precisely the area of interest for the control and release of peptides.

Some additional threads may be important for the antidepressant activity of ECT. Repeated seizures increase the permeability of the blood brain barrier (Bolwig et al., 1977a,b; Bolwig & Rafaelson, 1981). This observation has been repeatedly made, suggesting that a greater passage of substances into (or out of) the brain may contribute to the antidepressant efficacy of ECT. Also, while many observers have studied the changes in many chemical elements in the brain, CSF, blood, and urine, their association with outcome has generally been poor, except for measures of calcium.

Seizures increase the cerebral and cerebrospinal fluid content of most substances measured (Fink, 1979). Calcium levels in CSF, blood and urine, however, fall during a series of fits (Flach et al., 1960; Flach, 1964; Faragalla & Flach, 1970; Carman & Wyatt, 1977). The changes in calcium are measurable after three to five seizures, seemingly coincident with an emerging antidepressant effect. Since calcium excretion does not increase, it is likely that the free calcium in body fluids is transferred to intracellular storage. Like the change in cerebrovascular permeability, the decrease in calcium levels in brain fluids may be a factor in the antidepressant effects of repeated seizures. The time course is salutary, and there is one function which calcium may serve, that of an intracellular replacement for discharged hormonal substances.

These observations of the clinical and neuroendocrine aspects of melancholia and the changes observed in ECT led us to propose a neuroendocrine theory of its antidepressant efficacy. The theory has three components. Hypothalamic hypofunction, with a decreased release of mood maintaining factors, is a central feature of melancholia. The antidepressant efficacy of induced

119

seizures is due to the release of peptides with behavioral (antidepressant) effects. Stimulation occurs directly by the same processes that induce a grand mal seizure, and indirectly, by the release of acetylcholine and norepinephrine into the brain and cerebral circulation (Fink & Ottosson, 1980).

The changes in calcium metabolism and blood brain barrier are supporting events. In order for substances to be released from cells, calcium ions move from extracellular storage into neuroendocrine cells, thereby decreasing free calcium in the CSF, plasma and urine. The increased permeability of the blood brain barrier allows these behaviorally active substances (? peptides), which are largely liberated outside the brain, entry to the brain.

Such a hypothesis does not explain the relative efficacy of ECT in patients with mania, catatonia and schizophrenia, but it is a heuristic explanation of the antidepressant process in convulsive therapy. It takes into account disparate observations which show temporal relations in the ECT process: the specificity of the response in severely depressed patients and the significance of 'hypothalamic' symptoms; the decrease in CSF calcium; and the increase in permeability of the blood brain barrier. It allows numerous loci for testing — hypothalamic functions in responders and non-responders to ECT; the behavioral effects of substances released from the brain stem in response to elevations of brain acetylcholine and/or norepinephrine; and clinical trials of behaviourally active peptides as substitutes for ECT.

Discussion

Studies of the mode of action of convulsive therapy are compelling. After almost 50 years, the treatment is still widely used, with 100 000 patients treated annually in the United States, and about 20 000 patients in Great Britain (APA, 1978; Pippard & Ellam, 1981). Despite its confirmed efficacy and usage, the treatment is criticized, largely for its avowed abuses and persistent fears of persistent brain damage. The fears have gone so far in some localities, as in Berkeley, California in November, 1982, that the voters decided to interdict its use within their city.

What is to be done? Educate the public? Even if it were possible, it will only assuage feelings for the moment. Better education of practitioners and the medical community, from whose ranks some of the most vocal critics arise? Such efforts are needed, and may prove useful, particularly in improving the care of those receiving ECT. Or, support and encourage research efforts designed to understand the ECT process and thereby replace it with a more acceptable treatment? I believe such efforts are urgent. For only if we come to understand the ways in which repeated seizures alter brain chemistry, is there a likelihood that a successful replacement will be found.

Some writers doubt that a seizure is necessary, although the recent studies in Great Britain reinforce the belief that fits are necessary for an antidepressant effect (Palmer, 1981). Some writers are concerned with further improvement in safety, and undertake explorations of different electrode placements, current waveforms, and anesthetics. Such studies are necessary, for they improve the delivery of services. Some writers seek better prognostic tools, searching for predictors of good outcome and for criteria for an endpoint of treatment — and these studies are clearly useful. But it is an understanding of the mechanism of convulsive therapy that is essential, to improve both the efficacy and acceptability of our antidepressant regimens. Such studies will also improve our understanding of the pathophysiology of mood disorders.

The two theories that are currently under study, labeled the 'neuroendocrine' and the 'neurohumoral', deserve greater attention. Neither promises an understanding of the behavioral effects of repeated fits, but they do provide bases for study and encourage systematic investigation. Other hypotheses, focussed on other mechanisms, would be useful.

The convulsive therapy process is the last vestige of the heroic therapies developed in the wake of the enthusiasm for fever therapy of neurosyphilis. Other therapies, as leucotomy, insulin coma, regressive electroshock, electronarcosis, shock-countershock, CO_2 therapy, and Dauerschlaf (persistent sleep) have each been found wanting and have been replaced by pharmacotherapy. The persistent use of convulsive therapy is a challenge to researchers and theoreticians, to develop an understanding of its activity and persistence, and to achieve a satisfactory replacement.

Conclusion

The convulsive therapy process remains an enigma. By seeking explanations of its anti-depressant efficacy, we may achieve an understanding of the process itself, thereby hastening the day when a pharmacologic replacement is accepted. Theories of the antidepressant efficacy of ECT provide a framework for studies of the mechanism of its action and serve as explanations for treatments usually seen as barbaric, bizarre, and medieval. For the thoughtful citizen, observations on efficacy and safety of ECT and the mainstream nature of the theories of its mode of action should be reassuring, and should encourage an acceptance of the treatments for those severely ill patients for whom it is likely to be effective.

References

Albala, A. A., Greden, J. F., Tarika, J. & Carroll, B. J. (1981): Changes in serial dexamethasone suppression tests among unipolar depressives receiving electroconvulsive treatment. *Biol. Psychiat.* **16**, 551-560.

Altschule, M. D., Promisel, E., Parkhurst, B. H. & Grunebaum, H. (1950): Effects of ACTH in patients with mental disease. *Arch. Neurol. Psychiat.* **64**, 641-649.

American Psychiatric Association (1978): *Electroconvulsive Therapy.* Task Force Report No. 14, 200 pp., Washington, D.C.

Ashby, W. R. (1949): The effects of convulsive therapy on the excretion of cortins and ketosteroids. *J. ment. Sci.* **95**, 275-324.

Berger, P. A., Watson, S. J., Akil, H., Elliott, G. R., Rubin, R. T., Pfefferbaum, A., Davis, K. L., Barchas, J. D. & Li, C. H. (1980): Beta-endorphin and schizophrenia. *Arch. Gen. Psychiat.* **37**, 635-640.

Bliss, E. L., Migeon, C. J., Nelson, D. H., Samuels, L. T. & Branch, C. H. (1954): Influence of E.C.T. and insulin coma on level of adrenocortical steroids in peripheral circulation. *Arch. Neurol. Psychiat.* **72**, 352-361.

Bolwig, T. G., Herz, M. M. & Holm-Jensen, J. (1977*a*): Blood brain barrier permeability during electroshock seizures in the rat. *Eur. J. Clin. Invest.* **7**, 95-100.

Bolwig, T. G., Herz, M. M., Paulson, O. B., Spotoft, H. & Rafaelson, O. J. (1977*b*): The permeability of the blood brain barrier during electrically induced seizures in man. *Eur. J. Clin. Inves.* **7**, 87-93.

Bolwig, T. & Rafaelson, O. J. (1981): Working action of electroconvulsive therapy. In *Handbook of biological psychiatry*, Vol. 6, ed H. M. van Praag, M. H. Lader, O. J. Rafaelson & E. J. Sachar. Pp. 405-418.

Brown, W. A., Johnston, R. & Mayfield, D. (1979): The 24-hour dexamethasone suppression test in a clinical setting: Relationship to diagnosis, symptoms, and response to treatment. *Amer. J. Psychiat.* **136**, 543-547.

Carman, J. S. & Wyatt, R. J. (1977): Alterations in cerebrospinal fluid and serum total calcium with changes in psychiatric state. In *Neuroregulators and psychiatric disorders*, ed E. Usdin, D. Hamburg and J. Barchas. Pp. 488-494. New York: Oxford University Press.

Carroll, B. J., Greden, J. F., Feinberg, M., James, N. M., Haskett, R. F., Steiner, M. & Tarika, J. (1980): Neuro-endocrine dysfunction in genetic subtypes of primary unipolar depression. *Psychiat. Res.* **2**, 251-258.

Carroll, B. J., Feinberg, M., Greden, J. F., Tarika, J., Albala, A. A., Haskett, R., James, N. M., Kronfol, Z., Lohr, N., Steiner, M., deVigne, J. & Young, E. (1981): A specific laboratory test for the diagnosis of melancholia. *Arch. Gen. Psychiat.* **38**, 15-22.

Checkley, S. A. (1980): Neuroendocrine tests of monoamine function in man: A review of basic theory and its application to the study of depressive illness. *Psycholog. Med.* **10**, 35-53.

Checkley, S. A., Shur, E. & Slade, A. P. (1981): The biochemistry of depression: A review of the current status of the monoamine hypothesis. In: *Metabolic disorders of the nervous system*, ed F. C. Rose. Pp. 461-476. London: Pitman.

Cleghorn, R. A., Graham, B. F., Saffran, M. & Cameron, D. E. (1950): A study of the effect of pituitary ACTH in depressed patients. *Can. Med. Assoc. J.* **63**, 329-331.

Clower, C. G. & Migeon, C. J. (1967): Psychoendocrine aspects of depression and ECT. *Johns Hopkins Med. J.* **121**, 227-233.

Dysken, M., Pandey, G. N., Chang, S. S., Hicks, R. & Davis, J. M. (1979): Serial postdexamethasone cortisol levels in a patient undergoing ECT. *Am. J. Psychiat.* **136**, 1328-1329.

Elithorn, A., Bridges, P. K. & Hodge, J. R. (1968): Adrenocortical responsiveness during courses of electroconvulsive therapy. *Br. J. Psychiat.* **114**, 575-580.

Emrich, H. M., Höllt, V., Kissling, W., Fischler, M., Laspe, H., Heinemann, H., v. Zerssen, D. & Herz, A. (1979): Beta-Endorphin-like immunoreactivity in cerebrospinal fluid and plasma of patients with schizophrenia and other neuropsychiatric disorders. *Pharmakopsychiat. Neuro-Psychopharm.* **12**, 269-276.

Faragalla, F. F. & Flach, F. (1970): Studies of mineral metabolism in mental depression. I. The effects of imipramine and electric convulsive therapy on calcium balance and kinetics. *J. Nerv. Ment. Dis.* **151**, 120-129.

Fink, M. (1966): Cholinergic aspects of convulsive therapy. *J. Nerv. Ment. Dis.* **142**, 475-484.

Fink, M. (1979): *Convulsive therapy: theory and practice.* 308 pp. New York: Raven Press.

121

Fink, M. (1981): Convulsive and drug therapies of depression. *Ann. Rev. Med.* **32**, 405-412.

Fink, M. (1982): The enigma of convulsive therapy: an effective, safe and controversial treatment. In *Critical problems in psychiatry*, ed J. O. Cavenar & H. K. H. Brodie. Pp. 203-219. Philadelphia: J. B. Lippincott.

Fink, M. & Kahn, R. L. (1957): Relation of EEG delta activity to behavioral response in electroshock: Quantitative serial studies. *Archs Neurol. Psychiat.* **78**, 516-525.

Fink, M., Papakostas, Y., Lee, J., Meehan, T. and Johnson, L. (1981): Clinical trials with des-Tyr-gamma-Endorphin (GK-78). In *Biological Psychiatry 1981*, ed C. Perris, G. Struwe, & B. Jansson. Pp. 398-401.

Fink, M., Kety, S., McGaugh, J. & Williams, T. A. (1974): *Psychobiology of Convulsive Therapy.* 312 pp. Washington, D.C.: V. H. Winston & Sons.

Fink, M. & Ottosson, J.-O. (1980): A theory of convulsive therapy in endogenous depression: significance of hypothalamic functions. *Psych. Res.* **2**, 49-61.

Flach, F. F. (1964): Calcium metabolism in states of depression. *Br. J. Psychiat.* **110**, 588-593.

Flach, F. F., Liang, E. & Stokes, P. E. (1960): Effects of electric convulsive treatments on nitrogen, calcium, and phosphorous metabolism in psychiatric patients. *J. Ment. Sci.* **106**, 638-647.

Garfinkel, P. E., Brown, G. M., Warsh, J. J. & Stancer, H. C. (1979): Neuroendocrine responses to carbidopa in primary affective disorders. *Psychoneuroendocrin.* **4**, 13-20.

Gerner, R. H., Catlin, D. H., Gorelick, D. A., Hui, K. K. & Li, C. H. (1980): Beta-endorphin: Intravenous infusion causes behavioral change in psychiatric patients. *Arch. Gen. Psychiat.* **37**, 642-647.

Gold, M. S., Pottash, A. L. C., Ryan, N., Sweeney, D. R., Davies, R. K. & Martin, D. M. (1980): TRH-induced TSH response in unipolar bipolar, and secondary depressions: Possible utility in clinical assessment and differential diagnosis. *Psychoneuroendocrinol.* **5**, 147-155.

Grahame-Smith, D. G., Green, A. R. & Costain, D. W. (1978): Mechanism of the antidepressant action of electro-convulsive therapy. *Lancet* **1**, 254-256.

Grahame-Smith, D. G. The 1980s and beyond. In *Metabolic Disorders of the Nervous System*, ed F. C. Rose. Pp. 497-512. London: Pitman.

Green, A. R. (1980): The behavioral and biochemical consequences of repeated electroconvulsive shock administration to rats and the possible clinical relevance of these changes. In *Enzymes and neurotransmitters in mental disease*, ed E. Usdin, T. L. Sourkes & M. B. H. Youdim. Pp. 455-467. New York: John Wiley & Sons.

Kendell, R. E. (1981): The present status of electroconvulsive therapy. *Br. J. Psychiat.* **139**, 265-283.

Kety, S. (1974): Biochemical and neurochemical effects of electroconvulsive shock. In *Psychobiology of convulsive therapy*, ed M. Fink, S. Kety, J. McGaugh & T. Williams. Pp. 285-294. Washington, D.C.: V. H. Winston & Sons.

Kirkegaard, C. (1981): The thyrotropin response to thyrotropin-releasing hormone in endogenous depression. *Psychoneuroendocrinol.* **6**, 189-212.

Kirkegaard, C., Bjørum, N., Cohn, D. & Lauridsen, U. B. (1978): Thyrotrophin-releasing hormone (TRH) stimulation tests in manic-depressive illness. *Arch. Gen. Psychiat.* **35**, 1017-1021.

Lerer, B. & Belmaker, R. H. (1982): Receptors and the mechanism of action of ECT. *Biol. Psychiat.* **17**, 497-511.

Loosen, P. T. & Prange, A. J., Jr. (1980): Thyrotropin releasing hormone (TRH): A useful tool for psychoendocrine investigation. *Psychoneuroendocrinol.* **5**, 63-80.

Meco, G., Casacchia, M., Carchedi, F., Falaschi, P., Rocco, A. & Frajese, G. (1978): Prolactin response to repeated electroconvulsive therapy in acute schizophrenia. *Lancet* **1**, 999.

Modigh, K., Balldin, J., Eden, S., Granerus, A.-K. & Walinder, J. (1981): Electroconvulsive therapy and receptor sensitivity. *Acta Psychiat. Scand.* **63**, 91-99 (suppl. 290).

Nedophil, N. & Rütter, E. (1979): Effects of the synthetic analogue of methionine enkephalin FK 33-824 on psychotic symptoms. *Pharmakopsych. Neuro-Psychopharm.* **12**, 277-280.

O'Dea, J. P. K., Gould, D., Hallberg, M. & Wieland, R. G. (1978): Prolactin changes during electroconvulsive therapy. *Am. J. Psychiat.* **135**, 609-611.

Öhman, R., Balldin, J., Walinder, J. & Wallin, L. (1976): Prolactin response to electroconvulsive therapy. *Lancet* **1**, 936-938.

Palmer, R. L. (ed) (1981): *Electroconvulsive therapy: an appraisal.* Oxford: Oxford University Press.

Papakostas, Y., Fink, M., Lee, J., Johnson, L. & Irwin, P. (1981): Neuroendocrine measures in psychiatric patients: Course and outcome with ECT. *Psychiat. Res.* **4**, 55-64.

Pickar, D., Davis, G. C., Schulz, S. C., Extein, I., Wagner, R., Naber, D., Gold, P. W., van Kammen, D. P., Goodwin, F. K., Wyatt, R. J., Li, C. H. & Bunney, W. E. (1981): Behavioral and biological effects of acute beta-endorphin injection in schizophrenic and depressed patients. *Amer. J. Psychiat.* **138**, 160-166.

Pippard, J. & Ellam, L. (1981): *Electroconvulsive Treatment in Great Britain, 1980.* London: Gaskell.

Pitts, F. N. & Patterson, C. W. (1979): Electroconvulsive therapy for iatrogenic hypothalamic-hypopituitariam (CRF-ACTH type). *Am. J. Psychiat.* **136**, 1074-1077.

Pryor, G. T. (1974): Effects of repeated ECS on brain weight and brain enzymes. In *Psychobiology of convulsive therapy*, ed M. Fink, S. Kety, J. McGaugh & T. Williams. Pp. 171-184. Washington D.C.: V. H. Winston & Sons.

Raskind, M., Orenstein, H. & Weitzmann, R. E. (1979): Vasopressin in depression. *Lancet* **1**, 164.

Reis, R. & Bokan, J. (1979): Electroconvulsive therapy following pituitary surgery. *J. Nerv. Ment. Dis.* **167**, 767-768.

Roth, M. (1952): A theory of E.C.T. action and its bearing on the biological significance of epilepsy. *J. Ment. Sci.* **98**, 44-59.

Roth, M., Kay, D. W. K., Shaw, J. & Green, J. (1957): Prognosis and pentothal induced electroencephalographic changes in electroconvulsive treatment. *Electroenceph. Clin. Neurophysiol.* **9**, 225-237.

Schlesser, M. A., Winokur, G. & Sherman, B. M. (1979): Genetic subtypes of unipolar primary depressive illness distinguished by hypothalamic-pituitary-adrenal axis activity. *Lancet* **1**, 739-742.

Trimble, M. R. (1978): Serum prolactin in epilepsy and hysteria. *Br. Med. J.* **1**, 1682.

Verhoeven, W. M., van Praag, H. A., van Ree, J. M. & de Wied, D. (1979): Improvement of schizophrenic patients treated with (des-Tyr¹)-gamma-endorphin (DTgammaE). *Arch. Gen. Psychiat.* **36**, 294-302.

Verhoeven, W. M. A., van Ree, J. M., Heezius-van Bentum, A., de Wied, D. & van Praag, H. (1982): Antipsychotic properties of des-enkephalin-gamma-endorphin in treatment of schizophrenic patients. *Arch. Gen. Psychiat.* **39**, 648-654.

Volavka, J. (1974): Is EEG slowing related to therapeutic effect of convulsive therapy? In *Psychobiology of Convulsive Therapy*, ed M. Fink, S. Kety, J. McGaugh & T. A. Williams. Pp. 35-40. Washington, D.C.: V. H. Winston & Sons.

Volavka, J., Feldstein, S., Abrams, R., Dornbush, R. & Fink, M. (1972): EEG and clinical changes after bilateral and unilateral electroconvulsive therapy. *Electroenceph. Clin. Neurophysiol.* **32**, 631-639.

Weinstein, E. A. & Kahn, R. L. (1955): *Denial of illness*. Springfield, Ill.: C. C. Thomas.

Weinstein, E. A., Linn, L. & Kahn, R. L. (1952): Psychosis during electroshock therapy: Its relation to the theory of shock therapy. *Am. J. Psychiat.* **109**, 22-26.

15.
Changes in regional cerebral blood flow during ECT

P. SILFVERSKIÖLD, L. GUSTAFSON and J. RISBERG

Department of Psychiatry, Laboratory of Neuropsychology, University Hospital, S-221 85 Lund, Sweden.

Introduction

Electroconvulsive therapy (ECT) is today still an unsurpassed treatment for depressive states. Scientifically there has always been great interest in its mode of action and its influence on different structures and functions in the brain.

Several studies have been directed at answering the question of whether ECT causes brain damage or permanent psychological sequelae. In cats Hartelius (1952) reported mainly reversible changes in nerve cells and vessels and glial reactions following four daily electrically induced seizures. Reviews by Corsellis & Meyer (1954) and Corsellis & Meldrum (1976) concluded that uncomplicated ECT in man causes only minimal pathological changes in brain tissue. Negative effects of ECT on cognitive functions have been demonstrated (Cronholm & Molander, 1957); these may vary depending on the electrode placement. Unilateral ECT over the nondominant hemisphere causes less post-ictal confusion and disturbance of verbal memory than does bilateral ECT. Both types of ECT, however, appear to be clinically equally effective (d'Elia, 1970; d'Elia & Raotma, 1975, 1977; Strömgren, 1973).

The development of methods for measuring the cerebral blood flow (CBF) has opened a new pathway for understanding the function of the normal and the diseased brain. There is a tight coupling between the CBF, the cerebral oxygen consumption and the neuronal activity of the brain (Raichle *et al.*, 1976). The first clinical application of CBF measurements in the psychiatric field was made by Kety *et al.* (1948) using the nitrous oxide technique. They found a normal CBF level in 22 schizophrenic patients. Measurements following single ECT in seven patients showed a marked (35 per cent) decrease in CBF. With the same technique Wilson *et al.* (1952) studied a group of 22 psychotic patients (including 10 with depressive and 9 with schizophrenic illness) before and after an ECT series. They found a small, nonsignificant CBF decrease after an average of 10 treatments. This CBF change could neither be related to clinical improvement nor to occurrence of post-ictal confusion.

The intra-arterial ^{133}Xe clearance technique for measuring the *regional* CBF (rCBF) (Lassen & Ingvar, 1963, 1972) has been used in several clinical studies in the psychiatric field. A few of these have concerned affective disorders and ECT. In presenile dementia, the CBF level has been found to be subnormal (Gustafson *et al.*, 1981*b*) in demented patients; where symptoms of depression were also found, the flow level was higher than in patients lacking such symptoms (Gustafson & Risberg, 1974; Gustafson & Hagberg, 1975). In 11 patients receiving ECT with endogeneous depression, Broderson *et al.* (1973) found that the CBF and oxygen and glucose uptake doubled during seizures. Changes in the blood–brain barrier permeability during seizures have long been known (Aird *et al.*, 1956; Angel & Roberts, 1966) and a relationship to the therapeutic effect of ECT has been suggested. Bolwig *et al.* (1977*b*) found an increase in the permeability of the blood–brain barrier in rats after 10 electroshock stimuli. In man, Bolwig *et al.* (1977*a*) studied rCBF permeability of the blood–brain barrier, during and after ECT and during hypercapnia in 22 patients with endogeneous depression. The results in man indicated that the increased permeability of the blood–brain barrier in these high flow situations was related to the increase in CBF and not to the epileptic activity per se. In the animal study acute systemic hypertension was the suspected cause of the blood–brain barrier breakdown.

The development of the nontraumatic ^{133}Xe inhalation technique (Obrist *et al.*, 1967; Risberg, 1980) has reduced many technical and ethical problems associated with measuring rCBF in psychiatric patients. The method allows bilateral and repeated rCBF measurements and requires no premedication. Using this technique Mathew *et al.* (1980) reported a decreased rCBF in 13 depressed patients as compared to a control group. The results are, however, difficult to interpret since apCO$_2$ values are not reported. Furthermore the conclusion of the authors that depressive illness is coupled to a subnormal flow level seems doubtful, since the observed rCBF level was within the normal range of most other published reports (Blauenstein *et al.*, 1977; Prohovnik *et al.*, 1980). This conclusion (Mathew *et al.*, 1980) is also not supported by Bolwig *et al.* (1977*a*) who found rCBF levels to be normal (intra-arterial technique) in depressed patients prior to treatment. In addition, preliminary data related to the present study has revealed normal levels and distributions of rCBF in depression (Silfverskiöld *et al.*, 1979) in contrast to findings in patients of similar age with organic dementia (Gustafson *et al.*, 1981*a,b*).

A new area of research in affective disorders attracting increasing interest is the study of functional hemispheric asymmetries. There is now evidence that not only cognitive but also emotional functions are lateralized. Clinical studies indicate that different mental disorders, including affective illness as well as schizophrenia, could be related to functional differences between the two hemispheres (Flor-Henry, 1969; Gainotti, 1972; d'Elia & Perris, 1973; Yozawitz *et al.*, 1979; Flor-Henry & Koles, 1980). Bilateral rCBF measurements using the ^{133}Xe inhalation technique have been successful in studying the hemispheric and regional specialization of the brain for different cognitive and emotional functions (Risberg *et al.*, 1975; Gur & Reivich, 1980; Maximilian *et al.*, 1980; Risberg & Prohovnik, 1983; Johanson *et al.*, 1983).

The rCBF data reported here are part of a larger study attempting to elucidate cerebral mechanisms linked to single and serial unilateral and bilateral ECT in depressed patients. Data collected also included psychiatric ratings, psychometric testing and EEG. The results from these examinations are published elsewhere (Silfverskiöld *et al.*, 1983).

Patients and methods

Patients
Thirty-two patients referred for ECT with symptoms of depression were selected for the study. According to the diagnostic classification of DSM III (A.P.A. 1980) these included 22 patients with major depression, 5 patients with bipolar disorder, 1 case of dysthymic disorder and 4 cases of atypical affective disorder. None of the patients had received ECT within one year prior to the investigation. All patients reported right-handedness. Patients with neurological deficits, chronic psychosis or addiction were excluded from the study. Tricyclics, barbiturates and benzodiazepines were not used during the ECT series.

The sample was divided into two groups based on type of ECT:

Unilateral ECT group. 26 patients (13 men, 13 women), age 58.4 ± 13.8 years.

Bilateral ECT group. 9 patients (4 men, 5 women), age 67.2 ± 11.9 years. In this group one woman relapsed and was treated again with a bilateral ECT series. This woman and two of the men in the bilaterally treated group had been treated with unilateral ECT during previous depressive episodes and are therefore present in both groups. The current data are thus based on 10 series of bilateral and 26 series of unilateral ECT in 32 patients.

Methods
The patients were examined with psychiatric ratings, psychometric testing, EEG and rCBF immediately before and 60–90 min after ECT on three different occasions during the ECT

Table 1. *Effects of ECT in depression research design*

	Pre-ECT (1–2 days)	ECT 1 pre	ECT 1 post	ECT 3–4 pre	ECT 3–4 post	ECT 5–7 pre	ECT 5–7 post	Post-ECT controls
Psychiatric rating		X	X	X	X	X	X	X
EEG, frequency analysis		X	X	X	X	X	X	X
rCBF		X	X	X	X	X	X	X
Psychometric testing								
Extensive	X							X
Verbal memory		X	X	X	X	X	X	X

series (see Table 1)). Treatments were given two or three times a week. Only the rCBF data will be reported at this time.

rCBF measurements
The regional cerebral blood flow (rCBF) was measured during rest in 16 regions of each hemisphere by the ^{133}Xe inhalation technique (Obrist *et al.*, 1975; Risberg *et al.*, 1975) together with the arterial partial CO_2 pressure (apCO_2). A detailed description of the measurement system (NDS-Inhalation-Cerebrograph) and the methods of curve analysis are presented elsewhere (Risberg, 1980). In the present study the Initial Slope Index (ISI) (Risberg *et al.*, 1975) will be used. This index of mainly grey matter blood flow was selected due to its high reliability. The ISI flow values are presented as (i) absolute values or (ii) as relative distribution values (in per cent of the total mean of the two hemispheres). The mean of the relative distribution values in five frontal and fronto-temporal regions is called 'frontal per cent'.

Electroconvulsive therapy
A conventional ECT apparatus (Siemens Convulsator 622) and procedure were used. The electrode placement was either bifronto-temporal (bilateral ECT) or unilateral (nondominant) as described by d'Elia (1970). The brief narcosis included atropine, the ultrashort-acting barbiturate methohexital and a muscle relaxant.

Results
Fig. 1 shows the rCBF during rest in 32 depressed patients before the first ECT compared to a young (28 ± 7 years) and health reference group, previously studied in our laboratory (Prohovnik *et al.*, 1980).

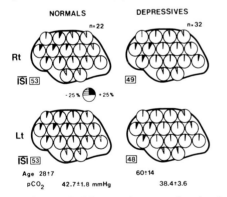

Fig. 1. *rCBF values (ISI) of the right (Rt) and left (Lt) hemispheres in normals (n = 22) and depressives (n = 32). The mean hemispheric flow values are shown in the squares. The clock symbols indicate the regional variation of the mean hemispheric flow values. Black means above, striped means below the mean hemispheric flow value. 90° indicates a 25 per cent deviation from the mean hemispheric value*

The small difference between flow levels of the two groups can be explained by differences in age (Lavy *et al.*, 1979) and apCO_2 (Maximilian *et al.*, 1980). The flow distribution was also very similar in the two groups with somewhat higher flow values in the frontal areas of the brain constituting the normal hyperfrontal rCBF pattern during rest (Wilkinson *et al.*, 1969; Ingvar, 1979; Prohovnik *et al.*, 1980).

Unilateral ECT

Table 2. *Changes of rCBF before and after unilateral ECT in depression.* Age 58.4 ± 13.8 years

	ECT 1 (n = 26)		ECT 3–4 (n = 21)		ECT 5–7 (n = 26)	
ISI	Left	Right	Left	Right	Left	Right
Pre-ECT	48.0 ± 6.7	48.2 ± 6.7	46.8 ± 7.4	47.3 ± 7.8	45.9 ± 8.9	46.1 ± 7.9
Post-ECT	45.5 ± 6.0	45.0 ± 6.2	44.6 ± 6.3	44.3 ± 6.8	44.6 ± 7.2	44.1 ± 7.2
t-test	$P < 0.05$	$P < 0.01$	$P < 0.05$	$P < 0.01$	n.s.	$P < 0.05$
apCO$_2$						
Pre-ECT		38.6 ± 3.8		37.6 ± 4.4		37.6 ± 3.6
Post-ECT		39.4 ± 3.7		38.4 ± 3.5		38.5 ± 3.6
t-test		n.s.		n.s.		$P < 0.01$

Table 2 shows mean hemispheric rCBF (ISI) before and after unilateral ECT 1, 3–4 and 5–7. Following ECT 1 and 3–4 the mean level decreased bilaterally with a tendency for a slightly larger decrease on the right side (5–7 per cent, $P < 0.01$ right, $P < 0.05$ left). A smaller but similar rCBF change was found at ECT 5–7 again with a somewhat larger reduction on the right side ($P < 0.05$). Before ECT 3–4 and 5–7 the rCBF level tended to approach the pre-ECT 1 level. On these three ECT occasions apCO$_2$ showed a small but consistent increase from pre- to post-ECT measurements being significant ($P < 0.01$) on the third ECT occasion.

Fig. 2 shows the regional rCBF results and Fig. 3 the differences between pre- and post-ECT values throughout the ECT series. Before ECT 1 there was, as previously stated, a normal, hyperfrontal and symmetric flow pattern. After ECT 1 there was a tendency for frontal areas to show larger flow decreases than other regions, especially on the right side. Before ECT 3–4 the regional distribution was equal to that found before ECT 1. After ECT 3–4 there was again a frontal decrease affecting the right more than the left side. On the third ECT occasion there was a change in flow distribution similar to but smaller than that following ECT 3–4.

Table 3 shows changes in frontal per cent from pre-ECT 1 to pre-ECT 5–7. There was a small rCBF reduction of about 2 per cent on the right side ($P < 0.01$) as compared to a 1 per cent reduction on the left side ($P < 0.05$).

Bilateral ECT
Table 4 shows the mean hemispheric rCBF data from the 10 series of bilateral ECT. The rCBF differences between pre- and post-ECT throughout the bilateral ECT series are shown in Fig. 5. The very pronounced flow reduction after ECT 1 is clearly seen. It involved all measured areas of the brain in contrast to later in the series, when the decreases were more marked in frontal areas. No significant right–left differences were found. There was no significant change in frontal per cent from pre-ECT 1 to pre-ECT 5–7.

Discussion
The results indicate that our depressed patients had normal rCBF levels and normal regional distributions before ECT. As discussed in the introduction, the results of Mathew *et al.* (1980) are within the normal range and thus agree with our findings. These normal findings in depressed patients differ considerably, however, from rCBF results in patients of similar age with organic dementia, who have subnormal flow levels and focal flow abnormalities (Gustafson *et al.*, 1981a,b). Although depressive symptoms may occur in connection with brain damage and dementia, our findings do not support any direct relation between depressive illness and global or regional cortical functional abnormalities. (Pathology in deeper, ie limbic structures, inaccessible by the present rCBF method, cannot of course be excluded.) The existence of a subgroup of depressed patients, who also have an organic brain disorder and abnormal rCBF values, has been suggested in a previous report from our laboratory (Silfverskiöld *et al.*, 1979). These results agree with the findings of Jacoby & Levy (1980), who in a study using computed tomography found abnormalities in a subgroup of elderly depressed patients.

127

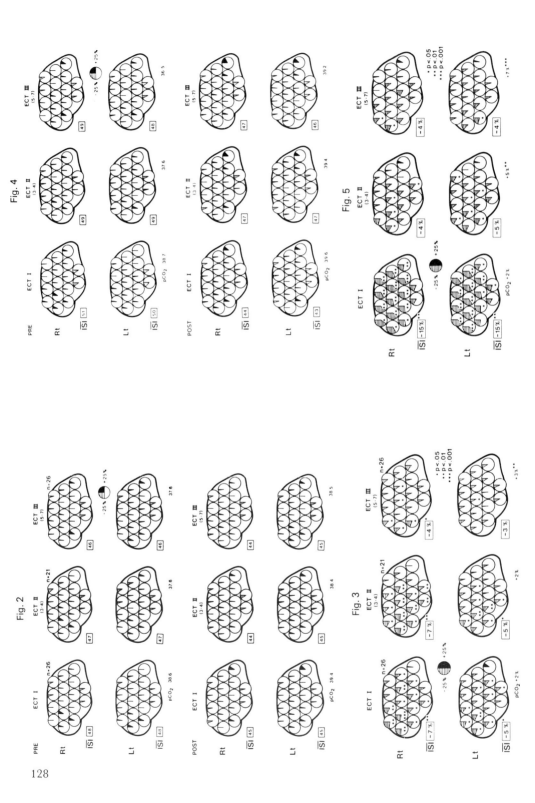

Fig. 2

Fig. 3

Fig. 4

Fig. 5

128

Table 3. *rCBF changes in frontal per cent during unilateral ECT in depression*
(*n* = 26) Age 56.4 ± 13.8 years

	Frontal per cent	
	Left	Right
Pre-ECT 1	104 ± 4.1	104 ± 3.1
Pre-ECT 5–7	103 ± 3.2	102 ± 3.8
t-test	$P < 0.05$	$P < 0.01$

Table 4. *Changes of rCBF during bilateral ECT in depression* (*n* = 10) Age 67.2 ± 11.9 years

	ECT 1		ECT 3–4		ECT 5–7	
ISI	Left	Right	Left	Right	Left	Right
Pre-ECT	50.3 ± 9.6	51.4 ± 9.6	48.9 ± 6.4	49.1 ± 6.6	48.1 ± 7.6	48.6 ± 7.9
Post-ECT	42.8 ± 5.3	43.6 ± 5.3	46.5 ± 6.9	47.1 ± 6.6	46.1 ± 5.2	46.5 ± 5.7
t-test	$P < 0.01$	$P < 0.01$	n.s.	n.s.	n.s.	n.s.
apCO$_2$						
Pre-ECT	38.7 ± 2.9		37.6 ± 3.6		36.5 ± 4.6	
Post-ECT	39.6 ± 2.8		39.4 ± 2.5		39.2 ± 4.6	
t-test	n.s.		$P < 0.01$		$P < 0.001$	

Table 5. *Changes of rCBF (corrected for apCO$_2$) during bilateral ECT in depression* (*n* = 10) Age 67.2 ±
11.9 years

	ECT 1		ECT 3–4		ECT 5–7	
ISI	Left	Right	Left	Right	Left	Right
Pre-ECT	51.3 ± 8.1	52.5 ± 8.2	50.6 ± 4.4	50.9 ± 4.6	50.7 ± 6.5	51.2 ± 6.5
Post-ECT	43.3 ± 4.1	44.0 ± 3.9	47.0 ± 5.9	47.6 ± 5.8	46.7 ± 5.4	47.2 ± 5.6
t-test	$P < 0.001$	$P < 0.001$	$P < 0.01$	$P < 0.05$	$P < 0.01$	$P < 0.01$

apCO$_2$ corrected to 40 mmHg

A very consistent decrease in flow level was found following each ECT occasion irrespective of electrode placement. This finding is in line with the results of Kety *et al.* (1948) and Bolwig *et al.* (1977a). Comparing the two types of ECT we did, however, find that bilateral ECT 1 was associated with twice the decrease found in the unilateral group. Later in the series the decreases were less pronounced and similar in both groups. The flow decreases cannot be explained by differences in apCO$_2$ nor by effects of medication given during ECT. The effects of atropine and narcosis (sham ECT) were investigated in a pilot study of four cases, where the mean hemispheric flow level (ISI) pre-ECT was 49.1 ± 6.2 and post-ECT 53.2 ± 7.1. It therefore seems likely that these decreases are related to cerebral functional changes associated with ECT.

The more marked flow reduction following bilateral ECT 1 indicates a difference between the stimulation techniques with a possibly stronger cortical involvement of the seizure activity following the initial bilateral ECT. This finding again raises the question of possible differences in therapeutic effects between uni- and bi-lateral ECT. Some authors have reported a better effect of bilateral ECT, especially in the early phase of a treatment series (Fleminger *et al.*, 1970; Cronin *et al.*, 1970; Abrams *et al.*, 1972; Abrams, 1982). Our results corroborate the EEG findings of d'Elia (1970) who demonstrated that bilateral ECT produced higher integrated voltage than did unilateral ECT.

The somewhat asymmetric flow decrease in frontal areas following unilateral ECT is probably directly linked to electrode placement with more seizure activity in the ipsilateral

---

Figures 2–4 opposite.
Fig. 2. *rCBF pre- and post-unilateral ECT.*
Fig. 3. *Changes in rCBF during unilateral ECT in depression. Differences in ISI from pre- to post-ECT. The difference in hemispheric means is expressed as per cent of the pre-ECT value in the squares. The clock symbols indicate the regional flow differences. 180° indicate a 25 per cent deviation from the pre-ECT value.*
Fig. 4. *rCBF pre- and post-bilateral ECT (n = 10).*
Fig. 5. *Changes in rCBF during bilateral depression. Differences in ISI from pre- to post-ECT (n = 10).*

cortical areas. This result is consistent with the asymmetric EEG findings following unilateral ECT discussed by d'Elia (1970). As expected the flow decrease found following bilateral ECT was symmetric.

Concerning the relation between the effects of ECT and rCBF changes, preliminary data have shown that in patients with a good therapeutic outcome, the rCBF level was well preserved after the ECT series compared to the pretreatment level. In patients with less improvement, however, the flow level decreased significantly from before to after the ECT series. We have also found that patients with a low initial rCBF level (compared to the other patients in the study) had a more pronounced vulnerability to disturbances of the memory consolidation process caused by ECT (Johanson et al., 1979).

While significant 'acute' changes of rCBF were recorded on the day of treatment, our results also indicate very small persistent changes during and after the ECT series. This will be further explored in forthcoming publications, which will include data from followup measurements after the ECT series. We will also correlate clinical, psychometric and EEG findings with the rCBF results to further elucidate the effects of ECT.

Acknowledgements — This investigation was supported by The Swedish Medical Research Council (projects No. 04969 and 03950), The King Gustaf V and Queen Victoria's Foundation, The Swedish Council for Social Science Research and The Medical Research Council of the Swedish Life Insurance Companies. The authors are indebted to Siv Karlson for his excellent technical assistance and to Mrs Maj Lantz for her efficient secretarial aid.

References

Abrams, R. (1982): Bilateral or unilateral ECT? *Lancet* **2**, 112.

Abrams, R., Fink, M., Dornbush, R. L., Feldstein, S., Volavka, J. & Roubicek, J. (1972): Unilateral and bilateral electroconvulsive therapy. *Arch. Gen. Psychiat.* **27**, 88–91.

Aird, R. B., Strait, L. A., Pace, J. W., Hrenoff, M. K. & Bowditch, S. (1956): Neurophysiologic effects of electrically induced convulsions. *A.M.A. Arch. Neurol. Psychiat.* **75**, 371–378.

American Psychiatric Association (1980): *Diagnostic and statistic manual of mental disorders (DSM III)*, 3rd edn. Washington D.C.: American Psychiatric Association.

Angel, C. & Roberts, A. J. (1966): Effect of electroshock and antidepressant drugs on cerebrovascular permeability to cocaine in the rat. *J. Nerve. Ment. Dis.* **142**, 376–380.

Blauenstein, U. W., Halsey, J. H., Wilson, E. M., Wills, E. H. & Risberg, J. (1977): 133-xenon inhalation method, analysis of reproducibility: some of its physiological implications. *Stroke* **8**, 92–102.

Bolwig, T. G., Hertz, M. M., Paulson, O. B., Spotoft, H. & Rafaelsen, O. J. (1977a): The permeability of the blood-brain barrier during electrically induced seizures in man. *Eur. J. Clin. Invest.* **7**, 87–93.

Bolwig, T. G., Hertz, M. M. & Westergaard, E. (1977b): Acute hypertension causing blood brain barrier breakdown during epileptic seizures. *Acta Neurol. Scand.* **56**, 335–342.

Brodersen, P., Paulson, O. B., Bolwig, T. G., Rogon, Z. E., Rafaelsen, O. J. & Laasen, N. A. (1973): Cerebral hyperemia in electrically induced epileptic seizures. *Arch. Neurol.* **28**, 334–338.

Corsellis, J. A. N. & Meldrum, B. S. (1976): The pathology of epilepsy. In *Greenfields Neuropathology*, 3rd edn, eds. W. Blackwood & J. A. N. Corsellis). Pp. 771–795. London: Edward Arnold.

Cronholm, B. & Molander, L. (1957): Memory disturbances after electroconvulsive therapy. *Acta Psychiat. Scand.* **32**, 280–306.

Cronin, D., Bodley, P., Potts, L., Mather, M. D., Gardner, R. K. & Tobin, J. C. (1970): Unilateral and bilateral ECT: a study of memory disturbance and relief from depression. *J. Neurol. Neurosurg. Psychiat.* **33**, 705–713.

d'Elia, G. (1970): Unilateral electroconvulsive therapy. *Acta Psychiat. Scand.* **215** suppl., 5–98.

d'Elia, G. and Perris, C. (1973): Cerebral functional dominance and depression. *Acta Psychiat. Scand.* **49**, 191–197.

d'Elia, G. & Raotma, H. (1975): Is unilateral ECT less effective than bilateral ECT? *Br. J. Psychiat.* **126**, 83–89.

d'Elia, G. & Raotma, H. (1977): Memory impairment after convulsive therapy. *Arch. Psychiat. Nervenkr.* **223**, 219–226.

Fleminger, J. J., de Horne, D. J., Nair, N. P. V. & Nott, P. N. (1970): Differential effect of unilateral and bilateral ECT. *Am. J. Psychiat.* **127**, 430–436.

Flor-Henry, P. (1969): Psychosis and temporal lobe epilepsy. A controlled investigation. *Epilepsia* **10**, 363–395.

Flor-Henry, P. & Koles, Z. J. (1980): EEG studies in depression, mania and normals: evidence for partial shifts of laterality in the affective psychoses. *Adv. Biol. Psychiat.* **4**, 21–43.

Gainotti, G. (1972): Emotional behaviour and hemispheric side of the lesion. *Cortex* **8**, 41–55.

Gur, R. C. & Reivich, M. (1980): Cognitive task effects on hemispheric blood flow in humans: Evidence for individual differences in hemispheric activation. *Brain Lang.* **9**, 78–92.

Gustafson, L. & Hagberg, B. (1975): Emotional behaviour, personality changes and cognitive reduction in presenile dementia related to regional cerebral blood flow. *Acta Psychiat. Scand.* **257** suppl., 39–68.

Gustafson, L. & Risberg, J. (1974): Regional cerebral blood flow related to psychiatric symptoms in dementia with onset in the presenile period. *Acta Psychiat. Scand.* **50**, 516–538.

Gustafson, L., Risberg, J. & Silfverskiöld, P. (1981a): Cerebral blood flow in dementia and depression. *Lancet* 1, 275.

Gustafson, L., Risberg, J. & Silfverskiöld, P. (1981b): Regional cerebral blood flow in organic dementia and affective disorders. *Adv. Biol. Psychiat.* 6, 109–116.

Hartelius, H. (1952): Cerebral changes following electrically induced convulsions. An experimental study on cata. *Acta Psychiat. Scand.* 77, 1–128.

Ingvar, D. H. (1979): 'Hyperfrontal' distribution of the cerebral grey matter flow in resting wakefulness: on the functional anatomy of the conscious state. *Acta Neurol. Scand.* 60, 2–25.

Jacoby, R. J. & Levy, R. (1980): Computed tomography in the elderly. 3. Affective disorder. *Br. J. Psychiat.* 136, 270–275.

Johanson, M., Risberg, J., Silfverskiöld, P. & Gustafson, L. (1979): Regional cerebral blood flow related to acute memory disturbances following electroconvulsive therapy in depression. Föredrag vid *9th International Symposium on Cerebral Blood Flow and Metabolism*, Tokyo 29 May–1 June 1979.

Johanson, M., Silfverskiöld, P., Smith, G. & Risberg, J. (1983): Regional cerebral blood flow in anxiety. *Acta Neurol. Scand.* 60 suppl. 72 534–535.

Kety, S. S., Woodford, R. B., Harmel, M. H., Freyhan, F. A., Appel, K. E. & Schmidt, C. F. (1948): Cerebral blood flow and metabolism in schizophrenia. *Am. J. Psychiat.* 104, 765–770.

Lassen, N. A. & Ingvar, D. H. (1963): Regional cerebral blood flow measurements in man. *Arch. Neurol.* 9, 615–622.

Lassen, N. A. & Ingvar, D. H. (1972): Radioisotopic assessment of regional cerebral blood flow. *Progr. Nucl. Med.* 1, 376–409.

Lavy, S., Melamed, E., Cooper, G., Bentin, S. & Rinot, Y. (1979): Regional cerebral blood flow in patients with Parkinson's Disease. *Arch. Neurol.* 36, 344–348.

Mathew, R. J., Meyer, J. S., Semchuk, K. M., Francis, D. J., Mortel, K. & Claghorn, J. L. (1980): Cerebral blood flow in depression. *Lancet*, 1308.

Maximilian, V. A., Prohovnik, I. & Risberg, J. (1980): Cerebral hemodynamic response to mental activation in normo- and hyper-capnia. *Stroke* 11, 342–347.

Obrist, W. D., Thompson Jr, H. K., King, C. H. & Wang, H. S. (1967): Determination of regional cerebral blood flow by inhalation of 133-xenon. *Circulation Res.* 20, 124–135.

Obrist, W. D., Thompson, H. K., Wang, H. S. & Wilkinson, W. E. (1975): Regional cerebral blood flow estimated by 133-xenon inhalation. *Stroke* 6, 245–256.

Prohovnik, I., Håkansson, K. & Risberg, J. (1980): Observations on the functional significance of regional cerebral blood flow in resting normal subjects. *Neuropsychologia* 18, 203–217.

Raichle, M. E., Grubb, R. L., Gado, M. H., Eichling, J. O. & Terpogossian, M. T. (1976): Correlation between regional cerebral blood flow and oxidative metabolism. *Arch. Neurol.* 8, 523–526.

Risberg, J. (1980): Regional cerebral blood flow measurements by 133-xenon inhalation: methodology and applications in neuropsychology and psychiatry. *Brain Lang.* 9, 9–34.

Risberg, J., Halsey, J. H., Wills, E. L. & Wilson, E. M. (1975): Hemispheric specialization in normal man studied by bilateral measurement of the regional cerebral blood flow. Brain 98, 511–524.

Risberg, J. & Prohovnik, I. (1983): Cortical processing of visual and tactile stimuli studied by noninvasive rCBF measurements. *Hum. Neurobiol.* 2, 5–10.

Silfverskiöld, P., Gustafson, L., Johanson, M. & Risberg, J. (1979): Regional cerebral blood flow related to the effect of electroconvulsive therapy in depression. In *Biological psychiatry today*, ed J. Obiols, C. Ballús, E. González & J. Pujol. Pp. 1178–1183. Amsterdam: Elsevier/North Holland.

Silfverskiöld, P., Gustafson, L., Johanson, M. & Risberg, J. (1983): Regional cerebral blood flow in affective disorders. In *Brain imaging and regional function in psychiatry and neurology: positron emission tomography and other techniques*, ed M. S. Buchsbaum, W. E. Bunney Jr, E. Usdin & D. H. Ingvar. Boxwood/Synapse.

Strömgren, L. S. (1973): Unilateral versus bilateral ECT. *Acta Psychiat. Scand.* 240 suppl.

Wilkinson, I. M. S., Bull, J. W. D., duBoulay, G. H., Marchall, J., Ross Russel, R. W., Symon, L. (1969): Regional blood flow in the normal cerebral hemisphere. *J. Neurol. Neurosurg. Psychiat.* 32, 367–378.

Wilson, W. P., Schieve, J. F. & Scheinberg, P. (1952): Effects of series of electric shock treatments on cerebral blood flow and metabolism. *Arch. Neurol. Psychiat.* 68, 651–654.

Yozawitz, A., Bruder, G., Sutton, S., Sharpe, L., Gurland, B., Fleiss, J. & Costa, L. (1979): Dichotic perception: Evidence for right hemisphere dysfunction in affective psychosis. *Br. J. Psychiat.* 135, 224–237.

131

16.
The influence of electrically-induced seizures on deep brain structures

T. G. BOLWIG

Department of Psychiatry, Rigshospitalet, Copenhagen, Denmark.

Introduction

Like other treatment modalities electroconvulsive therapy (ECT) has wanted and unwanted effects. The former is its superiority to other treatment approaches in the therapy of severe endogenous depression (for review, see Fink, 1979) and also certain other conditions, eg delirious states (Kramp & Bolwig, 1981). The latter is the well-known transient disturbance of cognitive functions induced by ECT (d'Elia & Raotma, 1977; Squire, 1975, 1977; Heshe *et al.*, 1978).

During a generalized epileptic seizure which is believed to underlie the therapeutic action of ECT, a multitude of physiological and biochemical events have been documented, both in experimental studies and in clinical investigations (for review, see Ottosson, 1962, 1974). Yet the mode of action of this therapeutic modality is not known even after more than 40 years of use. Although many theories have been proposed, so far no unified hypothesis seems justified. Recently Fink & Ottosson (1980) published a theory of convulsive therapy based on the findings of neuroendocrine abnormalities characterizing patients with endogenous depression — abnormalities reversed by convulsive therapy. Earlier, Ottosson's classical electrophysiological studies clearly pointed to the involvement of the diencephalon in the therapeutic process elicited by ECT (Ottosson, 1962). A series of studies performed in Copenhagen with the purpose of throwing light on the mechanism of action of ECT seem to support the above-mentioned theories and are described below.

Blood–brain barrier (BBB) studies

Most previous work concerning BBB and electrically induced seizures have been animal studies in which the effects of prolonged and repeated seiziures were studied (Angel & Roberts, 1966; Lorenzo *et al.*, 1972, 1975). An increased blood to brain transfer of both small and large molecules was demonstrated. These studies, however, seem more applicable to a model for epilepsy than to one for ECT.

We therefore decided to
(1) study in animals the effects of ECS given under such experimental conditions that a direct comparison with the clinical situation could be reasonably justified. We used the indicator dilution method originally described by Crone (1963) in studies of the transfer of small molecules across the cerebral vessels (Bolwig *et al.*, 1977a).
(2) Concomitantly this methodology was applied in a study of depressed patients undergoing ECT (Bolwig *et al.*, 1977b).
(3) Finally, when the similarity of findings was established, we studied in animals the morphology of some basic mechanisms underlying the pathophysiological observations.

The indicator dilution technique involves the rapid injection into the internal carotid artery of one or more labelled substances, whose passage is to be studied (test substances). In the same injectate a nonpermeable tracer (reference substance) is introduced and fractional sampling from the jugular vein in humans (Fig. 1) or the sagittal sinus (in rats) is carried out. Thereby the transcapillary escape of the substance(s) during a single passage through the brain can be estimated by comparing the areas under the venous outflow curves for reference and test substances. The fractional transcapillary permeability of a substance is termed the extraction coefficient (E) and is calculated at any point of the tracer dilution curve an example of which is seen in Fig. 2, according to the following equation:

$$E(t) = \frac{C_{\text{ref}(t)} - C_{\text{test}(t)}}{C_{\text{ref}(t)}} \tag{1}$$

where $C_{\text{ref}(t)}$ and $C_{\text{test}(t)}$ are the relative concentrations of the reference and the test substance, respectively, corresponding to the time, t.

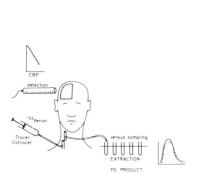

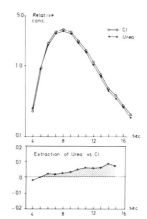

Fig. 1. *Blood–brain barrier study in man. Also see text*

Fig. 2. *Venous outflow and extraction curves of ^{14}C-urea (●) compared to the co-tracer $^{36}Cl-$(○). Also see text*

The best estimate of BBB-permeability for smaller molecules is the so called permeability surface area product (PS), or the capillary diffusion capacity (CDC), as it also takes into account the cerebral blood flow (CBF) as shown in equation (2):

$$PS = CBF \times \ln(1 - E) \tag{2}$$

Thus, PS and CBF have the same dimension, ie volume per weight per time.

As mentioned earlier, the animal study and the human investigation were performed under comparable circumstances: anaesthesia, muscular relaxation, artificial ventilation and with the application of a suprathreshold electrical stimulus eliciting generalized seizure activity lasting 40–60 s.

In the patient study we further induced hypercapnia for a brief period 15 min after seizure arrest, when CBF had been normalized, so as to create two different high flow situations, one with and one without seizures, ie two situations when coupling and uncoupling of flow and metabolism exist.

The main results for the two situations were as follows:

(1) The E value for small tracers such as $^{24}NA^+$, $^{36}Cl^-$, ^{14}C-urea and ^{14}C-thiourea did *not*

133

increase, as would have been the case if a 'breakdown' of the BBB had occurred. A dissociation between the curves for the test substances and the reference substance, which was ^{113}^{m}In-DTPA, would then have taken place.

(2) The PS value, however, rose, indicating a net increase in the outward transport of small molecules during both seizures and hypercapnia. The increase in PS was shortlived as 6 min after seizure arrest it was normal for all substances tested.

One conclusion is that at the capillary level the endothelial cells during high flow — with or without seizures — are stretched, and the area available for the passive diffusion of test substances is thereby enlarged. The possibility also exists, that in the high-flow situation some capillaries which are normally less perfused will open up, ie recruitment may take place.

In the animal study we tested the possibility that even the reference substance ^{113}In-DTPA might escape to a certain extent and thereby mask the fact that an opening in the capillary walls had actually taken place. However, when ^{113}^{m}In-DTPA was studied with ^{51}Cr-labelled red blood cells acting as reference substance, no dissociation of the venous out flow curves could be seen — a fact that supports the above-mentioned conclusion that it is the hyperperfusion and not the seizure activity *per se* that leads to the increased permeability of the BBB (Bolwig *et al.*, 1977*a,b*).

Our conclusions were further substantiated when in a study of a possible localized penetration of circulating horseradish peroxidase (HRP) (M:40.000) in rats undergoing repeated ECS we abolished the increase in systemic blood pressure by transsection of the spinal cord. We then found that only in those animals which had increased blood pressure during the seizure activity (measured by EEG), was a staining of the tissue along the vessels to be seen (Fig. 3) (Bolwig *et al.*, 1977*c*). Again, the seizure activity was found to play no specific role in the increased cerebrovascular premeability. Electron-microscopy studies of the stained areas showed that the vessels were intact, especially at the 'tight junctions' between endothelial cells, which probably represent the BBB. The escape of peroxidase across the vascular walls appeared to be due to an increased activity of pinocytotic vesicles (Fig. 4), a transport mechanism which is normally very modest in the arterioles (Westergaard & Brightman, 1973). These observations (Bolwig *et al.*, 1977*c*; Westergaard *et al.*, 1978) are similar to those published a few months earlier by Petito *et al.* (1977).

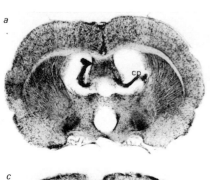

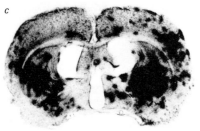

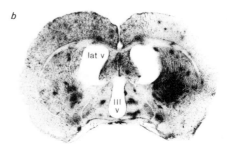

Fig. 3. *Frontal sections of brains from rats intravenously injected with HRP.* The sections are cleared. × 8. (*a*) The spinal cord has been transected and 10 ECS given. The distribution of tracer is as in rats injected with HRP only. The choroid plexus (cp) contains HRP. (*b*) One ECS has been given. Dark spots of reaction product occur in the neuropil without preference for a definite part of the brain. lat v., lateral ventricle; III v., third ventricle. (*c*) Ten ECS were given. The number of spots in the neuropil is greater than in (*b*). Furthermore, the extent of the spots is more pronounced and they often coalesce

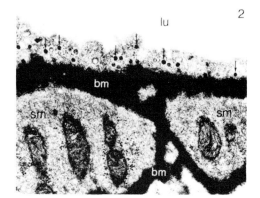

Fig. 4. *Detail of the endothelium in a venule after ten ECS.* The endothelial cells exhibited vesicles containing HRP (arrows). Most of these are circular with a diameter of about 400 nm. lu, lumen; bm, basement membrane. There is no disruption of the cell surface

It is noteworthy that the most marked changes in the permeability to peroxidase were found in central structures as opposed to the predominantly cortical changes found when peroxidase escapes across the vascular wall during chemically-induced hypertension with no seizure activity involved (v. Deurs *et al.*, 1977). Due to the very high staining capacity of horseradish peroxidase, these results do not contradict those from the indicator dilution studies of the cerebral capillary transfer of small molecules noted above. For all practical purposes the cerebrovascular structures must thus be considered not to be influenced by ECS as such.

Whether the increased permeability of the vessels during ECT plays some role in the therapeutic process and/or in the transient, unwanted effects on cognitive functions, is so far an unresolved issue. For either to be the case, then it must be the accumulation of the described observations that is important since each of them is a shortlasting phenomenon and the clinically important effects of the seizures are sustained.

Recent studies by Preskorn and co-workers (1981, 1982) also show an effect on the BBB of electrically induced seizures in animals. Very interestingly, these investigators also found that a tricyclic antidepressant and lithium exert an effect on BBB. These findings suggest a possible interrelationship between two hypotheses: the monoamine theory of affective disorders and the central adrenergic vasoregulatory hypothesis as both mechanisms are known in rats to be influenced by tricyclics and ECS (Modigh, 1976).

Synaptic protein studies

In an attempt to study some events connected with induced seizures at the neuronal level, we used the technique of crossed immunoelectrophoresis (Jørgensen & Bolwig, 1979) to measure specific synaptic proteins in rat brain after a number of ECS (three times per week for four weeks). We studied the following brain specific proteins:

Synaptin, which is present in subcellular fractions of both synaptic vesicles and synaptosomal plasma membranes, but absent from cultured astrocytes. This protein is assumed to act in the exo–endocytotic process of synaptic nerve transmission and may therefore be an indicator of the amount of synaptic vesicles.

D1, D2 and D3 are present in synaptosomal membrane fractions, but absent from synaptic vesicles and cultured astroglial cells; D2 is assumed to be involved in intercellular recognition during synaptogenesis and may be an indicator of both synaptogenesis and the amount of synapses. D3 and possibly also D1 indicate the amount of mature synapses.

14-3-2 has been localized to the neuronal cytoplasm and is a brain-specific form of the glycolytic enzyme enolase.

The results of this study appear in Table 1 and point to the following conclusions. There were changes indicative of an increase in the number of synaptic vesicles and an increased synaptic remodelling because synaptin and D2 were increased but not D1 and D3. Further, 14-3-2 increased considerably, consistent with a greater preparedness of the synapses to meet the heavy

Table 1. *Electroconvulsive stimulation of rats: effect on brain proteins and weight.* Rats were given ECS for four weeks or for four weeks followed by 12 weeks recovery. The results indicate percentage deviations between the littermate controls of the same age and ECS rats. Means and standard errors are given

	Four weeks ECS			Four weeks ECS + 12 weeks recovery		
	Whole forebrain	Occipital cortex	Hypothalamus	Whole forebrain	Occipital cortex	Hypothalamus
Weight	-0.8 ± 1.2	-4.7 ± 1.4†	15.6 ± 5.5*	0.3 ± 1.5	-2.3 ± 1.8	-0.2 ± 6.2
Protein	1.2 ± 2.2	-2.9 ± 3.2	15.2 ± 5.9	3.7 ± 2.0	-4.2 ± 1.9*	-6.5 ± 5.0
Synaptin	8.5 ± 2.3†	-8.8 ± 3.9*	7.5 ± 4.8	5.2 ± 3.0	-2.1 ± 2.6	-9.8 ± 4.9
D1	1.8 ± 2.1	-5.4 ± 2.3*	16.1 ± 5.6*	1.7 ± 2.2	-3.0 ± 2.3	-6.5 ± 6.5
D2	5.2 ± 2.3*	5.1 ± 2.1*	9.5 ± 4.6	1.4 ± 1.5	0.9 ± 2.1	-8.0 ± 4.4
D3	1.0 ± 2.9	1.9 ± 2.5	20.2 ± 7.2*	4.9 ± 3.4	-1.0 ± 3.1	-10.6 ± 7.7
14-3-2	9.7 ± 1.5‡	10.3 ± 4.3*	15.8 ± 3.5‡	0.3 ± 1.6	-1.9 ± 1.4	-2.3 ± 4.5
Glutamin synthetase	-4.0 ± 1.9	-10.1 ± 2.0‡	5.5 ± 3.5	-2.4 ± 3.5	-3.3 ± 1.4*	-6.1 ± 5.2
Body weight		-15.2% ± 1.6‡			-9.9% ± 3.6*	

Significance levels: $*P < 0.05$; $†P < 0.001$; $‡P < 0.001$ (Student's paired t-test.)

glycolytic demand following seizure activity. When different regions of the brain were studied it was notable that the hypothalamus differed from other regions mainly in that all proteins increased, especially D1 and D3. This suggests that an increase in the number of synapses may preferentially take place in this brain region.

Twelve weeks following the last in the series of ECS which were induced without anaesthesia and muscular relaxation, the changes in brain-specific proteins were normalized in the hypothalamus (Bolwig & Jørgensen, 1980). These experiments thus demonstrate a sustained, yet not permanent influence of a series of ECS on the synapses. The findings are in line with studies of Modigh (1976), Evans et al. (1976), Edén & Modigh (1977), and Green et al. (1977) who showed an increased effect on the postsynaptic membrane of receptor agonists following a series of ECS. Whether these findings may have some explanatory value is not known, but it should be noted that a single study of CSF brain-specific proteins has shown an increase of D2 in patients recovering from endogenous depression regardless of treatment modality (Jørgensen et al., 1977). This observation may make further studies of CSF brain-specific proteins in patients relevant to the search for a theory of antidepressant action.

Vasopressin studies

Vasopressin (AVP) is a peptide hormone with effects on behaviour (de Wied et al., 1976). Gold et al. (1978) have reported that the levels of this hormone are decreased in the plasma of endogenously depressed patients and return to normal with recovery from the depressive state. The retrograde amnesia following ECT has been said to be partially reversed by a vasopressin analog (Weingartner et al., 1981). This peptide has previously been reported to show a 100 per cent increase in activity in the plasma of schizophrenic patients 2–5 min after an ECT session (Narang et al., 1973). Also, prolactin (Öhmann et al., 1976; O'Dea et al., 1978) and LH, FSH and GH have been shown to increase in the plasma of some but not all patients undergoing ECT (Ryan et al., 1970; Delitala et al., 1977). Because of the reported effect of vasopressin on mental activity we found it of interest to measure the activity of this peptide in the plasma of patients treated with ECT.

Nine female patients were studied two or three times during series of ECT given with a MECTA machine. They fulfilled the criteria of Feighner et al. (1972) for primary affective disorder. Blood was sampled before anaesthesia and relaxation and 2, 3, 4, 5, 10 and 30 min after the onset of seizures. Plasma AVP was measured by radioimmunoassay (RIA) (Hammer, 1978).

From basal resting levels within the normal range a prompt rise in plasma AVP concentration was found 2 min after the electrical stimulus was given, and this rise was followed by a rapid fall to nearly baseline levels after 10 min. Before ECT which in all cases induced a grand mal pattern of at least 30 s duration on the EEG, the AVP values showed a value for 34 ECT sessions of 3.2 ± 0.5 ng/ml (mean ± s.e.m.) the 2-min post-seizure value was 18.6 ± 3.6 ng/ml and the 30-min post-seizure value was 3.9 ± 0.8 ng/ml.

136

Seven of the patients responded satisfactorily to ECT, represented by a score below 8 on the Hamilton Rating Scale for Depression. Two of the patients had a Hamilton score of 14 or above at the end of series. A trend towards a rise in basal plasma AVP-concentration could be demonstrated in patients with a good response to ECT.

The unwanted effects of ECT ie cognitive disturbances were measured by global assessment. These disturbances did not differ clinically from those previously psychometrically estimated in the study of ECT in our department (Heshe *et al.*, 1978). This means that on inquiry three months after the last ECT, no patient experienced subjective, cognitive deficits and the interviews revealed no clinical impression of such deficits.

Anaesthesia has been shown not to stimulate AVP release (Raskind *et al.*, 1979) and our findings thus indicate that electrically-elicited seizures are followed by a transient release of AVP into the blood. The extent of AVP release is high compared to those plasma AVP increases obtained under normal osmolar stimuli (Hammer *et al.*, 1980). The increases are of the same order of magnitude as AVP values following extreme stress situations such as profuse haemorrhage resulting in volume depletion or painful stimuli (Robertson, 1977).

ECT has been shown to produce signs of pituitary stimulation and increased autonomic activity (Beuret & Swanson, 1969). Changes in plasma concentrations of LH, FSH and GH in some but not all patients receiving ECT are additional evidence of changes in pituitary function (Ryan *et al.*, 1970; Delitala *et al.*, 1977).

It is still not proven whether the prompt response to ECT of AVP values in plasma has significance for the therapeutic effect and/or cognitive disturbances following this treatment of severe depressive illness. The question can only be resolved after further investigations of AVP activity in independent patient studies.

Concluding remarks

The studied cited here, however different they may be, have one common denominator. They seem to demonstrate a significant influence of ECT on deep brain structures. Although comparisons are made between human and animal studies the model for studying a possible antidepressant action seems to some degree justified. The investigations described here suggest that ECT exerts its biological action mainly in central structures which in accordance with previous findings by Ottosson (1962). They also seem to lend support to the theory of convulsive therapy which emphasizes the significance of hypothalamic functions, proposed by Fink & Ottosson (1980).

References

Angel, C. & Roberts, A. J. (1966): Effect of electroshock and drugs on cerebrovascular permeability to cocaine in the rat. *J. Nerv. Ment. Dis.* **142**, 376–380.

Beuret, L. & Swanson, D. W. (1969): Endocrine effects of electroconvulsive therapy: a review. *Psychiat. Quart.* **43**, 650–661.

Bolwig, T. G., Hertz, M. M. & Holm-Jensen, J. (1977a): Blood–brain barrier permeability during electroshock seizures in the rat. *Eur. J. Clin. Invest.* **7**, 95–100.

Bolwig, T. G., Hertz, M. M., Paulson, O. B., Spotoft, H. & Rafaelsen, O. J. (1977b): The permeability of the blood-brain barrier during electrically induced seizures in man. *Eur. J. Clin. Invest.* **7**, 87–93.

Bolwig, T. G., Hertz, M. M. & Westergaard, E. (1977c): Acute hypertension causing blood–brain barrier breakdown during epileptic seizures. *Acta Neurol. Scand.* **56**, 335–342.

Bolwig, T. G. & Jørgensen, O. S. (1980): Synaptic proteins after electroconvulsive stimulation: Reversibility and regional differences in the brain. *Acta Psychiat. Scand.* **62**, 486–493.

Crone, C. (1963): The permeability of capillaries in various organs as determined by use of the ''Indicator Diffusion'' method. *Acta Physiol. Scand.* **58**, 292–305.

d'Elia, G. & Raotma, H. (1977): Memory impairment after convulsive therapy. *Arch. Psychiat. Nervenkr.* **223**, 219–226.

Delitala, G., Masala, A., Rosati, G., Aiello, I. & Agnetti, V. (1977): Effect of electroconvulsive therapy (electroshock) on plasma ACTH, GH, LH, FSH, TSH and 11-OH-CS in patients with mental disorders. *Panminerva Med.* **19**, 237–243.

de Wied, D., van Wimersma Greidanus, T. B., Bohus, B., Urban, I. & Gispen, W. H. (1976): Vasopressin and memory consolidation. *Prog. Brain Res.* **45**, 181–194.

Edén, S. & Modigh, K. (1977): Effects of cypomorphine on rat plasma growth hormone after treatment with reserpine and electroconvulsive shocks. *Brain Res.* **179**, 379–384.

Evans, P. P. M., Grahame-Smith, D. G., Green, A. R. & Tordorff, A. F. C. (1976): Electroconvulsive shock increases the behavioural responses of rats to 5-HT accumulation and central nervous system stimulant drugs. *J. Pharmacol.* **56**, 193-199.

Feighner, J. P., Robins, E., Guze, S. B., Woodruff, R. A., Winokur, G. & Munoz, R. (1972): Diagnostic criteria for use in psychiatric research. *Arch. Gen. Psychiat.* **26**, 57-63.

Fink, M. (1979): *Convulsive therapy: theory and practice.* New York: Raven Press.

Fink, M. & Ottosson, J.-O. (1980): A theory of convulsive therapy in endogenous depression: significance of hypothalamic functions. *Psychiat. Res.* **2**, 49-61.

Gold, P. W., Goodwin, F. K. & Reus, V. I. (1978): *Vasopressin in affective illness. Lancet* **1**, 1233-1236.

Green, A. R., Heal, D. J. & Grahame-Smith, D. G. (1977): Further observations on the effect of repeated electroconvulsive shock on the behavioural responses of rats produced by increases in the functional activity of brain 5-HT and dopamine. *Psychopharmacology* **52**, 195-200.

Hammer, M. (1978): Radioimmunoassay of 8-arginine-vasopressin (antidiuretic hormone) in human plasma. *Scand. J. Clin. Lab. Invest.* **38**, 707-716.

Hammer, M., Ladefoged, J. & Ølgaard, K. (1980): Relationship between plasma osmolality and plasma vasopressin in human subjects. *Am. J. Physiol.* **238**, E313-E317.

Heshe, J., Röder, E. & Theilgaard, A. (1978): Unilateral and bilateral ECT. *Acta Psychiat. Scand.* Suppl. 275.

Jørgensen, O. S., Bock, E., Bech, P. & Rafaelsen, O. J. (1977): Synaptic membrane protein D2 in the cerebrospinal fluid of manic-melancholic patients. *Acta Psychiat. Scand.* **56**, 50-56.

Jørgensen, O. S. & Bolwig, T. G. (1979): Synaptic proteins after electroconvulsive stimulation. *Science* **205**, 705-707.

Kramp, P. & Bolwig, T. G. (1981): Electroconvulsive therapy in acute delirious states. *Compr. Psychiat.* **22**, 368-371.

Lorenzo, A. V., Shirahige, I., Liang, M. & Barlow, C. F. (1972): Temporary alteration of cerebrovascular permeability to plasma protein during drug-induced seizures. *Am. J. Physiol.* **223**, 268-277.

Lorenzo, A. V., Hedley-Whyte, E. T., Eisenberg, H. M. & Hsu, D. S. (1975): Increased penetration of horseradish peroxidase across the blood–brain barrier induced by Metrazol seizures. *Brain Res.* **88**, 136-140.

Modigh, K. (1976): Long-term effects of electroconvulsive shock therapy on synthesis turnover and uptake of brain monoamines. *Psychopharmacology* **49**, 179-185.

Narang, R. L., Chaudhury, R. R. & Wig, N. N. (1973): Effect of electroconvulsive therapy on the antidiuretic hormone level in the plasma of schizophrenia patients. *Indian J. Med. Res.* **61**, 766-770.

O'Dea, J. P. K., Gould, D., Hallberg, M. & Wieland, R. G. (1978): Prolactin changes during electroconvulsive therapy. *Am. J. Psychiat.* **135**, 609-611.

Öhman, R., Walinder, J., Balldin, J., Wallin, L. & Abrahamsson, L. (1976): Prolactin response to electroconvulsive therapy. *Lancet* **2**, 936-937.

Ottosson, J.-O. (1962): Electroconvulsive therapy of endogenous depression: An analysis of the influence of various factors on the efficacy of therapy. *J. Ment. Sci.* **108**, 694-703.

Ottosson, J.-O. (1974): Systemic biochemical effects of ECT. In *Psychobiology of convulsive therapy*, ed M. Fink, S. Kety, J. McGaugh and I. Williams. Pp. 209-220. Washington, D.C.: V. H. Winston & Sons.

Petito, C. K., Schaefer, J. A. & Plum, F. (1977): Ultrastructural characteristics of the brain and blood–brain barrier in experimental seizures. *Brain Res.* **127**, 251-267.

Preskorn, S. H., Irwin, G. H., Simpson, S., Friesen, D., Rinne, J. & Jerkovich, G. (1981): Medical therapies for mood disorders alter the blood–brain barrier. *Science* **213**, 469-471.

Preskorn, S. H., Raichle, M. E. & Hartman, B. K. (1982): Antidepressants alter cerebrovascular permeability and metabolic rate in primates. *Science* **217**, 250-252.

Raskind, M., Orenstein, H. & Weitzman, R. E. (1979): Vasopressin in depression. *Lancet* **1**, 164.

Robertson, G. L. (1977): The regulation of vasopressin in health and disease. *Rec. Prog. Horm. Res.* **133**, 333-385.

Ryan, R. J., Swanson, D. W., Faiman, G., Mayberry, W. E. & Spadoni, A. J. (1970): Effects of convulsive electroshock on serum concentrations of follicle stimulating hormone, luteinizing hormone, thyroid stimulating hormone and growth hormone in man. *J. Clin. Endocr. Metab.* **30**, 51-58.

Squire, L. R. (1975): A stable impairment in remote memory following electroconvulsive therapy. *Neuropsychologia* **13**, 51-58.

Squire, L. R. (1977): ECT and memory loss. *Am. J. Psychiat.* **134**, 997-1001.

v. Deurs, B., Brøndsted, H. E. & Westergaard, E. (1977): Increased vesicular transfer of exogenous peroxidase across cerebral endothelium evoked by acute hypertension. *Acta Physiol. Scand.* **34**, 141-152.

Weingartner, H., Gold, P., Ballenger, J. C., Smallberg, S. A., Summers, R., Rubinow, D. R., Post, R. M. & Goodwin, F. K. (1981): Effects of vasopressin on human memory functions. *Science* **211**, 601-603.

Westergaard, E. & Brightman, M. W. (1973): Transport of proteins across normal cerebral arterioles. *J. Comp. Neurol.* **152**, 17-44.

Westergaard, E., Hertz, M. M. & Bolwig, T. G. (1978): Increased permeability to horseradish peroxidase across cerebral vessels, evoked by electrically induced seizures in the rat. *Acta neuropath.* (Berl.) **41**, 73-80.

17.
ECT stimulus parameters and electrode placement: relevance to therapeutic and adverse effects

R. D. WEINER, H. J. ROGERS, C. A. WELCH, J. R. T. DAVIDSON,
R. D. MILLER, D. WEIR, J. F. CAHILL AND L. R. SQUIRE

Psychiatry Service, Durham VA Medical Center, Durham, NC 27705, USA (RDW, JRTD); Department of Psychiatry, Duke University Medical School, Durham, NC 27710, USA (RDW, HJR, JRTD); Somatic Therapies Consultation Service, Department of Psychiatry, Massachusetts General Hospital, Boston, MA 02124, USA (CAW, JFC); Department of Psychiatry, University of Wisconsin, Madison, WI, USA (RDM); 48 Glen Holm Avenue, Toronto, Ontario, Canada M6H 3A9 (DW); Psychology Service, San Diego VA Medical Centre, La Jolla, CA 92161, USA (LRS).

Introduction

Electroconvulsive therapy (ECT) involves the electrical induction of a series of generalized major motor type seizures in order to treat certain susceptible psychiatric disorders. This is most notably the case for major depressive episodes, where ECT still remains the most effective treatment available (Scovern & Kilmann, 1980). A great concern on the part of psychiatrists, other mental health professionals, and the general public regarding ECT has been the organic brain syndrome associated with ECT, particularly with respect to memory deficits. Beginning in the early 1940s, a variety of modifications in ECT technique were developed in order to minimize CNS sequelae. This paper will focus upon two of these: low-energy brief-pulse stimuli and unilateral nondominant stimulus electrode placement.

The ECT stimulus

As first used in 1938 (Cerletti & Bini, 1938), the ECT stimulus consisted of a 50 Hz (60 Hz in USA) sine wave, as shown in Fig. 1. This waveform was chosen by reason of convenience, as it represents what is directly available out of the wall socket. Although it was clear to early researchers that the depolarization and synchronization of neuronal tissue necessary to evoke a generalized seizure requires a series of electrical discharges, such as is available with the sine wave, it was also clear that this could be accomplished by using a briefer waveform, thereby delivering much less stimulus energy (Liberson, 1945; Offner, 1946). The brief-pulse stimulus, shown in Fig. 1, is close to the optimum waveform in this regard. Transitional waveforms between the sine wave and brief pulse were also developed and are currently widely used, particularly in Europe (Gordon, 1982). A contemporary brief pulse ECT device, the MECTA (Mecta, Inc.) produces a seizure with approximately a third of the stimulus energy of a sine wave device (Weiner, 1980).

Most early studies comparing the relative efficacy and safety of various waveform types claimed less confusion and amnesia and equivalent therapeutic efficacy for low-energy stimuli, but were confounded by concomitant differences in electrode placement between experimental groups (Pacella, 1949). Later work has tended to indicate a rough therapeutic equivalence between various combinations of stimulus waveform types (Liberson & Wilcox, 1945; Kendall *et al.*, 1956; Valentine *et al.*, 1968; Carney & Sheffield, 1974; Weaver *et al.*, 1977) except insofar as ultrabrief-pulse stimuli are not as effective (Cronholm & Ottosson, 1963*a,b*).

139

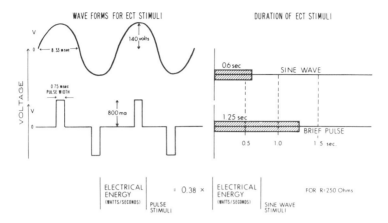

Fig. 1. *Electrical differences between the sine-wave (upper) and pulse (lower) stimulus, and their typical initial parameters.* (Medcraft B24 and MECTA ECT devices.)

Acute cognitive impairment was found to be somewhat less with lower energy stimuli by some investigators but not by others. The earliest study which allowed a true comparison of amnestic effects on the basis of waveform unfortunately contrasted the brief-pulse stimulus with that of a no longer marketed device which delivered a peculiar combination of sine waves and very high amplitude ultrabrief pulses (Liberson & Wilcox, 1945). Their finding, that the pulse stimulus is acutely less amnestic, is therefore of dubious contemporary relevance. Kendall *et al.* (1956) next compared a sine wave with a unidirectional interrupted sine-wave stimulus. They found a greater impairment in objective memory performance soon after the last treatment with the former, but this difference had disappeared by 14 days. Cronholm & Ottosson (1963*a,b*) compared a unidirectional interrupted sine wave with an ultrabrief-pulse stimulus and found both acute amnestic changes and therapeutic response less with the latter. Valentine *et al.* (1968) contrasted a sine wave with a brief-pulse stimulus, finding less amnestic change with the latter, though their results have been criticized since they were only collected during the immediate post-ictal period and were therefore contaminated by post-ictal confusion. Goldstein *et al.* (1977) compared a sine wave with bidirectional-pulse stimuli, using the Halstead Reitan Battery, a comprehensive neuropsychological assessment tool, and found no difference between the two groups either one day or three months following the course of ECT.

The animal literature is likewise equivocal with respect to amnestic differences on the basis of stimulus waveform. In a rat study, Docter (1957) found less amnesia with pulse stimuli during the acute post-ictal period, but also that this difference disappeared within 72 h. Recently, Spanis & Squire (1981) reported a series of studies in mice which, in general, demonstrated that sine-wave and bidirectional-pulse stimuli produce equivalent amnestic changes 24 h following a single electrically-induced seizure. Their widest pulse stimulus, however, was associated with a small but significant decrement in memory function as compared with the sine-wave stimulus. The findings of two electroanesthesia studies done in primates may have some bearing on this latter finding, as they both indicate that a lower scalp to brain impedance (and therefore higher transmission of stimulus current) occurs with pulse stimuli (Tatsuno *et al.*, 1967; Jarzembski *et al.*, 1970). Still, the differences in electrical tissue properties and current paths between human and animal preparations make the applicability of these experimental data unclear.

Electrode placement

Friedman & Wilcox (1942) were the first to suggest that unilateral nondominant stimulus electrode placement is associated with less amnestic impairment than the standard bilateral technique. It was not, however, until the landmark work of Lancaster *et al.* (1958) that this modification received widespread use. Since that time, there have been a relatively large number of studies which have indicated a rough equivalence on the basis of electrode placement with respect to efficacy (d'Elia & Raotma, 1975), but a large advantage for unilateral nondominant ECT with respect to memory function (Squire & Slater, 1978). It should be pointed out, however, that some studies, eg Abrams & Taylor, 1976; Reichert *et al.*, 1976; Heshe *et al.*, 1978; Abrams *et al.*, 1982, found bilateral ECT to be more effective. In terms of this discrepancy, it may be worthwhile to point out that all of the above studies which found a significant therapeutic advantage for bilateral ECT utilized the Lancaster *et al.* (1958) fronto-temporoparietal electrode placement, while those who utilized a larger inter-electrode distance (eg, that of d'Elia, 1970) have reported a relative therapeutic equivalence between the two types of electrode placement. Another possibility to explain potential differences in efficacy is the greater technical complexity in administering unilateral ECT, which may predispose this treatment modification to a greater number of missed or incomplete seizures. There is, however, some recent evidence suggesting that there may be a subgroup of depressed patients, so far not well described, which does not respond to unilateral ECT as well as to bilateral ECT (Heshe *et al.*, 1978; Price, 1981). Furthermore, it has been claimed that an interaction exists between electrode placement and stimulus waveform with respect to therapeutic response, eg, with the combination of brief-pulse stimuli with unilateral nondominant electrode placement showing less efficacy (Lambourn & Gill, 1978; Price, 1981).

A further index of brain impairment with ECT is bilateral electroencephalographic (EEG) slowing, which typically builds up over a course of ECT. While the situation with respect to stimulus waveform has not been well investigated, it is widely acknowledged that, as with memory deficits, less slowing occurs with unilateral electrode placement.

The need for further research

The above historical survey delineates the present situation with respect to the effects of stimulus waveform and electrode placement upon therapeutic and adverse responses to ECT. Although there is some data suggesting that low-energy stimuli and unilateral nondominant electrode placement both offer therapeutically effective means to minimize CNS sequelae with ECT, the literature does not yet offer a sufficiently convincing rationale to have significantly affected the clinical practice of ECT in this regard in most countries. In both the USA and Great Britain, for example, recent surveys have revealed that the use of high-energy stimuli and bilateral electrode placement continues to be widespread (APA, 1978; Pippard & Ellam, 1981).

Furthermore, there remain major unanswered questions as to the biologic bases for differences in safety and efficacy on the basis of ECT treatment modalities, ie, do such differences result from a direct effect of the intensity and distribution of the current flow, or are they related instead to the induced seizure activity. Answers to these questions may be important not only in attempting to explain observed differences in the effects of different treatment modifications, but also may shed some light upon the underlying biologic mechanisms of ECT's therapeutic and adverse effects.

Research design

In order to investigate these issues, a controlled prospective protocol was developed by which the therapeutic, mnestic, and EEG responses to unilateral nondominant vs bilateral electrode placement and pulse vs sine-wave stimuli could be ascertained. This study is still ongoing. Except for those assessed only on EEG measures, all subjects fit Research Diagnostic Criteria for major depressive disorder (Feigner *et al.*, 1972), and have no evidence of underlying organic brain dysfunction. Subjects who were referred by their clinical psychiatrist for ECT are randomly assigned to either bidirectional-pulse or sine-wave stimuli, and to either unilateral nondominant or bilateral electrode placement. Control subjects are chosen from those meeting all study criteria except for referral to ECT. For unilateral ECT the widespread parietofronto-temporal placement advocated by d'Elia (1970) is used. Any subjects demonstrating an equivocal response to a cerebral dominance performance battery are assigned to bilateral electrode placement. Stimuli are iteratively adjusted to achieve satisfactory seizures (greater than 25 s) with only mildly suprathreshold stimulus intensity, and a single channel of ictal EEG is recorded. ECT treatments are modified by atropine, methohexital and succinylcholine, with the number of treatments left open to the attending clinical psychiatrist, who traditionally bases the decision to terminate the course of treatments upon clinical response.

Testing consists of a variety of objective clinical, mnestic and EEG measures and is carried out within a few days prior to beginning ECT, two to three days following completion of ECT, and six months thereafter. Control subjects are tested at identical time intervals. The measures which have thus far received preliminary analysis consist of the Hamilton interviewer-rated Depression Scale (Hamilton, 1960), a newly designed personal memory questionnaire, and the quantitative level of bilateral frontocentral EEG slowing in the delta and theta range, as determined by the Fast Fourier Transform (Cooley et al., 1969). Only the baseline and acute post-ECT data have been analyzed so far. Topics covered by the personal memory questionnaire are shown in Table 1. All of these questions use the index hospitalization as a time reference and, as much as possible, the questions relate to recent as well as remote material and events. Portions of these data can be found in Weiner et al. (1982) and Welch et al. (1982).

Table 1. *Topics covered by personal memory questionnaire.* All questions refer to period prior to index hospitalization

Residence — Neighbors — Family (2 members) — Friends (2) — Last birthday — Last new year's eve — Last overnight trip out of town — Favorite TV show — Last movie seen at a theater — Current hospitalization — Recent outstanding experiences.

General results

Analysis has been carried out on a total of 93 subjects. Because data analysis for different measures was carried out at different times and because not all measures were assessed for every patient, the number of subjects reported for each test measure is smaller than the total population. So far there are no significant differences among the five treatment groups with respect to subject's age, sex, education, IQ or socioeconomic status. With respect to the four ECT groups, there are no intergroup differences on the basis of number of ECT treatments, seizure duration (by EEG criteria, overall mean of 55 s), or incidence of missed seizures (overall mean of 8 per cent).

Therapeutic response

The mean difference between the acute post-ECT and pre-ECT Hamilton Depression scores for the four experimental groups is shown in Fig. 2. These data cover a total of 59 subjects split evenly between two test sites: Durham, North Carolina and Boston, Massachusetts. An interrater reliability of 90–95 per cent was found within and between both test sites. There is no significant difference in efficacy on the basis of stimulus waveform, but subjects given unilateral nondominant ECT showed a greater therapeutic response at the $P < 0.05$ level (2-way ANOVA). Further analysis reveals that the therapeutic response is not related to either mean nor total seizure duration, as measured by EEG, and also is not related to the number of ECT treatments given.

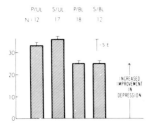

Fig. 2. *The acute effect of ECT upon severity of depression.* The difference between baseline and 2-3 day post-ECT Hamilton Depression Rating scores as a function of type of ECT is shown

Discussion of efficacy data. The present data suggest that, in our series of subjects, pulse stimuli are as effective as sine-wave stimuli in establishing a therapeutic ECT response as measured by the Hamilton Depression Scale. In addition, unilateral nondominant electrode placement is at least as therapeutically effective, and possibly even more effective than bilateral electrode placement. Of particular interest is the therapeutic response of the pulse unilateral group, which, as opposed to that reported by others (eg, Price, 1981), did not appear to be at a therapeutic disadvantage. These findings stand in contradistinction to most earlier research data, which indicate that nondominant ECT is at best as effective as bilateral ECT, and may require more treatments to reach such an equivalence. One possible explanation for these discrepancies could be that the Hamilton Scale may be confounded by differential levels of CNS organicity induced by ECT, with higher scores, and thereby greater apparent depressive symptomatology, in those who are more impaired. No evidence for such a relationship has been reported, but this is something which needs further study.

A second possible explanation may be that unilateral ECT in this study was carried out in a fashion so as to maximize its therapeutic potency. There are several factors involved in this. First, a wide interelectrode distance was utilized (d'Elia, 1970), thereby ensuring a more adequate intracerebral current flow than that associated with a shorter interelectrode distance (eg, Lancaster *et al.*, 1958). Second, a great deal of attention was given to the precise coupling of the stimulus electrodes to the scalp, thereby also acting to ensure a more consistent intensity and flow of the stimulus current. Finally, seizures were monitored electroencephalographically, with missed seizures noticed and managed with restimulation at a higher stimulus intensity. This last factor is of particular importance, since subthreshold seizures are not associated with as great a therapeutic potency (Fink, 1979). As mentioned earlier, missed seizures were also relatively infrequent in this study (8 per cent), and showed no difference on the basis of electrode placement or stimulus waveforms.

Memory function
The fraction of baseline personal memory data not recalled at the acute post-ECT test session is shown in Fig. 3 for 33 experimental and 8 control subjects tested at the Durham, North Carolina site (such testing was not carried out elsewhere). Using ANOVA's, ECT subjects are significantly more amnesic than controls ($P \leq 0.001$). With respect to stimulus electrode placement, subjects receiving bilateral ECT are significantly more amnesic than those receiving unilateral nondominant ECT ($P < 0.01$). There is, in addition, a nonsignificant trend ($P \cong 0.08$) for sine-wave stimuli to be associated with greater amnesia than pulse stimuli. No significant interaction exists between electrode placement and stimulus waveform. The degree of acute amnesic impairment is not related to either mean or cumulative EEG seizure duration, but is a function of the number of ECT treatments given ($P \leq 0.03$).

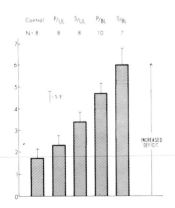

Fig. 3. *The acute effect of ECT upon personal memory function.* For each group, the fraction of baseline items not recalled 2-3 days post-ECT (or comparable time for controls) is shown

Discussion of memory data. The personal memory questionnaire appears to be quite sensitive to acute ECT-induced amnesia. With its use, a highly significant advantage for unilateral nondominant electrode placement was elicited, consistent with that already well described in the literature (eg, Squire & Slater, 1978). Potential explanations for less amnesia with unilateral nondominant electrode placement relate to differences in both stimulus current flow and induced seizure activity. Weaver *et al.* (1976) have provided some theoretical data, using a multicompartmental model of the human head, that intracerebral current density with unilateral electrode placement is not only significantly lower within the nonstimulated hemisphere, as compared with bilateral electrode placement, but is also less within the stimulated hemisphere as well. Assuming that the electrical stimulus itself has a disruptive effect upon memory function, independent of seizure activity, such a difference in the intensity and distribution of stimulus current could well explain the lesser degree of amnesia seen with unilateral ECT. Going against this assumption, however, are claims by some clinicians that amnesia does not occur with missed seizures, even with the application of high-intensity stimuli. Still, the study of graded levels of stimulus intensity upon memory performance in animals has indicated that both seizure activity and stimulus intensity may play a role (Zornetzer, 1974). If stimulus intensity is a factor, one would expect that a relationship exists between stimulus energy and degree of amnesia, particularly given the large range of seizure thresholds encountered in our series (eg, greater than 1000 per cent for pulse stimuli). Such a relationship will be closely investigated as the present study continues.

Observed ictal differences which have been reported to occur between unilateral and bilateral ECT (Small *et al.*, 1978; Staton *et al.*, 1981), suggest that the type of induced seizure may be an important factor in the lower degree of amnesic impairment seen with unilateral ECT. Although unilaterally induced seizures are bilaterally generalized in a qualitative sense, and do not differ in duration from those induced bilaterally (at least for pulse stimuli (Weiner, 1980)), they appear to be focal in onset and have a larger EEG amplitude over the stimulated hemisphere. In addition, less post-ictal EEG suppression is seen with unilateral ECT, particularly over the nonstimulated hemisphere. All of these differences suggest that a lesser degree of neuronal involvement in seizure activity occurs with unilateral electrode placement, at least within the nonstimulated hemisphere; a factor which could indeed provide an explanation for the lesser disruptive cognitive changes with unilateral ECT. In the future we hope to carry out a more complete evaluation of the qualitative and quantitative topographic EEG differences between unilateral and bilateral ECT in order to help resolve this issue.

The finding of a trend toward an advantage for pulse stimuli with respect to amnesic effects awaits the completion of the study protocol for definitive analysis. Still, present data indicate that even if such a relationship holds up, it will likely be of lesser magnitude than that demonstrated on the basis of electrode placement. If pulse stimuli are in fact associated with less amnesia than sine-wave stimuli, two possible explanations, similar to those described above for electrode placement, can be made. First, the difference may be a result of the greater stimulus energy which is known to occur with sine-wave stimuli. If this is the case, we would also expect that a waveform-independent correlation between stimulus intensity and memory impairment, as has been suggested by Ottosson (1960), is present; but, as mentioned above, this relationship awaits further analysis. Second, although seizure duration does not appear to be a function of stimulus waveform, other ictal differences may occur which may account for a lesser disruptive effect by pulse stimuli. Liberson (1948), Marshall & Dobbs (1959), and Valentine *et al.* (1968) among others, have noted in this regard that seizures induced by pulse stimuli appear to be less 'complete' than those induced by sine-wave stimuli, in that less intense convulsive movements are seen, post-ictal confusion appears to be less, and patients given unmodified pulse ECT would sometimes appear to wake up during the seizure itself. These anecdotal reports are in fact consistent with the lesser degree of EEG slowing seen following pulse ECT in the present study (see below). Potential associations between ictal parameters and ECT-induced amnesia are, as mentioned above, something we hope to investigate further.

The absence of a statistically significant interaction between electrode placement and stimulus waveform with respect to effects upon memory function suggests that the respective roles of the two are independent and additive. The absence of a significant correlation between degree of amnesia and mean or cumulative seizure duration, does not, for reasons already noted above, indicate that the seizure is not the major causal factor in the amnesic effect of ECT. It may instead indicate that, as with therapeutic effect, as long as the seizure is suprathreshold, its precise duration is relatively unimportant. The modest positive correlation between memory impairment and number of ECT treatments further supports this point, in that it suggests that the number of suprathreshold seizures, rather than the duration of seizure activity, is important in this regard. This fits well with numerous reports in the literature that memory loss builds up over a course of ECT, and is clearly more severe for those who received large numbers of treatments (Fink, 1979). Although a significant correlation between seizure length and amnesia might not emerge with a narrow distribution for either of the two parameters, the variances of both seizure length and amnesic impairment were quite high with reference to their respective means (variance to mean ratios of 0.30 and 0.47, respectively).

EEG slowing

The difference between the acute post-ECT and baseline levels of bilateral frontocentral EEG slowing (in arbitrary units) is shown in Fig. 4 for 54 experimental and 9 control subjects at the Durham, North Carolina site (such testing was not carried out elsewhere). Using ANOVA's, subjects receiving ECT have more EEG slowing than control subjects ($P < 0.02$) except for the pulse unilateral ECT group, which is statistically equivalent to the control with respect to EEG slowing. More slowing occurs with subjects receiving bilateral than unilateral ECT ($P < 0.01$), and also for those receiving sine-wave vs pulse stimuli ($P < 0.002$). The sine-wave bilateral ECT group clearly shows the most slowing (S/BL vs P/UL, $P < 0.0006$; S/BL vs S/UL, $P < 0.04$; S/BL vs P/BL, $P < 0.02$). No significant interaction between electrode placement and stimulus waveform takes place, however. The acute EEG slowing was further investigated for possible relationships to mean and cumulative EEG seizure duration, number of ECT treatments, and mean and cumulative stimulus energy (the latter determinations were carried out separately for pulse and sine wave conditions, as this variable itself introduces a major difference with respect to stimulus energy). No significant correlations between any of these variables and acute EEG slowing were found.

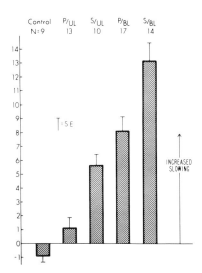

Fig. 4. *Acute EEG slowing with ECT*. For each group the difference in bifrontocentral theta and delta activity between 2-3 days post-ECT and baseline testing is shown. A commensurate time interval was used for control subjects

Discussion of EEG data. The lesser degree of EEG slowing following unilateral ECT is consistent with that reported elsewhere (Small *et al.*, 1978). This is more supportive of a hypothesis involving ictally-mediated differences rather than one presupposing a direct electrical effect, since EEG slowing with unilateral ECT is most often symmetrical. The symmetry of the EEG slowing with our data has yet to be analyzed, but preliminary indications suggest that there will probably not be large hemispheric differences. The large difference in slowing between pulse and sine-wave ECT reported here represents the first true demonstration of stimulus waveform effects upon electrophysiologic functioning. In this case, the absence of a correlation between EEG slowing and stimulus energy, when controlling for stimulus waveform type, strongly supports an ictal hypothesis for EEG slowing differences.

Since stimulus waveform appears to play a larger role in EEG slowing as opposed to in memory impairment, EEG slowing and amnesia may be to some degree independent. Hypothetically, it may be that EEG slowing reflects a nonspecific effect of induced seizure activity, while memory impairment represents a more specific involvement of limbic structures, with differences in ictal characteristics affecting both processes in a differential fashion. Further investigation of ictal parameters and also of possible correlations between EEG slowing and memory impairment should prove helpful in resolving this issue.

Conclusion

The present data indicate that unilateral nondominant electrode placement and pulse stimuli are as effective as bilateral electrode placement and sine-wave stimuli in the production of a clinical remission in severely depressed patients. In addition unilateral electrode placement was found to be associated with significantly less acute amnesia for personal memories than bilateral electrode placement. Furthermore, both unilateral nondominant electrode placement and brief-pulse stimuli produced less acute pathologic EEG slowing than did their counterparts. These findings suggest that the therapeutic and adverse effects of ECT may be relatively independent of one another, and raises the question of whether the characteristics of the induced seizure activity or the electrical stimulus itself are primarily responsible for these differences. It is proposed that ictal factors, perhaps reflecting diminished hypersynchrony with the two milder forms of ECT, are of primary importance. Further analysis, however, will be necessary before this issue can be considered fully clarified.

References
Abrams, R. & Taylor, M. A. (1976): Diencephalic stimulation and the effects of ECT in endogenous depression. *Br. J. Psychiat.* **129**, 482–485.
Abrams, R., Taylor, M. A., Faber, R., Ts'o, T.O.T., Williams, R. A. & Almy, G. (1983): Bilateral vs. unilateral ECT: some new data. *Am. J. Psychiat.*
American Psychiatric Association Task Force on ECT (1978): *Electroconvulsive Therapy*. Task Force Report #14, American Psychiatric Association, Washington, D.C.
Carney, M. W. P. & Sheffield, B. F. (1974): The effects of pulse ECT in neurotic and endogenous depression. *Br. J. Psychiat.* **125**, 91–94.
Cerletti, U. & Bini, L. (1938): Un neuvo metodo di shockterapie ''l'elettro-shock''. *Boll. Acad. Med., Roma* **64**, 36–138.
Cooley, J. W., Lewis, P. A. W. & Welch, P. D. (1969): The fast fourier transform and its applications. *IEEE Trans. Educ.* **E-12**, 27–33.
Cronholm, B. & Ottosson, J. W. (1963a): Ultrabrief stimulus techniques in ECT. I. Influence on retrograde amnesia. *J. Nerv. Ment. Dis.* **137**, 117–123.
Cronholm, B. & Ottosson, J. O. (1963b): Ultrabrief stimulus techniques in ECT. II. Comparative studies of therapeutic effects and memory disturbances in treatment of endogenous depressives with the Elther BS Apparatus and Siemens Konvulsator III. *J. Nerv. Ment. Dis.* **137**, 268–276.
d'Elia, G. (1970): Unilateral ECT. *Acta Psychiatr. Scand.*, Suppl. **215**, 5–98.
d'Elia, G. & Raotma, H. (1975): Is unilateral ECT less effective than bilateral ECT? *Br. J. Psychiat.* **126**, 83–89.
Docter, R. F. (1957): The effect of electroconvulsive shock (ECS) vs. ''brief stimulus therapy'' (BST) on memory and nest building in albino rats. *J. Comp. Physiol. Psychol.* **50**, 100–104.
Feighner, J. P., Robins, E., Guze, S. B., Woodruff, R. A., Winokur, A. & Munoz, R. (1972): Diagnostic criteria for use in psychiatric research. *Arch. Gen. Psychiat.* **26**, 57–63.
Fink, M. (1979): *Convulsive therapy: theory and practice.* New York: Raven Press.

Friedman, E. & Wilcox, P. H. (1942): Electrostimulated convulsive doses in intact humans by means of unidirectional currents. *J. Nerv. Ment. Dis.* **96**, 56-63.

Goldstein, S . G., Filskov, S. B., Weaver, L. A. & Ives, J. O. (1977): Neuropsychological effects of electroconvulsive therapy. *J. Clin. Psychol.* **33**, 798-806.

Gordon, D. (1982): Electroconvulsive therapy with minimum hazard. *Br. J. Psychiat.* **141**, 12-18.

Hamilton, M. (1960): A rating scale for depression. *J. Neurol. Neurosurg. Psychiat.* **23**, 56-62.

Heshe, J., Roeder, E. & Theilvarrd, A. (1978): Unilateral and bilateral ECT: a psychiatric and psychological study of therapeutic effects and of the side effects. *Acta Psychiatr. Scand.*, Suppl. **275**, 1-180.

Jarzembski, W. B., Larson, S. J. & Sances, A. (1970): Evaluation of specific cerebral impedance and cerebral current density. *Ann. N. Y. Acad. Sci.* **170**, 476-490.

Kendall, B. S., Mills, W. B. & Thale, T. (1956): Comparison of two methods of EST and their effects on cognitive functions. *J. Consulting Psychol.* **20**, 423-429.

Lambourn, J. & Gill, D. (1978): A controlled comparison of simulated and real ECT. *Br. J. Psychiat.* **133**, 514-519.

Lancaster, N. P., Steinert, R. R. & Frost, I. (1958): Unilateral electroconvulsive therapy. *J. Ment. Sci.* **104**, 221-227.

Liberson, W. T. (1945): Time factors in electric convulsive therapy. *Yale J. Biol. Med.* **17**, 571-578.

Liberson, W. T. (1948): Brief stimulus therapy: physiological and clinical observations. *Am. J. Psychiat.* **105**, 28-39.

Liberson, W. T. & Wilcox, P. H. (1945): Electric convulsive therapy: Comparison of 'brief stimuli technique' with Friedman-Wilcox-Reiter technique. *Dig. Neurol. Psychiat.* **13**, 292-302.

Marshall, T. J. & Dobbs, D. (1959): Treatment technique and apnea in electroshock. *Dis. Nerv. Syst.* **20**, 582-583.

Offner, F. (1946): Stimulation with minimum power. *J. Neurophysiol.* **9**, 387-390.

Ottosson, J. O. (1960): Experimental studies on the mode of action of electroconvulsive therapy. *Acta Psychiatr. Neurol. Scand.*, Suppl. 145 **35**, 1-141.

Pacella, B. L. (1949): Varieties of electrical shock therapy. *J. Nerv. Ment. Dis.* **109**, 396-404.

Pippard, J. & Ellam, L. (1981): Electroconvulsive treatment in Great Britain. *Br. J. Psychiat.* **139**, 563-568.

Price, T. R. P. (1981): Unilateral electroconvulsive therapy for depression. *New Eng. J. Med.* **304**, 53.

Reichert, H., Benjamin, J., Neufeldt, A. H. and Marjerrison, G. (1976): Bilateral and nondominant unilateral ECT: part II. Development of prograde effects. *Can. Psychiat. Assoc. J.* **21**, 79-86.

Scovern, A. W. & Kilmann, P. R. (1980): Status of ECT: A review of the outcome literature. *Psychol. Bull.* **87**, 260-303.

Small, J. G., Small, I. F. & Milstein, V. (1978): Electrophysiology of EST. In *Psychopharmacology: a generation of progress*, ed M. A. Lipton, A. Dimascio and K. F. Killam. Pp. 759-769. New York: Raven Press.

Spanis, C. W. & Squire, L. R. (1981): Memory and convulsive stimulation: effects of stimulus waveform. *Am. J. Psychiat.* **138**, 1177-1181.

Squire, L. R. & Slater, P. C. (1978): Bilateral and unilateral ECT effects on verbal and nonverbal memory. *Am. J. Psychiat.* **135**, 1316-1320.

Staton, R. D., Hass, P. J. & Brumback, R. A. (1981): Electroencephalographic recording during bitemporal and unilateral nondominant hemisphere (Lancaster position) electroconvulsive therapy. *J. Clin. Psychiat.* **42**, 264-269.

Tatsuno, J., Zouhar, R. L., Smith, R. H. & Cullens, S. C. (1967): Electroanesthesia study: The target area for electroanesthesia. *Anesthesia and Analgesia* **46**, 432-439.

Valentine, M., Keddie, K. M. G. & Dunne, D. (1968): A comparison of techniques in electroconvulsive therapy. *Br. J. Psychiat.* **114**, 989-996.

Weaver, L. A., Ives, J., Williams, R. & Nies, A. (1977): A comparison of standard alternating current and low-energy brief pulse electrotherapy. *Biol. Psychiat.* **12**, 525-543.

Weaver, L., Williams, R. & Rush, S. (1976): Current density in bilateral and unilateral ECT. *Biol. Psychiat.* **11**, 303-312.

Weiner, R. D. (1980): ECT and seizure threshold. *Biol. Psychiat.* **15**, 225-241.

Weiner, R. D., Rogers, H. J., Davidson, J. & Miller, R. D. (1982): Evaluation of the central nervous system risks of ECT. *Psychopharm. Bull.* **18**, 29-31.

Welch, C. A., Weiner, R. D., Weir, D., Cahill, J. F., Rogers, H. J., Davidson, J. & Mandel, M. R. (1982): Efficacy of ECT in the treatment of depression: Waveform and electrode placement considerations. *Psychopharm. Bull.* **18**, 31-34.

Zornetzer, S. (1974): Retrograde amnesia and brain seizures in rodents: electrophysiological and neuroanatomical analyses. In *Psychobiology of convulsive therapy*, ed M. Fink, S. Kety, J. McGaugh and T. A. Williams. Pp. 99-128. Washington, D.C.: V. H. Winston & Sons.

147

18.
Mechanism of action of ECT—relevance of clinical evidence: is noradrenergic failure associated with the development of depressive delusions?

T. J. CROW, J. F. W. DEAKIN, E. C. JOHNSTONE,
M. H. JOSEPH and P. D. LAWLER

Divisions of Psychiatry and Anaesthesia, Clinical Research Centre, Northwick Park Hospital, Harrow HA1 3UJ, England

Introduction

Recently the efficacy of electroconvulsive therapy has been the subject of debate. Whereas for many years it had been accepted that the electroconvulsion is the essential therapeutic element, this conclusion has now been called into question. Thus it has been pointed out (Crow & Johnstone, 1979) that in the study of Cronholm & Ottosson (1960) which examined the therapeutic effects of convulsive, sub-threshold and anticonvulsant-modified electroshocks, patients were not allocated to treatment groups at random. Moreover, some studies which have compared ECT with anaesthesia without electroshock (eg Miller *et al.*, 1953; Brill *et al.*, 1959) have not clearly demonstrated greater efficacy of the former, although these studies are susceptible to the criticism that they did not focus on the group of endogenous depressive patients for whom ECT is generally considered appropriate. These considerations have led to renewed interest in comparisons of real with pseudo-ECT. Four recent trials (Lambourn & Gill, 1978; Freeman *et al.*, 1978; Johnstone *et al.*, 1980; West, 1980) have addressed this issue. Of these the Northwick Park trial included the most detailed assessment of the patient population in an attempt to define potential predictors of response to electroconvulsive shock.

There has also been increased interest in the mechanisms of action of ECT. This chapter asks the question which component of depressive illness it is that responds to ECT, reviews some evidence from animal experiments on physiological changes induced by ECT, and proposes a theory of the mechanism of the therapeutic effect of ECT.

The Northwick Park trial

The design of the Northwick Park trial (Johnstone *et al.*, 1980) is presented in Fig. 1. Patients were included if they fulfilled each of three sets of selection criteria, and were stratified by the presence or absence of delusions, retardation and agitation before they were randomly allocated to real or pseudo-ECT. Patients were then assessed with the Hamilton Depression Scale (Hamilton, 1967) and the Leeds Self-rating Scale (Snaith *et al.*, 1976) at weekly intervals over the four-week course of the trial (with two treatments per week) and at one-month and six-months follow-up. The main findings of the trial are presented in Fig. 2. Patients in both treatment groups improved quite markedly but those who received real ECT were significantly better at the end of the trial period ($P < 0.05$ when account is taken of the differences in pretreatment ratings). This difference had, however, disappeared at the one-month and six-month followup points.

The treatment effect can be examined in relation to the substratification groups defined by

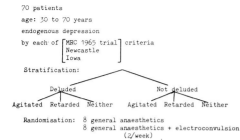

Fig. 1. *The design of the Northwick Park ECT trial.* Diagnostic criteria: MRC 1965 trial (Medical Research Council, 1965); Newcastle (Carney *et al.*, 1965); Iowa (Feighner *et al.*, 1972)

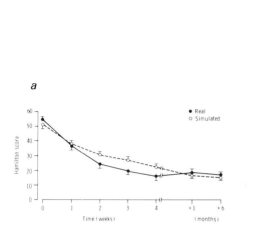

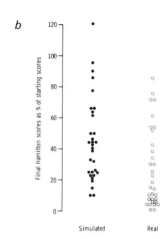

Fig. 2. *(a) Severity of depression in relation to the course of ECT and one and six months thereafter (from Johnstone* et al., *1980). (b) The scatter of improvement scores in patients treated with real and simulated ECT at the end of the treatment course*

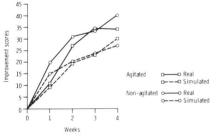

Fig. 3. *Improvement scores for patients on real and simulated ECT with the patient sample divided according to the presence* (n = 22) *or absence* (n = 40) *of agitation*

the presence or absence of retardation, agitation and delusions. The presence of agitation did not appear to be a predictor of response (Fig. 3). On the other hand examination of the sub-groups formed by the presence or absence of retardation and delusions suggested that these symptoms might be related to response (Figs 4 and 5). These factors can to a certain extent be separated by examining the two features in the absence of each other although the numbers of patients in the relevant groups are much reduced. Thus the presence or absence of retardation can be examined in the group of patients who lack delusions (Fig. 6) and the presence or absence of delusions can be examined in the group of patients who lack retardation (Fig. 7). The findings suggest that it is the presence of delusions that determines response to ECT. This conclusion is reinforced by an analysis (Division of Psychiatry, Northwick Park, 1983) of the

149

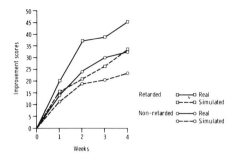

Fig. 4. *Improvement scores for patients on real and simulated ECT with the patient sample divided according to the presence (n = 25) or absence (n = 37) of retardation*

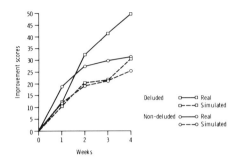

Fig. 5. *Improvement scores for patients on real and simulated ECT with the patient sample divided according to the presence (n = 22) or absence (n = 40) of delusions*

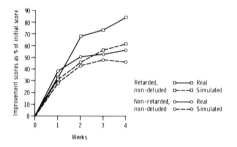

Fig. 6. *Improvement scores as a percentage of initial score in the population of nondeluded patients (n = 40) divided according to the presence (n = 15) or absence (n = 25) of retardation*

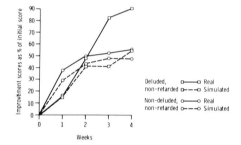

Fig. 7. *Improvement scores as a percentage of initial score in the population of patients without retardation (n = 37) divided according to the presence (n = 12) or absence (n = 25) of delusions*

number of delusions present on Present State Examination (PSE) at trial entry — response to ECT increased with increasing severity of delusions assessed by summing the 0, 1, 2 PSE ratings for each delusion assessed as present. From an extensive analysis of the data collected in this trial it was concluded that only the presence of delusions appeared to be an effective predictor of response. Neither the stereotype of endogenous depression nor analysis of the items of the Hamilton Scale provided effective predictors of response to real as compared to pseudo-ECT.

The mechanism of action of ECT

There is considerable evidence from animal experiments (Kety *et al.*, 1967; Musacchio *et al.*, 1969; Modigh, 1976) that ECS increases the turnover of noradrenaline. More recently ECS has also been shown to down-regulate β-noradrenergic receptors, assessed either as noradrenaline-sensitive adenylate cyclase (Vetulani & Sulser, 1975) or by ligand binding techniques (Bergstrom & Kellar, 1979; Pandey *et al.*, 1979). These effects may well be related since it has been found that 6-hydroxydopamine (6-OHDA) lesions of ascending noradrenergic neurones from the locus coeruleus, attenuates the decrease in [3H]-dihydroalprenolol binding observed after ECS (Fig. 8). This suggests that the reduction in β-noradrenergic receptors after electroshock is secondary to the increase in noradrenaline turnover. Some behavioural effects of electroshock are also reduced by 6-OHDA lesions of ascending noradrenergic neurones. Thus the enhancements of activity in response to the serotonin agonist quipazine and the dopamine

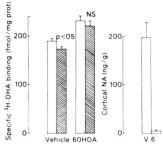

Fig. 8. *Effects of 6-hydroxydopamine (8 μg/2 μl) microinjected into the ascending fibres of the dorsal noradrenergic bundle on the cortical content of noradrenaline (right hand histogram) and the development of subsensitivity of β-adrenergic receptors (assessed by [³H]-dihydro-alprenolol binding) in rats treated with a course of ECS.* Hatched columns indicate ECT treated and open columns sham treated experimental groups (from Deakin & Owen, 1981)

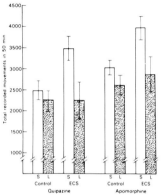

Fig. 9. *Effects of 6-OHDA microinjections into the dorsal noradrenergic bundle on the increase in locomotion activity induced by the sero-tonergic agonist quipazine and the dopaminergic agonist apomorphine which follows a course of ECS.* Open columns (marked S) show effects in sham-operated animals and stippled columns (L) indicate the effects in animals that have previously received bilateral micro-injections of 6-OHDA in the dorsal noradrenergic bundle (from Green & Deakin, 1980)

agonist apomorphine following electroshock are abolished by 6-OHDA lesions (Fig. 9). Thus it is possible that the primary neurochemical change induced by electroshock treatment is an increase in the turnover of noradrenaline.

Noradrenaline and learning

The concept that the noradrenergic innervation of the cerebral cortex is involved in learning (Crow, 1968, 1972; Kety, 1970) includes the hypothesis that this system delivers a 'reinforce-ment' or 'results of action' signal which initiates a process transforming a transient pattern of synaptic changes (representing information in a short-term memory store) into the more durable form of synaptic facilitation assumed to underly long-term memory. A role for the locus coeruleus system (which innervates the cerebral and other cortical areas) in reward mechanisms is supported by the observation that electrical self-stimulation can be obtained with electrodes located in the cell bodies of origin in the locus coeruleus (Crow *et al.*, 1972; Ritter & Stein, 1973). A more critical prediction is that interference with central noradrenergic transmission, including lesions of the locus coeruleus, should impair learning. This issue has proved controversial but there is evidence both from pharmacological and lesioning studies consistent with the hypothesis. Thus inhibition of the noradrenaline synthetic enzyme dopamine-β-hydroxylase, impairs learning of a passive avoidance task (Randt *et al.*, 1971) and such an impairment can be reversed by intraventricular administration of norepinephrine immediately after the learning experience (Stein *et al.*, 1975). In addition, impaired acquisition of runway performance was reported after bilateral electrolytic lesions of the locus coeruleus (Anlezark *et al.*, 1973; Crow, 1977). Similar deficits in motor learning were reported after intraventricular 6-OHDA injections (Mason & Iversen, 1975) but apparently were not seen after 6-OHDA injections into the ascending fibres of the dorsal noradrenergic bundle, which arise from the locus coeruleus (Mason & Iversen, 1978).

Impairments of passive avoidance acquisition however were seen after 6-OHDA injections into the locus coeruleus itself (Crow and Wendlandt, 1976) and learning deficits have been

151

observed in some situations following 6-OHDA injections into the dorsal noradrenergic bundle (Leconte & Hennevin, 1981; Mason & Fibiger, 1978; Robbins *et al.*, 1982). There is, therefore, support for the hypothesis that noradrenergic processes, specifically the locus coeruleus noradrenergic system, are involved in the acquisition of learned behaviours.

Noradrenaline and memory functions in depression
The concept that there is a failure of noradrenergic transmission in depression has long been considered (Schildkraut, 1965). If such a deficit included the locus coeruleus system, failures of learning function would be expected, and these have been documented by Cronholm & Ottosson (1963) and Sternberg & Jarvik (1976). Delusion formation can be considered as a more complex disturbance of learning. Depressive delusions have the characteristic that beliefs and expectations are acquired which are consistently biassed toward pessimism and focus on the negative aspects of the individual's life and his relations with the external world. It may be proposed that such distortions of perception could arise from a bias in those mechanisms of reward and punishment by which the organism acquires information concerning the external environment. There is a case (Crow & Deakin, 1979, 1983) that whereas the central mechanisms of reward are dependent upon noradrenergic transmission, those of punishment are serotonergic. Thus a shift in the balance between these systems from catecholaminergic to serotonergic could lead to a change in the individual's evaluation of the environment with the development of a bias toward the prediction of punishing as opposed to rewarding events. This change might represent either enhanced acquisition of expectations with this bias or could result from a change in the mechanisms of retrieval such that previous learning is recalled from a long-term store with a selective preference for memories associated with fear and prediction of danger. Assessment of new learning of patients in the Northwick Park trial (Frith *et al.*, in press) revealed no tendency for depressed patients to learn more words with unpleasant as compared to pleasant associations. This suggests that the cognitive bias does not relate to the acquisition process; it might however be present in retrieval, as suggested by Teasdale & Fogarty (1979).

The hypothesis may thus be stated: that one component of endogenous depression is a failure of noradrenergic transmission, and that this component is specifically related to the development of depressive delusions and responds to electroconvulsive therapy.

Evaluation of the hypothesis
Apparently consistent with the catecholamine hypothesis of depression, have been reports of reduced excretion of the noradrenaline metabolite 3-methoxy-4-hydroxy-phenylglycol (MHPG) in the urine of some depressed patients (eg Maas *et al.*, 1968). Moreover in one study (Sweeney *et al.*, 1978) low MHPG excretion was found to be correlated with delusions. In a study of the group of patients in the Northwick Park trial, MHPG excretion in the urine was substantially reduced in comparison with controls and various other groups of patients (Joseph *et al.*, 1982) (Fig. 10). This appears consistent with the catecholamine hypothesis. However in these patients urinary MHPG was not correlated with delusions, nor did it change with recovery either in response to ECT or in patients improving with pseudo-ECT. Urinary MHPG was found to be slightly lower in those patients who had received tricyclic anti-depressant medication before entry to the trial. Although they remained free of such medication during the trial, the patients did receive benzodiazepines, most commonly as night sedation. Such drugs have been reported to reduce MHPG excretion (Petursson *et al.*, 1983) and noradrenaline release in the periphery (Hossman *et al.*, 1980). It seems possible they may be responsible for some of the reducitons in MHPG excretion reported in depression.

A second approach to the neurochemistry of depression is through post-mortem brains. In a study of nine patients with depression and nine controls (Blessed *et al.*, 1982) MHPG concentrations were not reduced either in frontal cortex or hippocampus in depressed patients in comparison with controls, and the activity of the noradrenaline marker enzyme dopamine-β-hydroxylase was closely similar in these two areas in both groups.

Thus no unequivocal evidence for the catecholamine hypothesis of affective disorder has been

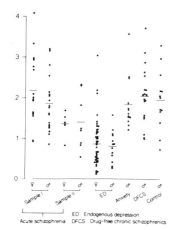

Fig. 10. *Urinary MHPG excretion in patients with endogenous depression (ED) in the Northwick Park ECT trial in comparison with two samples of patients with acute schizophrenia, patients with anxiety, a drug-free group of patients with chronic schizophrenia (DFCS) and a group of male controls* (data reported by Joseph et al., 1982)

ED Endogenous depression
Acute schizophrenia DFCS Drug-free chronic schizophrenics

forthcoming from these two studies. The development of more direct methods of assessing central catecholamine neurone function *in vivo* may be required in order to provide definitive data.

Conclusions

(1) In the Northwick Park ECT trial the presence of delusions was found to be the best predictor of response to real as compared to pseudo-ECT.

(2) There is evidence that adrenergic systems (specifically the locus coeruleus system) are involved in learning. It is suggested that depressive delusion formation is secondary to a failure of adrenergic transmission in endogenous depression, and may be associated with a shift from noradrenergic reward to serotonergic punishment systems in cognitive function.

(3) Although MHPG was found to be reduced in the urine of patients with endogenous depression in the Northwick Park trial, this change was not related to the presence of delusions, and did not respond to ECT. Moreover in a post-mortem study of a small number of patients with depression there was no evidence of decreased noradrenergic function. Evaluation of central monoamine function in depression may require the development of new techniques of *in vivo* assessment.

References

Anlezark, G. M., Crow, T. J. & Greenway, A. P. (1973): Impaired learning and decreased cortical norepinephrine after bilateral locus coeruleus lesions. *Science* **181**, 682–684.

Bergstrom, D. A. & Kellar, K. J. (1979): Effect of electroconvulsive shock on monoaminergic receptor binding sites in rat brain. *Nature* **278**, 464–466.

Blessed, G., Crow, T. J., Cross, A. J., Perry, E. K., Perry, R. H. & Tomlinson, B. E. (1982): Monoaminergic function in post-mortem brain in depression. *Abstracts of 13th CINP Congress*, p. 58.

Brill, N. Q., Crumpton, E., Eiduson, S., Grayson, M. H., Hellman, L. I. & Richards, P. A. (1959): Relative effectiveness of various components of electroconvulsive therapy. *Arch. Neurol. Psychiat.* **81**, 627–635.

Carney, M. W. P., Roth, M. & Garside, R. F. (1965): The diagnosis of depressive syndromes and the prediction of ECT response. *Br. J. Psychiat.* **111**, 659–674.

Cronholm, B. & Ottosson, J.-O. (1960): Experimental studies of the therapeutic action of electroconvulsive therapy in endogenous depression. *Acta Psychiat. Scand.*, suppl. 145 **35**, 69–101.

Cronholm, B. & Ottosson, J.-O. (1963): The experience of memory function after electroconvulsive therapy. *Br. J. Psychiat.* **109**, 251–258

Crow, T. J. (1977): A general catecholamine hypothesis. *Neurosci. Res. Prog. Bull.* **15**, 195–205.

Crow, T. J. (1968): Cortical synapses and reinforcements: an hypothesis. *Nature* **219**, 736–737.

Crow, T. J. (1972): A map of the rat mesencephalon for electrical self-stimulation. *Brain Res.* **36**, 265–273.

Crow, T. J. & Deakin, J. F. W. (1979). Monoamines and the psychoses. In *Chemical influences on behaviour*, ed S. J. Cooper & K. Brown, Pp. 503–532. London: Academic Press.

Crow, T. J. & Deakin, J. F. W. (1983): Neurohumoral transmission, behaviour and mental disorder. In *Handbook of psychiatry*, vol. 5 ed M. Shepherd. Cambridge: Cambridge University Press.

Crow, T. J. & Johnstone, E. C. (1979): Electroconvulsive therapy: efficacy, mechanism of action and adverse effects.

153

In *Psychopharmacology of affective disorders*, ed E. S. Paykel & A. Coppen. Pp. 108-122. Oxford: Oxford University Press.

Crow, T. J. & Wendlandt, S. (1976): Impaired acquisition of a passive avoidance response after lesions induced in the locus coeruleus by 6-OH-dopamine. *Nature* **259**, 42-44.

Crow, T. J., Spear, P. J. & Arbuthnott, G. W. (1972): Intracranial self-stimulation with electrodes in the region of the locus coeruleus. *Brain Res.* **36**, 275-287.

Deakin, J. F. W. & Owen, F. (1981): ECT — a noradrenergic mechanism of action? In *Electroconvulsive therapy — an appraisal*, ed R. I. Palmer. Pp. 150-158. Oxford: Oxford University Press.

Division of Psychiatry, Clinical Research Centre, Northwick Park (1983): ECT: Analysis of predictors of response to real and simulated ECT. *Br. J. Psychiat.* (in press).

Feighner, J. P., Robins, E., Guze, S. B., Woodruff, A., Winokur, G. & Munoz, R. (1972): Diagnostic criteria for use in psychiatric research. *Arch. Gen. Psychiat.* **26**, 57-63.

Freeman, C. P. L., Basson, J. V. & Crichton, A. (1978): Double-blind controlled trial of electroconvulsive therapy (ECT) and simulated ECT in depressive illness. *Lancet* **1**, 738-740.

Frith, C. D., Stevens, M., Johnstone, E. C., Deakin, J. F. W., Lawler, P. & Crow, T. J. The effects of ECT and depression on various aspects of memory. *Brit. J. Psychiat.* (in press).

Green, A. R. & Deakin, J. F. W. (1980): Depletion of brain noradrenaline prevents electroconvulsive shock induced enhancement of 5-hydroxytryptamine and dopamine mediated behaviour. *Nature* **285**, 232-233.

Hamilton, M. (1967): Development of a rating scale for primary depressive illness. *Br. J. Clin. Soc. Psychol.* **6**, 278-296.

Hossman, V., Maling, T. J. B., Hamilton, C. A., Reid, J. L. & Dollery, C. T. (1980): Sedative and cardiovascular effects of clonidine and nitrazepam. *Clin. Pharmacol. Ther.* **28**, 167-174.

Johnstone, E. C., Deakin, J. F. W., Lawler, P., Frith, C. D., Stevens, M., McPherson, K. & Crow, T. J. (1980): The Northwick Park ECT Trial. *Lancet* **2**, 1317-1320.

Joseph, M. H., Risby, D., Johnstone, E. C., Deakin, J. F. W., Lawler, P. & Crow, T. J. (1982): MHPG excretion in depressed patients and clinical response to ECT. *Abstracts of 13th CINP Congress*, p. 363.

Kety, S. S., Javoy, F., Thierry, A. M., Julou, L. & Glowinski, J. (1967): A sustained effect of electroconvulsive shock on the turnover of norepinephrine in the central nervous system of the rat. *Proc. Nat. Acad. Sci.* **58**, 1249-1254.

Kety, S. S. (1970): The biogenic amines in the central nervous system: their possible roles in arousal, emotion and learning. In *The neurosciences study program*, ed F. O. Schmitt. Pp. 324-336. New York: Rockerfeller University Press.

Lambourn, J. & Gill, D. (1978): A controlled comparison of simulated and real ECT. *Br. J. Psychiat.* **133**, 514-519.

Leconte, P. & Hennevin, E. (1981): Post-learning paradoxical sleep, reticular activation and noradrenergic activity. *Physiol. Behav.* **26**, 587-594.

Maas, J. W., Fawcett, J. & Dekirmenjian, H. (1968): 3-methoxy-4-hydroxy-phenylglycol (MHPG) excretion in depressive states. *Archs Gen. Psychiat.* **19**, 129-134.

Mason, S. T. & Iversen, S. D. (1978): Reward, attention and the dorsal noradrenergic bundle. *Brain Res.* **150**, 135-148.

Mason, S. T. & Fibiger, H. C. (1978): Noradrenaline and spatial memory. *Brain Res.* **156**, 382-386.

Mason, S. T. & Iversen, S. D. (1975): Learning in the absence of forebrain noradrenaline. *Nature* **258**, 422-424.

Medical Research Council (1965): Clinical trial of the treatment of depressive illness. *Br. Med. J.* **2**, 881-886.

Miller, D. H., Clancy, J. & Cumming, E. (1953): A comparison between unidirectional current non-convulsive electrical stimulation given with Reiter's machine, standard alternating current electroshock (Cerletti method) and pentothal in chronic schizophrenia. *Am. J. Psychiat.* **109**, 617-621.

Modigh, K. (1976): Long-term effects of electroconvulsive shock therapy on synthesis, turnover and uptake of brain monoamines. *Psychopharmacology* **49**, 179-185.

Musacchio, J. M., Julou, S., Kety, S. S. & Glowinski, J. (1969): Increase of brain tyrosine hydroxylase activity produced by electroconvulsive shock. *Proc. Nat. Acad. Sci. USA* **63**, 1117-1119.

Pandey, G. N., Heinze, W. J., Brown, B. D. and Davis, J. M. (1979): Electroconvulsive shock treatment decreases γ-adrenergic receptor sensitivity in rat brain. *Nature* **280**, 234-235.

Petursson, H., Bond, P. A., Smith, B. & Lader, M. H. (1983): Monoamine metabolism during chronic benzodiazepine treatment and withdrawal. *Biol. Psychiat.* **18**, 207-213.

Randt, C. T., Quartermain, M., Goldstein, M. & Anagnoste, B. (1971): Norepinephrine biosynthesis inhibition: effects on memory in mice. *Science* **172**, 498-499.

Ritter, S. & Stein, L. (1973): Self-stimulation of noradrenergic cell group (A6) in locus coeruleus of rats. *J. Comp. Physiol. Psychol.* **85**, 443-452.

Robbins, T. W., Everitt, B. J., Fray, P. J., Gaskin, M., Carli, M. & de la Riva, C. (1982): The roles of central catecholamines in attention and learning. In *Behavioural models and the analysis of drug action*, ed M. Y. Spiegelstein & A. Levy. Pp. 109-134. Amsterdam: Elsevier.

Schildkraut, J. J. (1965): The catecholamine hypothesis of affective disorders: a review of supporting evidence. *Am. J. Psychiat.* **112**, 509-522.

Snaith, R. P., Bridge, A. W. K. & Hamilton, M. (1976): The Leeds scale for the self-assessment of anxiety and depression. *Br. J. Psychiat.* **128**, 156-165.

Stein, L., Belluzi, J. D. & Wise, C. D. (1975): Memory enhancement by central administration of norepinephrine. *Brain Res.* **84**, 329-335.

Sternberg, D. E. & Jarvik, M. E. (1976): Memory functions in depression. *Arch. Gen. Psychiat.* **33**, 219-224.

Sweeney, D., Nelson, C., Bowers, M., Maas, J. & Heninger, G. (1978): Delusional vs. non-delusional depression: neurochemical differences. *Lancet* **2**, 100–101.

Teasdale, J. D. & Fogarty, S. J. (1979): Differential effects of induced mood on retrieval of pleasant and unpleasant events from episodic memory. *J. Abnorm. Psychol.* **88**, 248–257.

Vetulani, J. & Sulser, F. (1975): Action of various antidepressant treatments reduces reactivity of noradrenergic cyclic AMP-generating system in limbic forebrain. *Nature* **257**, 495–496.

West, E. D. (1980): Electric convulsion therapy in depression: a double-blind controlled trial. *Br. Med. J.* **282**, 355–357.

19.
ECT and memory dysfunction

L. R. SQUIRE

Veterans Administration Medical Center, San Diego and Department of Psychiatry, University of California, School of Medicine, La Jolla, California 92093, USA.

Introduction

Electroconvulsive therapy (ECT) has been the subject of increased attention in recent years, and a great deal of information has become available concerning its efficacy, mechanism of action, and side effects. Psychiatric Associations of three countries have prepared reports or position papers on ECT (Pankratz, 1980; Royal College of Psychiatrists, 1977; APA Task Force Report No. 14: ECT, 1977), and two books have appeared recently (Fink, 1979; Abrams & Essman, 1982). It is generally recognized that ECT is a safe and effective treatment for major depressive disorder, even for patients who have responded poorly to other treatments (Paul *et al.*, 1981).

Nevertheless, concern continues to be expressed about memory impairment, certainly the most prominent and troublesome of ECT's side effects. This chapter summarizes what is known about the memory impairment associated with ECT. Readers wishing more detailed information and more complete documentation of the relevant research findings are directed to recent review articles and the references therein (Harper & Wiens, 1975; Fink, 1979; Price, 1982; Squire, 1982*a*). This summary is organized around six topics: the anterograde amnesia or loss of new learning capacity associated with ECT; retrograde amnesia, or loss of memory for events that occurred before ECT; memory loss associated with bilateral vs right unilateral ECT; current parameters and memory loss; memory complaints, ie, the observation that patients often report memory problems long after a course of ECT; and the question of why memory loss occurs.

Anterograde amnesia

The impairment of new learning capacity associated with ECT has a characteristic form that distinguishes it from whatever learning difficulty might have already been present due to depression. Immediate recall is normal, as long as the to-be-remembered information does not consist of too great a quantity of material, but forgetting is abnormally rapid (Cronholm & Ottosson, 1961). Because forgetting occurs more rapidly than usual, the memory impairment appears more severe as retention is assessed at longer learning-retention intervals. The deficit diminishes in severity as learning is attempted at longer intervals after each treatment. It increases in severity as a function of the number of treatments given.

Fig. 1 shows good immediate recall and poor delayed recall for patients who learned a short prose passage 6–10 hours after the fifth treatment of a series. Interestingly, at this point in a treatment schedule, it is easy to have the impression that a patient's memory is adequate. This impression is due to the preserved ability of patients to recall information immediately after acquiring it. However, memory functions are markedly impaired at this time, as evidenced by how little can be recalled one day after learning. Only two of 15 patients in the illustrated study

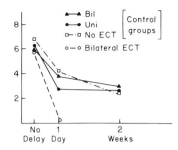

Fig. 1. *Recall of a short prose passage at different times after learning by patients in the midst of a course of bilateral ECT and by three other groups who had received bilateral ECT, unilateral ECT, or hospitalization for depression without ECT six to nine months previously.* The group tested during their course of treatment learned the prose passage between 6 and 10 hours after the fifth treatment. The follow-up groups had received a total of 10.1 treatments (bilateral group) or 9.2 treatments (unilateral group) (From Squire & Chace, 1975.)

recalled any of the passage at all, and some did not remember the experimenter or the fact that they had ever heard a piece of prose.

The anterograde amnesic disorder persists for a variable time after the completion of treatment, depending on the number of treatments in the series. Some prospective follow-up studies have concluded that new learning capacity can return to normal as early as a few weeks after treatment. Yet the tests used to measure learning ability vary so much in their sensitivity to memory impairment that it has been difficult to identify any one time after treatment when recovery is complete. In the study illustrated in Fig. 1, anterograde amnesia had subsided by six to nine months after treatment. Those who had received bilateral ECT six to nine months previously learned and remembered as well as those who had received unilateral ECT and as well as those who had been hospitalized for depression without ECT. In the same study, similar results were obtained for other memory tests, including a sensitive measure of incidental learning (Squire & Chace, 1975). It seems likely that normal learning ability is achieved well before six months after treatment. When 31 patients were asked seven months after bilateral treatment to estimate their own experience in quantitative terms, the median duration of perceived anterograde amnesia was three months (Fig. 2) (Squire & Slater, 1983).

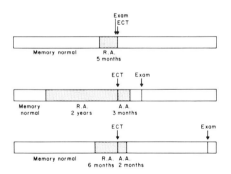

Fig. 2. *Estimates of time periods that were difficult to remember obtained from patients before (top bar), seven months after (middle bar), and three years after (bottom bar) bilateral ECT (n = 31).* Shaded areas represent the median time period perceived as affected from the period before ECT (ie, R.A., retrograde amnesia) and after ECT (ie, A.A., anterograde amnesia). Since the first time estimate was obtained just prior to ECT (top bar), the five months perceived as affected at that time presumably reflects memory problems associated with depressive illness (from Squire & Slater, 1983.)

Since anterograde amnesia is considered to be a failure in the formation and maintenance of memory (Squire, 1982*b*), when learning capacity recovers one would not expect there to be recovery of memory for the events that occurred during the period of anterograde amnesia. When 31 patients were asked three years after treatment to estimate their experience of anterograde amnesia, the median period after ECT perceived to have been affected was two months — about the same period of time judged to be affected at seven months after treatment (Squire & Slater, 1983).

Retrograde amnesia
Loss of memory for events that occurred before treatment has been studied by administering formal tests that ask questions about events that occurred during the previous months and

157

years. ECT is typically associated with a temporally-limited retrograde amnesia that affects recent memories to a greater extent than more remote memories. This impairment can include memory for events that occurred as long as a few years prior to treatment, or even longer before treatment in some circumstances. Fig. 3 shows the findings for patients who were asked questions about television programs that had been broadcast for no more than a single season each of the past several years. ECT affected memory for programs broadcast during the previous one to two years without affecting memory for programs from the period three to ten years before treatment. These and related findings show that ECT affects memory for past events in a way that depends on the age of memory at the time of treatment. Impairment of remote memory develops gradually during a series of treatments, and is then stable from day to day until treatment is completed. As might be expected, retrograde amnesia affects auto-biographical information as well as information about public events (Janis, 1950; Squire *et al.*, 1981).

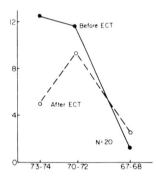

Fig. 3. *Recall of facts about former television programs that had been broadcast for a single season during each of several years prior to ECT. Testing was scheduled before bilateral treatment and one hour after the fifth bilateral treatment of the series.* Testing occurred in 1975–1976 (From Squire and Cohen, 1979.)

In clinical practice the temporally graded feature of retrograde amnesia is not always appreciated, because other factors can obscure direct observation of the phenomenon in a single patient. Thus, although the age of a memory is a powerful determinant of its vulnerability to ECT, the fate of a past memory after ECT is also determined by its importance, the number of times it has been rehearsed, as well as dynamic factors. For example, patients will sometimes remember coming to the treatment room in the morning just prior to their treatment. But this preserved recent memory for an important event in a patient's day occurs against a background of impairment of other recent memories and relative sparing of more remote memories.

Fig. 4 shows gradual recovery from retrograde amnesia during the months after treatment. As measured by this test, which sampled memories from each of several previous years, recovery seemed to be complete. Since the memory test used to demonstrate recovery assessed memory for relatively trivial information that was not likely to have been systematically

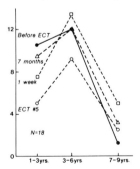

Fig. 4. *Recovery from retrograde amnesia after completion of a course of bilateral ECT.* The test used was the same as shown in Fig. 2, and it was given on four different occasions, at the times indicated (From Squire *et al.*, 1981.)

relearned (facts about defunct TV programs) it seems reasonable to presume that recovery from retrograde amnesia is spontaneous and not dependent on any special effort by the patient. By analogy to post-traumatic amnesia, which has been rather thoroughly studied (Russell & Nathan, 1946), recovery or shrinkage of retrograde amnesia appears to occur first for oldest memories and last for recent memories. Retrograde amnesia can continue to shrink after anterograde amnesia has fully subsided.

Some information is available about how completely retrograde amnesia disappears following the completion of treatment. Memory for events that occurred a year or more prior to ECT seems to recover rather well by seven months after ECT, as measured by the TV test and certain other tests of past public or personal events. Patients themselves, however, seem to feel that it takes longer than seven months for memory from this time period to return (see Fig. 2).

Though recovery from retrograde amnesia can be substantial, memory for events that occurred close to the time of treatment can be permanently lost (Squire *et al.*, 1981). The vulnerable period before treatment can be as long as a week or two and perhaps longer under some circumstances. Permanent retrograde amnesia is considered to occur because ECT disrupts the consolidation process, which must proceed for a period of time in order for memory to become stable. If this lengthy process, which ordinarily continues for years, is disrupted soon after it is initiated, memory loss can be permanent. If this process is disrupted longer after it is initiated, eg, a few months or a year, memory will be only temporarily affected.

A number of lines of evidence based on studies of memory loss from causes other than ECT (eg, head trauma, encephalitis), and recent ideas about how memory is organized in the brain (Squire *et al.*, 1983), suggest that the length of permanent retrograde amnesia after ECT is related to the duration of anterograde amnesia. The longer that anterograde amnesia persists, the longer will be the permanent retrograde amnesia that persists after anterograde amnesia has subsided.

Bilateral vs unilateral treatment

In all respects, the memory loss associated with bilateral ECT is greater than the memory loss associated with unilateral treatment. This is true for retrograde as well as for anterograde amnesia. Right unilateral treatment is associated with memory loss that is specific to nonverbal material, ie, memory for material like faces and shapes that depends especially on the integrity of the right cerebral hemisphere. Variation of electrode position over the right hemisphere does not seem to diminish memory impairment beyond that associated with conventional right unilateral electrode placement (d'Elia, 1976).

One might worry that right unilateral ECT, which concentrates the flow of current in the right hemisphere, might have a particularly deleterious effect on memory for nonverbal material. However, when memory was assessed with tests sensitive to the effects of right hemispheric dysfunction, bilateral ECT produced greater impairment than right unilateral ECT (Squire & Slater, 1978). The selective effect of left and right unilateral ECT on verbal and nonverbal memory respectively (Cohen *et al.*, 1968), suggests that the path of current flow between electrodes plays a significant role in determining the nature of memory dysfunction. For example, it is possible that the seizures associated with right unilateral, left unilateral, and bilateral electrode placement are qualitatively different, so that the hemisphere over which the electrodes are applied is affected more severely than the other hemisphere (Staton *et al.*, 1981).

Current parameters and memory loss

In addition to the reduction in memory loss that can be expected by favoring unilateral over bilateral ECT, one might also hope to reduce memory loss further by altering the parameters of electrical stimulation. One obvious away that this can be done is to administer the minimum amount of current needed to produce a seizure. It has been known for a long time that the seizure is responsible for ECT's therapeutic effects. Increasing the current above what is needed to elicit a seizure increases memory loss without improving efficacy. Administering the same amount of current, while partially blocking the seizure pharmacologically, markedly reduces

159

efficacy (Ottosson, 1962a,b). Finally, it is well known from studies of experimental amnesia in animals that memory loss is positively and monotonically related to the current intensity used to elicit a convulsion (Zornetzer & McGaugh, 1971).

Brief-pulse stimulation can elicit a seizure with approximately one-third of the electrical energy associated with conventional sine-wave stimulation. Accordingly, it might be supposed that memory loss would be less following brief-pulse stimulation than following sine-wave stimulation. However, this issue remains an open question. It is possible, for example, that reducing the total energy of an electrical stimulus will reduce memory loss only to the extent that the seizure-producing effects of the stimulus is also reduced. If this is true, then even though brief-pulse stimulation can produce a seizure with less electrical energy than sine-wave stimulation, memory loss would be similar when the two kinds of stimulation were each delivered at seizure threshold.

Studies with experimental animals are consistent with this idea. The ability of a sine-wave stimulus to produce memory loss was compared in mice in two conditions: when ether was administered before the convulsion to raise the seizure threshold, and without ether (Zornetzer & McGaugh, 1971). At seizure threshold memory loss was the same in the two conditions, even though three times as much electrical current was administered in the ether condition. In another study with mice, more relevant to questions about waveform and ECT, brief-pulse stimulation was compared to sine-wave stimulation in several conditions that equated for the ability of the two waveforms to produce seizures (Spanis & Squire, 1981). Brief-pulse stimulation caused as much memory loss as sine-wave stimulation and sometimes more.

Only one study of psychiatric patients receiving ECT has compared brief-pulse and sine-wave stimulation under conditions where seizure-producing efficacy of the two waveforms was equated and where the seizures were carefully monitored by EEG (Weiner et al., this volume). Brief-pulse stimulation produced somewhat less memory loss than sine-wave stimulation, but the difference did not reach statistical significance.

Memory complaints

Considering the evidence from formal tests about the course of recovery of memory functions after treatment, complaints of diminished memory abilities are heard longer after treatment than they might be expected. This issue has been addressed by questionnaire techniques, interviews and self-rating scales (Freeman & Kendall, 1980; Squire et al., 1979; Squire & Slater, 1983). It appears that these memory complaints are in part related to the ECT experience. Self-reports of memory functions are qualitatively different before treatment when patients are depressed, compared to self-reports obtained shortly after treatment when patients are amnesic. The self-reports seven months after treatment differ from the before-ECT, depressed pattern and resemble the reports obtained shortly after treatment. One possibility is that patients gradually recovering from anterograde amnesia come to doubt their memory abilities and tend to attribute even normal failures in recall to their course of ECT. Another possibility, not incompatible with the first, is that memory complaints refer in part to the real gap that exists in memory for the period of time surrounding ECT.

Freeman & Kendall (1980) recommend that patients be counseled after ECT as to what can be expected as far as memory is concerned. Patients typically forget this kind of information when they are given it before treatment. It is also worth pointing out that the simple explanation to a patient that 'memory will recover' is misleading. It is true in one sense, ie, that the ability to learn recovers and that retrograde amnesia substantially clears. But memory for events that occur shortly after the completion of treatment, during the period of anterograde amnesia, cannot be expected to recover. Similarly, some permanent memory loss must be expected from the time just prior to treatment.

Why memory loss occurs

Though it is by no means well understood, the therapeutic action of ECT is believed to be due to biochemical sequelae of the seizure. The memory loss associated with ECT is known to be unrelated to therapeutic efficacy, because clinical efficacy does not correlate with the severity of memory loss. Moreover, unilateral ECT is associated with much less memory loss than is bilateral ECT, even though their therapeutic efficacy is considered to be virtually the same (Small *et al.*, 1981; d'Elia & Raotma, 1975; Welch, 1982; but see Abrams, 1982). Accordingly, information about the mechanism of ECT's therapeutic efficacy is not likely to help us understand why memory loss occurs.

A number of considerations link memory loss after ECT to transient disruption of the medial temporal region of the brain. It has been known for nearly a century that memory loss occurs when there is damage to either of two brain regions. The diencephalic midline of the brain, especially the dorsal medial nucleus of the thalamus and the mammillary bodies, have been implicated in the amnesia associated with the alcoholic Korsakoff syndrome (Victor *et al.*, 1971; Mair *et al.*, 1979), and in the amnesia exhibited by a well-studied single case of memory disorder, case N.A. (Kaushall *et al.*, 1981). The medial temporal region, especially the hippocampal formation and the amygdala, have been implicated in the amnesia associated with bilateral medial temporal surgery, especially in the famous case H.M. (Scoville & Milner, 1957; Milner, 1972). Pointing to the great sensitivity of the hippocampal formation to seizures and to other indirect evidence, Inglis (1970) suggested that ECT effects on memory might constitute a special instance of medial temporal dysfunction.

It has recently become possible to test this idea in a somewhat more direct way. Studies of amnesic patients as well as studies of operated monkeys, prepared in an attempt to model the human amnesic syndrome, have shown that diencephalic and bitemporal amnesia differ in an interesting respect (Huppert & Piercy, 1979; Squire, 1981; Zola-Morgan & Squire, 1982). Bitemporal dysfunction is associated with rapid forgetting of material that can be learned, whereas diencephalic amnesia is associated with deficient learning and a normal rate of forgetting. The finding that ECT is associated with rapid forgetting tends to place this form of memory impairment alongside examples of medial temporal dysfunction, and differentiates it from cases of diencephalic dysfunction. Of course, one must also keep in mind the possibility that ECT might disrupt the integrity of the diencephalic structures important in memory as well as the integrity of medial temporal structures.

In any case, ECT is known to produce abnormal EEG findings, ie, hypersynchronous slow waves over each hemisphere, and these abnormalities gradually wane during the weeks and months following treatment (Weiner, 1980; Abrams & Volavka, 1982). It seems reasonable to suppose that these EEG changes are the signs of functional disturbances in those brain regions known to be critical for memory functions. As time passes after treatment and normal electrical activity can be recorded from these regions and their vicinity, new learning once again becomes possible; and recall becomes possible for those memories which were acquired a sufficient period of time before treatment.

Present understanding of memory and its organization in the brain is grossly incomplete. Nevertheless, progress is being made in understanding which specific brain regions are involved in memory functions. Better descriptions are also becoming available concerning the role that these regions play in accomplishing memory storage (Thompson *et al.*, 1983; Woody, 1983; Weiskrantz, 1982; Mishkin, 1982; Squire & Davis, 1981; Squire, 1983). The study of ECT has in fact contributed to this progress. One can hope that it will some day be possible to apply this knowledge to the treatment of memory disorders of the type that are associated with ECT. At the same time, as more is learned about the biology of memory and about how brain organization and function give rise to behavior, we should eventually come to a better understanding of ECT, as well as the psychiatric illnesses for which ECT is prescribed.

Acknowledgements — Supported by the Medical Research Service of the Veterans Administration and by NIMH Grant MH24600. I thank Dr Charles Rich for his helpful comments.

References

Abrams, R. (1982): Technique of electroconvulsive therapy. In *Electroconvulsive therapy: biological foundations and clinical applications*, ed R. Abrams & W. B. Essman. Pp. 41-55. New York: Spectrum Publications.

161

Abrams, R. & Essman, W. B. (ed), (1982): *Electroconvulsive therapy: biological foundations and clinical applications*. Jamaica, New York: Spectrum Publications.

Abrams, R. & Volavka, J. (1982): Electroencephalographic effects of convulsive therapy. In *Electroconvulsive therapy: biological foundations and clinical applications*, ed R. Abrams & W. B. Essman. Pp. 157–167. New York: Spectrum Publications.

APA Task Force Report No. 14: (1978): *Electroconvulsive therapy*, Washington, D.C.: American Psychiatric Association.

Cohen, B. D., Noblin, C. D. & Silverman, A. J. (1968): On the functional asymmetry of the human brain. *Science* **162**, 475–477.

Cronholm, B. & Ottosson, J.-O. (1961): Memory functions in endogenous depression before and after electroconvulsive therapy. *Arch. Gen. Psychiat.* **5**, 193–199.

d'Elia, G. (1976): Memory changes after unilateral electroconvulsive therapy with different electrode positions. *Cortex* **12**, 280–289.

d'Elia, G. & Raotma, H. (1975): Is unilateral ECT less effective than bilateral ECT? *Br. J. Psychiat.* **126**, 83–89.

Freeman, C. P. L. & Kendell, R. E. (1980): ECT: I. patients' experiences and attitudes. *Br. J. Psychiat.* **137**, 8–16.

Fink, M. (1979): *Convulsive therapy: theory and practice*. New York: Raven Press.

Harper, R. G. & Wiens, A. N. (1975): Electroconvulsive therapy and memory. *J. Nerv. Ment. Dis.* **161**, 245–254.

Huppert, F. A. & Piercy, M. (1979): Normal and abnormal forgetting in organic amnesia: effect of locus of lesion. *Cortex* **15**, 385–390.

Inglis, J. (1970): Shock, surgery, and cerebral asymmetry. *Br. J. Psychiat.* **117**, 143–148.

Janis, I. L. (1950): Psychologic effects of electric convulsive treatments. *J. Nerv. Ment. Dis.* **3**, 359–382.

Kaushall, P. I., Zetin, M. & Squire, L. R. (1981): A psychosocial study of chronic, circumscribed amnesia. *J. Nerv. Ment. Dis.* **169**, 383–389.

Mair, W. G. P., Warrington, E. K. & Weiskrantz, L. (1979): Memory disorder in Korsakoff's psychosis: a neuropathologcal and neuropsychological investigation of two cases. *Brain* **102**, 749–783.

Mishkin, M. (1982): A memory system in the monkey. In *Phil. Trans. Roy. Soc. London*, Vol. 297, ed D. E. Broadbent & L. Weiskrantz. Pp. 85–95. London: The Royal Society.

Milner, B. (1972): Disorders of learning and memory after temporal lobe lesions in man. *Clin. Neurosurg.* **19**, 421–446.

Ottosson, J.-O. (1962a): Electroconvulsive therapy — electrostimulatory or convulsive therapy? *J. Neuropsychiat.* **3**, 216–220.

Ottosson, J.-O. (1962b): Seizure characteristics and therapeutic efficiency in electroconvulsive therapy: an analysis of the antidepressive efficiency of grand mal and liodocaine-modified seizures. *J. Nerv. Ment. Dis.* **135**, 239–251.

Pankratz, W. J. (1980): Electroconvulsive therapy. *Can. J. Psychiat.* **25**, 509–514.

Paul, S. M., Extein, I., Calil, H., Potter, W. Z., Chodoff, P. & Goodwin, F. K. (1981): Use of ECT with treatment-resistant depressed patients at the National Institute of Mental Health. *Am. J. Psychiat.* **138**, 486–489.

Price, T. R. P. (1982): Short- and long-term cognitive effects of ECT: 1 — effects on memory. *Psychopharmacol. Bull.* **18**, 81–91.

Royal College of Psychiatrists (1977): Memorandum on the use of electroconvulsive therapy. *Br. J. Psychiat.* **131**, 261–272.

Russell, W. R. & Nathan, P. W. (1946): Traumatic amnesia, *Brain* **69**, 280–300.

Scoville, W. B. & Milner, B. (1957): Loss of recent memory after bilateral hippocampal lesions. *J. Neurol. Neurosurg. Psychiat.* **20**, 11–21.

Small, I. F., Milstein, V. & Small, J. G. (1981): Relationship between clinical and cognitive change with bilateral and unilateral ECT. *Biolog. Psychiat.* **16**, 793–794.

Spanis, C. W. & Squire, L. R. (1981): Memory and convulsive stimulation: effects of stimulus waveform. *Am. J. Psychiat.* **138**, 1177–1181.

Squire, L. R. (1981): Two forms of human amnesia: an analysis of forgetting. *J. Neurosci.* **1**, 635–640.

Squire, L. R. (1982a): The neuropsychology of human memory. *Ann. Rev. Neurosci.* **5**, 241–273.

Squire, L. R. (1982b): Neuropsychological effects of ECT. In *Electroconvulsive therapy: biological foundations and clinical applications*, ed R. Abrams & W. B. Essman. Pp. 169–186. New York: Spectrum Publications.

Squire, L. R. (1983): Memory and the brain. In *Brain, cognition and education*, ed S. Friedman *et al.* New York: Academic Press.

Squire, L. R. & Chace, P. M. (1975): Memory functions six to nine months after electroconvulsive therapy. *Arch. Gen. Psychiat.* **32**, 1157–1564.

Squire, L. R. & Cohen, N. (1979): Memory and amnesia: resistance to disruption develops for years after learning. *Behav. Neural. Biol.* **25**, 115–125.

Squire, L. R. & Davis, H. P. (1981): The pharmacology of memory: a neurobiological perspective. *Ann. Rev. Pharmacol. Toxicol.* **21**, 323–356.

Squire, L. R. & Slater, P. C. (1978): Bilateral and unilateral ECT: effects on verbal and nonverbal memory. *Am. J. Psychiat.* **11**, 1316–1320.

Squire, L. R. & Slater, P. C. (1983): Electroconvulsive therapy and complaints of memory dysfunction: a prospective three-year follow-up study. *Br. J. Psychiat.*, **142**, 1–8.

Squire, L. R., Cohen, N. & Nadel, L. (1983): The medial temporal region and memory consolidation: a new hypothesis. In *Memory consolidation*, ed H. Weingartner & E. Parker. Hillsdale, New Jersey: Lawrence Erlbaum Associates.

162

Squire, L. R., Slater, P. C. & Miller, P. (1981): Retrograde amnesia following ECT: long-term follow-up studies. *Arch. Gen. Psychiat.* **38**, 89-95.

Squire, L. R., Wetzel, D. C. & Slater, P. C. (1979): Memory complaint after electroconvulsive therapy: assessment with a new self-rating instrument. *Biol. Psychiat.* **14**, 791-801.

Staton, R. D., Hass, P. J. & Brumback, R. A. (1981): Electroencephalographic recording during bitemporal and unilateral nondominant hemisphere (Lancaster Position) electroconvulsive therapy, *J. Clin. Psychiat.* **42**, 264-269.

Thompson, R., Berger, T. & Madden, J. (1983): Cellular processes of learning and memory in the mammalian CNS. *Ann. Rev. Neurosci.* **6**, 447-492.

Victor, M., Adams, R. D. & Collins, G. H. (1971): In *The Wernicke-Korsakoff Syndrome*, ed F. Plum & F. H. McDowell. Philadelphia, Pennsylvania: Davis.

Weiner, R. D. (1980): The persistence of electroconvulsive therapy-induced changes in the electroencephalogram, *J. Nerv. Ment. Dis.* **168**, 224-228.

Weiskrantz, L. (1982): Comparative aspects of studies of amnesia. In *Phil. Trans. Roy. Soc. London*, Vol. 298, ed D. E. Broadbent & L. Weiskrantz. Pp. 97-109. London: The Royal Society.

Welch, C. A. (1982): The relative efficacy of unilateral nondominant and bilateral stimulation. *Psychopharm. Bull.* **18**, 68-70.

Woody, G. D. (ed) (1983): *Conditioning: representation of involved neural function*, New York: Plenum Press.

Zola-Morgan, S. & Squire, L. R. (1982): Two forms of amnesia in monkeys: rapid forgetting after medial temporal lesions but not diencephalic lesions. *Soc. Neurosci. Abstr.* **8**, 24.

Zornetzer, S. & McGaugh, J. L. (1971): Retrograde amnesia and brain seizures in mice. *Physiol. Behav.* **7**, 401-408.

163

20.
The psychobiology of ECT

J. P. BROWN

Department of Psychiatry, Hadassah University Hospital, Jerusalem, Israel.

Introduction

Miller's 1967 article *Psychological Theories of ECT: A Review* marked the watershed of scientific evaluations of the psychological contributions to the mechanism of ECT. Thirty years of experience with ECT had produced a plethora of theories (50 were reported by Gordon in 1948) and yet Miller was only able to conclude that ECT was still an empirical treatment. Although it is arguable whether this situation has changed radically in the succeeding 15 years, there has been a substantial advance in our psychiatric knowledge and conceptualisation of psychpath-ology and its somatic treatment by ECT. This will, perhaps, permit us to reconsider the mechanism of ECT from a psychobiological rather than a purely psychological frame of reference.

Up to 1967, psychological theories either drew on psychoanalytic metapsychology or on general psychological theories *vis-a-vis* disordered memory and cognition. Little attention was paid to experimental studies of electric shock eg, Gellhorn's (1949) finding that psychologically, ECS restores inhibited conditioned reflexes in animals, and that of Masserman & Jacques (1947) who successfully used ECS to reduce neurotic behaviours in cats. These experimental findings required, however, the development of adequate psychobiological models of depression in order to advance our investigation of the mechanism of psychiatric treatment and in particular of ECT. Before considering some of the contemporary work on the psychology of ECT, the historical background of psychological theories will be re-reviewed, and then the evidence for the convulsion as the therapeutic factor will be evaluated.

Historical background of psychological theories

Perhaps it is not surprising that psychological theories of the mechanism of ECT were prevalent in the early days following the introduction of this treatment. Rollin (1980) has called ECT the most important advance in treatment in our time; the following quote from Gordon (1948) explains why . . .

> Particularly receptive to this new method were those on duty within crowded mental institutions, moving through wards of humans seemingly doomed to incessant inner turmoil, to regression down to the level of dumb animal or even the vegetable stratum; mute, motionless, filthy and slowly deteriorating or belligerent and self-destructive. These workers who do not deal with a few selected psychoneurotics in their offices or with chosen demonstration samples presented in a university lecture-hall, but with thousands upon thousands of wretched lives for whom prolonged individual attention is impossible, couldn't resist any straw of salvation given to them.

ECT was seen as producing 'electric miracles' and psychoanalytically orientated psychiatrists rapidly introduced metapsychological investigations into its mechanism of action. The patient was frequently seen as the passive and helpless recipient of the therapist's power and fantasies in an agonising process of death and rebirth (Clare, 1976). Millet & Moss (1945) saw as the positive indications for ECT: patients inaccessible to psychotherapy; patients who had undergone an unsuccessful course of psychotherapy, and to make patients accessible to psychotherapy. Gordon (1948) saw ECT as acting at a physiological level on the brain mechanism which expressed interpersonal tendencies. He favoured a regression model of mental illness and asked, 'How does electrical energy achieve the inactivation of the phylogenetic and the reactivation of the ontogenetic functions at a new level of maturity?' Drawing upon 23 psychogenic theories (out of a total of 50 reviews) he saw ECT as allaying primitive libidinal surges and unconscious conflicts and desensitising the psyche to traumata principally through its amnesic effect. In the same vein, Cameron (1960) advocated massed ECT (large numbers of treatments given at brief intervals), which was said to produce differential deficits in the memories of highly cathected (mostly negative) emotional experiences, with a subsequently more healthy psychological reintegration.

Much of this theorising, however, was based on the electroconvulsive treatment of schizophrenics, in whom ECT was seen as fostering regression of psychotic habits and experiences, or even as restructuring the 'psychotic personality' through a putative exploitation of the post-treatment organic-shock syndrome and re-education of the nascent personality by deep intensive psychotherapy. Frosch & Impastato (1948) focused on individualised explanatory patient paradigms, such as shock-induced weakening of the integrative functions of the ego (though the mechanism was unspecified), regression to the narcissistic stage, and a subsequent higher re-integration. Abse (1944) believed both habitual and idiosyncratic defences, and repression in particular, to be increased in response to ECT administration. It was soon realised, however, that this apparent repression actually represented nothing more than regressive symptomatology associated with the transitory organic-shock syndrome.

By the time Miller (1967) came to review 75 studies carried out over a period of 30 years, he had little to add in the way of plausible metapsychological theories. At that time he saw as needing explanation: the therapeutic effect of ECT, the memory disturbance, confusion and the neuropsychological test results. Miller rightly noted that the repression theories were unverified and that the fear hypothesis (Abse, 1944) was negated, for example, by studies showing an inverse relationship between fear and treatment outcome (Cook, 1940). Punishment theories in which guilt is assuaged by electric shocks were then, as now, not seen as borne out by clinical experience.

For his own hypothesis, Miller proposed a two-factor model for the action of ECT, in which amnesia and confusion were seen as the aetiological agents. In terms of evidence against this, studies with unilateral ECT by Cannicott (1963) and numerous others showed that amnesia could be reduced to a transient and momentary loss while retaining therapeutic efficacy. It has also been suggested that the events forgotten are independent of psychological importance (Williams, 1966). Ottosson (1968) came closer to the point by drawing attention to the fact that memory loss and confusion are part of an organo-mental syndrome due to the treatments administered: a combination of neocortical attention deficit alongside transient limbic disorder of memory retention and consolidation. While such deficits might account for the nonspecific antipsychotic effects of ECT, they did not appear to be of importance in the treatment of affective disorders. Furthermore, a substantial degree of memory deficit is also present in depressed patients prior to ECT (Cronholm & Ottosson, 1960; Sternberg & Jarvik, 1976). Even though such deficits differ in some ways from those related to ECT, this finding still serves to confound attempts to assess the contribution of amnesia to the antidepressive therapeutic effect of ECT.

Still, Lambourn (1981) has argued that retrograde amnesia, the principal feature of cognitive dysfunction following ECT, remains one of several therapeutic components of this treatment. Based upon an analysis of cases in which the diagnosis and treatment of hysterical states was facilitated by ECT, he concluded that ECT might act by helping patients to forget both their misery and their delusional beliefs. He supported this view by the finding that there was a trend for those treatments associated with a larger amnestic effect (eg, bilateral electrode placement and sine-wave stimuli) to be the most effective. Lambourn (1981) suggested a prospective double-blind study comparing randomly allocated groups of these four treatment modalities. Paradoxically, however, his own double-blind study comparing real with sham ECT (Lambourn & Gill, 1978) employed unilateral, brief-pulse electroshock, ostensibly to reduce cognitive dysfunction and generate more reliable double-blind experimental conditions. Three other double-blind studies (which will be described subsequently) each used bilateral sine-wave ECT.

An additional potential psychological factor involved in the therapeutic action of ECT was proposed by Fink (1979), who based this work upon Weinstein's (1952) studies of organo-mental denial (anosognosia). Fink (1979) attempted to relate ECT-induced changes in brain function to pre-existing life history and personality structure, but he concluded that no predictors were better than clinical diagnosis.

At the present time, it is probably fair to say that metapsychological and personality studies no longer play a fundamental role in elucidating the mechanism of ECT. Although psychological effects occur, this does not mean that they represent psychological causes, and it is more likely that ECT acts via a complex psychobiological interaction. Miller (1967) evaluated three such hypotheses, each supported by animal ECS studies: neural consolidation, aversion, and competing responses, but none of these is now favoured as an explanatory approach. He also called for better experimental design, for conceptualisation of hypotheses to be more closely tied to the experimental findings, and for a more thorough consideration of potentially relevant parameters.

Since that time, however, there has been little direct use of experimental animals in the investigation of the relevant behavioural consequences of ECT. Horrell (1981) summarised the available research on the effect of ECT on specific behaviours believed analogous to those of endogenous depression. Such data, which was frequently equivocal, consisted of findings in experimental animals (mostly in rats) that ECT (1) improves food intake and augments body weight; (2) reduces REM sleep and REM sleep rebound; (3) increases psychomotor activity (open-field activity), (4) suppresses aggression (muricide in rats); and (5) disrupts the normal oestrus cycle.

In addition to such effects, others have focused upon the role of the induced seizures themselves in ECT mechanisms (Weiner, 1979). Before further discussion of these matters, however, it would be prudent to examine the evidence for the efficacy of ECT, particularly to consider which of the various components of the ECT process appear to be most closely linked to a therapeutic response.

Efficacy and effective components of ECT: evidence from controlled trials
The Royal College of Psychiatrists (1977) described the therapeutic efficacy of ECT in depression as substantial and incontravertible, although the majority of clinical trials were poorly controlled. Wechsler (1965) reviewed 153 such trials reported in the USA, Canadian and UK literature between 1958 and 1963 and quoted 72 per cent efficacy for ECT, against 23.2 per cent for placebo control. Up to 1966 Barton (1977) could only find six trials which he felt conformed to methodological requirements which included the presence of a 'sham ECT' control group among other conditions. He therefore did not include the two large multicentre trials of ECT, both of which are frequently quoted in favour of ECT. Greenblatt's USA study (Greenblatt *et al.*, 1962, 1964) achieved 76 per cent improvement in marked depression and 92 per cent if marked and moderate depressions were combined, with a corresponding 46 per cent and 69 per cent improvement on placebo. In the Medical Research Council trial (1965), 72 per cent were improved on ECT and 39 per cent on placebo. Recently, Pippard and Ellam (1981) sampled 2755 British psychiatrists: 87 per cent found ECT at least occasionally useful particularly in endogenous depression, depressive psychosis and involutional melancholia, while only 1 per cent were wholly opposed to its use. A subsequent three-month prospective study involving 2594 courses of ECT (80 per cent of all ECT carried out in UK ECT clinics)

reported the incidence of at least some improvement, without relapse in the first month, to be 75 per cent. In all, ECT appears, from such studies, to have been shown to be as effective if not superior to placebo control.

Findings from some double-blind controlled trials evaluating the seizure component have, however, proven more equivocal. Earlier trials were methodologically inadequate in a number of areas (Miller, 1953; Brill, 1959; Sainz, 1959; Robin & Harris, 1962; Fahy et al., 1973). Cronholm & Ottosson (1960), by shortening the fit with lidocaine, were able to infer the necessity of an adequate seizure for therapeutic benefit. The impetus for the most recent generation of trials evaluating the therapeutic value of ECT, and of electrically induced cerebral seizures in particular, was provided by a combination of media-sensationalism and public outcry. In 1974, a report in World Medicine (Jones, 1974) described 'effective' ECT administration for two years using a machine incapable of delivering an electric shock. A growing media-inspired public reaction to shock treatment (eg, 'One Flew Over the Cuckoo's Nest') augmented by alarmist pronouncements in the professional psychiatric and medical literature eg, that of Friedberg (1977), stimulated four double-blind clinical trials in depressed patients in the UK alone.

For a period of decades prior to this time, the ethics of withholding an increasingly substantiated effective treatment, albeit to investigate the contribution of electrically-induced seizure, precluded use of simulated ECT on its own. The present four studies, those of Lambourn & Gill (1978), Freeman et al. (1978), Johnstone et al. (1980), and West (1981), all had in common the use of a double-blind sham ECT procedure, by which control subjects underwent the entire ECT procedure except for the passage of an electric current. Two of these double-blind studies supported the role of seizure while the other two were less certain. Freeman et al.'s (1978) study divided 40 depressed inpatients randomly and equally between a real ECT group and a group in which the real ECT was preceded by two sham ECTs. These investigators found a significantly greater therapeutic response after the first two treatments in the real ECT group and that a delayed, but commensurate response occurred in those receiving the sham/real ECT combination. They also observed a greater number of treatments in the sham/real ECT group, further supporting a true effect for the induction of seizures. West (1981), in a smaller study of depressed inpatients showed no treatment effect of simulated ECT in 11 control subjects as opposed to 11 ECT subjects who improved on their Hamilton means from 68 to 16. Ten out of the 11 patients from the simulated ECT group subsequently improved significantly on real ECT.

Lambourn & Gill (1978) administered real vs simulated ECT to two equally divided groups of depressed inpatients and outpatients. The real ECT group received six ultrabrief-pulse unilateral ECT, a relatively untried method of electric shock administration. No significant difference in improvement on mean Hamilton scores between real ECT and simulated ECT was found. The overall improvement was less than would normally be expected for ECT and has led to some doubt as to the adequacy of the administration of ECT, particularly given the concomitant use of benzodiazepines and the use of ultrabrief stimuli. Not surprisingly, however, Lambourn & Gill (1978) argued for placebo effects and spoke of the 'mystique' of ECT.

Perhaps the most controversial of the four double-blind studies is that of the Northwick Park group (Johnstone et al., 1980). These investigators found real ECT to be more effective than simulated ECT by the end of the course, but not at one- and six-month follow-up testing sessions. Sixty-two inpatient depressives completed this trial. Eight bi-weekly, bilateral ECTs were administered to the real ECT patients group over four weeks. Controls were similar in all respects apart from the absence of electrical stimulation. After four weeks of treatment, Hamilton mean score differences were 38 for the real ECT group and 28 for the simulated group. Further analysis revealed that this early response to ECT was predicted by the presence of delusions. At one and six months after treatment had been completed, however, there were no significant differences between groups. Johnstone et al. argued for a more rapid speed of response to real ECT, and mentioned the possibility that either the anesthetic or intensive nursing and medical care could account for the large 'placebo' effect. They concluded that (1) the effects of electric convulsion are probably small by comparison with other changes taking place; (2) these effects develop slowly; and (3) are not long-lasting. Their study has been criticised, however, for not including a typical population of depressed subjects along with a variety of other factors which may have minimised intergroup differences, including the use of minor tranquillisers during the index treatment period and the use of antidepressant drugs during the follow-up period.

In summary, the methodologic insufficiencies of early studies and the conflicting results of more well-controlled recent studies of the therapeutic effect of ECT, make the issue of whether and to what degree ECT is more effective than alternative treatments still somewhat unresolved, particularly regarding a specific therapeutic role for the induced-seizure activity. Crow et al. (this volume), along with others, have postulated roles for other factors which may account for at least part of the apparent strong therapeutic response to ECT. To a large degree, these reflect both an augmentation of placebo components to the response such as loss of consciousness and the administration of an elaborate somatic treatment in an emotionally charged treatment environment (Overall et al., 1962; Hollister et al., 1967), along with subtle investigator-related influences (Mason, 1962; Lowinger & Dobie, 1969). Because of this continued uncertainty, the issue of psychobiological factors in the mechanism of ECT remains open. Before looking at animal experimental paradigms for evaluating the psychobiological mechanisms of ECT, the most comprehensive psychobiological overview of depression to date, that of Akiskal & McKinney (1973, 1975), will be described.

The psychobiology of depressive disorders

Proposal of a psychobiological mechanism of ECT in the treatment of depression requires at least a minimal psychobiological understanding of its psychopathological substrates. A clear theoretical integration of depressive disorder was expressed by Akiskal & McKinney (1973, 1975), who stated that "certain forms of depression result from interpersonal factors that secondarily induce biochemical changes in those areas of the brain that moderate affect". These investigators integrated 10 models of depression, representing five schools of thought: psycho-analytical (aggression turned inward, object loss, loss of self esteem, negative cognitive set), behavioural (learned helplessness, loss of reinforcement), sociological, existential, and biological (biogenic amine, neurophysiological). Akiskal & McKinney (1973, 1975) argued for depressive disorders as a final common path in which genetic, developmental, pharmacological and interpersonal factors converge in the midbrain to produce a reversible functional derangement of the neurophysiological substrates of reinforcement.

These pathways have been conceptualised by Stein (1971) and Olds (1977) as comprising (1) the medial forbrain bundle (MFB), the anatomical substrate for the 'reward system' which originates in the locus coerulus, and the adjacent reticular formation, both of which make noradrenergic synapses in the lateral hypothalamus, at higher levels in the limbic system, and in the frontal cortex; and (2) the periventricular system (PVS), the anatomical substrate for the 'punishment system' arising in the dorso-medial region of the midbrain, making cholinergic synapses in the medial hypothalamus and also in the limbic system. The MFB initiates facilitatory feedback and increases the probability that the behaviours concerned will be completed — a system of primary reinforcers upon which the PVS exerts inhibitory control.

Akiskal & McKinney (1973, 1975) also describe three further components closely coupled with the reinforcement system: the stress system (hypothalamo-pituitary), the arousal system (reticular activating system), and the psychomotor system (pyramidal and extrapyramidal pathways). In the development of a depressive episode, perturbations in any of these three systems would act by exacerbating a postulated functional impairment of the reward system. These authors attempted to resolve the controversy whether altered catecholamine metabolism is a cause or an effect of depression by stating that 'lowering of noradrenaline in the reinforcement system would contribute to functional impairment whether it is primary or secondary', and that 'noradrenaline depletion can be an effect that, in its own right, can serve as a cause in the pathogenetic chain of events'. Akiskal & McKinney (1973, 1975) summarised the data by providing a unified model of human depression in which (1) chemical factors (current infections, drugs such as reserpine) may interfere with the monoaminergic receptor; (2) genetic factors (in some disorders) determine enzymatic defects with subsequent failure to respond to reinforcement; (3) genetic-interpersonal factors are expressed by a 'labile' diencephalic reinforcement system; (4) developmental factors lead to a disruption of attachment bonds in early life resulting in 'fragile' reward systems; and (5) interpersonal factors produce interpersonally-induced states of frustration and helplessness.

In considering a psychobiological model of ECT, it may be worthwhile to examine these developmental and interpersonal factors which appear to be affected by ECT. In particular the results of three closely related putative aetiological phenomena in depression are said to be reversed by ECT: chronic aversive stimulation (Wolpe, 1971), loss of reinforcers (Bowlby, 1979) and loss of control over reinforcement, or learned helplessness (Overmeier & Seligmann, 1967). Akiskal & McKinney (1973, 1975) proposed two possible mechanisms for these three phenomena in contributing to severe depression: (1) that interpersonally elicited and maintained depression becomes biologically autonomous and thus require somatic treatment; (2) that severe depression ultimately 'requires' a fundamental genetic-biochemical predisposition. In support of the first of these two putative aetiologies, Lewis & McKinney (1976) investigated the effect of electrically-induced seizures on the social deprivation syndrome produced by early separation of Rhesus monkeys from their mothers and solitary confinement. Monkeys with this experimentally induced syndrome responded, ie, demonstrated more normal behaviour, to real ECT, but not to sham ECT. Although these authors state that 'what human psychopathological syndrome is being modelled by these monkeys is not yet clear', their results do provide the groundwork for an experimental psychobiological model for the therapeutic effects of ECT.

Learned helplessness and the psychobiology of ECT

The learned helplessness model is based upon a conception of affective illness as a disorder of the mechanisms for responding to rewarding and punishing stimuli. Although learned helplessness is a laboratory-defined phenomenon, and it is not clear, for example, that failure of control over reinforcers plays a major role in the development of a depressed mood in humans, this model has provided some useful insights into the aetiology, treatment, and prevention of depressive disorders (Seligman, 1978).

Animals which are exposed to inescapable electric shocks are subsequently passive in the face of trauma (motivational impairment) and have more difficulty in learning that their responses can be effective in bringing about relief (negative cognitive set). This finding generalises across many species (rats, dogs, humans), both in weanlings and in adults. Other unconditioned stimuli than shock, eg, tumbling and noise are also effective, and interference may be produced in a variety of adaptive behaviours, such as escape-avoidance training and appetitive discriminant learning. The behavioural effects of learned helplessness, all of which dissipate with time, include anorexia and weight loss.

Weiss et al. (1976) have hypothesised that this phenomenon reflects a specific stress-induced CNS disturbance which is manifested by a biological deficit consisting of noradrenaline depletion and altered noradrenaline turnover. Weiss et al. support their noradrenaline depletion hypothesis with the following lines of evidence. Firstly, those experiments in which helplessness was not found to be associated with noradrenaline depletion did not lead to escape-avoidance deficits. Secondly, experiments not involving helplessness, but which were associated with noradrenaline depletion did lead to escape-avoidance deficits. Finally, animals receiving monoamine-oxidase inhibitor drugs (and not controls) were protected from escape-avoidance deficits.

The learned helplessness model is congruent with other aetiological theories of depression: Bibring's helpless ego (Bibring, 1965), Bowlby's ineffective action (Robertson & Bowlby, 1952) and Beck's negative cognitive set (Beck, 1967). In all of these, loss of control over gratification is

169

seen as inducing helplessness. Seligman (1968) found only one cure for learned helplessness in his dogs: dragging the animals to safety across the shuttlebox. Similarly, in the treatment of depression, directed exposure to a positive response may produce successful relief, eg, Bibring's ego psychology, Beck's cognitive therapy, Lazarus' assertiveness training and cathartic release of anger.

Alternatively, Seligman et al. (1968) were able to produce behavioural 'immunisation' against learned helplessness by giving escape-avoidance trials prior to the administration of inescapable shock. This finding is in line with the fact that a life history of mastery may mitigate against depression. In any event, it appears clear that the history of experimental animals may significantly affect outcomes in testing as part of the learned helplessness model. Recent studies with weanling rats (Gerber et al., 1979) show that inescapable shock administered early in life impairs subsequent adult appetitive discrimination learning, a finding which also generalises across a variety of different motivational states. The report of Seligman & Groves (1970) that isolation rearing of laboratory rats (equivalent to traumatic child-rearing) leads to impaired performance on the shuttlebox escape-avoidance training schedule is also consistent with this.

Dorworth & Overmier (1977) looked at the effect of ECS on dogs which had been rendered helpless by inescapable shock. They conducted a four-part experiment in which 19 dogs were given a series of 67 unavoidable, inescapable hindfood electric shocks while confined to a harness. Twenty-four hours later 10 trials of escape-avoidance training in a shuttlebox were administered to these and two control groups (eight dogs which received no footshocks and eight dogs which received no manipulation at all). Ten of the pre-shocked dogs never showed escape-avoidance learning. These ten maximally helpless dogs were further subdivided into two groups for the main experimental manipulation. Over a period of three days, one group received a total of six ECS through temporoparietal electrodes, while the other group received an equivalent amount of handling but no ECS therapy. In the final phase, all 10 dogs were tested for escape-avoidance in the shuttlebox. Dorworth & Overmier (1977) state that 'the experimental ECS therapy and no ECS groups differed markedly in the final test, with the former showing improved responsiveness attributable to the ECS therapy' and, furthermore, that 'those ECS therapy dogs which escaped and avoided shock in the final test did so for the first time only after being given ECT'. Similar findings were reported by Petty & Sherman (1980), who compared the effects of convulsive and sub-convulsive electrical stimuli in rats.

In summary, both learned helplessness and depression show not only behavioural effects eg, motivational deficits and negative cognitive set, but also biologic manifestation eg, vegetative symptomatology and catecholamine dysfunction. By acting therapeutically on the biological substrates of learning and reinforcement, ECT may also act to restore normal motivation and appropriate cognitive sets, and thereby relieve the depressive episode. Still, such a conclusion must be considered tentative, particularly in the light of the philosophical and methodological problems which must first be overcome.

ECT and the problems of psychobiological psychiatry

There is no generally accepted conception of the psychobiological basis of meaningful behaviour and even less of the basis of somatic treatment in psychiatry. While seizure activity itself clearly appears to act on the biological substrates of depression, this, as was noted from the double-blind controlled studies of ECT, may not account for all of its therapeutic efficacy. Behavioural change, even if it is clearly linked to the presence of an electrically induced seizure, occurs in the context of a complex set of meanings, both personal (self system) and shared (socio-cultural values). An interactionist approach (Popper & Eccles, 1977) to model building and model testing may be necessary to deal with the complex relationships of the different factors which underlie ECT's therapeutic effect.

Lerer & Belmaker (1982), for example, in reviewing neurotransmitter receptors and the mechanism of action of ECT, noted a discrepancy between biochemical and behavioural indices of receptor sensitivity. They saw this as requiring a postulation of differential receptor sensitivities depending, among other things, on the 'state of the organism'. Akiskal &

McKinney's (1973, 1975) model of depression provides just such a scheme for relating biological with psychosocial variables. These latter investigators argued that Schildkraut's (1970) pharmacological bridge between brain and behaviour must be two-way, so that the biological substrate of depression can be affected not only by somatic interference but also by complex psychosocial variables. These variables may be conceived of as either positive or negative reinforcers, and include the impact of the patient's attitudes to ECT and mental status at the time of treatment, the patient's personality and history, the attitudes and behaviours of the treatment team, the therapeutic atmosphere in the clinical setting, the quality of the social network to which the patient returns, and the overall attitudes towards ECT in society at large. The impact of such psychosocial processes may be seen as becoming more significant as the relatively biological autonomous aspects of depression are gradually relieved by ECT.

Unfortunately, an adequate methodologic evaluation of the roles of nonbiologic factors in the mechanism of ECT has proved wanting, much as it has for therapy in general, be it somatic, psychotherapeutic, or behavioural. Studies such as that of Freeman & Kendall (1980), which focused upon various facets of patient's attitudes to ECT, provide a preliminary means to define the specific nature of such parameters. It is left to the future, however, to come up with a meaningful solution to this problem; one in which a true psychobiologic synthesis of ECT mechanisms can be established.

References
Abse, D. W. (1944): Theory of the rationale of convulsion therapy. *Br. J. Med. Psychol.* **20**, 35-50.
Akiskal, H. S. & McKinney, W. T. (1973): Depressive disorders: toward a unified hypothesis. *Science* **182**, 20-29.
Akiskal, H. S. & McKinney, W. T. (1975): Overview of recent research in depression. *Arch. Gen. Psychiat.* **32**, 285-305.
Barton, J. L. (1977): ECT in depression: the evidence of controlled studies. *Biolog. Psychiat.* **12**, 687-695.
Beck, A. (1967): *Depression: clinical, experimental and theoretical aspects.* New York: Harper and Row Publishers Inc.
Bibring, E. (1965): The mechanism of depression. In *Affective Disorders*, ed P. Greenacre. Pp. 13-48. New York: International Universities Press.
Bowlby, J. (1979): *The making and breaking of affectional bonds.* London: Tavistock Press.
Brill, N. Q., Crumpton, E., Eiduson, S., Grayson, H. M., Hellman, L. I. & Richards, P. A. (1959): Relative effectiveness of various components of electroconvulsive therapy. *Arch. Neurol. Psychiat.* **81**, 627-635.
Cameron, D. E. (1960): Production of differential amnesia as a factor in the treatment of schizophrenia. *Comprehen. Psychiat.* **1**, 26-34.
Cannicott, S. M. (1963): Technique of unilateral electroconvulsive therapy. *Am. J. Psychiat.* **120**, 447-480.
Clare, A. (1976): *Psychiatry in dissent.* London: Tavistock Press.
Cook, L. C. (1940): Has fear any therapeutic significance in convulsion therapy? *J. Ment. Sci.* **86**, 484-490.
Crohholm, B. & Ottosson, J. O. (1960): Experimental studies of the therapeutic action of electroconvulsive therapy in endogenous depression. *Acta Psychiat. Scand.*, suppl. 145; **35**, 69-101.
Dorworth, T. R. & Overmier, J. B. (1977): On learned helplessness: the therapeutic effect of ECS shocks. *Physiolog. Psychol.* **5**, 355-358.
Fahy, P., Imlah, H. & Harrington, J. (1968): A controlled comparison of convulsive therapy, imipramine and thiopentone sleep in depression. *J. Neuropsychiat.* **4**, 310-314.
Fink, M. (1979): *Convulsive therapy: theory and practice.* New York: Raven Press.
Freeman, C. P. L., Basson, J. V. & Crighton, A. (1978): Double-blind controlled trial of electroconvulsive therapy (ECT) and simulated ECT in depressive illness. *Lancet* **1**, 738-740.
Freeman, C. P. L. & Kendell, R. E. (1980): 1. Patients' experiences and attitudes to ECT. *Br. J. Psychiat.* **137**, 8-16.
Friedberg, J. (1977): Shock treatment, brain damage and memory loss: a neurological perspective. *Am. J. Psychiat.* **134**, 1010-1013.
Frosch, J. & Impastato, D. (1948): The effects of shock treatment on the ego. *Psychoanal. Quart.* **17**, 226-239.
Gellhorn, E. (1949): Psychological basis of shock therapy. *Proc. Roy. Soc. Med.* **4**, 55.
Gerber, J., Fencil-Morse, E., Rosellini, R. A. & Seligman, M. E. P. (1979): Abnormal fixations and learned helplessness: inescapable shock as a weanling impairs adult discrimination learning in rats. *Behav. Res. Therapy* **17**, 197-206.
Gordon, M. (1948): Fifty shock therapy theories. *Milit. Surgeon* **103**, 397-401.
Greenblatt, M., Grosser, H. & Wechsler, H. (1962): A comparative study of selected antidepressant medications and ECT. *Am. J. Psychiat.* **119**, 144-153.
Greenblatt, M., Grosser, H. & Wechsler, H. (1964): Differential response of hospitalised depressed patients to somatic therapy. *Am. J. Psychiat.* **120**, 935-943.
Hollister, L. E., Overall, J. E., Shelton, J., Pennington, V., Kimball, I. & Johnson, M. (1967): Drug therapy of depression, amitryptiline, perphenazine and their combinations in different syndromes. *Arch. Gen. Psychiat.* **17**, 486-493.

Horrell, R. I. (1981): Specific antidepressant-like behavioral consequences of electroconvulsive shock in experimental animals. In *Electroconvulsive therapy: an appraisal*, ed R. L. Palmer. Pp. 125-149. Oxford: Oxford University Press.

Johnstone, E. C., Deakin, J. F. W., Lawler, P., Firth, C. D., Stevens, M., Mcpherson, K. & Crow, T. J. (1980): The Northwick Park ECT trial. *Lancet* **2**, 1317-1320.

Jones, J. E. (1974): Non ECT. *World Med.* **10**, 24.

Lambourn, J. (1981): Is cognitive impairment one of the therapeutic ingredients of ECT? In *Electroconvulsive therapy: an appraisal*, ed R. Palmer. Pp. 97-105. Oxford: Oxford University Press.

Lambourn, J. & Gill, D. (1978): A controlled comparison of real and simulated ECT. *Br. J. Psychiat.* **133**, 514-519.

Lazarus, A. (1960): Learning theory and the treatment of depression. *Behav. Res. Therapy* **6**, 83-89.

Lerer, B. & Belmaker, R. H. (1982): Receptors and the mechanism of action of ECT. *Biol. Psychiat.* **17**, 497-511.

Lewis, J. K. & McKinney, W. T. (1976): The effect of electrically-induced convulsions on the behavior of normal and abnormal rhesus monkeys. *Dis. Ner. Syst.* **37**, 687-693.

Lowinger, P. & Dobie, S. (1969): What makes placebo work? A study of placebo response rates. *Arch. Gen. Psychiat.* **20**, 84-88.

Mason, R. M. (1962): Clinical trials. *Proceed. Roy. Soc. Med.* **55**, 512-516.

Masserman, J. H. & Jacques, M. G. (1947): The effects of cerebral electroshock on experimental neurosis in cats. *Am. J. Psychiat.* **104**, 92-97.

Medical Research Council (1965): Report by Clinical Psychiatry Committee. Clinical trial of the treatment of depressive illness. *Br. Med. J.* **1**, 881-886.

Miller, D. H., Clancy, J. & Cumming, E. (1953): A comparison between unidirectional current non-convulsive electrical stimulation given with Reiter's machine, standard alternating current electroshock (Cerletti method) and pentothal in chronic schizophrenia. *Am. J. Psychiat.* **109**, 617-621.

Miller, E. (1967): Psychological theories of ECT, a review. *Br. J. Psychiat.* **113**, 301-311.

Millet, J. A. P. & Mosse, E. P. (1945): On certain psychological aspects of electroshock therapy. *Psychosom. Med.* **6**, 226-236.

Olds, J. (1977): *Drives and reinforcements*. New York: Raven Press.

Ottosson, J. O. (1968): Psychological or physiological theories of ECT. *Internat. J. Psychiat.* **5**, 170-174.

Overall, J. E., Hollister, L. E., Pokorny, A. D., Casey, J. F. & Katz, G. (1962): Drug therapy in depressions, controlled evaluation of imipramine, isocarboxazide, dextroamphetamine, amobarbital and placebo. *Clin. Pharmacol. Therapy* **3**, 16-22.

Overmier, J. B. & Seligman, M. E. P. (1967): Effects of inescapable shock upon subsequent escape-avoidance learning. *J. Compar. Physiol. Psychol.* **63**, 23-33.

Petty & Sherman (1980): Quoted by Kendell, R. E. in The Present Status of ECT. *Br. J. Psychiat.* 1981, **139**, 265-283.

Pippard, J. & Ellam, L. (1981): Electroconvulsive treatment in Great Britain: A report to The College. *Br. J. Psychiat.* **139**, 563-568.

Popper, K. R. & Eccles, J. C. (1977): *The self and its brain*. New York: Springer International.

Robertson, J. & Bowlby, J. (1952): Responses of young children to separation from their mothers. *Courrier Centre Inter Enfance* **2**. 131-142.

Robin, A. A. & Harris, J. A. (1962): A controlled comparison of imipramine and electroplexy. *J. Ment. Sci.* **108**, 217-219.

Rollin, H. R. (1980): The impact of ECT in electroconvulsive therapy. In *Electroconvulsive therapy: an appraisal*, ed R. L. Palmer. Pp. 11-18. Oxford: Oxford University Press.

Royal College of Psychiatrists (1977): Memorandum on the use of electroconvulsive therapy. *Br. J. Psychiat.* **131**, 261-272.

Sainz, A. (1959): Clarification of the action of successful treatment in the depressions. *Disorders Ner. Syst.* suppl. **20**, 53-57.

Schildkraut, J. (1970): *Neuropsychopharmacology and the affective disorders*. Boston: Little & Brown.

Seligman, M. E. P. (1978): Depression and learned helplessness. In *Research in Neurosis*, ed H. M. van Praag. Pp. 72-107. Utrecht: Bohn, Scheltma Holkema.

Seligman, M. E. P., Maier, S. F. & Geer, J. (1968): The alleviation of learned helplessness in the dog. *J. Abnor. Psychol.* **73**, 256-262.

Stein, L. (1971): Neurochemistry of reward and punishment: some implications for the aetiology of schizophrenia. *J. Psychiat. Res.* **8**, 354-361.

Sternberg, D. E. & Jarvik, M. E. (1976): Memory functions in depression. *Arch. Gen. Psychiat.* **33**, 219-224.

Wechsler, H., Grosser, G. M. & Greenblatt, M. (1965): Research evaluating antidepressant medication on hospitalized mental patients: a survey of published reports during a 5 year period. *J. Ner. Ment. Dis.* **141**, 231-239.

Weiner, R. D. (1979): The psychiatric use of electrically induced seizures. *Am. J. Psychiat.* **136**, 1507-1519.

Weinstein, E. A., Linn, L. & Kahn, R. L. (1952): Psychosis during electroshock therapy: Its relation to the theory of shock therapy. *Am. J. Psychiat.* **109**, 22-26.

Weiss, J. M., Glazer, H. I. & Pohorecky, L. A. (1976): coping, behaviour, and neurochemical changes. In *Animal models in human psychobiology*, ed G. Serban & A. Kling. Pp. 141-173. New York: Plenum.

West, E. (1981): Electric convulsion therapy in depression: a double-blind controlled trial. *British Medical Journal* **282**, 355-357.

Williams, M. (1966): Memory disorders associated with electroconvulsive therapy. In *Amnesia*, ed C. W. M. Whitty & O. L. Zangwill. Pp. 139-149. London: Butterworth.

Wolpe, J. (1971): Neurotic depression: experimental analog, clinical syndromes and treatment. *Am. J. Psychother.* **25**, 362-368.

21.
ECT mechanisms: current perspectives and future directions

B. LERER, R. D. WEINER and R. H. BELMAKER

Jerusalem Mental Health Center, POB 140, Jerusalem, Israel (BL & RHB); Psychiatry Service, Durham VA Medical Center, Durham, NC 27705, USA; Department of Psychiatry, Wayne State University and Lafayette Clinic, 951 E. Lafayette, Detroit, MI 48207, USA (BL, present address)

Introduction

ECT 'involves massive discharge over wide areas of the brain, activation of the peripheral autonomic nervous system, release of the secretions of many endocrine glands and, unless there is neuromuscular blockade, tonic and clonic convulsions of much of the muscle mass of the body. All these activities cause so many changes in the chemical homeostasis of the body, that . . . the difficulty lies not in demonstrating such changes, but in differentiating . . . which of the changes may be related to the important antidepressive and amnestic effects and which are quite irrelevant to these' (Kety, 1974). The ostensibly impossible task involved in such an undertaking led Van Praag (1977) to conclude that 'only an incorrigible optimist could hope to select from the numerous changes precisely those which determine the therapeutic effect'.

It is intriguing that two innovative investigators should take so pessimistic a view especially when, in retrospect, the bewildering array of effects attributed to psychopharmacologic agents such as the neuroleptics and antidepressants, are considered. While single, systematically investigated mechanisms of action have been suggested for both the latter agents, it is questionable whether hypotheses regarding either have been definitively proven. That the impressive body of work presented in this volume has not established a proven mechanism of action for ECT must also be clearly noted at this juncture. The findings presented speak for themselves in suggesting that a number of directions remain open for potentially fruitful study. The purpose of this concluding chapter is not to draw the debate to a premature or artificially parsimonious closure but to place these findings in a wider scientific and clinical perspective by considering the nature of the investigative methodology employed thus far, relevance to knowledge acquired from the clinical setting and potentially fruitful newer approaches.

Effects of ECT in animals

Much of the data presented in this volume derives from studies on the effects of ECS in animals, particularly rodents. The phylogenetic gap between rodents and humans is an obvious shortcoming in attempting to interpret these findings. To this may be added the fact that the animals studied are (at the outset at least) essentially normal while ECT is administered to depressed, or otherwise ill, patients. A number of clinically-oriented adjustments in experimental design have been proposed (Kety, 1974; Grahame-Smith *et al.*, 1978) in order to mitigate some of these shortcomings. Most have been followed by contributors to this volume and they may be briefly summarized as follows:

(1) Findings should be demonstrable after repeated rather than single ECS.
(2) The same changes should occur after repeated seizures induced by nonelectrical means, as after ECS.

(3) Changes should be clearly attributable to the seizure and not derive from nonspecific effects such as repeated handling, sub-convulsive shock, stress or anoxia.

(4) Changes should be relatively persistent, ie, should be present after recovery from the acute effects of the last of a series of shocks.

Notwithstanding the shortcomings discussed above, the assertion that findings relevant to therapeutic mechanisms in humans can be extrapolated from animal studies is clearly defensible. This is particularly so when data can be cross-correlated with available clinical parameters. The highly significant correlation between dopamine receptor blockade by neuroleptic drugs and their antipsychotic potency, is a case in point (Snyder, 1976). Even when human evidence proves to be less forthcoming, such as the absence, thus far, of corroborating support for the catecholamine hypothesis of affective disorder (Schildkraut, 1965), the heuristic impact of a hypothesis of therapeutic action derived from animal findings may be enormous.

An approach taken by a number of investigators has been to seek parallels between the effects of ECS and those of psychopharmacologic treatments with similar clinical spectra. The fact that ECS is devoid of pharmacokinetic interactions which may confound neurochemical studies makes it an ideal research tool. The possibility that a single mechanism of action may underlie the therapeutic efficacy of treatments as diverse in their nature as the tricyclic antidepressants, monoamine oxidase inhibitors, lithium and ECT is an exciting one. Yet this possibility should not be translated into a rigid prerequisite. A variety of mechanisms of action may lead to a final common therapeutic pathway. For example, antihypertensive agents may act via diuretic mechanisms, cardiac β-blocking mechanisms or peripheral vasodilatory mechanisms yet all these agents achieve a drop in blood pressure. Moreover, the clinical spectra of ECT and the chemical antidepressants are by no means identical, the antimanic and possibly antischizophrenic efficacy of ECT representing a clinical difference. A common mode of action should therefore not be too stringently demanded. Yet, as an increasing number of putative neurotransmitters, receptors, co-transmitters and neuromodulators emerge from the investigative efforts of basic researchers, ECS may prove to affect some or many of them to a greater or lesser extent. A comparison between the effects of ECT and those of other agents with clinically similar actions therefore remains an important step in defining the relevance of such effects.

An important clinical issue which may be investigated in the context of an animal study is the question of the relationship between seizure length and therapeutic efficacy. Short seizures are regarded by clinicians as clinically ineffective. Although an optimum seizure length has not been experimentally defined, most clinicians advise that the monitored seizure should not be shorter than 30 s. Reported effects of ECS on monoamine-mediated behaviours are not demonstrable after sub-convulsive shocks (Grahame-Smith *et al.*, 1978) but it is not clear whether there is a difference in the effect of 'short' (clinically ineffective) seizures as opposed to full-length seizures on these and other ECS effects. Animals treated with 'short' seizures or pharmacologically-attenuated seizures may be a better control group for 'sham ECS' effects than the handled controls usually used.

Findings derived from ECS effects in animals may also be of practical value in developing compounds with a potential 'ECT-like' action. The series of behavioral screening tests used to screen potential neuroleptic agents is an example which might be applied to findings from ECS studies. Further study of putative antidepressant compounds with possible 'ECT-like' activity on a series of screening tests could also have important theoretical implications. Such an approach is preliminarily explored by Green (this volume).

Studies in humans

Human studies on ECT mechanisms provide a unique opportunity for evaluating which of the animal effects of ECS are likely to be pertinent to the therapeutic effect of ECT. An added advantage is that studies in humans provide the opportunity to compare effects between patients who are ECT-responsive and those who are nonresponders. Human studies are, of course, limited by ethical considerations which dictate that brain functions can be studied only by

174

indirect means. Notwithstanding these limitations, a number of potential approaches are available, most of which have been only minimally explored.

Until recently, the central role of the seizure in mediating the therapeutic effect of ECT had seemed firmly established. The pioneering studies of Ottosson (1960) who demonstrated attenuation of therapeutic efficacy by pharmacological attenuation of the seizure, had seemed to clearly corroborate the original conceptualizations of Meduna (1935) and Cerletti & Bini (1938). Yet two recent clinical trials comparing 'real' vs 'sham' ECT have raised doubts on this issue (Lambourn & Gill, 1978; Johnstone et al., 1980). The findings from these trials appear to contradict a vast body of clinical experience which is supported by findings from two other recent trials using similar methodology (West, 1981; Freeman et al., 1978). Yet the disconcerting results of the two essentially negative studies cannot be summarily dismissed since their implications for the clinical practice of ECT as well as for animal ECS research are enormous. As reviewed earlier, most of the philosophy behind animal ECS studies that are considered more clinically relevant derives from the ascribed centrality of the seizure to the therapeutic process. Even if the findings from a trial such as that conducted at Northwick Park (Crow et al., this volume) are interpreted as narrowing the therapeutic spectrum of ECT rather than questioning its basic efficacy, this does not substantially alter their impact.

The question can, of course, only be resolved by further well-controlled double-blind studies. In view of the still extensive clinical use of ECT, the ethical validity of such studies in consenting subjects, seems beyond question. The enormous practical as well as ethical commitment involved should make it mandatory that further studies of this kind also evaluate effects upon neurochemical and physiological measures relevant to basic mechanisms of ECT. The opportunity to compare findings in responders and nonresponders to both ECT and sham ECT should yield valuable information.

Of the indirect approaches available for the study of brain function in ECT-treated patients, neuroendocrine probes have been the most extensively used. Results from such studies directed at testing neurotransmitter and receptor function involved in the release (or inhibition of release) of the hormone being tested, have thus far yielded inconclusive correlations with data from animal ECS studies. While neuroendocrine probes have been extensively used in studying untreated depressed patients or the effects of antidepressant treatment on receptor sensitivity, their application to ECT has, nevertheless, been relatively minimal (Lerer & Sitaram, 1983). The scope remaining for further studies is enormous.

Other indirect approaches which may be utilized include studies employing peripheral or central physiological responses as measures of receptor sensitivity (eg, blood pressure, heart rate, thermoregulation, REM sleep induction, pupillary diameter, sedation, arousal and mood changes) or peripheral biochemical markers (eg, monoamine metabolites, cyclic nucleotides and receptors on blood cells or other peripheral tissue) for the same purpose (Lerer & Sitaram, 1983). In general, the use of challenge strategies rather than the measurement of baseline levels or resting function, would seem likely to be the more productive strategy. Earlier studies on cerebrospinal fluid (CSF) monoamine metabolite levels following ECT had proved inconclusive (Lerer & Belmaker, 1982) but recent CSF findings further linking abnormalities in indolamine metabolites to depression and suicidality constitute a major impetus to further studies of this kind with ECT. More direct approaches to radioligand-binding studies of receptors in human brain may well be made possible by advances in visual imaging techniques such as provided by positron emission tomography (PET) and nuclear magnetic resonance (NMR) (Brownell et al., 1982) and these could provide valuable information previously available only from neurochemical studies in animals.

Mechanisms of adverse effects

Post-treatment memory deficits are the major adverse effect associated with the anesthetic- and muscle-relaxant modified ECT techniques used today. Although the nature of the ECT-induced memory impairment has been carefully defined (Squire, this volume), little is known of its biological underpinnings. The most generally accepted assumption is that while the therapeutic effects of ECT may be ascribed to the seizure, it is the passage of the electrical current through the brain which is responsible for the ECT-induced amnesia. The lesser degree of amnesia (but equivalent therapeutic efficacy), associated with unilateral electrode placement and, possibly, lower intensity, brief-pulse stimuli, would seem to support this viewpoint. A clear, quantitative relationship between ECT-induced memory impairment and the amount of electricity applied to the brain or the quantity of brain tissue traversed by the current has, however, yet to be definitively established. The clinical impression of many ECT-practitioners that 'missed seizures' are not associated with amnesia, should be noted in this regard. Moreover, reports suggesting that pharmacological attenuation of the seizure may also reduce the memory deficit (Ottosson, 1960) or that a degree of memory impairment equivalent to that induced by bilateral ECT follows fluorythyl-induced seizures (Fink *et al.*, 1961), tend to contradict a definitive association of ECT-induced amnesia with electrical factors.

The precise role of the seizure versus the electricity in the causation of ECT-induced amnesia, clearly needs to be further studied. Advanced EEG techniques involving power density spectral analysis of pre- vs post-ECT recordings, have contributed preliminary, relevant information (Weiner *et al.*, this volume). There is also evidence to suggest that differences in the electroencephalographic nature of the seizure itself may underlie EEG slowing following unilateral versus bilateral ECT and sine-wave versus brief-pulse electrical stimuli. Such differences in the nature of the induced seizure rather than in electrode placement or current parameters, may account for variations in the degree of amnesia induced with different ECT techniques. Studies investigating topographic EEG correlates of different forms of electrically-induced seizures along with a consideration of alterations in regional cerebral blood flow with unilateral vs bilateral ECT (Silfverskiold *et al.*, this volume), may yield further relevant information.

The clinical implications of this issue as well as its relevance to studies aimed at defining the neurochemical basis of ECT-induced amnesia (Lerer *et al.*, this volume) are clearly evident. The emphasis of such studies should be placed on possible correlations between ECS-induced memory impairment and neurochemical changes induced by repeated seizures versus changes induced by repeated exposure of the brain to electrical stimuli (with the seizure modified or prevented). Concurrent EEG monitoring of the seizure would provide an added dimension in interpreting the data obtained. A more clinically-relevant rodent model of ECS-induced amnesia based on repeated exposure to ECS in which contamination by the acute effects of the last ECS is avoided, should be studied. Such a model would also allow for further testing the therapeutic potential of memory-active peptides which have been preliminarily investigated in ECT-induced amnesia (Weingartner *et al.*, 1981; Lerer *et al.*, 1983).

Conclusions

It is abundantly clear that a wealth of data is available on the effects of ECT on neurochemical and other parameters, particularly on the basis of animal ECS studies. Such studies are likely to generate further data as newer techniques in neurochemistry and neuropharmacology are applied to ECT mechanisms. As long as ECT retains a central role in psychiatric treatment, studies of this kind are likely to continue. Human studies seeking support for a relationship between ECS effects in animals and the clinical efficacy of the treatment, have been fewer and have thus far yielded inconclusive results although many approaches remain to be explored. Studies on the basic mechanisms of ECS-induced amnesia have thus far not utilized a design which would enable the results to be definitively applied to the clinical situation. Taken together, the data already reported and that likely to be generated if potentially promising strategies are applied, suggest that the mechanism of action of ECT may be far more amenable to understanding than may at first seem apparent. A close interaction between basic and clinically-oriented researchers holds the key to designing studies which can answer critical questions rather than simply generating further data.

References

Brownell, G. L., Budinger, T. F., Lauterbur, P. C. & McGeer, P. L. (1982): Positron tomography and nuclear magnetic resonance imaging. *Science* **215**, 619–626.

Cerletti, V. & Bini, L. (1938): Un nuevo metodo di shock-terapie 'L'elettro-shock'. *Boll Acad. Med. Roma* **64**, 136–138.

Fink, M., Kahn, R. L., Kárp, K., Green, M., Alan, B. & Lefkowits, H. J. (1961): Inhalant-induced convulsions: Significance for the theory of the convulsive process. *Arch. Gen. Psychiat.* **4**, 259–266.

Freeman, C. P. L., Basson, J. V. & Crighton, A. (1978): Double-blind controlled study of electroconvulsive therapy and simulated ECT in depressive illness. *Lancet* **1**, 738–740.

Grahame-Smith, D. G., Green, A. R. & Costain, D. W. (1978): Mechanism of the antidepressant action of electroconvulsive therapy. *Lancet* **1**, 245–256.

Johnstone, E. C., Lawler, P., Stevens, M., Deakin, J. F. W., Frith, C. D., McPherson, K. & Crow, T. J. (1980): The Northwick Park electroconvulsive therapy trial. *Lancet* **2**, 1317–1320.

Kety, S. (1974): Effects of repeated electroconvulsive shock on brain catecholamines. In *Psychobiology of convulsive therapy*, ed M. Fink, S. Kety, J. McGaugh & T. Williams. Washington, D.C.: H. J. Winston & Sons.

Lambourn, J. & Gill, D. (1978): A controlled comparison of simulated and real ECT. *Br. J. Psychiat.* **133**, 514–519.

Lerer, B. & Belmaker, R. H. (1982): Receptors and the mechanism of action of ECT. *Biol. Psychiat.* **17**, 497–511.

Lerer, B. & Sitaram, N. (1983): Clinical strategies evaluating ECT mechanisms — pharmacological, biochemical and psychophysiological approaches. *Progr. Neuropsychopharmacol. Biol. Psychiat.*, in press.

Lerer, B., Zabow, T., Egnal, N. & Belmaker, R. H. (1983): Effect of vasopressin on memory following ECT. *Biol. Psychiat.*, in press.

Ottosson, J.-O. (1960): Experimental studies of the mode of action of electroconvulsive therapy. *Acta Psychiatr. Neurol. Scand.*, Suppl. 14S **35**, 1–141.

van Praag, H. M. (1977): *Depression and schizophrenia: a contribution on their chemical pathologies.* Pp. 119–121. New York: Spectrum.

Schildkraut, J. J. (1965): The catecholamine hypothesis of affective disorders: A review of supporting evidence. *Am. J. Psychiat.* **122**, 509–522.

Snyder, S. H. (1976): The dopamine hypothesis of schizophrenia: focus on the dopamine receptor. *Am. J. Psychiat.* **133**, 197–202.

Weingartner, H., Gold, P., Ballanger, J. C., Smallberg, S. A., Summers, R., Rubinow, D. R., Post, R. M. & Goodwin, F. F. (1981): Effect of vasopressin on human memory function. *Science* **211**, 601–603.

West, E. D. (1981): Electric convulsion therapy in depression. A double-blind controlled trial. *Br. Med. J.* **282**, 355–357.

Subject Index

180

181